Law, Leverage and Litigation in Late Medieval Bruges

Law, Leverage and Litigation in Late Medieval Bruges

Foreign Merchants in a City of Justice

Niels Fieremans

EDINBURGH
University Press

Edinburgh University Press is one of the leading university presses in the UK. Publishing new research in the arts and humanities, EUP connects people and ideas to inspire creative thinking, open new perspectives and shape the world we live in. For more information, visit www.edinburghuniversitypress.com.

Edinburgh University Press Ltd
13 Infirmary Street, Edinburgh EH1 1LT

Typeset in 10/12 Goudy Old Style by
IDSUK (DataConnection) Ltd, and
Printed and bound in the UK using 100% renewable electricity by
CPI Group (UK) Ltd

A CIP record for this book is available from the British Library

ISBN 978 1 3995 4586 0 (hardback)
ISBN 978 1 3995 4588 4 (webready PDF)
ISBN 978 1 3995 4587 7 (epub)

EU Authorised Representative:
Easy Access System Europe
Mustamäe tee 50, 10621 Tallinn, Estonia
gpsr.requests@easproject.com

MIX
Paper | Supporting responsible forestry
FSC
www.fsc.org
FSC® C013604

This book is printed using paper from well-managed forests, recycling and other controlled sources

Contents

Abbreviations vi
Preface vii

1. Introduction 1

Part I Law: The Legal Framework of Late Medieval Bruges

2. The Procedures of the Aldermen 19
3. The Usage of Procedures 37
4. The Goal of Procedures 48

Part II Leverage: Group Strategies to Adapt the Framework

5. The Strategy of Economic Leverage: The Hanseatic, English and Scottish Communities 77
6. The Strategy of Political Leverage: The Iberian Communities 96
7. Strategies Without Privileges: The Italian Communities 116

Part III Litigation: Individual Strategies Adapting the Framework

8. Princely Courts. A New Framework for Late Medieval Bruges 143
9. Merchants Using the Princely Courts 162
10. The End of Bruges' Legal Dominance 177

11. Conclusion 188

Bibliography 193
Index 237

Abbreviations

ARCHIVES

ADNB	Archives Départementales du Nord, Serie B (Departemental Archive Lille)
AN	Archives Nationales (National Archives France)
ARA	Algemeen Rijksarchief Brussel (National Archive Belgium)
ASF	Archivio di Stato di Firenze (State Archive Florence)
ASL	Archivio di Stato di Lucca (State Archive Lucca)
ASV	Archivio di Stato di Venezia (State Archive Venice)
BN	Bibliotheca Nationale Firenze (National Library Florence)
CAA	Municipal Archives Aberdeen
FA	Felixarchief (Municipal Archive Antwerp)
MAL	Municipal Archives London
NADG	Nationaal Archief Den Haag (National Archives of the Netherlands)
NAK	National Archives Kew
RAB	Rijksarchief Brugge (State Archive Bruges)
RAG	Rijksarchief Gent (State Archive Ghent)
SAB	Stadsarchief Brugge (City Archive Bruges)
SNSP	Scuola Normale Superiore Pisa

COINS

d. gr.	denarii (penningen)
s. gr.	solidi (schellingen)
lib. gr.	Ponden Vlaamse Groten/Pounds Flemish Groats
par.	Parisis

Preface

This work is the result of a doctoral dissertation in both history and law. I have had the privilege of enjoying the best of both worlds. I am indebted to my three supervisors, professors Jan Dumolyn (Ghent University), Dave De ruysscher (Vrije Universiteit Brussel), and Dirk Heirbaut (Ghent University), for their wise counsel and occasional jokes throughout my four-year research period. Their support and guidance proved to be essential. It was a privilege to work with them. Additionally, I am grateful for the intellectually stimulating environment provided by the respective departments. In particular, I would like to thank my colleagues at the 'Bureau Dhondt' and my two *compaignons de route* Filip Batselé and Florenz Volkaert.

During my time, I have had the opportunity to visit some of the most magnificent archives and libraries around Europe. I would like to express my gratitude to the personnel at the Municipal Archives in Bruges, the Municipal Archives of Aberdeen, the National Archives of Brussels, Kew, Den Haag, France and the State Archives in Ghent, Lucca, Firenze and Venice, the University Library of Ghent University, and the Bibliotheque nationale de Paris for their assistance in browsing through the fifteenth-century documents. I would like to express my gratitude to professors John Cairns (Edinburgh University), Julie Claustre (Paris I Sorbonne), and Francesco Guidi-Bruscoli (Florence University), as well as the numerous scholars I have encountered during my research stays, for their hospitality and engaging discussions. Lastly, I am grateful to Maxim De Schepper for – besides his friendship – proofreading my English, which was crucial for completing this work.

I am grateful to my wider 'framework'. During the last few years, I have been fortunate to receive support from my friends and family, who have provided the necessary distractions that made these last years a joy. I would like to express my gratitude to Matthias, Jelle, Sebbe, Dennis, Sander, Simon, Liesbeth, Aaron, Elisabeth, Ruben, Arno, Jef, Swaaf, Van Hove, Jonas, Romeo, Laura, Fedra, Anjoeta, Lotte, and Stijn. I would also like to thank my parents, grandmother, and partner for the unwavering support, love and warmth they have given me.

A final special mention must be given to Sander D'haese, not only for being a true friend throughout these past years, but also for lending his artistic talents in creating a miniature depicting not only the aldermen of Bruges, but also a section of Gerard David's renowned painting, *The Judgement of Cambyses*, set in the aldermen's hall. The artwork also features prominent merchants such as Tommaso Portinari, Piero Bandini, Giovanni Arnolfini, and Angelo Tani. I am deeply grateful for both the hours of work dedicated to this project and the years of valued friendship.

1

Introduction

In 1498, the aldermen of Bruges acquired a new painting for their aldermen's court. Gerard David's artwork 'The Judgment of Cambyses' was considered an 'exemplum virtutis' or an 'exemplum iustitiae' – a painting that conveyed the principles of virtue and justice. It depicted the aldermen witnessing both the arrest of a corrupt judge and his subsequent punishment. The painting tells the story of corrupt judge Sisamnes. According to Herodotus, Sisamnes, an ancient Persian judge, had accepted bribes in a case. The King of Persia, Cambyses, refused to tolerate such misconduct and selected one of the most gruesome punishments imaginable. Sisamnes was to be skinned alive, a procedure conducted in an excruciatingly painful manner. Subsequently, the skin of the unfortunate judge was draped over the judgment chair of his son, Otanes. Otanes was appointed as the new judge, and his father's skin was placed there as a reminder of 'what good justice was'. The painting commemorating this event was displayed in the aldermen's court, visible to both the aldermen and the litigants, serving as a cautionary reminder of the consequences for 'bad judges'. What does the choice of this scene tell us about the attitude of the judges of Bruges, and what must the litigants have thought when they entered the courtroom?[1]

In the fourteenth and fifteenth century the city of Bruges was considered to be the nexus between the northern Baltic and North Sea trade, the southern Mediterranean, and from the fifteenth century, upcoming Atlantic trade.[2] While London fulfilled a similar function, it could not boast of having so many nationalities within the city.[3] Italians, Aragonese, Spaniards, Portuguese, French, English, Scottish, Hanseatic and South German merchants were regular visitors.[4] Larger ships docked at Bruges' outport Sluis, unloaded their merchandise into smaller vessels and sailed it to Bruges.[5] During the fourteenth century, Bruges had made significant efforts to assert legal control over the outports of Sluis and Damme, seeking to bring them under its influence and make sure the transit to Bruges occurred. Once in Bruges, merchants could stock their merchandise in the cellars of hostellers or houses of their merchant community.[6] These hostellers were inn-keepers who provided accommodation, advice and were the necessary middle-men in all commercial transactions taking place in Bruges. The city was unparalleled in North Europe in both economic and financial techniques.[7] According to the Castilian traveller Pero Tafur (1438), Bruges was the place where all commodities in the world came together and dispersed again.[8] The presence of so many foreign nationalities must have been an active concern for the aldermen. However, according to Pero Tafur, Sluis was the only place in the world where all the nationalities could sit at the same table and leave their national disputes behind. In 1438, Pero Tafur noted that, in addition to the incomparable splendour, there was an exquisite justice system.[9] Interestingly enough, he was not the only one to make this observation. In the sixteenth century, after Bruges' commercial demise, the Italian Lodovico Guicciardini described Bruges as the city where justice reigned.[10]

Guicciardini wrote at a time that Bruges was no longer the most important commercial centre of the Burgundian Netherlands. Since the 1490s, Bruges had been in a state of decay and its commercial rival Antwerp was on the rise. Trade flows were changing, the access to Bruges, called the Zwin, was silting and all merchants had left the city during the last rebellion (1488–1492). In this context, it is not unthinkable that Bruges tried to promote itself as a city of justice eager to bring back merchants. Still, it remains a striking observation. In a city like medieval Bruges, law was based on customs, experience and good governance.[11] The aldermen applied law in a way they believed to be equitable and expedient.[12] Its legal framework was unwritten and based on the insights of the aldermen, not on written law. Crafty litigants could definitely sway the aldermen, foresee exemptions and make the system work for them. To convince the aldermen, they needed to know the vulnerabilities of both the system and the persons before them. Yet, the aldermen of Bruges still spoke about a feeling of careful justice, most likely delivered by them. This justice, as a practice and as a point of reference will be used in this study as the legal framework. Such a framework is hard to define. When the sources spoke about the aldermen, they used the term the 'law of Bruges' (*wet van Brugge*). However, the law these aldermen spoke was pragmatic rather than principled, and depended on the contextual influences. The word 'framework' is used to refer to the complex collection of written and unwritten regulations, anticipations and wishes that influenced the way justice was accomplished. In this framework, the aldermen were not the only ones making the definitions. It was the result of interactions between aldermen, merchants, and later on, princely courts.

This book will focus on the interaction between law and commerce and its impact on the concept of justice held by the aldermen. There are three main groups influencing this interaction. One of the central actors in this study are the aldermen, who determined how conflicts should be resolved in the city, adopted initiatives, and tried to control what law was in the city. The merchants make a second group. They formed communities that could leverage Bruges into adapting its framework to the community's advantage. I will examine their litigation strategies as a group and their level of success. Lastly, there were princely courts that offered alternatives through litigation. Merchants could seize the initiative and use contextual developments to their advantage. In so doing, they were also affecting the original framework of Bruges. The law of Bruges was not exclusively defined by the aldermen, but emerged as a product of the influence exerted by economic communities on the city, as well as the outcomes of litigation before the princely court. Law in Bruges was shaped through the interaction of these three key groups.

First and foremost, there were the aldermen of Bruges. These annually elected judges governed the city politically, financially and judicially. In most cases, the aldermen had not enjoyed a university training and relied on the expertise of pensionaries (*pensionarissen*) for legal expertise. However, experience was the point of reference for the settlement of judgments, not university-learned law.[13] This was amplified by the fact that often the richest, most important, and influential families had generations of scions on the aldermen bench. The commercial families Van der Buerse, Van Aertrike, Metteneye, Coolbrandt, Heldebolle were frequent suspects in the division of the aldermen bench.[14] In medieval Bruges, the commercial elite was definitely involved in the government of the city.[15] However, the different guilds were also represented in the aldermen bench. Hence, in the evaluation of rules and cases, or in the assessment of the value of a merchant community for Bruges, communal and commercial interests could collide.

The second group was the merchants. In the fifteenth century, the aldermen decided their cases according to customs, experience and expediency, and as such, they were under the constant influence of contextual events. One of these were the merchant communities. The foreign nations in Bruges were an influential group.[16] For example in 1456, the Genoese merchants made a deal with the Bruges city administration regarding the execution of debt settlement and the settlement of gambling debts.[17] However, the most important influences on the system of Bruges were the privileges foreign communities received. These privileges were charters granting a specified group a certain set of rights that deviated from the general rule set applied to a foreigner. Such a charter was a legal – enforceable – document bestowed by the prince. Whether merchants received these privileges and the desired rights depended on the leverage a community could provide to Bruges. This leverage was the amalgam of reasons why Bruges should give them preferential treatment. This could vary from political relations, economic dependency or just a market niche that was sought after in Bruges. In brief, there were rules on paper and there was what merchants could present to Bruges to bend the rules a little. Merchants did not simply bend the system, but studied it, overcame it and made it work for them. When the aldermen of Bruges did not grant a favourable decision, they could seek out another court and use it to their advantage. In other words, these merchants could forum shop.

In the fifteenth century, the prince offered these opportunities for forum shopping. Bruges lay in the County of Flanders with the Count of Flanders as its prince. The Flemish cities were among the largest of Europe and would develop a clear political ambition from early on, but they never achieved independence in the Italian style.[18] The count never ceased to be an influential figure. The cities were largely free to organise matters in their own territory, and they could occasionally weigh in on the foreign policy of the Count of Flanders. From 1369 onwards, the Dukes of Burgundy became major players in the county. The Burgundian dukes combined the County of Flanders with their other dominions into a personal union making them one of the most influential princes of Europe.[19] During the fifteenth century, these Burgundian dukes ruled the County of Flanders free from kingly influence and focused on building a power base from their collection of duchies and counties.[20] One of the biggest influences on Bruges' legal system would be the introduction of the princely courts in the form of the Council of Flanders (1386) and the Great Council of the Duke (1440s).[21] Although these courts rarely called cases from Bruges to their court (a procedure called *evocation*), the appeals that were lodged by, for example, merchants, and the possible condemnation for a spurious judgment, severely distressed the aldermen.[22]

These actors had diverging motivations, goals, and desired results. How creative merchants or merchant communities challenged the existing framework, sought alternative means of conflict resolution and, in so doing, changed the framework will be our central focus. The goal of this book is to understand how these merchants influenced the legal system of Bruges during its commercial zenith (1252–1492) and how they used this system and made it work for them. I use the term 'legal system' because I argue that the norms and customs valued by the aldermen of Bruges were challenged by the expectations of the merchants and influenced by the practices of princely courts, shaping a new legal reality. The 'law' of the aldermen did not exist in a vacuum. On the basis of commercial privileges, court registers and city accounts, I will investigate the conflict resolution of the foreign merchant communities of late medieval Bruges, its legal aspects but also its contextual influence. As will be shown, this will encompass more than just the litigation found in the registers of the aldermen of Bruges. In order to do so, I will look at the rules of the game (Part I), the modification that took place (Part II), and how some merchants played the game (Part III).

HISTORIOGRAPHY AND CONTRIBUTION

This book aims to contribute to the three main debates concerning medieval Bruges: the national debate on the causes of the decline of Bruges and the role of Bruges legal system (customary law) in it, the commercial debate on the role of institutions on commerce and the legal debate on the influence of law on commerce in a medieval city. In what follows, I will discuss the main questions that remain in each of these debates and how I will contribute to them.

To begin with, there is the question of trade flows and what made Bruges decline and Antwerp rise. Although the reasons for Bruges' success or decline were never monocausal, the position of Bruges has intrigued historians. The city of Bruges relied on its many guilds who provided several services: stevedores, shippers, weighters and so on. Rudolf Häpke even called Bruges a 'Rechtsstadt' because of its far-reaching involvement in commercial affairs.[23] However, historians such as Van Houtte and Van Werveke have disagreed on whether the high level of regulation was detrimental to the city. For example, in Bruges, brokers were the essential go-between for commercial transactions. Nevertheless, it is still debated whether these brokers provided an essential service or were an obstruction to private initiative?[24] It was one of the reasons why Van Houtte called Bruges a regional centre of trade, whereas Bruges' commercial successor Antwerp was truly international.[25] Similarly, we can ask whether Bruges' legal involvement in mercantile cases put a strain on relations between merchants and eventually pushed them towards Antwerp. As we do not know how merchants operated in Bruges, we cannot precisely estimate the role of Bruges.[26]

This begs the question as to how Bruges' institutions worked and what benefits merchants could obtain from them. Also, on the institutional level, the issue of what made Bruges so effective seems to trigger debate among historians. Fifteenth-century Bruges was unique in the size of its different merchant communities. As such the city has received much scholarly attention.[27] However, the scope of this attention is not on a par with Antwerp, which is thoroughly researched in both its commercial and legal aspects.[28] How Bruges managed all those merchants with different backgrounds has remained a mystery until now. According to Henri Pirenne, it was commerce that assured the rise of law, merchant law and eventually justice.[29] The concept of *lex mercatoria* has been refuted several times.[30] However, merchants operating in their own commercial and legal world still hold significant power. In his *Cradle of Capitalism*, James Murray stressed the networks that made Bruges so special. In the line of private conflict resolution, the consular courts of the different communities were also network-building institutions central to the resolution of conflicts.[31]

Similarly, the question of what made Bruges so special also stood at the centre of Gelderblom's work *Cities of Commerce*.[32] Interestingly enough, Gelderblom credits Bruges with a strong respect for the merchant communities and the desire for merchants to solve their problems with each other on their own terms. Arbitration, where peers decided the outcome of quarrels, was seen as a fast, inexpensive and impartial legal procedure capable of meeting the needs of merchants. Arbiters could deviate from local customs and sideline the aldermen of Bruges.[33] As such, Bruges provided the institutional framework for merchants to prosper. Although the networks of close-knit communities were essential in Bruges, Gelderblom cannot surmount the apparent paradox between the two debates: on the one side we have a highly regulated commercial sphere; and on the other, a loosely regulated legal sphere. Therefore, in this book I will incorporate the legal framework of Bruges, but instead of regarding it as something created for a large anonymous merchant community, I will question the choices the aldermen of Bruges made and stress the legal initiatives they took for some merchants. Crucial to this are the different expectations from the merchant communities. These communities were exceptionally heterogenous with varied norms, behaviours and values that differed from other groups.[34] However, scholars have often failed to appreciate the diversity in these merchant communities regarding the resolution of their conflicts.[35] Different merchants and different backgrounds also imply different strategies of conflict resolution. All too often, historians have perceived the merchants of Bruges as one community that followed an economic logic that is uncomfortably close to a modern one.[36]

In addition to this, these merchants were confronted with a normative hybrid world. Multiple – often overlapping – authorities operated at the same time and gave merchants the option to make decisions.[37] In the fourteenth century, the Four Members of Flanders, an alliance of Bruges, Ghent, Ieper and the Liberty of Bruges (the rich region surrounding Bruges), could resolve commercial disputes.[38] However, their power was gradually eroded during the fifteenth century. During that century, princely courts such as the Council of Flanders and the Great Council confronted the aldermen of Bruges. As argued by Jan Dumolyn and Bart Lambert, the activities of the higher princely courts cannot be taken out of the equation.[39] In the fifteenth century, the courts, their jurisdictions, and even their picking order were not inscribed in stone, and would only rise after a long process of negotiation – a negotiation that was influenced by contextual factors. Merchants could take the initiative and seek redress in a court other than the aldermen of Bruges. In the fourteenth century, Bruges dealt with almost all mercantile cases. In the sixteenth century, Bruges did not question the sovereignty of a princely court. What happened in between? Interestingly for our research, the lack of such a monopoly also ensured that Bruges had to define what good justice was, and actively seek it. If it failed to do so, it risked losing these cases to a higher court.

The contribution to these debates centres on three questions. How did the Bruges aldermen, who had both political and judicial responsibilities, control such a vast gathering of merchants, with different backgrounds and diverging goals? One of these diverging aspects between the different merchant communities were their privileges. In legally enforceable charters, the merchants gained rights that exempted them from the common statute of a foreigner. However, what these rights entailed, how they fitted in the commercial framework and what consequences they had on the litigation strategies of Bruges are still in the balance. In addition, Bruges may have been the prime source of justice in the city, but its relation to the princely courts and how merchants used the various courts to their advantage is still unanswered.

We will approach this from the viewpoint of the players and how the customs, usages and guidelines were used and shaped by these contextual factors. There are few indications of a conscious strategy of Bruges to influence commerce through litigation, but there are plenty of indications of commerce influencing law. Honest intentions, deceitful tricks, and violence were all a part of their framework.[40] Merchants were not always impartial actors selecting the most favourable option. A prime example of merchants making poor decisions can be found in the accounts of various comital officers of justice. The fines imposed on these merchants demonstrate that some had indeed made ill-considered choices.[41]

SOURCES

As the object of our study is to investigate how the aldermen made their justice system work and how foreign merchants adapted to this system, we should first look at the court registers of the aldermen of Bruges. The court of aldermen consisted of twelve aldermen, a burgomaster of the aldermen and twelve councillors. They held two sessions, one in the *vierschaar* and one in the Chamber.

Unfortunately, the registers for the *vierschaar* are lost for most of the fifteenth century. Fortunately, merchants were obliged to use the chamber procedure. This was a faster, but also a less elaborate procedure where the aldermen held a daily session. The registers of the chamber are (fragmentarily) preserved for the periods 1424–1425, 1433–1436, 1447–1461 and 1465–1471 and we have the drafts of these registers for 1439–1441, 1473–1475, 1478–1479, 1487–1490.[42] The aldermen pronounced the decisions, and the clerks wrote them down. These clerks were required to make notes during the procedure in a small booklet in cursive writing. The clerks had to present these to the aldermen for control and were subsequently allowed to write them in a larger register which was checked again by the aldermen.[43] Everybody could visit these registers for 2 s. gr. and for an additional 2 s. gr. they could have a copy of a specific case.[44] Decisions made by the aldermen were in middle Flemish or middle French. The aldermen probably accommodated the merchants by using languages they could understand. Italians, Castilians, and Portuguese received their decisions in French while Germans, English and, of course, Flemings received them in middle Flemish. Sometimes decisions were also written in Latin.[45] The scribes who registered the decisions of the aldermen could also intervene in small matters of voluntary jurisdiction. These scribes could draft deeds from immovable properties, donations and inheritances.[46]

Our other main source, the registers of the Council of Flanders, has a somewhat distinct structure. The princely court, the Council of Flanders has two main series of registers for the fifteenth century. The first ones are the *Acten en Sententiën* and the *Interlocutoire Sententiën*. The *acten en sententiën* (acts and sentences) is the most complete series. The councillors held sessions on Tuesdays and Fridays where they followed the cause-list, and then the result of this cause-list and a secretary registered the procedural steps in the *acten en sententiën*. Unfortunately, the registrations are often brief and do not include the narration of the case. Therefore, we do know which merchants appeared and which procedural steps they took, but not why they were there.[47] Only when the Council pronounced a decision was an account of the events given. These pronunciations, whether they were interim or final judgments, were written down in the *interlocutoire sententiën*.

Unfortunately, these sources are far from complete. If we compare the registers of the *interlocutoire sententiën* and the *akten en sententiën* of the Council of Flanders, it is clear that not all (interlocutory) decisions were registered. In addition, we can be quite confident that a substantial number of cases that appeared before the Council of Flanders did not reach a conclusion. The procedure was long, cases were transferred to a different court or litigants just gave up. In addition, the courts often did not provide grounds for their decisions.[48]

By contrast, for the Great Council we lack the sources to know how many cases appeared (and did not reach a conclusion), but we do have their eventual decisions. The Great Council of the Duke of Burgundy was an ambulant court until the 1470s, making it very challenging to research. It is only from 1470 onwards that we have fragmentary registers with decisions from the court.[49] The problem here is determining how often merchants looked to the Great Council for help. Especially in the period preceding 1470, where decisions are scarce, it is hard to determine the activity of this princely court and how often merchants turned to this court.[50]

Some courts have no surviving register. The chamber of accounts at Lille and the consular courts of the merchant communities at Bruges have no surviving records of court decisions.[51] The chamber of accounts could sanction Burgundian officials, but in the preserved letters we see that the main solicitors of the chamber were the princely courts seeking advice.[52] As we were unable to discover any examples of merchants taking advantage of the chamber of Lille, we will not dwell on this further. The consular courts of the merchant's nations are another mystery. Due to their strong connection with their home cities, we have examined the local archives for any relevant connections. For communities like the Scottish, English and Italians it was meaningful to study their relations with their 'home' courts, how these courts in London, Lucca or Florence behaved towards the merchants in Bruges and whether they tried to influence conflicts in Bruges.[53]

In the end, the Parliament of Paris, the high court of the King of France, has the best level of preservation. Besides the decisions of the parliament, there were also registers with the arguments and even the informal dealings. But not all registers have survived, and not all dealings, acts and resolutions were written down in these registers.

In addition, the court registers only tell a part of the story. The registers rarely contain all acts in a procedure, and often do not include an eventual decision; and even when decisions are recorded, the underlying reasoning is not. Therefore, we have to be aware of a 'survivor bias'. Some merchant communities did not trade in Bruges for several years, making their presence in the surviving registers very variable. For example, the Hanseatic merchants boycotted Bruges from 1451 until 1457, or the Venetian fleet occasionally skipped Bruges in the second half of the century.[54] As a consequence, their presence in Bruges, and also its registers, is minimal for those years. A considerable number of sources were lost. Short-lived privileges that were not registered, urban ordinances that may alter our view, or simply a register with a final decision in it may have altered our conclusions.[55] The problem can be eased by looking at references in the surviving sources, cartularies containing decisions of the aldermen, or even a compilation of (copied and confirmed) treaties.[56] Reading between the lines remains vital. To understand the procedures of the Council of Flanders, it can help to consult the jurists who wrote a treatise on the practice of princely courts such as Filips Wielant, Frans de Rycke and the anonymous 'costume van de Rade'.[57] Although each of these authors probably knew the procedure of the Council of Flanders in the fifteenth century, they wrote their conclusions down in the sixteenth century. We have to be aware of their own motivations and bias. These scholars do provide a helpful insight in understanding the procedure of a court, as long as we remember that their learned law is not necessarily a reflection of the legal practice in the fifteenth century.[58]

Nevertheless it is difficult to distinguish the coincidental decision from the structural and exemplary decision. For some courts or merchant communities, only a few traces survived in the court registers and for each 'litigation strategy' this work discusses, it is important to avoid a deterministic view. As I will argue, merchants were not absolutely bound by their community and could take the initiative. Likewise, it was not because the aldermen decided in a particular context, that they could not – in a different context – decide something else. Therefore, our main interest will not be in 'what the aldermen decided' or 'who won the case', it is in 'how they decided something' and 'why they decided something'. The procedure is more important than the outcome.

Therefore, the court registers were supplemented with the true indicators for medieval courts: their accounts. In these accounts the court registered expenses and incomes and justified why they were made. For example in the accounts of the Great Council we can see the fines cities had to pay for a false appeal or for a spurious judgment by the Great Council.[59] As such it is immediately evident that Bruges was rarely condemned for such spurious judgments in the fifteenth century.[60] In addition, the costs for the messengers were registered and show how the Great Council or the Council of Flanders sent several messengers to solve problems on the spot.[61] Such a form of informal dispute settlement is not found in the registers, but was a real aspect of conflict resolution in late medieval Flanders.

In a similar fashion, the Bruges city accounts show the game that took place next to the formal litigation of the aldermen. Messengers were sent and gifts were given. These accounts were an integral part of the communal identity.[62] At the end of the twelfth and thirteenth centuries, when the guilds achieved more political power, they also wished for participation in government.[63] The financial accounts, which were normally discussed behind closed doors, were opened for the public and checked by the citizens when the accounts were read aloud.[64] The duke on the other hand tried to demand the inspection of these accounts by his chamber of accounts. The cities would refuse this as long as possible, but would send copies nonetheless from at least the middle of the fifteenth century.[65] Hence, the city accounts that were lost can be found in the archive of the chamber of accounts which also made small remarks on the accounting practices of Bruges. These remarks are also interesting for our research, as they indicate the more devious practices of the aldermen.

Tampering with these accounts did occur and, occasionally, urban administrators were chastised for taking too much private profit.[66] The payments in these accounts will not indicate corrupt activities, though several payments find themselves in grey areas. Gifts implied reciprocity, and payments to smooth matters were written down.[67] Fortunately for us, this also included some informal influence the aldermen of Bruges tried to exercise. The costs registered tell us not only of emissaries for negotiations but also the influence the city tried to exert, dubious gifts it gave or the kind of information it wanted to gather. In some cases, the aldermen were explicit as to why they were given and occasionally as to what the aldermen tried to obtain but this was not always the case.[68] For example, in

1453, the aldermen of Bruges paid 300 lib. gr. 'for the advancement and proper result of certain difficult procedures'.[69] The aldermen did not specify the person receiving these gifts or for what precise reason. The aldermen were so kind as to mention that the payments resulted from cases before the Council of Flanders, the Parliament of Paris and the Great Council. Medieval courts systems needed some motivation to work properly: some drinking money here, payment for a document there. Procedures were expensive, but such payments remain an enormous amount.[70] It immediately illustrates the problem with these sources. The goal of these registers was quick justification of an expense that had already been incurred. The accounts were not complete, they contained mistakes, and the aldermen used vague descriptions.[71]

PLAN OF THE BOOK

My argument unfolds across three major parts. Part I addresses the institutional framework of the aldermen; Part II examines the leverage merchants employed to modify this framework; and Part III focuses on the pressure exerted on the aldermen through merchant litigation before princely courts. The legal framework of Bruges extended beyond the formal rules governing the aldermen and was shaped by their interactions with merchants. Consequently, both formal and informal means of conflict resolution emerged through these mutual exchanges. Some merchants received more favourable treatment from the aldermen than others, a disparity largely influenced by the leverage individual merchants or merchant communities could exert over the authorities in Bruges.

Each merchant community had a distinct legal status within the city. To secure privileges, these communities leveraged their economic or political significance to persuade the city and the Count of Flanders to grant them specific rights. I will explore what factors convinced Bruges to extend these privileges, how these privileges shaped the strategies of merchants within their communities, and whether the aldermen adhered to these privileges in legal proceedings, such as litigation. The extent to which these privileges were respected provides a key indicator of the merchants' true influence at any given time.

However, merchants cannot always be neatly categorised by their community affiliations. As previously discussed, individual actors often took initiative. While a merchant's community could impose constraints, there are numerous instances where merchants transcended the formal boundaries of their community and navigated the complex judicial landscape independently. This was particularly true for a select group of 'forum shoppers' who sought out favourable legal forums across different jurisdictions.

In the final part, I will look at the individual merchants who wanted to escape the initial framework by using the opportunities presented to them, appealed decisions before a princely court, and challenged the aldermen of Bruges. Consequently, these merchants created options for other merchants and, in turn, changed the framework. The merchants travelling to the different courts are our research subjects in this part. Although these merchants were the exceptions, they also illustrate the boundaries of the system and what was possible. I will investigate which cases tended to go to the higher courts, why merchants chose these courts and how the aldermen of Bruges reacted.

Our main focus is on the fifteenth century. It is the nexus of several elements. Bruges was still a major centre of commerce, we have the court registers for most of the period, and even the foreign archives of merchant communities can supplement our material. However, the fifteenth century was also contextually interesting. Times were changing and Bruges was coming under more and more pressure to adapt. Princely courts intervened in what the aldermen of Bruges believed to be their jurisdiction, the Burgundian duke was becoming more powerful, and Bruges was increasingly feeling the hot breath of Antwerp. When Antwerp had usurped the commercial position of Bruges, the latter altered its system, and in these alterations, we can see how carefully Bruges had treasured its legal position in the previous years.

NOTES

1. Van Miegroet, 'Gerard David's "Justice of Cambyses"', 116–133; Verstegen, 'The Judgement of Cambyses', 125–147; van der Velden, 'Cambyses for example', 41–44; Martyn, 'Cambyses aan de Vlaamse kust', 126–127.
2. Blockmans et al., 'Maritime trade around Europe 1300–1600', 9; Jansen, 'Voies commerciales aux Pays-Bas', 21–26; Esch, 'Brügge als Umschlagplatz', 112.
3. Spindler, 'Between sea and city', 181–199.
4. Maréchal, *Europese aanwezigheid te Brugge*, 173–174, 211–227.
5. Sicking, *La naissance d'une thalassocratie*, 51–55; Degryse, 'Brugge en de pilotage van de Spaanse vloot', 105–107; Degryse, 'Brugge en de organisatie van loodswezen', 61–130. See on these outports: De Clercq et al. 'Turning back the tide', 305–321; Verhulst, 'Kort overzicht van de geschiedenis van de Zwinstreek', 191–198.
6. A merchant nation will be used as a synonym for merchant community. Some communities defined themselves as 'nations' while other did not. As I will discuss the legal statute of all communities, the difference is purely semantic.
7. Aerts, 'Italian presence in late medieval Bruges', 177–178.
8. Labarge, 'Pero Tafur', 238.
9. Devliegher, 'Pero Tafur', 272.
10. Guicciardini, *Descrittione*, 227. There is a difference between fair and equal. The aldermen of Bruges respected the privileges of the Hanse to the best of their ability. However, the modern notion of equality was unknown to them; De Boodt, 'An instrumental take on Justitia', 150–152.
11. Van Caenegem defined customary law 'as having grown spontaneously through repeated use and the consent of the people or at least the sectors of public life. These customs come into the legally enforceable sphere because they are enshrined in judgements'; Van Caenegem, 'Aantekeningen bij het middeleeuwse gewoonterecht', 97.
12. However, we should not equal the 'reasonability' of the aldermen with the Roman law notion of *Aequitas*: City Archive Bruges (Hereinafter: SAB) 157, *Civiele Sententiën*, 1453–1461, fol. 38 v.–39 v.; Donahue Jr, 'Equity in the courts of merchants', 11–16.

13. De ruysscher, 'Over themis en mercurius', 1110–1111; De Schepper and Cauchies, 'Legal tools of the public power', 239–246.
14. For example, the hosteller family 'Metteneye' delivered the first alderman in the years 1416, 1420, 1424, 1435, 1441, 1447, 1464, 1467, and the important mayor of the commune in the years 1386, 1418, 1421, 1430, 1434, 1455, 1461, 1470, 1474, 1498; SAB 114, *Wetsvernieuwingen*, 1386–1387, fol. 95 r. v.; SAB 114, *Wetsvernieuwingen*, 1397–1421, fol. 147 r.–v., 158 v.–159, 173 r.–v., 180 r.; SAB 114, *Wetsvernieuwingen*, 1422–1433, fol. 16 v., 57 r.–v., 94 r., 102 r.–v., 139 v.–140 r.; SAB 114, *Wetsvernieuwingen*, 1468–1501, fol. 17 v., 51 v., 249 v.
15. Blockmans, 'Mutaties van het politiek personeel', 92–103; Mertens, 'De Brugse ambachtsbesturen', 185–198; Sosson, *Les travaux pulics de la ville de Bruges*, 193–201; Vandewalle, 'De Brugse stadsmagistraat', 232.
16. See the famous episode during the marriage of Charles the Bold: Olivier de la Marche, *Mémoires*, vol. III, 113; Vandewalle, 'De vreemde naties in Brugge', 27–42; Degryse, 'De schepen in de haven van Sluis', 95–106.
17. SAB 96, *Rodenboek*, fol. 233 r.–234 v.
18. Boone, 'Le rêve de l'état-ville', 375–399.
19. Dumolyn and Haemers, 'Patterns of urban rebellion', 377; Blockmans, 'Villes et monarchies', 7–30; Prevenier, *The promised lands*, 141–174; Stein, *Magnanimous dukes and rising states*.
20. Flanders was divided into royal Flanders (everything west of the river schelde) and imperial Flanders (east of the river schelde). The King of Flance and the Holy Roman Emperor were the feudal lords. However, their actual influence was limited.
21. For the Council of Flanders see Dumolyn, *De raad van Vlaanderen*. For the Great Council: Van Rompaey, *De Grote Raad van de hertogen*.
22. See on evocation: RAG 146, 'Style van procederen', in de Raad van Vlaanderen, fol. 60 v.–61 r.
23. Häpke, *Brügges Entwicklung*, 256.
24. Van Houtte, 'Les courtiers aux Moyen Age', 134–135; Van Houtte, 'Makelaars en waarden', 1–30; 177–197; Van Houtte, 'Herbergwesen und Gastlichkeit', 177–88; Verbist, 'Traditie of innovatie?' 348–349; Puttevils, Stabel and Verbist. 'Een eenduidig pad van modernisering', 39–54.
25. Van Houtte, 'Bruges et Anvers', 89–108; Van Houtte, 'The rise and decline of the market of Bruges', 29–47; Van Houtte, 'Anvers aux XVe et XVIe siècles', 248–278. See also van Werveke, *Bruges et Anvers*; Asaert, 'Gasten uit Brugge', 23–41.
26. Lambert, 'A legal world market?' 171.
27. Brown and Dumolyn, eds. *Medieval Bruges*; Murray, *Bruges, Cradle of capitalism*; Brown, *Civic ceremony and religion*; Van Houtte, *De opkomst van een grote middeleeuwse markt: Brugge*; Van Houte et al., *De Geschiedenis van Brugge*; Gelderblom, *Cities of commerce*; Stabel, 'Organisation corporative', 91–134.
28. De ruysscher, 'From usages of merchants', 3–29; De ruysscher, *Handel en recht in de Antwerpse rechtbank*, 31–98; Van Hoftstraeten, *Juridisch humanisme en costumiere acculturatie*, 55–201.
29. Pirenne, 'Villes, marchés et marchands au Moyen Âge', 60; Pirenne, *l'origine des constitutions urbaines*, 31, 49.
30. Kadens, 'The myth of the customary law merchant', 1153–1206. De ruysscher, 'La lex mercatoria', 501–503; Donahue, 'Medieval and early modern lex mercatoria', 29–30.

31. See for Bruges as a network: Murray, *Bruges, Cradle of capitalism*, 228–229; Hunt and Murray, *A history of business*, 164; Murray, 'Of nodes and networks', 1–14.
32. Gelderblom, *Cities of commerce*, 104–105.
33. Ibid. 105–6, 108; Gelderblom, *The resolution of commercial conflicts*, 34.
34. Cordes and Höhn, 'Extra-legal and legal conflict management', 512–513. Höhn, *Kaufleute in Konflikt*, 279.
35. Most prominent in: Gelderblom, *Cities of commerce*; von Seggern, 'Fremde Kaufleute in Brügge', 111–123.
36. See the critique uttered by Cordes and Höhn, '"Per amorem vel per iusticiam"', 54.
37. Duve, 'Was ist "Multinormativität"?' 88–101; Decock, *Theologians and Contract Law*, 9, 29; Van Caenegem, 'Law in the medieval world', 18; Donlan, 'To hybridity and beyond', 17–32; Donlan, 'Comparative? Legal? History? Crossing boundaries', 82, 86.
38. Blockmans, *De volksvertegenwoordiging in Vlaanderen*; M. Boone, 'Urban Space and political conflict', 633. See on the Liberty of Bruges: Prevenier, 'Réalité et histoire', 5–14.
39. Dumolyn and Lambert, 'Cities of commerce, cities of constraints', 91–92.
40. Heebøll-Holm et al. 'Introduction', 14.
41. See, for example, the notable merchants Bernardo Cambi, Jacopo Strozzi, Allessandro Boromei and Jehan de Pin being slammed with a fine of the officer of justice due to infringements against communal law; General Archive Brussels, *Account of Joos van Varsenare*, 1447–1447, fol. 25 r.
42. SAB 157, *Civiele Sententiën Vierschaar*, 1424–1425; 1433–1436; 1447–1453; 1453–1461; 1465–1469, 1469–1471; SAB 164, *Memoriaal van de Kamere*, 1439–1441 and 1473–1474; SAB 165, *Sententiën Kamer*, 1474–1475 and 1478–1479. The Bruges archives make a division between the *Memoriaal* and the *Sententiën*. There is no reason for this, they were both a memorial of the procedure in camera. The difference with the Civiele Sententiën vierschaar is that the latter is the formal document that could be displayed in public, while the other two (numbers 164 and 165) were draft versions. There are also two incomplete parts of the formal registers for 1423–1424 and 1433–1436.
43. SAB 164, *Memoriaal van de kamer*, 1439–1441; SAB 157, *Civiele Sententiën*, 1453–1461, fol. 48 v.; Dendooven, 'De Brugse klerken in de veertiende eeuw', 85.
44. SAB 157, *Civiele Sententiën*, 1453–1461, fol. 48 v.
45. See on multilingualism in Bruges: Demets, 'Bruges as a multilingual contact zone', 313–332; Carlier, 'Taaldiversiteit in de kosmopolitische stad'. Although a unified Italian or German state did not exist in the middle ages, there was the common identity of 'Italians' or merchants from 'Allemange'. The sources also group them together. In 1493 the 'Italian merchants' received privileges.
46. From the city accounts and the 1491–1492 register of the *vierschaar* we learn that both procedure happened before the *vierschaar*; SAB 828bis, *Klerken vierschaar*, 1484–1488, fol. 53r.; SAB 216, *Stadsrekeningen Brugge*, 1470–1471, fol. 122 r. – 124 r.; SAB 216, *Stadsrekeningen Brugge*, 1443–1444, fol. 56 r.; SAB 216, *Stadsrekeningen Brugge*, 1471–1472, fol. 116 r.; Schouteet, *De klerken van de vierschaar*, 319. For foreigners appearing in this procedure see: SAB 828bis, *Klerken vierschaar*, 1484–1488, fol. 32 v., 33 r., 115 r.
47. From the *Acten en Sententiën*, we have a partial (per trimester) register for almost every year, and for interlocutory decisions we have registers for the periods between 1412–1440, 1450–1454 and from 1493 onwards. In these registers are the formal

decisions and often a narration of the case making them priceless. RAG 7508, *Raad van Vlaanderen, Interlocutoire Sententiën*, 1412–1427; RAG 7509, *Raad van Vlaanderen, Interlocutoire Sententiën*, 1437–1439 and 1421–1421; RAG 7510, *Raad van Vlaanderen, Interlocutoire Sententiën*, 1434–1441 and 1494–1496; 7511, *Raad van Vlaanderen, Interlocutoire Sententiën*, 1447–1458; RAG 7512, *Raad van Vlaanderen, Interlocutoire Sententiën*, 1483–1485; RAG 7513, *Raad van Vlaanderen, Interlocutoire Sententiën*, 1490–1493; RAG 7514, *Raad van Vlaanderen, Interlocutoire Sententiën*, 1496–1498; RAG 7515, *Raad van Vlaanderen, Interlocutoire Sententiën*, 1498–1503.

48. Dauchy, 'La non-motivation des décisions', 171–188.
49. Strubbe and De Smidt, *Chronologische lijsten*.
50. The aldermen of Bruges just speak about 'Grote Raad' or 'Grans Conseil' of the Duke. This can be both the Council of Flanders and the Great Council; SAB 157, *Civiele Sententiën*, 1465–1469, fol. 39 v.; RAG 2386, *Raad van Vlaanderen, Acten en Sententiën*, 1463–1464, fol. 290 r.
51. For example, the Portuguese nation transferred its documents to Antwerp when the community left Bruges. The archive of the Hanse Kontor is in Cologne. See, for example, for the original 1307 and 1309 privileges: Historische Archiv Köln, Hanseurkunden bis 1400, U 2/5–15; Vandewalle, 'Das Archiv der Hansestadt Lübeck,' 271–280; The archive of the Portuguese nation was transferred to Antwerp and partially to Lisbon: Braamcamp, *Noticias da feitoria*.
52. See on the chamber of accounts: Jean, *La chambre des comptes de Lille*, 104–106; Santamaria, *La chambre des comptes de Lille*, 325–362; den Hollander, 'Comparative cultures of accountability', 169. See for such a case of a princely court seeking advice: ADNB 17883, *Lettres missives et dêpéches*, Destroci.
53. Obviously, due to the abundance of materials, we had to take samples. It was interesting to see whether there was a link and how this court behaved towards Bruges. See, for example, the London municipal court drawing up rules for the English nation in Bruges: London Metropolitan Archives, *Common Council*, Journal 8, fol. 18 v. and LMA, *Common Council*, Journal 9, fol. 101 r.–v.
54. Pichierri, *Die Hanse*, 37–45. See on embargoes: Stantchev, 'The medieval origins of embargo', 388–389.
55. For example, the 'Hallegeboden' only survive from 1490 onwards. They contained a wealth of information on procedural matters in Bruges.
56. RAG 691, *Raad van Vlaanderen, Placcaaten en ordonantiën (1416–1475)*; Felixarchief Antwerpen 1070, Privilegiekamer, Vreemde natiën, Natie van Portugal, 1411–1650.
57. On Wielant and his career, see Kerckhoffs-De Hey, *De Grote Raad en zijn functionarissen* 157–161; Buntinx, 'Wielant, Philips', 279–298; Monballyu, 'Philips Wielant', 22. We consulted both the Dutch version of the *Practijke civile* and the French (better edited) version *Causes Civiles*: Wielant, *Practijke Civile*; Wielant, *Briève instruction en causes civiles*. There are numerous copies of the 'Style van Procederen' attributed to Frans de Rycke. We focused on the edition with early sixteenth-century handwriting: RAG 146, 'Style ende maniere van procederen' in de Raad van Vlaanderen. See for these seventeenth-century copies: RAG, 1127, Documenten met betrekking tot de 'stijl ende maniere van procederen in de Raad van Vlaanderen'. There is some overlap between de Rycke and the *Costume*, but the *Costume* seems to be a source where general rules were extracted from decisions that were made in the council; RAG 1259, Varia 2, *Costumen en Privileges van de Raad van Vlaanderen*; J. Monballyu, 'De style ende maniere van procederen in de camere van den raede in Vlaenderen (1521) van

Fransoys de Rycke (1525) ten onrechte toegeschreven aan Lambrecht van den Bryaerde, president van de Grote Raad van Mechelen,' *Tijdschrift voor Rechtsgeschiedenis* 49, nr. 3 (1981), 370–371.

58. The customs are a compilation of general rule written between folios 21 r. and 44 v. and are probably from the fifteenth century thanks to the various references to persons (Jan van Overbeke) and cases; RAG 1259, Varia 2, *Costumen en Privileges van de Raad van Vlaanderen*, 21 r.–44 v.
59. See for a vexatious appeal: ARA, CC, 21434, *Ontvanger van Exploten, Grote Raad*, fol. 6 r.
60. ARA, CC, 21436, *Ontvanger van Exploten, Grote Raad*, fol. 7 v.; ARA 21438, *Ontvanger van Exploten van de Grote Raad*, fol. 1 r. See also RAG 8495–8496, *Boeten*.
61. ARA, CC, 21440, *Ontvanger van Exploten van de Grote Raad*, fol. 16 r.; ARA, CC, 21445, *Ontvanger van Exploten van de Grote Raad*, fol. 24 r.; 38 r.; ARA, CC, 24803, *Ontvanger van Exploten, Raad van Vlaanderen*, 1427–1429, fol. 19 r.–19 v., 23 r.
62. Prevenier, 'Quelques aspects des comptes communaux', 144–145; Bosch, *Stedelijke macht*, 61–63.
63. Boone, 'Stedelijke financiën', 121–122.
64. Van Werveke, *De Gentsche stadsfinanciën*, 80–83.
65. Boone, 'L'influence des pratiques', 206.
66. Boone, *Geld en macht*, 32–34.
67. Groebner, 'The city guard's salute', 249; Groebner, *Liquid assets, dangerous gifts*, 20–22.
68. Fieremans, 'Give and Ye Shall Receive?', 83–87.
69. SAB 216, *Stadsrekeningen Brugge*, 1453–1454, fol. 53 v. Such payments increased as courts were becoming more involved in urban cases; SAB 216, *Stadsrekeningen Brugge*, 1512–1513, fol. 152 r. 300 Pounds Flemish Groat was, in 1453, around twenty-four' years work for a master stone mason. We calculated that an average stone mason worked about 250 days a year at a rate of 12 s. gr. a day.
70. Blockmans, 'Corruptie, patronage en makelaardij', 237–238; Derville, 'Pots-de-vin', 359–362; A. Derville, 'Les pots-de-vin', 449–469.
71. Van Werveke, *De Gentsche stadsfinanciën*, 93–99.

Part I

Law: The Legal Framework of Late Medieval Bruges

2

The Procedures of the Aldermen

The aldermen court was first and foremost a customary court. Although, there were certainly written ordinances and municipal guidelines, the aldermen founded the bulk of their decisions on unwritten rules or customs. These customs were created by implied consent and repeated practice. Thus, the aldermen were not very different from all other city courts in the County of Flanders.[1] Although the procedure before these courts started to be influenced by aspects of the Roman-Canonical procedural law, their decisions were based on experience and convenience.[2] Yet there is one essential difference. In medieval Bruges, there was an enormous presence of international merchants and a complex web of privileges and courts with overlapping jurisdictions. How this influenced the perceived justice of the city is the object of our study. Bart Lambert has already argued that the aldermen of Bruges did not have a habit of applying foreign customs. Foreign merchants would rather use Bruges' principles in court, rather than flaunting their customs.[3] According to Gelderblom, the Bruges aldermen allowed foreign merchants enough freedom to use the Bruges system in the most expedient way for them. Through consular courts, procedures such as arbitrations where peers decided upon a quarrel, and the leniency of the aldermen, merchants could influence the commercial city.[4] Or was it the commercial city that influenced merchants?

What merchants wanted remains a moot point. Of course, expectations varied from situation to situation and profile to profile. However, in this equation, it is important to confront the expectations of the merchants to the framework of the aldermen – how these groups interacted and how they changed each other. Older scholarship has often omitted the aldermen as active players. In the opinion of such scholars, parties would appear before the court, present their case, and the aldermen would decide. The court of aldermen was not able to intervene.[5] However, focusing solely on the merchants overlooks the presumption that the law mainly derived from the interaction between courts and litigants. While the merchants had a definition of justice, the aldermen also had their own definition and expectations for how a law court should function. It is important to consider the perspective of the aldermen as they established the framework within which the merchants operated.

The aldermen played a significant role in the definition of this framework. I will argue that the aldermen were able to intervene in the cases they deemed necessary. The Bruges' court still had mechanisms with which they tried to provide the most suitable possible outcome for all parties involved.

This is important because when the aldermen played an active role in shaping the framework, litigants could adjust their strategies accordingly to suit these judges. A merchant keen on winning his case was always smarter if he adapted to the judge, instead of asking the judge to adapt to him. As such, in every successful litigation strategy, merchants had to include, anticipate and convince the aldermen of Bruges. In the next section I will focus on the framework itself. This includes both the formal procedures and the less formal or even informal institutions that were present in Bruges.

THE VIERSCHAAR AND CHAMBER PROCEDURE

The aldermen had two formal procedures in the fifteenth century: the *vierschaar* and the chamber procedure. The first was the oldest.[6] In theory, the aldermen convened twice a week for this procedure and dealt with the matters at hand. As there are no registers preserved for the *vierschaar* before 1490, it is hard to say what this procedure exactly entailed. We have to be careful using the registers after 1490 as an example of the fifteenth century. When Bruges lost its commercial dominance, it changed its legal framework profoundly. Based on the registers of the chamber, the following section will try to outline the main differences and the role merchants played in them.

Merchants in the fourteenth century had few alternatives to appearing before the *vierschaar*. From the early fifteenth century, the aldermen had introduced another type of session called 'camere' or chamber procedure. Unfortunately, we lack any ordinances on what exactly these procedures entailed, who appeared where and what the difference in authority was.[7] Based on the registers of the aldermen, I will try to sketch the outlines of these procedures.

It is likely that the chamber procedure was the backbone of the judicial activity of the aldermen by the fifteenth century. The daily session was divided into two parts. The aldermen held the formal cases in the morning, while two aldermen and two council members provided a reduced court presence in the afternoon.[8] During this second part, the aldermen offered services such as the authentication of documents, the registration of sureties or the acceptance of small procedural acts.[9] These were minor acts that did not require a full assembly. In general, decisions from the chamber did not require the entire assembly to come to a decision. A full daily court was impossible if we consider the political responsibility, diplomatic missions, and communal care the aldermen undertook.

Furthermore, the intensity of the sessions varied daily. Similar cases were often evaluated on the same day, and not all the aldermen were consistently present. On important days, such as when conclusions were reached, the majority of councillors were present. On other days, only some were present. The aldermen also decreed that the members who were not present on the court days – and thus failed in their duties – would lose their remuneration *pro rata*. The registers ranging from 1447 to 1461 also mention the aldermen who were present at each decision. These witnesses were registered so the same aldermen could be questioned on their knowledge should the case be deliberated on. Important decisions were often made in the name of the entire council.[10]

There was little distinction *ratio materiae* on what could and could not appear before the *vierschaar* or the chamber. In addition to criminal procedures, people discussing inheritances, debts or insults appeared before the *vierschaar*. However, among the people who appeared, only a few were foreign merchants. The difference between both procedures is immediately apparent regarding nationality and the weight of the case. Which of these was more salient was discussed in 1478 before the Council of Flanders, the princely court in Flanders. In 1478, Colaert Willems complained that the aldermen had not considered his case according to the proper procedure. He stated that civil cases amounting to 30 lib. gr. should be held before the chamber and civil cases with a value over 30 lib. gr. should go before the *vierschaar*.[11] Although the aldermen did not dispute this rule, they stated that Colaert Willems had acted as a representative for some foreign merchants from Holland. As such, the aldermen believed that the correct procedure was applied since foreign merchants were bound to appear before the chamber. The Council of Flanders confirmed this and condemned Colaert Willems for a vexatious appeal. The procedure should continue according to the 'customs of the aforementioned city'.[12]

The alderman based their decision on who appeared before the *vierschaar* and who appeared in the chamber procedure on two considerations. The first was the rule that the *vierschaar* should have the financially impactful cases. The second was clearer: foreign merchants or people working for foreign merchants could not appear before the *vierschaar*. When someone was identified as a foreign merchant, the case should be decided in the chamber. The aldermen accepted even the faintest link as a relation. If a merchant made a surety for one of the litigants or even a merchant was indirectly involved, the case was transferred to the chamber.[13]

This was not a strict divide. Conflicts of all sorts between citizens could certainly be held before the *vierschaar* and occasionally a conflict between merchants must have appeared before the *vierschaar* as well.[14] When litigants wanted to change the procedure, the argument of being a 'foreigner' was adduced, and the aldermen agreed to transfer the case to the chamber procedure, but the parties needed to request this.[15] If none of the parties had a problem with having the case before the *vierschaar*, it was also acceptable for the aldermen.[16]

We should bear in mind that the same aldermen presided over a case in different procedures, and the *vierschaar* and the chamber could overlap.[17] As the *vierschaar* only sat in session twice a week, and the chamber daily, someone could present a surety before the chamber for a case that was pending at the *vierschaar*, which must have led to confusion regarding its registration in the registers.[18] Sometimes decisions taken in the *vierschaar* were subsequently written in the chamber's register. These decisions are relatively scant but show how vaguely defined the judicial system was. Take the arbitration between Saldone Ferrier from Catalonia and Marco Morosini from Venice, for example. Apparently, the *compromissum* or agreement to proceed to an arbitration, was presented when the *vierschaar* held its session. However, both of the parties were merchants and arbitrations were dealt in chamber procedure, so the aldermen wrote it down in the chamber register.[19]

The attitude of the aldermen towards this confusion between chamber and *vierschaar* would become stricter. Previously, the rule was that if the parties made no fuss about it, the aldermen would have no problem. Nevertheless, we can see that they are moving cases automatically in the 1460s. Already in 1457, the aldermen requested Bonnore Olivier, a citizen of Bruges originating from Genoa and receiver of extraordinary expenses, to move his case from the *vierschaar* to the chamber. Franchois Olivier and Colin de Laweye gave a surety that this would happen.[20] Jean de Lingui who acted on behalf of the Count of Saint-Pol was forbidden to appear before the *vierschaar*. As he was a foreigner, the aldermen decided he should appear before the chamber.[21] Moving cases also happened the other way around. There are a few people who wanted to appear before the chamber, but they were sent to the *vierschaar*. Unfortunately, we do not know what their cases were about since no registers prior to the 1490s were preserved.[22] It is nevertheless meaningful that appearing before the *vierschaar* was considered to be a privilege reserved for citizens.[23] As such, merchants were not allowed to appear before it, though exceptions were made.[24]

Why were some merchants eager to have their case before the *vierschaar*? It is possible that most were satisfied with the chamber procedure, yet some litigants preferred the *vierschaar* and were refused. It is hard to determine what exactly made them choose the *vierschaar*, because the sources do not reveal the intentions of the litigants.

Despite this clear obstacle, I propose the following hypothesis. Appearing before the chamber was known to be a faster procedure, probably because the aldermen held a daily court, but also because cases were less thoroughly developed.[25] There is truth to the argument that a faster procedure was sometimes necessary in fast-changing commercial relations. One of the arguments citizens used in their plea to appear before the chamber, was that the slow procedure of the *vierschaar* was detrimental to commerce.[26] However, there are various vague references that the chamber procedure was seen as less authoritative because of its speed. Some decisions even refer to the *vierschaar* as treating cases 'fully' (*gheheel*).[27] This is confirmed in the few civil cases we can find in the *vierschaar* register.[28] The chamber procedure was therefore not entirely satisfactory for some merchants. This might not have been a problem for citizens with claims of under 30 Flemish pounds. But we have seen for foreign merchants that nationality triumphed over value. These merchants had to appear before the chamber, even if damages rose above 30 lib. gr. It is therefore logical that if the stakes were high, these merchants would prefer elaborate procedures.

The role of the chamber procedure was to enforce debts when necessary. The aldermen listened to the arguments, inspected the presented evidence, and subsequently decided who was in the right or how the matter should proceed. By the second half of the fifteenth century, the aldermen employed the adversarial procedure that was becoming ubiquitous in fifteenth century Flanders. A claimant (*heesschere*) made a claim against the defendant (*verweerere*). The latter had the option to acknowledge the claim and settle the dispute, or to defy (*loochenen*) the claim and start a case.[29] Each party had the chance to make their claim, state their arguments, answer to these arguments and answer again to the reply. Parties were not obliged to prove their claims unless the aldermen demanded that they do so by an interlocutory judgment (a decision that did not decide the case). Of course, parties were free to prove their case before this point.

The evolution to a written procedure is of the essence here. Decisions pronounced – and written down – by the aldermen multiplied rapidly from the 1460s onwards. The number of merchants appearing before the court would stay largely the same as in the previous years. The rise is mainly the result of a rising number of citizens appearing in the chamber procedure and a rising number of procedural acts.[30] For example, if someone made a renunciation, the act where someone stated that no further arguments would follow, this was noted in the register.[31] The introduction of the written procedure might explain why the chamber became a more elaborate procedure. A smoking gun can be found in the scribes who complained about the 'multiplying of procedures, cases and persecutions' (*vermenichtheden vanden processen, ghedinghen ende vervolghen*), and demanded a raise because of 'the heavy burden they had to bear on a daily basis in the exercise of their office' (*zwaren lasten die zij daghelicx hadden int excerceren van haerlieder officien*).[32]

The evidence suggests that the written procedure made its introduction in Bruges from the late 1450s onwards and definitely by the late 1460s.[33] Parties were more prone to putting their arguments in writing, delivering them through representatives, and evading an appearance before the court in so doing. Sometimes the aldermen even required that the arguments were put in writing.[34] The booklets delivered by the parties were not registered by the aldermen except some small annotations.[35] Progress towards a solely written procedure was slow and the procedures existed side by side. This suggests a tendency, instead of a clean break with the past.

The incentive is unclear and was in all likelihood not monocausal. Jos Monballyu provides an explanation in the form of the Council of Flanders. As we will see later, the number of appeals against the aldermen of Bruges would rise in the 1460s and become a problem for Bruges. In case of an appeal, the Council of Flanders would assess whether the aldermen of Bruges had done their job.[36] The person who invoked the appeal accused the aldermen of rendering a poor judgment. When a written procedure occurred, the councillors would revisit the existing arguments. However, when an oral procedure had taken place, the councillors had to redo the procedure as there was no written argumentation.[37] The problem was that the parties could bring new arguments before the Council of Flanders that were previously unknown to the aldermen. In such a case, the aldermen could be condemned for a spurious decision founded on arguments that were previously unknown.[38]

This was problematic for the aldermen. Not surprisingly the cities of Flanders would forbid condemnations based on additional arguments in 1477.[39] The Council ignored this, and it would take until 1495 before the order was carried out.[40] This took quite some time, and it is not implausible that the aldermen tried to avoid this problem by simply investing more time in the written procedure. Since appeals were becoming more frequent in the second half of the fifteenth century, the aldermen defended themselves by providing written documentation.

In Antwerp, the increased formality of the court gave these merchants a familiar playing field (in the form of Roman law) and the necessary tools to play on it. In Bruges, customary law prevailed and, with some exceptions, evidence for Roman law is scarce. The court had spokespersons (*taelmannen*) in its service who assisted the parties on both law and facts.[41] However, they were not legal scholars. Specialists in Roman law rarely appear.[42] In most cases people represented themselves or were defended by colleagues or family members. In this respect it is also interesting to note that there are no signs that the aldermen's justice was an expensive one. As we have already indicated, litigants had to pay scribes a small fee if they wanted a consultation or a copy of a verdict. However, there are no systematic traces of this in the city accounts.

THE MERCHANTS THEIR INITIATIVE: ARBITRATION

The aldermen of Bruges encountered a structural issue: foreign merchants were restricted to appearing only before the chamber procedure, which lacked the depth of the *vierschaar* procedure. While some merchants found comfort in the 'in chamber' procedure, others did not. Time constraints often meant insufficient opportunities to gather arguments, hear testimonies, or seek expert opinions. To address this, the aldermen turned to arbitration, a voluntary process in which parties withdrew a conflict from the official judicial sphere to settle it informally.[43]

An appointed arbiter or several arbiters would decide upon the matter, thus avoiding a lengthy and expensive court procedure. Many historians argue that arbitration served as an exemplary form of conflict resolution among merchants in medieval Bruges.[44] Arbitration in Bruges satisfied the merchants' desires and also helped alleviate the workload of the aldermen. Despite being a private conflict resolution method, I will contend that arbitration in Bruges was both a form of private resolution for merchants and an integral part of the city's legal framework. Arbitration was essential for the aldermen to obtain justice. In medieval Bruges, most arbitrations were described as conducted by 'arbiters, arbitrators and common friends', a phrase that carried paradoxical yet precise implications. On one hand, it adhered to the Roman tradition of arbiters, who followed established laws, procedures, and wielded powers akin to court judges. On the other hand, the notion of an arbitrator arose from canon law and meant someone who judged according to equity and without a strict procedure. The precise interpretation and implications of both terms were subject to debate, and certainly, the Roman law 'arbiter' had to be adjusted to the legal practice of the Middle Ages by medieval jurists.[45]

In practice, the distinction was eroded in the thirteenth century. The decisions passed by an arbiter (called *arbitrium*) and those passed by an arbitrator (called *arbitrates*) gradually became more similar. This led to the use of the phrase 'arbiters, arbitrators and common friend', a combination that promoted flexibility.[46] According to some legal historians, it combined the best of both worlds, and arbitration therefore became a procedure readily adaptable according to the circumstances.[47] Despite the advantages of flexibility achieved through this amalgamation, historical records in Bruges reveal limited evidence of merchants freely interpreting or changing the rules of an arbitration.

This is primarily because the arbitrations were closely monitored by the aldermen. When parties agreed to arbitration, the aldermen recorded it in their registers. The agreement, called the *compromissum*, outlined essential aspects of the procedure to follow, including the selection of arbiters and the time frame for resolving the conflict. They agreed that they would respect their decision or otherwise would pay a fine.

The problem was that the aldermen never bothered to specify what those arbiters could and could not do. A first indication that these arbitrations were more or less the same is that the aldermen did not record the changing modalities of these arbitrations. It is likely that the aldermen had a certain expectation of what an arbitration should be and how it should be decided. In such a case, the sentence 'arbiters, arbitrators and common friends' must have had a precise meaning in Bruges that did not necessarily match its usage in arbitrations in other places. In fact, both parties were more or less aware of what was expected from them.

In the rare instance the Parliament of Paris talked about arbitrations in Bruges, it denominated the arbiters as 'arbitros simpliciter'.[48] Although that was hardly an indication on how arbitration was perceived in Bruges, it illustrates how arbitration was perceived by the Parliament. The Parliament of Paris saw a form of arbitration in Bruges that was not free to determine. Apparently, the aspect of the arbiter as a judge was deemed crucial by the Parliament in understanding arbitration in Bruges.

This emphasis on the arbiter's judicial role was also reflected in the way arbitration decisions were documented. Arbiters autonomously decided on the presented matters, and their decisions were recorded not as advice for the aldermen but as independent rulings.[49] Surviving arbitration records indicate that the arbitration process involved both parties presenting their arguments, and the arbiters subsequently made decisions. This contrasted with sixteenth-century Antwerp, where arbitration records were presented as advice for the aldermen's final decision-making. Furthermore, the eventual arbitration decisions were rarely registered, suggesting that they did not require formal approval from the aldermen. The registered cases usually pertained to situations expected to lead to further conflict.[50]

In this respect, we cannot neglect the private side of the arbitration. Arbiters were also considered as common friends. Although arbitrations were in principle conducted by neutral peers, we can see that in arbitrations the networks of merchants remained a vital aspect of how these conflicts were resolved. Most cases that were resolved through arbitration had the common feature that parties often made several claims and needed the in-depth involvement of a specialist or an experienced third party.[51] These arbiters still evaluated each claim according to their experience, the prevailing Bruges customs, and what they believed was reasonable.[52] For example, when Battista Gambaro claimed that the judgment of the arbiters was unreasonable, the arbiters answered that it had been drawn up according to their best knowledge.[53] They hoped that they had given a good ruling, although it had been made on the basis of their knowledge as merchants, not as scholars or doctors in law.

What did a ruling made by merchants imply? It seems to simultaneously indicate expertise and authority. The arbiters were not jurists, and they did not practice law, but in the matters set before them, they were presumably specialists. Parties had a say in the number and selection of the arbiters, the time limits on their decision, and could even determine whether or not they ratified the arbitration before the aldermen. Parties could choose their arbiter, but there seem to have been some rules in place.[54] Members of a party's own merchant community were often not eligible to be arbiters, and the arbiters in a case were often drawn from different merchant communities. A frequent combination consisted of three arbiters. Each party chose an arbiter, and the third person would be someone who provided common ground. It was also possible that only two arbiters were chosen, sometimes four or more, and some arbitration agreements included the option of co-opting an extra arbiter, the so-called *tiers-arbitre*. This person would try to force a decision before bringing the case back to the aldermen when the arbiters could not come to an agreement.

The chosen arbiters were not only capable but also respected and trusted figures in their communities. Although direct links between arbiters and parties were avoided, arbiters who appeared before the aldermen were often heads of firms, notable representatives, or consuls of merchant communities.[55] For instance, Battista Aliate, the head of a trading firm from Pisa, was a member of the Florentine merchant community while also assuming a more neutral role in arbitration. The vast number of arbitrations in which he participated is an indication of both his expertise and is intermediate role.[56]

In addition to specialist knowledge, networks were of utmost importance, becoming clearly visible in cases between citizens and international merchants.[57] When citizens of Bruges entered into arbitration with international merchants, one of the arbiters was often also a citizen. In such cases, the panel of arbiters would consist of at least one international merchant and at least one Bruges citizen. Hostellers were the exception. These hostellers had evolved from being innkeepers providing accommodation to brokers providing specialised knowledge about the market at hand. They provided several services to their customers, one of which was probably legal aid. They had often come to specialise in hosting specific groups of foreign merchants, offering guidance in the economic and social spheres, but they could also act as confidants in legal matters. In some cases, they were obliged to take responsibility for the merchants in their care.[58] As such, they would also act as arbiters because of their role as intermediaries.[59]

In summary, the figures who were chosen as arbiters were part of the agreement between the parties. The arbiters were chosen to represent them, defend them, but also to seek a solution between them. In cases between international merchants, they were often international merchants. Some had a clear link with one of the two parties, but this is not always easy to determine. Kin and people who had the same origins were often excluded from acting as arbiters. Respect, expertise and trustworthiness were needed, and the hostellers proved to take an important role in this. In cases involving citizens, we generally notice a combination of citizens and international merchants, or two hostellers as compromise figures.

There is some logic to this. These merchants had the combination of knowledge and networks and would give the parties assurance that their case would be treated as equitably as could be expected. At the same time, they had the authority of a judge who closed the matter. This authority was due to their expertise but also because the judicial system of Bruges required it. A frequently made statement was that the arbiters had viewed all the relevant documents and had heard all the arguments from the parties. They referred to and based their findings on as much evidence as possible, including a plethora of written arguments. These arguments were not discussed before or by the aldermen if the case was presented before their court.

In conclusion, we have arbitrations that were resolved according to the arbitrator's rule of equity but with the authority of the arbiter. Arbiters in Bruges were neither fully arbiters, nor arbitrators: they combined certain parts of both procedures. However, this does not mean that the parties were free to choose how they envisioned their arbitration. In medieval Bruges, all arbitrations agreed before the aldermen had the same structure and the same authority. In addition, if the aldermen checked the arbitration, they checked whether the arbitration was carried out according to the customs of Bruges. The Bruges aldermen played an important role in that they controlled the procedure to some extent and acted as a back-up if arbitration failed.

THE INITIATIVE OF THE ALDERMEN

The *vierschaar* or chamber procedures were the official side of proceeding before the aldermen. Merchants could bring their quarrels to the aldermen for a decision. The aldermen could decide on the matter as it lay before them, or they could demand further information and even take the initiative to obtain this information themselves. Besides their active role in a procedure, the aldermen could also opt to diverge from the normal procedure when they believed this to be expedient. Arbitration was a first example of a method of conflict resolution through peers instead of a court. These were conducted by merchants and took more time than the usual procedure. There might be an explanation why the aldermen used arbitration and why the aldermen supervised them closely. As we will see in more detail, arbitration was used as an alternative to the (overly) fast chamber procedure. The parties took their time, and the arbiters assessed all the arguments that could be provided and took the most informed decision. The aldermen saved effort by delegating some matters to arbiters, and offered a chance at proper justice for these merchants.

Yet the aldermen did not always relinquish the decision-making of all major cases to arbiters. In the most important cases the aldermen could also seize the initiative. In 1473, the banker Nicolas de May and the Hanseatic merchant Renault Roetaert appeared before the aldermen. Roetaert complained that payment was due for a bill of exchange, something Nicolas de May refused. The reaction of the aldermen is telling. In the proceedings, the aldermen appointed a committee from their midst to look into the matter. The aldermen did not specify the members of this committee, but in all likelihood, they were the hostellers and other specialists among them. In addition to their own expertise, the aldermen in the committee also sought advice from certain members of the bourse.[60] The committee gathered the arguments and then reported back to the general assembly of aldermen. The purpose of the committee was to provide the eventual judgment with authority. With the committee's work in mind, the aldermen passed their judgment.[61]

When in doubt about the evidence or the claims of a certain party, the aldermen could enquire on their own behalf. Although it happened rarely, it demonstrates the initiative they could take. It is therefore not a question of whether the aldermen could do this, but rather why and for whom they did this.

For instance, the aldermen could select a committee from among themselves to handle a difficult case in greater depth. Such a committee was called 'aldermen's deputation' (*schepenen deputatie*).[62] It was a very informal procedure and there are only indirect references to it in the written sources. The aldermen appointed commissioners who would then consider a case 'in the assessment of the parties' (*zittende in berechtene van de partijen*).[63] These aldermen assessed the case, decided on it and ended the matter, and reported the decision to the chamber.[64] The procedure had the advantage of resolving a matter quickly but also entailed a decreased legal certainty.[65]

This reduced legal certainty was apparent when Thideman Hoonin appeared before the aldermen against Jan van Remagen who acted as proctor for Leonardo Lomellini. During the session, the aldermen Jan Stockman and Jan Everyday had decided that Thideman Hoonin should pay Lomellini twenty-six Flemish pounds.[66] However, when Thideman refused, he was imprisoned on behalf of the Italian. Thideman claimed before the chamber that this was done abusively. He had two arguments. He claimed that the way the debt imprisonment happened was actually through a procuration, which was against the customs of Bruges. The second point was, however, more of a problem for the aldermen. Thideman claimed that the decision was a ruling 'outside of the chamber' (*buter camere*). There were no registers kept, hence, there was no written evidence. Thideman stated that any decision taken outside the chamber would only be valid for that legal year because of its informality.[67] He succeeded in confusing the aldermen who needed to consult 'various clerks and previous aldermen' before they were sure that this was a false interpretation.[68]

In an aldermen deputation, the aldermen's more informal and probably more conciliatory power counted, though it was at the expense of legal certainty.[69] If the aldermen wanted to make sure that the parties adhered to an informal judgment, they undertook another procedure called a submission (*submissie*). In such a case, one or more aldermen would be appointed as arbiters to decide on the conflict. The aldermen sought a compromise as mediators, used the expertise in their ranks, and gave more care to the cases at hand. For example, the alderman Filip van Aertrike was appointed in 1465 to decide on a case between the Portuguese Roys Vas and citizen Jan Allecaes.[70] Filip van Aertrike was part of the powerful van Aertrike family who combined the economic power of the hostellers with the political power of aldermanship. He was an expert who was chosen by the parties to end the case. Prior to the judgment from Filips van Aertrike, both parties had agreed to respect his judgment no matter the outcome.[71] These submissions took time and effort. Therefore, the aldermen employed them from the most important cases as an act of good governance.

The importance of this informal, fast and enforceable procedure becomes apparent in the conflict between the Castilian community and the Bruges guild of shippers in 1447. The shippers were responsible for vessels sailing between Sluis and Bruges.[72] The bigger ships docking at Sluis transferred their cargo onto these vessels and the shippers brought them to the Bruges market. These shippers held a monopoly on these services and believed in 1447 that their remuneration should rise. The Castilian community refused, and the aldermen quickly intervened. The Castilians were too essential to leave frustrated, the shippers vital for the transport of cargo between Sluis and Bruges, and the aldermen acted accordingly. The aldermen proposed a submission by two of their colleagues. The Castilians accepted and several shippers also agreed. The two aldermen heard both cases and concluded that the condition of the shippers was unreasonable and annulled it. The aldermen registered the judgment, stressed that the aldermen had listened to the parties, obtained advice and concluded their judgment in all fairness.[73] Of course, we do not know for sure whether that was indeed the case, but it is the narrative that counts here. Spanish wool was too crucial for the aldermen and they needed a quick solution to defuse the conflict.[74]

The communal accounts show each year the earnings of submissions, indicating that there was some regularity to the procedure.[75] However, the amounts were not a fee that litigants had to pay to initiate the procedure. They resemble the plea bargains (*compositie*) officers of justice offered.[76] These plea bargains were the prerogative of a ducal bailiff which meant that if the bailiff was convinced of a criminal's guilt but lacked enough evidence or lacked people claiming damages, he could propose a deal. The suspect would pay a fixed amount and the bailiff would dismiss the case. The incomes from a submission written in the city accounts point to a fine, but there is more to it.

Most of the submissions involved citizens and merchants only appeared sporadically, except for one type of case: infringements against the Bruges rights of staple. This is rather odd. The right of staple stated that merchants arriving in the Zwin should offer their merchandise for sale on the Bruges market before they could sell them elsewhere in Flanders. It assured the vitality of Bruges as a commercial centre. There is little doubt among historians that Bruges treasured its staple rights, enforced them, and protected them against any infringements. While one would expect that the aldermen of Bruges would make a show of transgressions they deemed particularly important, the city consequently opted for the less rigid way of conflict resolution.[77] In doing so, the aldermen demonstrate their leniency and how they use justice for their own municipal policy.

The staple was an assurance that certain commodities would flow to the city, yet Bruges depended on the good graces of the merchant communities to 'hold their staple'. Such a staple was often just held as long as the merchants were satisfied. The only thing Bruges could enforce was that merchants within Flanders prioritised Bruges over other ports.[78] The city maintained a particularly contentious relationship with Sluis, its outport. Sluis had the potential to surpass Bruges and emerge as a commercial hub in its own right. Throughout the fourteenth and early fifteenth centuries, Bruges vigorously sought privileges affirming that merchants were required to bypass Sluis and conduct their trade in Bruges. To enforce these privileges, Bruges relied on the *waterbaljuw* (officer of justice with competency 'on the water'), and from 1441 onwards, appointed its own official to oversee the staple regulations. The effectiveness of this official is evident in the data, as the city saw significant revenue increases during the 1440s and 1450s.[79] However, while we can presume that the disregard for the staple only increased when merchants sailed more frequently to Antwerp towards the end of the century, the fines quickly decreased. This sudden change is mysterious, but it is our hypothesis that the fluctuation can be explained from the conflict resolution Bruges applied to these cases. We should remember that the power of Bruges in cases of staple conflicts was exceedingly limited. The privileges only applied to the County of Flanders and not to Antwerp, which was located in Brabant. Therefore, the aldermen could not officially fine merchants going to Antwerp, as they did not violate Flemish privileges by going to Antwerp. Furthermore, if merchants disregarded the staple and travelled to Antwerp or Bergen-op-Zoom, Bruges could only penalise them upon their arrival in Bruges. A careful balance was to be observed. It was not the purpose of these fines to punish and estrange these merchants from Bruges. If Bruges fined these merchants beyond reason, they might just avoid Bruges altogether.

Therefore, Bruges dealt with these cases in submission. I argue that there were three reasons for Bruges to opt for this procedure: they could alter the interpretation of the right in the light of the common good; they could make a symbolical statement; and they could not be questioned on how they did this.[80]

There is a curious transformation of revenues from the staple in the city accounts. In the early fifteenth century, the city received numerous payments from citizens who wished to make 'amends' (*beteringhe te doen*). We do not know what these citizens had done to be penalised. The accounts only register that they had to pay or even perform acts or contribute to the common good (through public works). These citizens had to 'repay' the city because they had committed a violation (*ghemesuseert*) against the city and were now at 'the disposal of the aldermen'.[81] The citizen paid the city of Bruges back in natura: they provided building materials or did a good deed.[82]

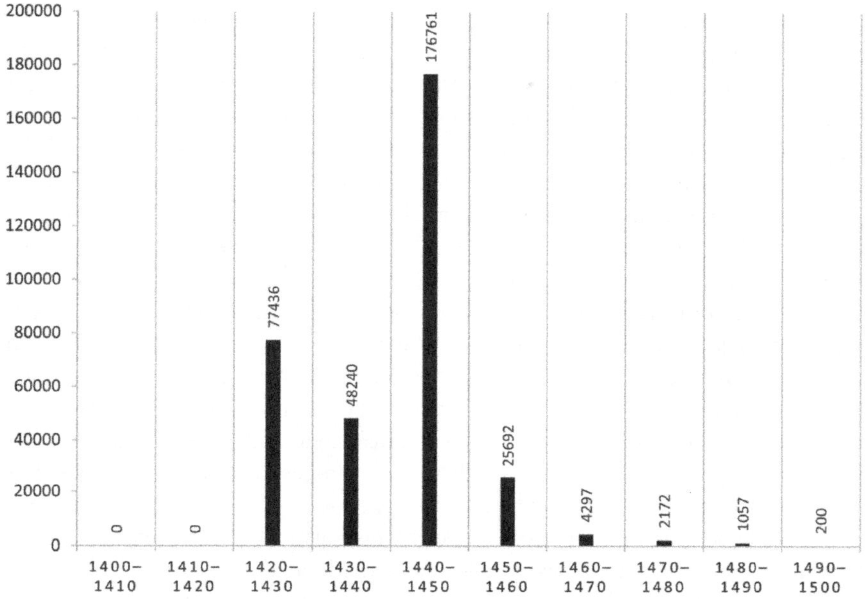

Figure 2.1 Fines collected by the aldermen of Bruges for staple infringements
Source: ARA, Dubbels van de rekenkamer, 1400–1500

This last category disappeared after the Bruges rebellion of 1438 when a new category was raised at the same time. In the accounts of 1438, we can see the aldermen registering the submissions for the first time. The Bruges rebellion, of course, is the big variable that changed relations between the prince and the city. The controllers of the chamber of accounts noted on the accounts of Bruges in 1438–1439 that the aldermen kept a separate account of all submissions.[83] Of course, Bruges was probably obliged by the Chamber of accounts to register this previously unregistered account. However, it is also remarkable that just as with the '*beteringhen*', submissions were initially mainly paid in natura where citizens were obliged to provide tiles. We can see that the 'importance' of the staple to the city remains the main ground on which the submissions were pronounced.[84] In paying this fine, the merchant was again contributing to the common good.

A condemnation in submission was also a symbolic gesture. The amount of the fines for staple infringements dropped radically during the 1450s and 1460s.[85] The drop coincides with the collapse of outports such as Damme. In the thirteenth and fourteenth centuries, ports like Damme and Sluis were considered as existential threats to the economic life of Bruges.[86] The staple ensured that merchants travelled to Bruges and not the other ports to sell their commodities. The new competitor was Antwerp and its yearly markets. This was a difficulty for Bruges, as the staple privileges were of great importance to Flanders, yet had no legal basis in Antwerp. Prior to 1441, the fines were large sums for individual merchants. These fines continued to fall after 1450, and certainly after 1460. In 1474, Tommaso Portinari had to pay 9 s. 1 d. gr. when he unloaded some merchandise in Sluis that he had bought in Bergen-op-Zoom.[87] Such a sum was probably small change for the Italian. Yet it was also a symbolic sanction to remind these merchants what had to be done.[88] By proposing these submissions, the Bruges aldermen could clearly deviate from formal procedures, apply their privileges in a symbolic (and wrongful) manner and propose a compromise. For example, Simon de Lalaing arrested some ships with Rhenish wines in Sluis. The staple for wine was in Damme, but because several ships were involved, it must have been a large quantity. Rather than having the strictest application of justice, the aldermen asked for the release of the wine on the condition that it was brought to the 'right' staple.[89] How Bruges convinced Simon de Lalaing remains a mystery.[90] Equally important was the fact that Bruges discarded some cases for merchants as 'being too small for punishment' and accepted the – small – financial compensation.[91] This may indicate that Bruges prioritised good trade flow over strict observance of the staple.

Furthermore, submissions offered some interesting procedural advantages. As we have already indicated, a submission allowed Bruges to include the water bailiff in the decision and it allowed Bruges to take notice of cases happening in the Zwin. It was an informal procedure where the aldermen dealt with a pending problem with discretion.[92] The merchants submitted themselves to the wise council of Bruges and the water bailiff and also avoided other aldermen benches by doing so, in particular Sluis or Damme.[93] By submitting themselves, the merchants accepted that the aldermen of Bruges were the competent judges to solve the matter. When a transgressor paid a fine, the fine confirmed the justness of Bruges' claim on the staple. The merchant admitted fault in paying a fine, even if it was just a small symbolic sum.

In addition, the aldermen did not pursue a longer procedure against the merchant and saw the matter as finished once the fine was paid.[94] In theory, submissions were not subject to appeal because there was no court decision.[95] Since it was a form of plea bargain between Bruges and another merchant, merchants were not able to appeal the accusations against them.[96] In addition, when the fines were low, these merchants were not severely punished and had very little incentive to appeal the decision. If a case was appealed, a princely court like the Council of Flanders would suddenly state its opinion on the matter.[97] This was something Bruges tried to avoid.

In conclusion, it is evident that the aldermen intervened in cases they considered significant. The judicial structure of Bruges was inherently flawed, as the procedure of the *vierschaar* was insufficient to meet the demands of a thriving commercial city. To address these shortcomings, certain adaptations were introduced: merchants were required to appear before the fast chamber procedure, and important cases were often resolved through arbitration. Arbitration allowed for a more thorough and extended process when necessary. Additionally, the aldermen utilised informal procedures to protect the interests of the city. These informal methods were primarily driven by communal concerns, such as maintaining the staple or ensuring the presence of merchants. For Bruges, it was crucial to retain control over merchants and prevent any harm to the city's interests. As the next chapter will demonstrate, the city employed innovative strategies to achieve this goal.

NOTES

1. De ruysscher, 'Customs and municipal law', 107.
2. Staelens, 'De schepenbank van Dendermonde', 89–92; De Smet, 'Het archief van Gent', 274; Monballyu, 'Het gerecht in de kasselrij Kortrijk', 657–664.
3. Lambert, 'A legal world market', 170–172.
4. Gelderblom, *Cities of commerce*, 106.
5. Gilliodts-Van Severen, *Inventaire des archives*, vol. II, 285; Boumans, 'Wethouders en stedelijk functionarissen,' 400; Janssens, 'Macht en onmacht van de Brugse schepenbank', 19–25.
6. Van den Auweele, 'Schepenbank en schepenen te Brugge', 281–282; Mertens, 'Bestuursinstellingen', 323–324.
7. It is highly hypothetical, but the two sessions may also indicate a distinction in locality. In 1410, the aldermen built a 'nieuwe camere' in the aldermen house. In 1424–1426, the aldermen already used the chamber procedure; Vanderwalle, 'Het Brugs stadhuis', 74.
8. SAB 157, *Civiele Sententiën*, 1453–1461, fol. 65 v.
9. There was some specialisation. For example the seventh and eight aldermen were responsible for matters relating to prison.
10. See for example: SAB 157, *Civiele Sententiën*, 1453–1461, fol. 42 r.
11. SAB 157, *Civiele Sententiën*, Snaggaertsvonnissen, fol. 87 v.; Mertens, 'Bestuursinstellingen van de stad Brugge', 324.
12. SAB 157, *Civiele Sententiën*, Snaggaertsvonnissen, fol. 87 r.–88 r.
13. SAB 157, *Civiele Sententiën*, 1447–1448, fol. 17 v.; SAB 157, *Civiele Sententiën*, 1447–1453, fol. 31 v.
14. SAB 157, *Civiele Sententiën* 1469–1471, fol. 67 v.
15. SAB 157, *Civiele Sententiën*, 1453–1461, fol. 72 r.
16. SAB 157, *Civiele Sententiën*, 1453–1461, fol. 37 r.–37 v.; SAB 157, *Civiele Sententiën*, 1453–1461, fol. 210 v., 212 r.
17. SAB 157, *Civiele Sententiën*, 1453–1461, fol. 37 r. See also: SAB 157, *Civiele Sententiën*, 1453–1461, fol. 279 r.
18. SAB 157, *Civiele Sententiën*, 1465–1469, fol. 120 v., zie ook SAB 157, *Civiele Sententiën*, 1469–1471, fol. 69 v. and 73 r.
19. SAB 157, *Civiele Sententiën*, 1453–1461, fol. 364 r.
20. Braekevelt and Lambert, 'Bonnore Olivier', 1155–1191.
21. SAB 157, *Civiele Sententiën*, 1453–1461, fol. 274 r.
22. SAB 157, *Civiele Sententiën*, 1469–1471, 119 r., see also fol. 34 v. and 62 r.
23. SAB 157, *Civiele Sententiën*, 1447–1453, fol. 324 v.
24. Of course, if a merchant decided to become a citizen of Bruges, they would also enjoy these rights and could follow a procedure before the *vierschaar*. See for example the process between Lijsbette Spapen and Rodrigo Catalaen; RAG 23720, Raad van Vlaanderen, Lijsbet Spapen, wed. van Willem de Ferrest c. Rodrigo Cathelaen.
25. It was stated in the 1304 charter that everyone who was imprisoned should receive justice within three to eight days; Gilliodts-Van Severen, *Coutume de Bruges*, vol. 2, 307.

26. SAB 96, *Rodenboek* A, fol. 303 r.
27. SAB 157, *Civiele Sententiën*, 1465–1469, fol. 218v. Submissions were seen as having authority like the vierschaar: SAB 157, *Civiele Sententiën*, 1469–1471, fol. 85 r.
28. SAB 157, *Civiele Sententiën*, 1491–1492; fol. 69 r.–77 r.
29. Stallaert, *Glossarium van verouderde rechtstermen*, 55.
30. This was only formally allowed in 1481; SAB 96, *Rodenboek* A, fol. 303 r. The year 1470–1471 only spans the period between September 1470 and January 1471, suggesting that it was an equally high year.
31. SAB 157, *Civiele Sententiën*, 1465–1469, fol. 220 r.
32. SAB 157, *Civiele Sententiën*, 1465–1469, fol. 53 r.
33. SAB 157, *Civiele Sententiën*, 1465–1469, fol. 119 r; SAB 157, *Civiele Sententiën*, 1465–1469, fol. 80 v.–81 r.
34. SAB 157, *Civiele Sententiën*, 1465–1469, fol. 132 v.
35. SAB 157, *Civiele Sententiën*, 1453–1461, fol. 278 r.; SAB 157, *Civiele Sententiën*, 1465–1469, fol. 120 v.
36. In late medieval Flanders, most appeals were in fact called reformations (*reformatiën*). The difference between an appeal were some procedures to be respected and the general antipathy the Flemish cities had towards appeals (so they had another name); Monballyu, 'Van appelatien ende reformatien', 237–276. See also RAG 146, 'Style van procederen', fol. 34 v.–48 v.
37. Monballyu, 'Van appelatien ende reformatien', 249; Wielant, 'Recueil des antiquités de Flandre', 111; Ganshof, *Etude sur le faussement de jugement*, 138–140.
38. Monballyu, 'Van appelatien ende reformatien', 253.
39. SAB 95, *Zwartenboek*, art. 25 en art. 26, fol. 20 r.
40. Monballyu, 'Van appelatien ende reformatien', 254; SAB 96, *Groenenboek B*, fol. 117 v.–118 v.
41. In later periods these '*taelmannen*' were considered as advocates. In Bruges, they seem to have a somewhat different function. Rather than a representative for one of the parties, the *taelmannen* worked for the court and were a service from the court towards the parties. See: Van Caenegem, 'Law in the medieval world', 37; Martyn, 'La "purge d'héritages"', 305.
42. See on proctors: Brundage, *The Medieval Origins*, 355; Falzone, 'Procureurs ad litem', 247; Guenée, 'Tribunaux et gens de justice', 202–212. In Flanders, all individuals could receive representation from a proctor. SAB, *Rodenboek*, fol. 204 r.–205 r.
43. Roebuck, *Mediation and arbitration*, 79–86; Biancalana, 'The legal framework of arbitration', 347–382; Oppetit, *Théorie de l'arbitrage*, 22.
44. See Gelderbom, *Cities of commerce*, 112.
45. Jeanclos, *L'arbitrage en Bourgogne*, 217–218.
46. Ziegler, 'Arbiter, arbitrator', 378–379; Lefebvre-Teillard, 'L'arbitrage en droit canonique', 28–33; Bader, 'Arbiter arbitrator seu amicabilis compositur', 276; Lefebvre-Teillard, 'Arbiter, arbitrator seu amicabilis compositor', 372–375.
47. Fowler, 'Forms of arbitration', 143–144.
48. Van Caenegem, *Les arrêts et jugés*, 613.
49. See for example: SAB 157, *Civiele Sententiën*, 1453–1461, fol. 96 r.; SAB 157, *Civiele Sententiën*, 1453–1461, fol. 91 r.; SAB 157, *Civiele Sententiën*, 1453–1461, fol. 79 r.
50. De ruysscher, 'Antwerp commercial law', 77–78.
51. Stevens, 'Failed arbitrations', 40.

52. SAB 157, *Civiele Sententiën*, 1453–1461, fol. 30 v.; SAB 157, *Civiele Sententiën*, 1465–1469, fol. 204 v.
53. SAB 157, *Civiele Sententiën*, 1447–1453, fol. 36 r.
54. SAB 157, *Civiele Sententiën*, 1447–1453, fol. 55 r.; SAB 157, *Civiele Sententiën*, 1453–1461, fol. 38 r.; SAB 157, *Civiele Sententiën*, 1447–1453, fol. 92 r.
55. SAB 157, *Civiele Sententiën*, 1469–1471, fol. 29 r.
56. See, for example: SAB 157, *Civiele Sententiën*, 1447–1453, fol. 249 v., 255 r., 304 r, 328 v., 320 r. 323 r.; SAB 157, *Civiele Sententiën*, 1453–1461, fol. 15 r., 25 r.–v., 30 v.–31 r., 38 r.–v., 61r.–62 r., 75 v.; 92 r., 142 r., 153 r., 158 v., 338 r., 361 v., 364 r.
57. SAB 157, *Civiele Sententiën*, 1447–1453, fol. 251 v.–252 r.; Jeanclos, *L'arbitrage en Bourgogne*, 97–98.
58. They were an essential witness when a case came before a court; SAB 165, Civiele Sententiën Kamer, 1474–1475, fol. 26 r.; Stabel et al. *Production, markets socio-economic structures*, 210–211; Murray, *Bruges, cradle of capitalism*, 196–202; Verbist, '*Traditie of innovatie*', 116.
59. SAB 157, *Civiele Sententiën*, 1453–1461, fol. 214 v.
60. SAB 165, *Civiele Sententiën Kamer*, 1473–1474, fol. 9 v.
61. This was not a strange procedure. The Council of Flanders could also appoint commissioners or decide a case through these commissioners. Likewise, the aldermen of Bruges could also demand a *turbe enquiry*. Evidence for this procedure is scarce.
62. SAB 157, *Civiele Sententiën*, 1465–1469, fol. 4 v.
63. SAB 157, *Civiele Sententiën*, 1447–1453, fol. 60 v.
64. It was not necessary to have the chamber's official approval, although some peer review may have been possible.
65. Sometimes even having a case before the parliament of Paris. Van Caenegem, *Le arrêts et jugés*, 480.
66. Approximately three years of work for a stone mason.
67. The aldermen started on 2 September and held office for one year. This legal year is the year one specific aldermen bench held power. In Dutch this would be called a '*jaerschare*'.
68. SAB 157, *Civiele Sententiën*, 1453–1461, fol. 36 v.
69. See for example: SAB 157, *Civiele Sententiën*, 1453–1461, fol. 40 v.
70. SAB 157, *Civiele Sententiën*, 1465–1469, fol. 3 v.
71. Buylaert et al., 'La loge des bourgeois de Bruges', 56–57.
72. See Vandewalle, 'Schippers', 85–111.
73. SAB 157, *Civiele Sententiën*, 1447–1453, fol. 40 v.–41 r.
74. SAB 157, *Civiele Sententiën*, 1447–1453, fol. 41 r.
75. SAB 216, *Stadsrekeningen Brugge*, 1473–1474, fol. 33 v.
76. See on these plea bargains: Van Rompaey, *Het grafelijk baljuwsambt*. However, the gains from submissions were written at a different part than the compositions for the bailiff; ARA, CC, 13781, *Accounts of the city bailiff of Bruges*, Antoine de la Vichte, 1478–1479, fol. 12 v.
77. This is to say, we do not have the registers of the *vierschaar* who might alter this view.
78. SAB, Politieke Charters, nr. 1323, SAB 96, *Rodenboek*, fol. 83 v.–84 r.; SAB 96, *Purperenboek*, fol. 91 r.–v.; CAB 96 96, *Rodenboek* A, fol. 7 r.–8 v.; Gilliodts-Van Severen, Coutumes des petites villes, IV, 502–504; Gilliodts-Van Severen, *Cartulaire de l'ancien consulat d'Espagne*, 158–159; SAB 96, *Rodenboek*, fol. 8 r.–v.; 83 r.–90 r.; UAG. HS.2570, *Privilegiën van Brugge en Sluis*, fol. 2 r.–3; SAB 522, *Waterrecht*, *De regulen*

ende sentencien vanden stapele, fol. 2 r.; Gilliodts-Van Severen, *Inventaire des chartes*, nr. 1023, p. 251. See for the case of 'subordination' of Sluis by granting a yearly gift. It came before the Council of Flanders and eventually before the Parliament of Paris. Before the Parliament, Sluis and Bruges made a deal; AN, X^{1A}, 4800, *Parliament de Paris, Plaidoires*, fol. 113 r.; AN, X^{1A}, 8304, *Parliament de Paris, Plaidoires*, fol. 136 r.; AN, X^{1C}, 172, *Parliament de Paris, Accords*, fol. 51 r.–54 r.r.

79. Lambert, 'Offences in the outport', 167–184; Lambert, 'Merchants on the margins', 237.
80. See on the common good in late medieval cities: Dumolyn, 'The common good', 70–71; Prevenier, 'Utilitas communis', 205–216.
81. ARA, CC, 32483, *Dubbels van de stadsrekeningen Brugge*, 1428–1429, fol. 26 r.
82. ARA, CC, 32472, *Dubbels van de stadsrekeningen Brugge*, 1417–1418, fol. 32 r.
83. Unfortunatly, there are no signs of submissions before 1438; ARA, CC, 32492, *Dubbels van de stadsrekeningen Brugge*, 1438–1439, fol. 19 r.; ARA, CC, 32493, *Dubbels van de stadsrekeningen Brugge*, 1438–1439, fol. 14 r.
84. ARA, CC, 32492, *Dubbels van de stadsrekeningen Brugge*, 1438–1439, fol. 19 r.; This occasionally returned in the later decades. ARA, CC, 32539, *Dubbels van de stadsrekeningen Brugge*, 1487–1488, fol. 28 r.; ARA 32529, *Stadsrekeningen Brugge*, 1478–1479, fol. 40 v.–41 r.
85. ARA, CC, 32517, *Dubbels van de stadsrekeningen Brugge*, 1450–1451, fol. 18 v.
86. Leloup and Dumolyn, 'The Zwin estuary', 201–202. The aldermen of Bruges forbade the aldermen of Damme to make plea deals with merchants ignoring the staple: SAB, *Politieke Charters*, 968, Gilliodts-Van Severen, *Inventaire des chartes*, vol. 4, 493.
87. SAB 216, *Stadsrekeningen Brugge*, 1473–1474, fol. 41 r. A year later, however, the water bailiff fined the man 13 lib. 6 s. 8 d. gr.; ADNB 6152, *Account of the watter bailiff*, fol. 1 r.
88. See for example: SAB 216, *Stadsrekeningen Brugge*, 1478–1479, fol. 47 r.–v.
89. SAB 216, *Stadsrekeningen Brugge*, 1452–1453, fol. 36 r.
90. Simon de Lalaing was also involved in the wine trade; Buylaert, 'Lordship, urbanization and social change', 61; De Win, 'Lalaing, Simon', 389–395.
91. SAB 216, *Stadsrekeningen Brugge*, 1459–1460, fol. 13 v.
92. SAB 216, *Stadsrekeningen Brugge*, 1461–1462, fol. 15 r. We can observe the same attitude in criminal cases. The city bailiff of Bruges occasionally organised compositions in accordance with the city council; ARA, CC, 13781, *Accounts of the city bailiff of Bruges*, 1477–1478, fol. 2 v.–3 r.
93. The bailiff of Damme occasionally punished merchants for staple transgressions (mainly wine): ARA, C.C., *Accounts of the bailiff of Damme*, 1445–1446, fol. 1 r.–1 v.
94. The aldermen tried to use the structures of arbitration here. In some submissions, we can see that aldermen acted as 'an arbitrator'; SAB 157, *Civiele Sententiën*, 1465–1469, fol. 3 v.
95. SAB 216, *Stadsrekeningen Brugge*, fol. 1461–1462, fol. 15 r. Although it was still possible that a staple infringement was dealt with a formal procedure; SAB 165, *Civiele Sententiën Kamer*, 1487–1488, fol. 15 r.
96. RAG 2385, *Raad van Vlaanderen, Acten en Sententien*, 1462–1463, fol. 193 v.
97. For example, in 1462, Sluis decided that herrings could also be sold in Sluis and had to explain its stance before a higher court; SAB 216, *Stadsrekeningen Brugge*, fol. 1461–1462, fol. 28 r.–v, 50 r.; SAB 216, *Stadsrekeningen Brugge*, 1463–1464, fol. 26 r. See also for a dispute between Sluis and Bruges: Archives Nationales, X^{1C}, 172, Parliament de Paris, Accords, nr. 51–54.

3

The Usage of Procedures

Arbitration was an essential part of Bruges' legal framework. The procedure allowed the aldermen to deal with cases in depth and attribute authority to decisions. Its observance was assured by the *compromissum* and if the aldermen were in doubt, they required additional sureties so the execution of the decision was assured. It illustrates the ambivalence between the public necessity and the private tools the aldermen wielded. Necessity prompted them to such alternatives, but we have to remember that the prime goal of the aldermen was the proper flow of justice.

The aldermen gave parties the space to solve quarrels privately, but still required guaranties that justice would prevail. The most essential mechanism of control was the promise of sureties. A surety was a guarantee for the creditor in case the debtor did not meet his obligation.[1] The act of standing guarantee for another person was nothing new in Bruges, but it received a particular function. It created a network of obligations. As such, guarantors appeared frequently before the aldermen of Bruges. In medieval Bruges, sureties were demanded for various reasons. There were procedural sureties for the respect of a court procedure, for the respect of a court decision or as the assurance for the good behaviour of a litigant. In addition, sureties could be given for the release of arrested merchandise or an arrested debtor and they could be demanded by the aldermen of Bruges for the safekeeping of the city. The city of Bruges could not be damaged, a procedure would be respected and the guarantor giving the surety was financially liable.

Almost one-fifth of the annotations in the registers of the aldermen relate to sureties.[2] The present chapter argues that the networks that were created and used were the fabric of Bruges society and the key to understand how the Bruges court operated. However, in practice the sureties that were given were often confounded, not systematised and cannot be reduced to a couple of axioms. It was a wasps' nest. I will limit myself here. The foundations, goals and precise legal ground merit their own study. The importance of sureties in late medieval Bruges is not so much in the legal figures that appeared, but in how it was used by the aldermen of Bruges. As such, I will focus on the role of these sureties, and the network that was made by them, in the litigation strategies of merchants. Therefore, I will only discuss two types of sureties: the sureties given in case of an arrest and those that were demanded by the Bruges court. The first was a private assurance to the creditor that a formal procedure would be followed, while the second was a promise to the aldermen of Bruges that the city would not be harmed. The aldermen used the network that was already in place to control the merchant communities and outrun damages.

MAKING NETWORKS

In its simplest form, three parties were involved in a surety. The debtor owned a debt to the creditor. However, the latter was not sure whether the debtor would fulfil this obligation. The surety guaranteed the payment.[3] If the debtor refused to fulfil the obligation, or just disappeared, the creditor could call upon the guarantor for the debt.

There were two essential ways for a creditor to make sure that the debtor provided sureties. The creditor could arrest the merchandise (attachment) or the debtor (coercion). An attachment was the most practised of both options. Creditors had to seize the goods for example during transports, when they were stored in an unprotected place or when these goods were in the ships in the harbour. When an attachment happened, the merchandise had to be kept, stored or at least the value preserved for one year and a day. If nobody disputed the attachment, the merchandise could be sold at a public auction.[4] However, the aldermen still demanded sureties from the seizing creditor. This creditor had to find someone to assure that the term of one year and a day would be respected and the merchandise would not be prematurely sold. In addition, if a debtor complained, the one making the arrest would abide by the judgment of the aldermen. In this way, possible debtors had the time to protest the arrest and, if applicable, see their merchandise returned. However, if a debtor claimed the merchandise, the aldermen demanded sureties for the release of the merchandise. The debtor had to find a man (or woman) who assured that the court procedure would be respected and the decision of the aldermen was carried out.

It was, of course, equally important to the aldermen that the seizer would also appear before the court and not keep all the profits. The hostellers Clais Pagant and Roegier Scaec illustrate this. They stood surety in 1455 for the Scottish merchant Henric Cups who had made an attachment on a ship – called the Kyele – to recover a debt from the Scottish nobleman Sir John Crichton. These guarantors promised Henric Cups would go to court if someone protested against his attachment.[5]

However, it was the other way around in most cases. The debtor was confronted with an attachment and had to provide sureties to see the merchandise returned. The broker Jacob Metteneye intervened on behalf of the bishop of Galway when Victor Pierens had seized the bishop's horses.[6] The guarantors provided by the bishop of Galway ensured the respect of the aldermen's decision and the return of the horses to its owner. As such, a surety was a precondition to the return of their merchandise.[7]

Debt imprisonment was an easier option. Creditors used one of the legal captors (*wettelijke vangers*), the people qualified to arrest people, and ordered debtors into prison.[8] The debtors lost their freedom, but the prison had to provide for them, and they maintained contact with the outside world and could continue commercial dealings. Once in prison, the debtor had to remain there until procuring a guarantor who made a surety for the debtor's release. The promise entailed that the debtor would not flee but agreed to solve the case before the aldermen of Bruges and would respect the decision of the aldermen.[9] When the debt imprisonment was done maliciously, the creditor had to pay for the sustenance of the debtor during the period of imprisonment. Several merchant communities had exceptions to this system. It barred some communities from direct imprisonment, while others had the assurance of release upon surety. When merchants lacked privileges protecting them, the consent of the creditor was essential.[10] The guarantor had to promise to bring the debtor to court, bring the case before the aldermen and to uphold the aldermen's ruling. If it was impossible to release the debtor, the guarantors promised to contend with the prison guardian so the debtor would not escape.[11]

Imprisonment comprised a higher liability for creditors, but they had to act fast before another creditor seized the opportunity. The aldermen frowned upon the practice of imposing a 'burden' (*verzwaren*) on a debtor with several claims at the same time.[12] A debtor could only be imprisoned and released on surety for one creditor (or a group of creditors making the same arrest) at the time. Although it was envisioned as a protective stance for the debtor, this motivated creditors to act swiftly in arresting debtors.[13] It was crucial to be the first to lock up the debtor. Once surety was obtained and proceedings had started, this creditor would be the first to receive a slice of the cake. Others would have to wait for the outcome of the proceedings and could only repeat the process.[14]

Obviously, the guarantors protected themselves.[15] Debtors and guarantors were free to make a contract setting the modalities for the surety. For example, when the English merchant William Bentham sued the citizen Antheunis Minne because he had promised to pay Hughe Went, a little document appears that stated there was a promise to keep the guarantor without any damage (*costeloos ende scadeloos*). The aldermen eventually forced Antheunis Minne to repay his guarantor.[16] Although the agreement between debtor and guarantor was not documented in the aldermen's register, the aldermen often wrote, next to the name and for what amount they made the surety, whether the surety included a formula indemnifying the guarantor.[17] In addition to the essential assurance that the debtor would appear before the court, this formula ensured that debtors would not run away and leave the guarantors to their fate.[18] A web of obligations had arisen with no way out for the debtor. The guarantor promised the creditor that the debtor would appear before the court and respect the judgment. If not, the guarantor would be liable to do so. However, for their part, guarantors demanded that they would suffer no damage from the debtor. Of course, what was to stop the debtor breaking this promise? The problem was that the surety was often made by family members, commercial partners, and hostellers. In some cases, the aldermen demanded that the guarantor was a citizen. When this happened, it was highly unlikely that both the guarantor and the debtor would disappear. In addition, if the citizen was a hosteller, the latter was the key to commerce in Bruges. If the merchants fooled the hosteller, it would damage their career beyond compare. As most hostellers worked with a limited number of merchant communities and specialised in certain networks, the debtor in question would quickly be excluded from the commercial community.[19]

Thus, the people who were released from prison or received their merchandise back were not genuinely free to do as they pleased.[20] The debtors were kept in an 'open prison'. The arrest did not aim for physical closure, but a symbolic one where the debtors could not escape their responsibilities. They were a fly in a web of obligations, in which the aldermen of Bruges used already existing networks in the form of commercial partnerships, merchant communities, and the services provided by hostellers to their advantage.[21] Bruges used the unique networks at hand to their benefit.

MERCHANTS USING NETWORKS

The main objective of the surety was the assurance of a fair procedure. Hence, the aldermen of Bruges were at the centre of the surety. Once a case was brought before the aldermen, the court had every interest in bringing it to a good conclusion. In order to do this, they had to ensure that both parties agreed that the aldermen court was the competent institution, that the parties would keep their case before the aldermen during the proceedings and eventually accept the judgment of the aldermen and pay what was decided. Whereas the aldermen's authority over its citizens was obvious, its authority over foreigners was a different case. Foreign merchants operated under princely safe conduct, and in many cases, they already had ways to solve quarrels without the intervention of the aldermen. Nonetheless, when a merchant initiated a case before the aldermen, these judges had a duty to find a resolution and solve the quarrel. However, what if one of the two parties disagreed and refused to appear before the aldermen?

In criminal cases, some enforcement mechanisms were present. Together with the city bailiff (*schout*), the burgomaster of the commune could apprehend criminals. However, the aldermen had to use more guile in civil cases. *Contumacia* or contumacy was the act of failing to appear before a court (*contumacia de non comparendo*), or failing to provide procedural acts (*contumacia de non agendo*). Contumacy was a plague faced regularly by pre-modern courts.[22] The punishment could be severe, but in reality, it hampered the efficiency of most courts.[23] Also, many cases in the princely courts were postponed several times due to the absence of a litigant, and a substantial number of them never reached another stage of proceedings.[24]

As such, sureties were essential for the avoidance of contumacy. In 1454, the aldermen decreed that anyone who was summoned three times, without appearing before the court or without sending a legal representative, and thus skipped three sessions, would be liable for capture for 'disobedience' (*onverhoorlichheden*).[25] By making these persistent defaulters liable for imprisonment, these people could also be included in the web of obligations without a prior debt.[26] These people could be imprisoned for refusing to appear before the court, and forced to provide sureties which would assure the proper procedure before the court if they wanted to be released. By providing a surety, the debtor also agreed that the aldermen were the competent court to discuss the matter. In this way, the aldermen tried to avoid contumacy. It was the aldermen's conviction that as long as both parties tried to achieve justice before their court, proper justice would be provided.

Needless to say, the aldermen favoured these sureties. It is a marker for the intelligence and insight in the aldermen's case law that litigants engaged with this surety system to convince the aldermen of their stance. When a Gordian knot presented itself and there was no easy solution, the aldermen often hesitated and quickly demanded sureties from the parties. A skilful litigant would foresee this and use the promise of a surety to sway the aldermen in his or her direction. This is illustrated by Cornelie. On 5 January 1457, the aldermen considered the case between Henric Peterszuene of Zeeland and a certain Cornelie. She was detained for her husband's debts. Her husband, Lauwerijns, was a shipmaster who arrived in England without a ship and its cargo of candles and soot. Aggrieved by this, the merchant Henric Peterszuene imprisoned Mr Lauwerijns immediately for outstanding debts. Since the latter was imprisoned in England, the competent court would be there. However, as Cornelie was imprisoned by the same captor in Bruges, she could bring the case before the aldermen of Bruges. Before the court, she lamented the behaviour of Henric Peterszuene who had also imprisoned her husband and now imprisoned a married woman who was not the principal of the debt.[27] When the aldermen asked her the reason for the imprisonment, she answered that Henric had imprisoned her husband Lauwerijns, through an English representative (*facteur*), while neither she nor Lauwerijns 'ever had anything to do with the aforesaid Henric'.[28] Henric, however, objected and claimed that Cornelie's husband was responsible as shipmaster for a disappeared cargo of candles and soot and that he had imprisoned him because these candles could only be retrieved with the greatest difficulty. According to Henric, Lauwerijns had acted as shipmaster of the cargo and could be held accountable for his presumed misconduct.[29]

Cornelie acted cunningly and wanted to present sureties in return for the release of her husband. By so doing, she demonstrated her good intentions to abide by the decision of the aldermen. The aldermen agreed. Cornelie was released, and the aldermen ordered the release of her husband, on the condition that Cornelie provided sufficient sureties.[30] Although Cornelie was caught in the web of obligations, and a court procedure probably followed, she also obtained reassurances that her husband, who was still in England, would be released. If Henric was to have any hope of retrieving anything from the couple, he had to abide by the procedure before the aldermen. If he refused, he would probably provoke the ire of the aldermen and lose the case. By using the *quid pro quo*, Cornelie, in all likelihood, convinced the aldermen to release the captive. Cornelie obtained the release of her husband and facilitated the costs she had to make for it.[31] Not to say that such activities were always this efficient, but by providing sureties and promising to abide by their procedures, she had bought the goodwill of the aldermen.

Coline Joos Bochoutswijve demonstrated how litigants could use this in their favour in 1465. She had obtained a letter of obligation from Jan Heyns of London.

The letter stipulated that Jan Heyns promised to pay the amount of 49 lib. gr. to another merchant Willem Stocker. The obligation could be paid out to Willem Stocker, his servants or someone who carried the letter. We do not know how Coline came into possession of the letter, but she handed it over to an agent of Willem Stocker in the hope of receiving payment.[32] However, after Coline entrusted the letter to Stocker's agent, it disappeared, along with the claim she had attached to it. Although Stocker's representative proclaimed before the aldermen that he had given Coline a chirograph, Coline declared she had suffered and would suffer more damage unless she had a written statement verified by the aldermen. She convinced the aldermen to keep her without damage (*quite ende scadeloos*). The factor had to provide guarantors that ensured the letter of obligation against Coline. In brief, Coline could convince the aldermen to give her sureties, and by doing so, the aldermen gave her a strong claim on the letter of obligation. For us, it is something of a mystery how she got the letter of obligation, but at the end of the process, she played the case to her advantage.[33]

THE CITY USING NETWORKS

In addition to litigants using a procedural surety to their advantage, the network was also consciously used to prevent Bruges, as a city, from suffering any damage. Informal conflict resolution is often combined with formal conflict resolution. Sureties were essential in keeping everyone in check. The guarantors assured that debtors would not incur damage to opponents by just disappearing, but also that they would not damage the vested interests of the aldermen. As such, the aldermen used the surety to safeguard individuals, but also to safeguard the city as a whole.

For example, Bruges could use the hostellers as a local network to keep merchants in check. As we have mentioned, one of the services these hostellers provided were legal tasks.[34] Making a surety before the aldermen could lead to accountability. However, there are cases where the aldermen considered the hostellers accountable even when they had not previously made a surety.[35] The city could additionally demand a surety from the hostellers so they would ensure the good conduct of their guests.

For example, in 1467, the hosteller Jacob van Dorle was forced by the aldermen to make some sureties in order to assure that his guests would not harm the Castilian nation.[36] The Castilian nation was a prominent and large merchant community with a firm presence in Bruges. For the Castilians, violence was a viable option to protect their interests. The hostellers had to make sureties to placate the Castilians and promise that the conflict would not escalate. One can only guess who these merchants were, but it is not unlikely they came from one of the other unrulier nations. The German sailors, for example, are usual suspects in the accounts of the officers of justice. This is a logical consequence of their large presence in Bruges. A large mass of people from one nation or another was also a danger for Bruges. At the time Spain and the Hanse were frequently attacking each other's vessels and could bring their violence to Bruges.[37] If these merchants were indeed Hanseatic, the Bruges aldermen used a smart way to control them. The aldermen could probably not ask the Hanseatic Kontor to discipline its merchants without running into lengthy discussions on who was actually at fault. However, by demanding one of their own hostellers to make the surety and control the merchants living in the hosteller's establishments, the aldermen might have reached the same result without disturbing the Hanse.

In the same year 1467, Bruges was again demanding sureties after Castilian shippers had attacked the vessel of the German merchant Matijs Priffel. The Hanseatic Kontor demanded justice from the Bruges aldermen. If the aldermen refused to provide justice, the Hanseatic merchants would do it themselves. Their privileges stated that in cases of maritime plunder the aldermen should bring their loot back without any form of trial.[38] However, the Castilian nation was not planning on surrendering their merchandise without a fight. If the aldermen hesitated, both parties could take matters into their own hands and escalate the situation. The threat of violence was considerable. The Bruges aldermen agreed that the consuls and several merchants of the North Spanish nation of Biscay should intervene as mediators, stand as sureties that nothing would happen and provide guarantors that the matter would be settled before a court. The Germans accepted the surety, and the Castilians were granted safe conduct in the Zwin to allow them to enter Bruges to discuss the conflict.[39] If the Germans did not respect this, the sureties would be annulled. Apparently, it worked. Later, the Hanseatic Kontor declared before the aldermen that the sureties were no longer necessary.[40]

The sureties had a safety function allowing the aldermen to defuse tensions between both parties, preventing them from taking matters into their own hands and resorting to violent alternatives. By providing sureties, both parties were assured that the matter would be resolved peacefully. It also had the added benefit of Bruges avoiding liability. When a member of the Hanse had taken French ships and brought them to Dunkirk, the Hanseatic Kontor in Bruges vowed to protect its merchants. Nevertheless, Bruges demanded a formal promise that they would be left without any damage.[41] The aldermen considered the network at hand one of the biggest tools they had to assure safe commerce and the orderly conduct of the merchants within their city. When the court deemed this necessary, the aldermen could demand that one of the parties should provide sureties. In such cases, the surety was not a measure to gain something like a release, nor a personal assurance; instead it provided an assurance for the city as a whole.

The Hanse had obtained a clause in 1309 stating that the city's money changers were under the responsibility of the aldermen of Bruges.[42] If a money changer disappeared, Hanseatic merchants would suffer damage.[43] Hence, according to the Hanse, the aldermen were accountable and should indemnify these merchants. Such a clause was augmented in 1359 when the mistakes of hostellers also fell under this responsibility.[44] The Hanseatic merchants were the biggest community and were highly persistent in enforcing these privileges. Subsequently, the Spanish and English would also acquire this right for indemnification when money changers defaulted.[45]

Of course, Bruges was never particularly happy to pay. To prevent this scenario, the aldermen had to work proactively and control individuals who could harm the city. For example, the aldermen obliged the hosteller Johan vanden Walle in 1465 to provide sureties. He presented a flight risk according to the aldermen and they realised that the city of Bruges would incur damage if he fled. Therefore, he was to provide sureties so he would not harm the city.[46] When the Bruges hosteller and money changer Pieter de Ceur went beyond the limits of reasonableness and defaulted too many times on the payment of the letters of exchange, the aldermen took resolute action. The Burgomaster of the commune arrested the latter 'in the interest of the city'.[47] The burgomaster locked Pieter up in prison, but also demanded several sureties so that he would remain and that unfortunate merchants could demand compensation. It must have been a large amount because the initial guarantors, his brother Hewin de Ceur, Antheunis den Pieyere and Simon de Cockere, were not sufficient. In addition to those sureties, influential people such as Pieter Bladelin, a member of the personal council of the Duke of Burgundy, Joos van Varsenare and Jan de Baenst, both prominent citizens of Bruges, became guarantors for Pieter de Ceur so he would pay his debt.[48] Nevertheless, even this had its limits. The aldermen had no intention of keeping these sureties liable 'until eternity'. Potential claimants had a year and a day to make their claim.[49]

As all merchant firms of note were present in Bruges, very few merchants could ignore the networks that were in place. For such a system to work, the city needed a critical mass. Networks and merchants who were reliant on these networks were the conditions to ensure these sureties worked. Damaging your name in Bruges would have dire consequences throughout the commercial world. The aldermen used the networks that were present to assure that they were the competent judges, and their decisions would have consequences, but also to make sure that they would not be damaged.

The aldermen tried to foresee these liabilities and acted quickly in demanding a surety if necessary. The network of sureties also had the consequence that it suited their concept of justice. Generally speaking, the aldermen refrained from interrupting commercial flows. Through sureties, creditors were assured that funds would not disappear and the normal flow of commerce could continue. The owners received their merchandise back and were not completely ruined. In case of debt imprisonment, it was more difficult. Debt imprisonment was a network-making institution: it bound the merchants to the Bruges court, it assured the creditor of the enforcement of the decision of the aldermen, and for those aware of the intricacies of the system, it could be used to get themselves out of a difficult situation. The informality of the practice led to some ingenious solutions on the part of merchants. When a debt could be substantiated, a merchant could be arrested. This was a very intrusive way of dealing with debtors. In most cases, merchants endeavoured to stay within the confines of what was permitted. Bruges remained vigilant, and if the aldermen ruled against the imprisoning merchant, the consequences could be dire. Fines could ensue, and the creditor had to bear the cost of maintaining their debtor. Still, the main objective was to get debtors out of prison as quickly as possible and, in so doing, he became a part of a powerful network. The biggest disadvantage to debtors was, of course, the limited chance of escape. Debtors were bound by their promises. This gave rise to a particular situation where creditors had many opportunities to make sure they received their dues. Debtors on the other hand could not use mechanisms such as bankruptcy to escape their obligations. The network was present, and the aldermen used it to their advantage. However, as we noted in the last section, the aldermen were focused on their own prerogatives. Such a stance raises questions on how far the aldermen concerned themselves with the safety of the merchants, the private sphere of conflict resolution, and what the true objectives of the aldermen were.

NOTES

1. Godding, *Le droit privé dans les Pays-Bas*, 441; Godding, 'Les sûretés personnelles', 305; Hattenhauer, 'Bürgschaft', 770–772.
2. More precisely 21 per cent.
3. SAB 157, *Civiele Sententiën* 1447–1453, fol. 34 r. Gilissen, 'L'évolution de la plévine', 180, 184–185.
4. In some cases they could do this with the permission of the aldermen, see for example: SAB 157, *Civiele Sententiën*, 1469–1471, fol. 35 r.; 73 v.
5. SAB 157, *Civiele Sententiën*, 1453–1461, fol. 65 v.
6. SAB 157, *Civiele Sententiën*, 1447–1453, fol. 309 v.
7. SAB 157, *Civiele Sententiën*, 1447–1453, fol. 324 r.
8. Smail, 'Debt, humiliation', 251–252. See also Smail, 'Legal plunder' and Smail, 'Violence and predation'.
9. In Flemish: 'het gewijsde betalen'.
10. SAB 157, *Civiele Sententiën*, 1465–1469, fol. 2 v.
11. SAB 157, *Civiele Sententiën*, 1447–1453, fol. 101 v.
12. Although there were numerous exceptions to this; SAB 96, *Groenenboek Ongecotteerd*, fol. 264 r.
13. In the case of distraints on merchandise, the aldermen allowed an equal division. This was not always the case in debt imprisonment.
14. However, there were numerous exceptions to the rule formulated by the aldermen in their cartularies. It seems that Wielants allowed this, which leaves us wondering how far this was a practice in other cities; Wielant, *Causes Civiles*, cap. 59, nr. 3; Bissaud, *Le créancier 'premier saisissant'*.
15. SAB 157, *Civiele Sententiën*, 1447–1453, fol. 38 v.
16. SAB 165, *Civiele Sententiën Kamer*, 1473–1474, fol. 2 v–3 r.
17. See for such a document: SAB, *Archief van de Adornes van Jeruzalem*, nr 18.
18. See for some examples: SAB 157, *Civiele Sententiën*, 1447–1453, fol. 59 r., 62 r.; SAB 157, *Civiele Sententiën*, 1453–1461, fol. 335 v., 351 r.; SAB 157, *Civiele Sententiën*, 1465–1469, fol. 18 r., 37 r., 59 r., 67 r., 86 v., 125 v., 128 r.; SAB 157, *Civiele Sententiën*, 1469–1471, fol. 55 v., 88 r., 127 r.
19. SAB 165, *Civiele Sententiën Kamer*, 1473–1474, fol. 32 r.; SAB 157, *Civiele Sententiën*, 1465–1469, fol. 59 r.

20. Some guarantors promised the debtor would not leave the city; SAB 157, *Civiele Sententiën*, 1453–1461, fol. 173 r.; SAB 157, *Civiele Sententiën*, 1465–1469, fol. 15 r., 24 v.
21. De Carbonnieres, 'Prison ouverte, prison fermée', 185–186.
22. Van der Tanerijen, *Boec van der Loopender Pracktijken*, deel I, Captut III.
23. Van Rhee, *Litigation and Legislation*, 289–297.
24. The Council of Flanders did not allow *contumax pro confessor habetur*: RAG 2359, *Raad van Vlaanderen, Acten en Sententiën*, 1441–1442, fol. 232 v.
25. SAB 157, *Civiele Sententiën*, 1453–1461, fol. 49 r.
26. Although there are cases where the aldermen of Bruges allowed the judgment to be carried out in contumacia; ADNB, *Lettres missives et dépêches*, 17683.
27. Which is interesting. Wielant also claimed that 'decent' women were not liable for arrest. This does not seem to be a strict rule in Bruges, but such captures remained unusual.
28. SAB 157, *Civiele Sententiën*, 1453–1461, fol. 161 r.
29. Without stating it clearly, Henry probably claimed barratry. The shipmaster had wilfully and due to his actions lost the cargo, and should therefore be held accountable for this. This would be one of the only figures making Lauwerijns a debtor.
30. SAB 157, *Civiele Sententiën*, 1453–1461, fol. 161 r.
31. SAB 157, *Civiele Sententiën*, 1469–1471, fol. 32 r.
32. A possibility might have been that she operated as a broker/hosteller. Although there is a lack of research on this subject, and I am not sure how many female brokers there were, we know that widows could ensure the continuation of the enterprise in other guilds.
33. SAB 157, *Civiele Sententiën*, 1465–1469, fol. 13 r.
34. SAB 157, *Civiele Sententiën*, 1465–1469, fol. 65 v.
35. Greve, 'Hoteliers en Hanzekooplieden', 102.
36. SAB 157, *Civiele Sententiën*, 1465–1469, fol. 65 v.; Greve, *Hansen, Hosteliers und Herbergen*, 121–122.
37. See Abraham-Thisse, 'Les relations hispano-hanséates', 281–282; Phillips, 'The Spanish kingdoms', 424–425.
38. Gilliodts-Van Severen, *Inventaire des chartes*, vol. 2, 52.
39. SAB 157, *Civiele Sententiën*, 1465–1469, fol. 84 r.–v.
40. SAB 157, *Civiele Sententiën*, 1465–1469, fol. 122 r.
41. SAB 157, *Civiele Sententiën*, 1465–1469, fol. 29 v.
42. See this privilege: Hohlbaum, *Hansische Urkundenbuch*, vol. I, 65, n. 154, art. 24.
43. Although the Hanse received privileges, they would still have many complaints about their execution. The Bruges aldermen often had the difficult choice between their own citizens and the privileges of the nation. When Laurens vander Buerse died in 1351, the aldermen of Bruges seized the inheritance in order to make sure that their own citizen would have their share as creditors, while leaving the Hanseatic creditors in the cold; Beuken, *De Hanze en Vlaanderen*, 44; Koppmann, *Hanserecesse* I, Vol. 3, n. 240. pp. 235–236.
44. However, when discussion arose in 1374, the Bruges aldermen gave this stipulation a rather wide interpretation and turned it to their benefit; Gilliodts-Van Severen, *Inventaire des chartes*, vol. 2, 51.
45. Gilliodts-Van Severen, *Inventaire des chartes*, vol. 2, 138, art. 48; SAB 96, *Ouden Wittenboek*, fol. 26 r.
46. SAB 157, *Civiele Sententiën*, 1465–1469, fol. 17 v.

47. SAB 157, *Civiele Sententiën*, 1453–1461, fol. 158 r.
48. The family De Baenst would deliver many aldermen, councillors and bailiffs of Bruges. Joos van Varsenare was a knight who won several tournaments and would become the city bailiff in the 1470s; Milis-Proost', Pieter Bladelin', vol. II, 61; Buylaert, 'Baenst, Jan III', vol. XVII, 44–49; Brown, 'Urban jousts', 321; SAB 157, *Civiele Sententiën*, 1453–1461, fol. 158 r.
49. SAB 157, *Civiele Sententiën*, 1453–1461, fol. 158 r.–v.

4

The Goal of Procedures

'And I will do everything good merchants have to do' to prove the claim, boasted Bernardo Cambi.[1] The Florentine was very confident. Cambi would appear in court and show all his accounts, as any good merchant would. It was a bluff, and the aldermen saw through it. Bernardo Cambi should have known that the aldermen regularly tested such confidence. In matters of finance, merchants were eager to gain profits and avoid losses. In doing so, they would not always be as honest as they appeared. Dave De ruysscher has shown that Antwerp municipal council had to intervene so insurers would not maliciously stall procedures and evade damage claims.[2] Loaded with experience in financial techniques, these merchants knew the details of their contracts when they appeared before the aldermen. When trouble arose, these merchants could make bold statements; but the aldermen were not naive and made the merchants substantiate their claims.

Since the fourteenth century, Bruges had developed into a financial centre beyond compare.[3] With so many merchants and so much expertise, the demand for good justice was not easily met. Knowledge was a key asset and as we have seen, the aldermen tried to meet this demand by allowing supervised arbitrations through peers. Nonetheless, not all merchants were bona fide. The limits of the system were sought, found and, occasionally, the aldermen of Bruges were confronted by crafty litigants who did everything to win their case. When the stakes were high, it was not always thought expedient to have specialists look at the case. Sometimes, the litigants preferred the aldermen.

How the aldermen dealt with these cases will be our object of study in this chapter. The court's main goal was to provide good governance and a proper procedure was vital for this. If the truth-finding process was based on trial by combat, merchants could find themselves easily disadvantaged in a foreign country.[4] In fifteenth-century Bruges, trial by combat was already a long-gone relic of the past.[5] In addition, the act of giving an oath in order to have a case decided, still happened in medieval Bruges, but was avoided as much as possible. In numerous proceedings, foreign merchants offered their oath in order to decide the case in their favour.[6] In almost as many cases, the aldermen refused this act. For example, in 1474, a litigant claimed that the party who was most likely to know the truth should also be the one performing the oath. The aldermen disagreed.[7] The court decided, often through an interlocutory judgment, who performed an oath. The issue of who was expected to deliver evidence was a decision of the aldermen.[8]

In addition, we see that the aldermen preferred written evidence over oral testimonies.[9] In 1474 they even decreed that any claimant who could not prove a claim would automatically be condemned for the claimed sum.[10] Things could be easy in case of written obligations. A litigant claimed a sum and provided a document attesting this claim.[11]

Still, some cases became complicated if national boundaries were passed or the damage claimed had occurred at sea. Bruges was a commercial and financial centre, and thus litigants could choose to present their trans-regional case before the aldermen. As long as the litigants had performed some actions in Bruges, the aldermen of Bruges could consider themselves competent to judge upon these cases. Take for instance, the case between Piero Battista Guistiniani and Johan Battista Fiers from Genoa and Gabriel Gonçalves. Once Gabriel Gonçalves arrived in the port of Sluis, his cargo was seized by Genoese merchants. The Genoese claimed that the merchandise, a cargo of crossbows, was theirs, as these weapons bore their marks.[12] The Genoese merchants explained that on its way to Bruges, the ship had perished, and its cargo had washed ashore in Portugal. In such a case, the right of shipwreck would come into effect, and the merchandise would become the property of the Portuguese king. According to the right of shipwreck, any goods that washed ashore in a principality would become the possession of the prince.[13] Of course, when goods were recovered after a shipwreck by a princely officer, the unfortunate merchants wanted to reclaim their belongings.

The Genoese contended that the king had shown mercy and ordered the delivery of these weapons to fre Vasco de Atíde, the prior of Crato, with the sole intention of giving the merchandise back to the Genoese.[14] However, against the king's wishes, this prior or his representatives sold the weapons and kept the profit. As the weapons had arrived in Bruges, the Genoese claimed that they were the rightful owners, and demanded a restitution of their property. Gonçalves did not deny these facts but claimed that he had bought these goods faithfully. The case resolved around the role of this prior and whether the Portuguese king had promised the return of those goods. The Genoese could not prove this statement and Gonçalves could not deny it. The aldermen bench ordered that both parties would have a period of a year and a day to prove this claim. However, in the meantime, Gonçalves would have the enjoyment (*jouissance*) of the goods and could sell them on the condition of a surety. If Gonçalves was ordered to do so by the aldermen, he would give the money back.[15]

As we will see, the goals of the aldermen resonate through their reaction to such cases. A good procedure was key to delivering adequate justice. The aldermen were mainly interested in the latter, but were faced with a considerable workload. It was impossible to appoint a commission of aldermen for each claim that came before them. Consequently, they had to make choices, and these choices will be of interest to us. In the previous chapters, we have seen how the aldermen valued a legal system. Merchants knew these rules, and knew how to bend the framework in their favour. The interpretation of these rules and the interaction with the aldermen remains to be discussed. Therefore, I will focus in the next sections on the decisions of the aldermen on three specific topics: maritime customs, maritime insurance, and bills of exchange. Each of these topics merits its own study. I will have to limit myself to the strategies that were played out. How did the merchants behave towards these (foreign) rules and how did this relate to practice in the Bruges court?

CLAIMS IN (INTER)NATIONAL CUSTOMS: MARITIME RULES

Although Bruges was one of the main commercial centres in Western Europe, the aldermen of Bruges were not specialists in everything. The diverse variety of merchant communities came with an array of rules. Parties could try to confuse the aldermen and convince the court to apply interpretations favourable to their situation. The strategy of claiming maritime customs before the aldermen court would not be the most efficient one, but it had its merits. Although these customs were both ancient, and sometimes even indigenous to the County of Flanders, the expertise lay elsewhere. Since the high medieval period compilations such as the *rôles of Oléron*, the *waterrecht van Damme* or the *Vonnesse van Amsterdam*, regulated international (or at least trans-regional) shipping disputes. However, everything still depended on local, regional and national differences.[16] In the case of Flanders, these maritime customs were the competence of the nearby community of Damme.[17] In the thirteenth and fourteenth centuries, Damme handled the events happening on the water: jettison, collisions and most maritime affairs appeared before these aldermen.[18] From the second half of the fifteenth century, the ports of Damme, Hoeke and Monnikrede lost their significance. Bruges controlled the Zwin area. This becomes clear in the accounts of the city of Mude, which indicate how high-profile cases in relation to maritime customs were referred to Bruges.[19]

Although the Bruges aldermen had only a slight interest in maritime laws, I will argue that certainly in the case of jettison and its treatment under the rules of general average, the Bruges aldermen were (unwillingly?) involved. Cases of jettison were the only maritime customs appearing with some regularity before the aldermen of Bruges. There are two sides of jettison. First there is the arrangement between merchants. Here, general average is of the essence. Second, there is the arrangement between the prince and the merchants. As jettisoned merchandise tended to wash ashore, merchants tried to retrieve their losses. However, the prince claimed all beached merchandise (the right of shipwreck). Merchants had privileges exempting them, but the numerous cases before the aldermen court indicate that the situation is somewhat more complicated.

The rule of general average was a mechanism of risk spreading. When caught in violent storms, the shipmaster had to make quick decisions and could decide to jettison merchandise. Throwing part of the cargo overboard would make the ship less heavy, giving it a better chance of survival. However, whose shipment was to be jettisoned? It was a decision of the shipmaster, but the rule of general average ensured that the unfortunate parties would be indemnified by the other merchants benefiting from the deed. The ship and the rest of its cargo were saved thanks to the cargo that was jettisoned. We find the first mention of such a rule in the *Lex Rhodia de iactu*. Digest D.14.2.1 stated that if merchandise was thrown overboard, the loss was compensated by all those who benefited from this act of jettison.[20] In the medieval period, however, different interpretations existed for these risk-sharing techniques.[21] Customs were accommodated, changed and communicated.[22] As Gijs Dreijer indicated, there were several averages simultaneously. There were the principles of general average and small average with their local differences. The Iberian nations protected themselves against jettison through the rules of general average, which required all members to contribute to a fund for unfortunate merchants and, last but not least, established contractual stipulations diverging from the general rule.[23] Of interest in this chapter is mainly how the Bruges aldermen dealt with the different forms of jettison and the subsequent rules of general average.

Initially, cases dealing with maritime customs that happened to find their way to Bruges were mainly resolved through arbitrations. As previously mentioned, arbitration was an informal procedure that gave arbiters more time to settle the matter, and provided the conflict with more expertise than could be expected from the aldermen of Bruges. This was perhaps necessary because rules could differ among nations. The Bruges Hanse Kontor applied the so-called *waterrecht*. This was a combination from the regulations from the maritime law from Gotland, the Vonnesse van Damme and the Amsterdam Ordonnancie.[24] Catalan merchants had the stipulations of the *Consulat del Mar*, and the Spanish (Castilian and Biscayan) communities had their funds for *avaria*.[25]

The latter was normally within the competence of the nation and not the aldermen. Even when cases of general average appeared before their court, the aldermen referred the conflict to experts. In cases pertaining to Spanish merchants and the *averia de nación*, this could be the Castilian nation; and if this would not solve the matter, arbitration was still an option.[26] The case between Jehan Martines of Biscay and several Spanish iron merchants illustrates why they did this.

In August 1452, a ship of Jehan Martines met with a tempest while transporting iron ore to Flanders. To save the ship and the rest of the cargo, the shipmaster threw a large quantity of iron ore overboard. However, once in Bruges, several merchants claimed that their jettisoned merchandise was not mentioned on the document attesting the losses. This document should attest the jettisoned merchandise so the other merchants could be compensated. However, several Spanish merchants asked for mediation from the aldermen of Bruges. The aldermen hesitated. The veracity of each merchant's claim had to be checked, the arguments had to be presented and the proper customs on the division and distribution of these claims were also not entirely apparent to the aldermen. The aldermen and parties agreed to save time, money and effort, and gave the dispute to arbiters, who were all Spanish.[27]

The shipmaster claimed that there was no record of the iron ore. It was not present in a public document nor in the registers of the shipmaster, which he was willing to prove through witnesses. But he was contradicted by the iron merchants who claimed he acted maliciously.[28] Fortunately, the Bruges clerks recorded the arbitral award in the registers. We can see a number of things in the award. The arbiters heard the pleas of both parties, they also saw the disputed document, visited witnesses in Spain to assess the price of the iron ore that was absent in the *avaria*, the memorial of the master and the advice from other shipmasters, merchants and people of renown.[29] Of course, such clauses were added to give the decision some weight. Obviously, the arbiters underlined their efforts. The arbiters could confirm that there was a difference between the actual cargo on the ship, the memorial of the shipmaster and, consequently, the goods that were thrown overboard. As the shipmaster had clearly maliciously falsified the document, the arbiters had to repeat the entire procedure.[30] Our (rhetorical) question is: if the aldermen had conducted the normal procedure, would the result have been the same?

Using arbiters in cases of maritime average was a recurring strategy for the Bruges aldermen.[31] These arbiters had more time and expertise to assess the different claims that came before them. In addition, an arbitration was an agreement. As the aldermen had no clear competency on these cases, they could still bring these cases under their authority via arbitration. As all parties had agreed on an arbitration, another court could not question the competence of the aldermen.

This changed from the 1460s. The procedures before the aldermen became more thorough, and the number of arbitrations fell sharply. When the merchants Loys Bastre and Christoforo Dalo demanded the transfer of their merchandise from the shipmaster Natalo Salomon, the shipmaster refused. The shipmaster had suffered damage and requested that he be compensated before he returned the merchandise. The merchants claimed that the shipmaster could not withhold the merchandise but had to content himself with sureties, assuring that the case of general average would be discussed. As was customary, an arbitration was set up to discuss the matter. Again, the aldermen stressed that the parties had had the time to narrate their side of the story and that the arbiters came to a decision.[32] However, the arbitration was afterwards not only confirmed, the aldermen used the arbitration to state their own decision that the shipmaster should return the merchandise and provide two guarantors to assure the decision.[33] In previous cases, the arbiters would go to work and decide upon the matter, which would be the end of the case. Cases of general average would prove to be the exceptions to this rule. The arbiters gave the case the time it needed and were the experts on the matter, but then the aldermen had the final say.

In 1467, the dispute between Frenchman Guerin Moysant and the Genoese Lazzaro Lomellini appeared before the aldermen of Bruges. The case was not referred to arbiters. The aldermen settled the case entirely before their court in a more thorough procedure. The aldermen stressed that they had heard all sides in all their arguments.[34] Of course, coincidence might be at play here. We only have court registers for the period between 1447 and 1470, and cases of general averages do not make up the bulk of it. However, the above-mentioned evolution is in line with the general one. Cases of general average remained difficult and needed specific attention. The aldermen did this with the risk of their competency being questioned.[35]

This debate on competency becomes apparent in cases where the ducal officer of the extraordinary expenses is involved. Since the 1440s, the Duke of Burgundy had attempted to streamline his revenues by appointing a special officer for extraordinary revenues. One of those princely revenues was the right of shipwreck. If a ship perished and its goods washed ashore, the prince would claim this merchandise. Since ancient times, this right was questioned by locals who considered it their right to keep what they found on the beach, and merchants who believed it unjust to be confronted with an overeager prince in their times of loss. When the Duke of Burgundy commissioned Bonnore Olivier, a Genoese merchant and confidant of the duke, the aldermen would have numerous discussions. The predicament was that merchants had received privileges exempting them from the right of shipwreck and assuring them the return of their merchandise. However, Bonnore Olivier was not engaged in charity. The receiver often demanded considerable compensation for the work carried out to retrieve goods.[36] The receiver of ordinary expenses regularly ignored privileges, jurisdictions of aldermen benches and sometimes refused to return merchandise.[37] In order to defuse these cases, the aldermen would regularly appoint arbiters, but the receiver of extraordinary expenses tended to ignore their judgments.[38] In addition, Bonnore Olivier tried to avoid the aldermen of Bruges as much as possible. He litigated his cases before the aldermen of Damme or even the Council of Flanders.[39] Once he even tried to drag the aldermen of Bruges before the Council of Flanders.[40]

Arbitration offered useful advantages. It allowed experts to take their time, investigate claims and study all the available evidence. It was also an agreement. The aldermen had questionable competency in cases of maritime law. Therefore, if they referred these cases to an arbitration, it could not be appealed.

CLAIMS IN FOREIGN CUSTOMS: MARITIME INSURANCE

Whereas maritime customs were mostly indigenous, maritime insurance found its origins in the Mediterranean.[41] In its essence, insurance entails the (partial) transfer of the risk of cargo losses arising from wreck, capture or arrest to insurers. However, it was a contract between two parties made in the city of departure. When a merchant arrived in a foreign commercial centre, the competent court did not necessarily abide by the expected set of rules. There are no indications that the aldermen drew up regulation in regard to maritime insurance. They assessed circumstances case by case. Yet, whereas the compilations of maritime customs gave some form of systematic ordering, maritime insurance depended on the contract made in the city of departure.[42] The working of a rule depended on the city of origin, the contract and the expectations of both insured and insurers. In the fifteenth century, insurance evolved rapidly and different rules were confronted one another. Although there were some basic premises to maritime insurance, which were understood by the aldermen, the nuances could still differ.[43] As insurance did not originate in Flanders, the aldermen of Bruges were less experienced with the foreign customs surrounding the practice.[44] Their main concern was the enforcement of debts. As the aldermen of Bruges had no strict rules on the basis of their territorial jurisdiction, the parties were free to regulate contracts as they pleased. However, when disputes came before the aldermen, the application of a foreign rule was far from certain. Some litigants exploited this uncertainty to confuse the aldermen. As such, I will delve into maritime insurance as an example that illustrates how various and contrasting rules were introduced in Bruges, and how parties tried to bring their own customs before the court.

The so-called 'commercial revolution' provided the backdrop to the rise of maritime insurance. This commercial revolution changed the face of commerce. Instead of directly travelling to the land of trade, merchants could stay in one place, and arrange their affairs through a system of factors.[45] Eventually, this led to the development of financial techniques such as maritime insurance, making it possible to spread risk at sea. Initially, trade was organised through agreements such as the *commenda*. In this system a creditor, or group of creditors, provided an agent with merchandise or credit. The latter was to trade with this and then return to investors their share of the profits. However, the risk was borne solely by the investors.[46] Insurance transferred the risk to someone who did not partake in the enterprise but was willing to take on the risk for a premium.

In medieval Bruges, when merchants wanted to cover a risk, they contacted a broker (a hosteller) who would then provide them with merchants willing to insure the risks. These merchants were the underwriters (*soubscriptures*) who insured the ship or a part of the cargo for a premium. The premium was often expressed as a part of the insured value. To determine this equation, it was essential to estimate the risk and thus provide sufficient information to fix the premium. The route of the ship, its state, its captain, and the season for the voyage had to be communicated. Merchants could redice risks by dividing cargoes over multiple ships and voyages, they could arm ships and/or sail in convoys.[47] In the case of high risks, the insurers would demand a high premium.

This practice originated from medieval Italian cities and was introduced relatively fast in Bruges. Luisa Piccinno refers to a notarial deed dated 9 March 1350 concerning a shipment of alum from Genoa to Bruges. The document was described as a (chance) contract. Piccinno believes it to be a disguised insurance, though there is no mention of the premium.[48] While this does not prove that insurance was a daily occurrence in medieval Bruges, it is a reminder that Genoese experts of the practice were present in Bruges. It was only a matter of time before parties would dispute their insurance policies before the aldermen court. The oldest of such conflicts is dated 1444, but in all probability there were prior cases.[49] When an insured cargo was lost, a debt arose that could be enforced before the aldermen. Here, it had to be determined whether the insured could claim the promised insurance from the underwriters.[50] Maritime insurance was a trans-regional practice, yet as the rules could differ, merchants could also alternate in the customs they claimed, and use the different customs to develop a strategy.[51]

If risks turned into losses, this would result in protracted litigation before the Bruges aldermen court. In its essence, maritime insurance was still a contract between two parties.[52] As such, the insured and the underwriter were free to determine the modalities of the contract. Princely legislation and the concern to offer a clear framework for insurance only began in the mid-sixteenth century.[53] By consequence, the aldermen of Bruges referred these cases to arbitrations. Just as in maritime customs, expert arbiters would deal with these foreign customs. In medieval Bruges, most underwriters were Italian or Spanish. This makes for an interesting combination due to the lack of their legislative framework and the omnipresence of Mediterranean-style premium insurance.[54] As Guido Rossi noted, insurance was a risk-taking practice that was easily gripped by the distrust and hysteria that could dominate a market.[55] The reason for this was the notorious fraudulent behaviour of both insured and insurers. Given their peculiar expertise, insurers-buyers could try to mislead their underwriters by overstating the value of their cargo, searching out policies for already perished ships, or by intentionally losing their ship. For example, in case of maritime plunder, the insured could just abandon their ship instead of risking their life.

Usually, a conflict regarding insurance would be referred to arbiters to decide the matter.[56] Yet from the mid-1450s we can see merchants preferring litigation over arbitration. This happened, for example, when the Genoese merchant Marco Gentile sued Carlo Lomellini, Michele Arnolfini and Angelo Tani for not paying out insurance compensation and the Italian merchants sued Marco Gentile for salvaging items from his ship.[57] Both claimants, albeit for different reasons, claimed customs 'in the matter of insurance' (*entretenu en matière d'asseurance*).[58] In this case, both parties believed that litigation before the aldermen was preferable. The aldermen appointed a specialist on the case who reported to the aldermen, and subsequently, the judges overruled the acclaimed custom and demanded that the Marco Gentile be paid.[59]

From the 1460s, the aldermen of Bruges considered these cases, often in full, before their own court.[60] The aldermen never addressed what motivated their choice, but insurance cases are almost always well documented. This may be so because of the aldermen's uncertainty – an uncertainty in which the litigation parties could play a part. Problems often arose around the modalities of the insurance and whether the contract had to be respected. In this light, underwriters often sought to invoke vague 'customs of assurances' to lead the aldermen astray.

For instance, in a case between Pierre Noel and Piero da Rabata, both litigants tried to prolong the proceedings, confuse the aldermen, and claimed vague notions over what should be done. Pierre Noel was a merchant from La Rochelle and had insured his ship, *Saint Jaques de la Rochelle*, for the value of 45 lib. gr. with several underwriters.

In January 1458, Pierre Noel argued before the aldermen that the ship was insured and outfitted in La Rochelle, but after the ship had set sail to the Low Countries, it perished somewhere at sea. As Pierre Noel could prove, the obligation of insurance existed, and these letters, under the seal of La Rochelle, were presented in the aldermen's court. The claimant concluded that he should receive the promised amounts.[61] Piero da Rabata, one of the underwriters, answered and acknowledged the existence of these insurance letters but argued that the letters were null and void. Since the vessel had never left its port and sank in La Rochelle itself, there could be no insurance for the voyage as it had never taken place. According to the usage in this matter, da Rabata continued, he was not responsible. Da Rabata added that he was willing to prove this custom if necessary.[62] Furthermore, the Italian claimed that these letters under the seal of La Rochelle should be invalid because the witnesses of the ship's demise were the sailors of that same ship. Since they were testifying for their ship and their captain, they were not reliable witnesses. Hence, these letters should not hold up in court. The aldermen gave each side an opportunity to discharge their opponent's claims and gave them one month to search for this evidence. Da Rabata succeeded in confusing the aldermen who postponed the case. Each party had the chance to dismiss the claims of the other. Proving that something was not a custom, as the shipmaster had to do, seemed to be quite difficult.[63]

In the subsequent month, the other underwriters Alvere de Vega, Jehan Corubeas, and Borromei Salviati, as proctor of Piero da Rabata, succeeded in futher delaying the case. The delays that were allowed, each time three or four months, were significantly longer than the usual interplay of sessions that the aldermen used.[64] In February 1459, Alvere de Vega represented everyone in court. Again, Pierre Noel claimed that as the ship was insured, and thus the insurers should pay him. Alvere de Vega had a different explanation. The underwriters agreed that the ship had set sail, but to counter an upcoming storm and not for the voyage to Flanders. As proof, the underwriters stated that the ship had not unfurled its large sails and was sailing against the wind.[65] The underwriters concluded that as the ship was not yet ready for the voyage, the insurance should not be paid for the agreed voyage. Again, the underwriters tried to buy time by stating that they wished to prove their claim. However, despite their confidence, the evidence they gathered (after a year) was circumstantial. The invoked customs did not hold up in court and the aldermen decided against them.[66]

Was the strategy of claiming a foreign custom effective? As the sources never specified what the maritime custom was, it is hard for us to assess its veracity. The reaction of the aldermen is telling. The court demanded further investigation in the case, but in the meantime, the aldermen also decreed that the insurers should already provide Pierre Noel with the sum claimed and that Pierre Noel would provide the insurers with sufficient sureties if the trial might conclude otherwise.[67] In this way, the lengthy court procedures would not bring Pierre Noel to the brink of bankruptcy but still assured that the case would be held before the aldermen.

In 1456, the citizen Gérard Plouvier and the Spanish merchant Saldone Ferrier demanded that the underwriters Giorgio Spinola, Francesco Sandei, Michele Arnolfini, Simon Larcar should pay for the goods of a perished vessel. The underwriters protested and stated that they were not obliged to pay the insurance because the shipmaster, Jacques Ribijs de Collier, had committed 'fraud de ribaudise', meaning that he had exceeded the liberties that were granted to a shipmaster during the trip. If the insurers could prove that the load perished because of a fault of the shipmaster, they could evade the claims. However, the insurers had to prove *dolus*, meaning that the man in question knowingly and wilfully lost the cargo.[68] As Guido Rossi has stressed, barratry or conscious deceit on the part of a shipmaster, was a much-theorised legal concept that only found its application in the most limited sense possible. The reason was that the court would have such high standards that barratry was rarely accepted.[69]

The aldermen immediately appointed members to find the authenticity of this custom. The aldermen did not state that they agreed with the custom, but they gave the Italian merchants a year and a day to prove the excesses and fraud.[70] Again, we see the aldermen adjourning, granting significant extra time to the underwriters to prove their claims, and demanding all the potential evidence.[71] In brief, the aldermen significantly raised the standards of their usual proceedings. When one of the two parties claimed the existence of such customs, the aldermen demanded all available evidence.[72] Sometimes, they tried to search the veracity of the different claims by appointing two of their aldermen to a particular case who would later report their findings back to the aldermen.

This was also something the parties exploited: every time insurers made an unlikely claim of a custom in maritime affairs, they also signalled that they wanted to prove this. However, if a party made a claim in an insurance case, the aldermen nearly always required it to be substantiated. In addition to this evidence, the aldermen demanded a guaranty from the party to make sure that the case was observed. At first, they mainly worked with sureties, but from the 1460s we see them systematically demanding a *namptissement*. The insurer had to deliver upfront the money that was at stake.[73] This was a legal consignment that had to guarantee a proper process. Instead of giving a surety, the debtors transferred some valuable – mostly non-perishable – items to the aldermen, and the latter kept it until the final decision.[74] The aldermen kept these goods and assured that the parties would respect the judgment. If we compare this court procedure with Antwerp, where the aldermen imposed oaths on plaintiffs or defendants in order to assess their pleas, a big difference in ethics is evident. Only in 1537 does princely law require insurers to deposit the indemnity sought before contesting insureds' claims.[75]

CLAIMS IN COMMERCIAL TECHNIQUES: BILLS OF EXCHANGE

Although, Bruges would lose its colours as a commercial centre by the end of the fifteenth century, the city remained the main financial centre of the Burgundian and Habsburg Netherlands until well into the sixteenth century.[76] The maritime customs were either a local matter for the aldermen of Damme, or a princely matter in cases of shipwreck. Maritime insurance was more of a foreign matter. Although well known in Bruges, the practice, its customs and the events leading to the insurance being triggered did not originate in the Flemish city. As we have seen, the aldermen of Bruges dealt these with cases with care, but were also often confused by these customs.

Letters of exchange were a different matter. Although this method of credit transfer was first introduced by Italian merchants travelling to the north, the city of Bruges would be one of the most influential centres. Each day at the Florentine nation on the Bourse square the rates of exchange were fixed, all respected banking houses had agents in the city, and the aldermen of Bruges were well aware of the financial techniques of the practice.[77] The financial elite of Bruges were well represented in the aldermen bench and, in case of doubt, the aldermen could always consult the leading merchants on the bourse.[78]

In the last section, we explored how merchants played with the rules of evidence and how the aldermen reacted. This section will go deeper into what the bill of exchange was and where it could go wrong, before we go on to examine the litigation strategies of merchants and the Achilles' heel of the aldermen of Bruges in treating these cases so thoroughly.

The prime function of a bill of exchange was to exchange one currency for another over an interval of time and space. With its origin in the Italian banking system, the bill of exchange was a way of providing credit from one region to another without the actual transfer of bullion.[79] Four parties were involved: two in the place where the bill of exchange was drawn up and two at the place where it was carried out. First, there is the deliverer (it. *datore*) who gives value for a bill of exchange by buying it from the taker (it. *penditore*). The taker accepts the money advanced by the deliverer and draws up a bill of exchange addressed to the person designated by the deliverer. The bill of exchange travelled into the hands of a payee who presents the bills of exchange to a drawee or payor. By accepting the bill of exchange, the payor had to pay the bill upon its maturity.[80]

Important in bills of exchange is that there should always be a change in place and time. Two time factors were essential. First, there was the time the bill needed to go from one financial centre to another. This was called the usance and was often a fixed period. These intervals were more or less predictable, but still brought a level of unpredictability. Raymond de Roover estimates that the 'mail pouch of the Catalans', which left two or three times a month, arrived in Barcelona after a voyage of twenty-two or twenty-three days.[81] Additionally, there was often an interval between the usance of the bill and its maturity. This was the time given to the payor in the financial centre to amass the money. When the bill was presented, the maturity started. This could be fixed, or could start after the bill of exchange had reached its destination and was presented by the payee to the payor.

There was always an exchange of currency and the time lapse made the two different currencies fluctuate. Because of this exchange in coins over time, a speculative element was incorporated. The exchange rate was the price of the bill. Supply and demand regulated this and made the exchange rates fluctuate.

In addition to the transfer and exchange of money, Raymond de Roover added a third use to the bill of exchange: the covered loan. De Roover noticed suspicious protestations of some letters of exchange. The taker might have accepted the bill of exchange, and sent it to the payee, but after seeing the bill of exchange, the payor protested it. In such cases, the bill of exchange would be returned to the taker, and the deliverer would receive a refund. However, because of the time lapse, this was not the original sum. This way, one of the two parties could make a profit. At the same time, the amount of money the deliverer gave to the taker was 'loaned' and repaid in a couple of months. By tweaking the exchange rates, the parties agreed on a loan.[82]

For De Roover, these letters of exchange were an example of how bankers used the laws on usury to their advantage. Medieval theologians defined usury very strictly as profit deriving from loans. As these exchange operations provided value, were speculative in nature and were not a clear-cut loan, bankers could escape the stigma of usurers.[83] The banker could not charge interest openly but had to disguise it in the exchange rate.[84]

Recently, Francesco Guidi-Bruscoli and Jim Bolton have maintained that, although this loan was possible, the primary purpose of the letter of exchange remained the transfer and the exchange of money. In their research, they could only find a small number of protested bills, thus implying that the goal of exchange letters was the transfer of money and not the exchange and re-exchange.[85] De Roover and Mueller based their findings on the Medici archives or the books of Andrea Barbarigo, Guidi-Bruscoli and Bolton on the Borromei archive.[86] In each case, the evidence is relatively scarce and even in our court registers, the exact goal of the letter of exchange is often omitted. After all, the merchants were not going to admit that it was a disguised loan. Nevertheless, it may be clear that there could be some tweaking on these letters of exchange and that they were highly flexible.[87]

Because of its interregional aspect, Bruges' jurisdiction was somewhat tricky. According to the *ius commune*, if a letter of exchange arrived in Bruges but the payor did not want to pay the payee, the payee could not claim an action from this fact.[88] The contract was between the deliverer and the taker and the deliverer had recourse where the initial contract was drawn.[89] Despite this rule, the aldermen of Bruges accepted the cases presented to them, if the payor acknowledged the validity of the letter of exchange, and thus the existence of a debt.[90] Hence, the aldermen did not develop a set of rules on the letters of exchange, but they did acknowledge the importance of Bruges as a centre of exchange and 'the customs of the bourse' as an authority in the matter.[91] Two types of disputes came before the aldermen of Bruges.

The first was between the payee and the payor about the exchange rates. As the currencies could fluctuate, there was always a risk.[92] The exchange rates worked according to two moments in time: the first when the bill of exchange is drafted and a second when the bill of exchange matured. The period between the exchange rates at two financial centres means that the buyer/lender would receive a positive return. To be profitable for the payor, the currency in the destination needed to be lower than in the place of origin.[93] However, in times of poor or slow communication, the exchange rates could be lower or higher than expected and weaker currencies could overtake stronger ones. In such a case, the bankers would lose money if they exchanged.[94] Since successful trading involved an up-to-date knowledge of the exchange rates, the best-informed merchants had a competitive advantage over their less well-informed peers.[95]

Some bankers just refused to take their losses. When the Genoese merchant Lazzaro Lomellini wanted to withdraw his letter of exchange for the value of 350 golden crowns from the Spanish merchant Alonso Pardo, the Spanish merchant refused. Alonso Pardo acknowledged the existence and confirmed the veracity of the bill of exchange, but offered to Lazzaro Lomellini to pay it in silver and gold. Presumably, the exchange rates had changed between the issuing and the checking of the bill, and the Spanish merchant tried to evade a loss by offering gold and silver.[96] Lomellini probably sniffed a gain and refused to cooperate. He brought his case to the aldermen, and the aldermen decreed that Alonso Pardo should abide by the contract and pay it in full golden crown according to the estimation of 50 g. Vl. per crown.[97]

In the second type of dispute, irregularities happened with the protestation. A protestation meant that the bill was rejected at its intended destination and sent back to its place of origin for restitution. If the bill of exchange was delivered but protested, it was the deliverer who had a right of recourse against the taker. In 1447 Asselin Spinola claimed that Bernardo Cambi had accepted and protested the bill at the same time. In Bruges, he had used the letter of exchange and was paid by Marian Rau. However, for some unknown reason, Bernardo Cambi also succeeded in protesting the bill, and Marian Rau had to send it back to Avignon, where it was paid back to the deliverer. Because of this, as claimed by Asselin Spinola, Cambi had received money both in Bruges and in Avignon.[98] Perhaps for obvious reasons, the Rau family was in dire financial straits, and Spinola offered his help against the suspected freeloader Cambi.

A couple of years later, Bernardo Cambi was again accused of malpractice involving letters of exchange. This time Richard Burk claimed that he had a letter of exchange and wanted to be paid. Bernardo Cambi had drafted a letter to his proxy in London, Renaldo Baroncelli so Diederik Vanden Goude, or whoever brought the letter, would be paid the amount of twenty English pounds sterling.[99] Richard Burke now claimed before the aldermen that this sum was never paid in London. To prove his claims, he brought both the letter of exchange and the protestation before the aldermen. Bernardo Cambi argued that he should not pay Richard Burke because Diederik Vanden Goude was the principal of the letter of exchange, and the letter was drafted with the intention of providing Van der Goude credit in London.[100] However, once the letter was in England, nobody accepted it and it could not be paid. How Richard obtained this letter was not known to Cambi. The latter did not recognise Richard or did not have any previous dealings with him, and therefore, he should not pay him. Richard responded that he received the letter validly (*deuchdelik*) and that Bernardo Cambi even made an oral promise to Burke that he would pay for the bill. Bernardo Cambi denied this claim.[101] The aldermen faced a stalemate. Richard Burk could prove the existence of debt and the fact that the letter of exchange should be reimbursed. In most cases, such proof sufficed for condemnation, but in this case, there was still some ambiguity about how Richard got his hands on the letter. He only claimed that he received it faithfully, but not how.

Therefore, the aldermen stated that, since there was a debt, Bernardo Cambi should have paid these twenty pounds sterling, but as there was still some uncertainty, Richard should provide sureties upon the payment and deliver within a year an authenticated proof that Diederik Vanden Goude had received no money. Again, sureties were the typical response.[102] If Richard could not substantiate his claim (thus making his claim was malicious), Richard or the sureties would have to reimburse Bernardo Cambi.[103]

The aldermen chose a solution with the highest chance of benefiting the faithful party. It is impossible to know whether Bernardo Cambi used the vagueness surrounding the actual owner of the bill of exchange to his advantage or not. However, the aldermen still sought a compromise solution. This response coincides with the aldermen's wish to provide adequate justice. The three aspects we have observed with maritime customs and maritime insurance were also present: a higher burden of proof, more time to gather evidence, and a reliance on external expertise.

To begin with, the aldermen increased the burden of proof. For example take the case between Willem Ceton from Scotland and the Florentine Piero Bandini. Willem claimed he had a letter of exchange that needed to be paid by Piero Bandini. Piero Bandini protested the bill and showed that the letter of exchange was already paid in Rome. He had a small note proving this fact. The aldermen concluded that such a note was insufficient to resolve the case and demanded that each party provide more evidence. Now, the parties each had to verify their claims. Willem Ceton had to prove that Piero Bandini did not pay the bill in Rome, and Piero had to prove that Willem had no claim to this money. In this way, the aldermen considerably increased the burden of proof that lay on the parties.[104]

In addition, the aldermen took more time for the procedure.[105] When in February 1457, the Aragonese merchants Antonio de Zaragoza and Sancho Pinello presented themselves before the aldermen, they had prepared their case. The Spaniards sued the Nuremberg merchant Stevin Pulcher for outstanding debts from a letter of exchange. Zaragoza and Pinello provided the aldermen with a letter of exchange indicating Stevin Pulcher's name. They also also had a document stating that Stevin was at least a factor or partner in his company and as such, personally liable.[106] Despite all this proof, Stevin Pulcher still denied the letters, the factorship and all promises of payment. Notwithstanding the proof that the Aragonese merchants provided, the aldermen agreed that both parties should be granted six months to provide more arguments.[107] Only after the Aragonese provided extra proof that the letter of exchange was truly from Pulcher, did the aldermen order him to pay the sum.[108]

Furthermore, the aldermen demanded expertise. This was because of the interregional aspect of letters of exchange and the higher complexity of the cases.[109] It is in this respect relevant to note that the aldermen quickly used the more extensive procedures they had at their disposal. Complex issues concerning letters of exchange were rapidly referred to arbiters who provided a more in-depth insight and advised the aldermen, or were even appointed to decide the matter.[110] In other cases, the aldermen sent a deputation from their number to investigate the case.[111] In the early 1450s, we can even see a case that was dealt with before the *vierschaar* and where the duration of the case caused problems for the levied arrests.[112]

When, in 1473, the Hanseatic merchant Renault Roetaert complained about the professional moneychanger Nicholas de May, he asked the aldermen to condemn De May to pay the sum of 27 lib. gr.[113] However, Nicholas argued that in a previous transaction, Henric Hoochins had acquired a letter of exchange for Raesse vanden Hove for 21 lib. 9 s. and that Renault Roetaert had brought this into accounts of Nicholas de May while he was not indebted to Henric. With the proof in his books of exchange, Nicholas de May brought other claims upfront to defend himself. Not only did he give a poor reason why he should not pay for the letter of exchange, he also claimed that Renault Roetaert should repay these 21 lib. gr. The case quickly became exceedingly complicated, and even though Nicholas de May could prove his dealings through his books of exchange, the aldermen appointed a couple of commissioners and requested advice from specific 'merchants of the bourse', before ordering Nicholas to pay the 27 lib. gr. and demanding that Raesse substantiate his claims.[114]

The added involvement of the aldermen of Bruges also had (probably unwarranted) consequences. There was an increased paper trail that the Council of Flanders happily used in its proceedings. The case between Pietro de Nyeto and Alonso de Larmes is an excellent example of this problem. Pietro de Nyeto had requested a letter of exchange from the compagnie of Couveroignes, represented by Jehan Zeboel in London. The letter of exchange should be sent to Jehan Louppes in Bruges, with Alonso de Larmes, from the same compagnie of Couveroignes, as the payor. Pietro de Nyeto transferred the money, and a letter of exchange was sent to Jehan Louppes. Jehan Louppes received the letter and presented it to Alonso de Larmes, although the amount was only to be paid in August 1474.[115] Alonso de Larmes acknowledged the letter, but never showed the money. Once Pietro de Nyeto was in Bruges, and the letter of exchange remained unpaid, de Nyeto wanted to bring Alonso de Larmes before the aldermen of Bruges.[116] Before the aldermen, he claimed that Alonso de Larmes had accepted the letter of exchange and should, therefore, also pay the agreed amount. Alonso de Larmes, however, was displeased with the case and refuted this claim by stating that he could not be bullied into paying through legal action. It was a custom that the payor should pay if this pleased him. He even claimed that this was 'familiar to merchants'.[117] In addition, he also believed that he was not bound to pay this, but could only voluntarily provide payment after the expiration. Pietro de Nyeto strongly disagreed, and the aldermen, as usual, ordered more information. In the tourbe-enquiry, the most important merchants from Bruges testified. Tommaso Portinari confirmed that in Bruges, the custom was such that if a merchant showed a letter of exchange, with expiration or not, the letter should be paid.[118] The aldermen drew their conclusion, and Alonso de Larmes was ordered to pay.[119]

The reason we know so much is that Alonso de Larmes appealed the judgment before the Council of Flanders. Immediately, we see that the aldermen of Bruges had to transfer all the documents to the princely court. All the relevant documents were transferred to the Council of Flanders.[120] This immediately reveals a sensitive spot on the part of the aldermen. Undoubtedly, they used a written procedure. In so doing, the aldermen informed themselves on several points and unconsciously prepared the way for the Council of Flanders to take note of the situation. We cannot know how well-versed the council members were in letters of exchange. But the documents that the aldermen of Bruges had to provide facilitated the job the council members had to do. Unfortunately, we do not know how far the case came or whether the Council of Flanders accepted it. Alonso de Larmes seems to have had several cases in 1480–1482 where he appealed against the aldermen of Bruges. Still, the registers of the Council of Flanders do not provide any details on the content of these cases themselves.[121]

Be that as it may, it signifies the problem confronting Bruges. Cases of maritime insurance, sea customs or even bills of exchange were specialised matters. Bruges knew that they needed to bring these cases to a respectable end. It was very rare for cases of maritime insurance, general average or even bills of exchange to appear before the Council of Flanders, but the more thorough procedure could also lead to an easier appeal.

It is in the most difficult cases that the aldermen showed their hand. Maritime customs, marine insurance and letters of exchange complicated cases. The aldermen were cautious in these commercial cases and clung to their belief of what good justice was. On each occasion they opted for more time, more expertise and a higher burden of proof. It was a choice the aldermen made. The fact that so few cases relating to maritime law, marine insurance and letters of exchange found their way to the Council of Flanders may be a sign of how appreciated the increased procedure was.

NOTES

1. SAB 157, *Civiele Sententiën*, 1447–1453, fol. 37 v.
2. De ruysscher, 'Antwerp 1490–1590', 79.
3. Spufford, 'From Genoa to London', 280; D. De ruysscher, 'Antwerp 1490–1590', 81.
4. Van Caenegem, *La preuve*, 379. P. Godding, 'La preuve en matière civile', 111–128.
5. Van Caengem, *La preuve*, 386, 389; Van Caenegem, 'Reflexions on rational and irrational modes of proof', 264–265; Damaska, 'Rational and irrational proof revisited', 25–40.
6. See SAB 157, *Civiele Sententiën*, 1447–1453, fol. 308 v.; SAB 157, *Civiele Sententiën*, 1453–1461, fol. 271 v.–272 r.
7. SAB 157, *Civiele Sententiën*, 1465–1469, fol. 102 r.
8. Van Caenegem, *La Preuve*, 412–413; SAB 157, *Civiele Sententiën*, 1465–1469, fol. 9 v.; 41 v.; 50 r.; 50 r.–52 r.
9. Van Caenegem, *La preuve*, 404.
10. SAB 165, *Civiele Sententiën kamer*, 1473–1474, fol. 13 r.

11. SAB 165, *Civiele Sententiën kamer*, 1473–1474, fol. 21 r.; SAB 157, *Civiele Sententiën*, 1465–1469, fol. 86 v. Although see Puttevils, 'Tweaking financial instruments', 337–361.
12. SAB 157, *Civiele Sententiën*, 1453–1461, fol. 254 v.
13. Sicking and De Klerk, 'The law of wreck in Flanders', 201–232; Levy-Bruhl, 'Droit de naufrage', 35; de Groote, 'Strandvonsten', 44–51; Hansen, 'Strandrecht und Strandraub', 51–78; Niitemaa, *Des Strandrecht in Nordeuropa im Mittelalter*.
14. The Prior of Crato was the traditional title given to the head of the Order of the Knights of Saint John of Jerusalem in Portugal, see on Fre Vasco; Neto, 'As relações sociais do Prior D. Vasco de Ataíde', 113–115.
15. SAB 157, *Civiele Sententiën*, 1453–1461, fol. 219 r.
16. SAB 96, *Purperenboek*, fol. 3 r.–5 v.; Rijksarchief Brugge, 3568, *Zeerechten*. See for edition of the Rôles de oléron and het waterrecht van Damme: Pardessus, *Collection de lois maritimes*, 283–354 and 355–392; Pardessus, *Collection de lois maritimes*, vol. 4, 19–29; Frankot, 'Medieval maritime law', 155–156; Cordes, 'Maritime Law. Western Europe'.
17. Although Bruges was the legal head of Damme and Mude, and was thus nominally competent in relation to these laws, it is likely that most cases were resolved there. However, we lack the court proceedings of both the aldermen of Damme and Sluis; Vanden Aauweele, 'Het Brugse zeerecht', 150.
18. Unfortunately, no registers of the aldermen of Damme were preserved. We have to rely on the city accounts for any reference to their law: ARA, CC, 33627, *Accounts of the city of Damme*, 1488, fol. 31 r.; ARA, CC, 33554, *Accounts of the city of Damme*, 1405, fol. 12v.; 18 r.
19. ARA, CC, *Accounts of the city of Mude*, 36563, 1431, fol. 17 v.; ARA, CC, 36585, *Accounts of the city of Mude*, 1454, fol. 9 v.; ARA, CC, 36589, *Accounts of the city of Mude*, 1458, fol. 14 v.
20. D. 14.2.1; Spruit et al. *Corpus Iuris* Civiles, 198–204; Aubert, 'Dealing with the Abyss', 157–161.
21. Frankot, *'Of laws of ships and shipmen'*, 27–52.
22. Cordes, 'Die Regelung von Interessenkonflikten', 52–90; Schweitzer, *Schiffer und Schiffsmann*.
23. Dreijer, 'Maritime averages', 31–54; Dreijer, *The power and pains of polysemy*, 105–129.
24. Cordes, 'Flandrischer Copiar', 127–128; Frankot, 'De "Ordinancie van Staveren"', 9.
25. With the 1407 Valencian customs and the 1435 Barcelonese; Dreijer, 'The powers and pains of polysemy', 136–137.
26. See for example, SAB, *Spaans Consulaat*, nr. 22.
27. SAB 157, *Civiele Sententiën*, 1453–1461, fol. 39 r.; SAB 157, *Civiele Sententiën*, 1453–1461, fol. 38 v.–39 r.
28. SAB 157, *Civiele Sententiën*, 1453–1461, fol. 38 v.–39 r.
29. SAB 157, *Civiele Sententiën*, 1453–1461, fol. 39 r.
30. The arbiters assessed point by point and stated several times 'que nous trouvons'; SAB 157, *Civiele Sententiën*, 1453–1461, fol. 39 v.–fol. 40 v.
31. SAB 157, *Civiele Sententiën*, 1453–1461, fol. 147 r.
32. SAB 157, *Civiele Sententiën*, 1465–1469, fol. 68 v.
33. SAB 157, *Civiele Sententiën*, 1465–1469, fol. 69 r.
34. SAB 157, *Civiele Sententiën*, 1465–1469, fol. 203 v.
35. SAB 157, *Civiele Sententiën*, 1469–1471, fol. 42 v. and 130 v.
36. ARA 3154, *Account of Bonnore Olivier*, fol. 15 v., 16 v.–17 r.

37. SAB 157, *Civiele Sententiën*, 1447–1453, fol. 77 v.; 382 v.; SAB 157, *Civiele Sententiën*, 1453–1461, fol. 35 v.–36 v.
38. SAB 157, *Civiele Sententiën*, 1447–1453, fol. 87r.–88 r.; 311 r.–v.; 320 r.
39. SAB 157, *Civiele Sententiën*, 1447–1453, fol. 78 r. As a ducal officer, the Flemish citizen often litigated against men before a princely court. Transgressions of ducal officers clearly fell within the competence of the Council of Flanders. However, Bonnora Oliviera also used it to his own advantage. See cases against the ducal receiver: RAG 2388, *Raad van Vlaanderen, Acten en Sententien*, 1464–1465, fol. 429 r.; RAG 2384, *Raad van Vlaanderen, Acten en Sententien*, 1462–1462, fol. 240 r., 307 v.; Offensive: RAG 2380, *Raad van Vlaanderen, Acten en Sententien*, 1460–1460, fol. 320 r.; RAG 2387, *Raad van Vlaanderen, Acten en Sententien*, 1464–1464, fol. 12 r.–v.
40. RAG 2385, *Raad van Vlaanderen, Acten en Sententien*, 1462–1463, fol. 193 v.
41. Hellwege, 'A comparative history', 67; Ebert, 'Early modern Atlantic trade', 102–103; Rossi, *Insurance in Elizabethan England*, 27–52.
42. Of course, there is a difference between the standard terms that derived from a normative practice and the negotiated terms. Nevertheless, it remained a mercantile transplant; De ruysscher, 'Normative hybridity in Antwerp Marine Insurance', 148; De ruysscher, 'Belgium. Marine Insurance', 113; Rossi, 'Civilians and insurance', 323–364.
43. As we are mainly interested in the strategies before the aldermen, I will not go into the particularities of insurance too much see: De Roover, 'The cambium maritimum', 15–33; Van Doosselaere, *Commercial agreements*, 182–196.
44. Illustrative in this respect are the debates surrounding the framework of insurance in sixteenth-century Antwerp: De ruysscher, 'Consulter, débattre, négocier', 1–9.
45. Lopez, *The commercial revolution*, 103–105. Bryer, 'Double-entry bookkeeping', 113–140.
46. Weber, *The history of commercial* partnerships, 63–84; Udovitch, 'At the origins of the Western commenda', 19–199.
47. Deloof and Puttevils, 'Marketing and pricing risk', 805–808.
48. Piccinno, 'Genoa, 1340–1620', 32.
49. SAB 96, *Groenenboek* A, fol. 230 r.
50. van Niekerk, *The development of the principles of insurance* law, 201–202.
51. See, for example, in the case of abandonment; Rossi, 'The abandonment to the insurers', 98–100; Ibbetson, 'Law and custom', 293.
52. De ruysscher and Puttevils, 'The art of compromise', 29–31; 39; Stevens, 'The contribution of Antwerp', 15.
53. De ruysscher, 'Antwerp 1490–1590', 79.
54. De ruysscher, 'Antwerp, 1490–1590', 85. Nevertheless, there were also Flemish insurers; SAB 157, *Civiele Sententiën*, 1469–1471, fol. 180 r.
55. Rossi, 'England 1523–1601', 139–140.
56. SAB 157, *Civiele Sententiën*, 1465–1469, fol. 204 v. and fol. 206 r.–207 r.
57. Of course, it was impossible to have the best of both worlds. If he called upon his insurance, any goods that were preserved were also for the insurers. See for example in the case of abandonment; G. Rossi, 'The abandonment to the insurers', 98–100. These Italian merchants were Michele Arnulphin from Lucca, Carlo Lomellino from Genua and Angelo Tani from Firenze; SAB 157, *Civiele Sententiën*, 1453–1461, fol. 274 v.
58. SAB 157, *Civiele Sententiën*, 1453–1461, fol. 274 v.

59. SAB 157, *Civiele Sententiën*, 1453–1461, fol. 274 v.
60. See for a similar process in England: Ibbetson, 'Insurance in sixteenth century England', 297.
61. SAB 157, *Civiele Sententiën*, 1453–1461, fol. 221 r.
62. SAB 157, *Civiele Sententiën*, 1453–1461, fol. 211 v.
63. Renaldo Baroncelli had to stand surety; SAB 157, *Civiele Sententiën*, 1453–1461, fol. 217 r.
64. SAB 157, *Civiele Sententiën*, 1453–1461, fol. 217 v. and 218 v. Borromei Salviati is described as a 'compagnon' of the company; SAB 157, *Civiele Sententiën*, 1453–1461, fol. 354 v.
65. SAB 157, *Civiele Sententiën*, 1453–1461, fol. 256 v.
66. SAB 157, *Civiele Sententiën*, 1453–1461, fol. 256 v.
67. SAB 157, *Civiele Sententiën*, 1453–1461, fol. 218 v. 219 v., 243 r.
68. Rossi, 'Early modern maritime insurance', 243.
69. Rossi, 'The liability of the shipmaster', 1–47; Rossi, 'The barratry of the shipmaster', 65–85; Rossi, 'The barratry of the shipmaster in early modern law', 504–574.
70. SAB 157, *Civiele sententiën*, 1453–1461, fol. 155 v.
71. SAB 157, *Civiele Sententiën*, 1469–1471, fol. 31 v.; 81 r.; SAB 157 *Civiele Sententiën*, 1469–1471, fol. 175 r.
72. SAB 157, *Civiele Sententiën*, 1453–1461, fol. 372 r.
73. Wielant, *Pracktijke Civiele*, 84; Gilliodts-Van Severen, *Coutumes de Bruges*, vol. 2, 141–142; Saelens, 'Consignatie bij de Gentse schepenbanken', 125.
74. Monballyu, 'Het costumiere recht', 150.
75. De ruysscher, 'Antwerp 1490–1590', 85
76. De Roover, *Money, banking and credit*, 11.
77. De Roover, 'Renseignements complémentaires', 68–69; Maréchal, 'Het internationale karakter van de Brugsche handelsbeurs', 89; Murray, *A history of business*, 160–163.
78. Aerts, 'Historici over bankiers in het laatmiddeleewse Brugge', 62; Murray, *Bruges cradle of capitalism*, 210–212; Flume, 'Constructing the stock exchange', 416–418; Braudel, *Les jeux* de l'échange, 117–124.
79. Aerts, 'Wisselruiterij in de Lage Landen', 38.
80. De Roover, *The rise and decline*, 109; Szramkiewicz and Descamps, *Histoire du droit des affaires*, 108–114; De Roover, 'Le contrat de change', 119.
81. De Roover, *The Bruges money market*, 22.
82. De Roover, 'Cambium ad Venetias', 240–242.
83. De Roover, 'The Scholastics, usury and foreign exchange', 259; Wood, *Medieval economic thought*, 174; De Roover, *The rise and decline*, 109; De Roover, 'Le contrat de change', 122.
84. Bell, Brooks, and Moore, 'Cambium non est mutuum', 377.
85. Bolton and Guidi-Bruscoli, 'Borromei', 473–474; Bolton and Guidi-Bruscoli, 'Your flexible friend', 889.
86. De Roover, *Rise and decline*, 108–141; Mueller, *The Venetian money market*, 327–337.
87. Bolton and Guidi-Bruscoli, 'Your flexible friend', 890.
88. However, the reality is more complex than the theory. For example, in 1448, Niccolao Burlamachi wrote a letter of exchange in Bruges to be delivered on the night of May 1448 in Genua. However, the Lucchese court decided that since the debtor (Geoffredo de Foya) was Lucchese, and thus, his case could be heard in Lucca. Achivio di Stato di Lucca, Corte de Mercantei, Cause civile, 1457–1458, fol. 165 r.

89. De ruysscher, 'L'acculturation juridique', 154–156.
90. See for example: SAB 157, *Civiele Sententiën*, 1447–1453, fol. 66 v., 129 r., 130 v.
91. Neither did the aldermen who had to order information to find out what the usual rule was.
92. As is recently proved based on the Datini letters; Bell et al. 'Cambium non est mutuum', 390.
93. In the middle ages, the people who occupied themselves with letters of exchange were called bankers. People who occupied themselves with loans were called Lombards; De Roover, 'Le contrat de change', 119.
94. De Roover, *The Bruges money market*, 34.
95. Bell et al., 'Cambium non est mutuum', 379.
96. The case may refer to the ducal monetary reform in 1410. In order to boost his currency in silver and ban foreign currencies, the duke ordered that all letters of exchange should be paid in both silver and gold. The reform was met with hard criticism from Italian merchants and was modified on their request; Gilliodts-Van Severen, *Coutume de Bruges*, vol. I, 457; van der Wee, 'L'echec de la réforme monétaire de 1407', 587; De Roover, *The Bruges money market around 1400*, 67–78; Zoete, *Handelingen van de leden en van de staten*, vol. I, p. 216–223; 431, 468–469, nr. 148–153, 301–319.
97. SAB 157, *Civiele Sententiën*, 1465–1469, fol. 137 r.
98. SAB 157, *Civiele Sententiën*, 1447–1453, fol. 37 r.
99. As the confusion of this case also indicates, this should not be seen as an early example of *endossement*: De Roover, *L'évolution de la lettre de change*, 88–89.
100. But Bernardo Cambi remained vague about why Diederik did this. He said that Diederik 'had some reason instigating him'; SAB 157, *Civiele Sententiën*, 1447–1453, fol. 127 r.
101. SAB 157, *Civiele Sententiën*, 1447–1453, fol. 127 r.
102. SAB 157, *Civiele Sententiën*, 1447–1453, fol. 127 r.
103. SAB 157, *Civiele Sententiën*, 1447–1453, fol. 127 v.
104. SAB 157, *Civiele Sententiën*, 1469–1470, fol. 110 r.
105. See for example: SAB 157, *Civiele Sententiën*, 1453–1461, 179 r.
106. SAB 157, *Civiele Sententiën*, 1453–1461, fol. 166 v.
107. SAB 157, *Civiele Sententiën*, 1453–1461, fol. 166 v.
108. SAB 157, *Civiele Sententiën*, 1453–1461, fol. 179 r.
109. See for aldermen deputation: SAB 157, *Civiele Sententiën*, 1453–1461, 53 r.–54 v. See for arbiters assisting the aldermen; SAB 157, *Civiele Sententiën*, 1447–1453, fol. 37 v.; SAB 157, *Civiele Sententiën*, 1465–1469, 173 v.
110. See for example: SAB 157, *Civiele Sententiën*, 1447–1453, 66 v.
111. See for example: SAB 157, *Civiele Sententiën*, 1453–1461, fol. 53 v.–54 v., 158 r.
112. SAB 157, *Civiele Sententiën*, 1453–1461, fol. 37 r.–v.
113. There was a difference between the merchant/bankers and the professional exchangers who operated exchange offices. The usual suspects in exchange operations were the merchants/bankers such as the Lomellini, Da Rabata and Medici. The family De May seems to have focused on banking services. In Bruges there were about fifteen or sixteen local private money changers who had developed along the lines of the Italian *cambiatoris*. See De Roover, *Money, Banking and Credit*, passim; Murray, *Bruges, Cradle of Capitalism*, 153–155; Aerts, 'The absence of public exchange', 94–95.
114. SAB 165, *Civiele Sententiën Kamer*, 1473–1474, fol. 9 r.

115. RAG 23705, Processen par Escript, Pietro de Nyeto vs. Alonso de Larmes, 1475–1482, demande.
116. To do this, he needed the claim from Jehan Loupes. He threatened him into delivering the bill of exchange of pay up the amount; RAG 23705, Pietro de Nyeto vs. Alonso de Larmes, 1475–1482, demande; RAG 23705, Pietro de Nyeto vs. Alonso de Larmes, 1475–1482, decision of the aldermen.
117. SAG 23705, Pietro de Nyeto vs. Alonso de Larmes, 1475–1482, response, fol. 3 r.–v.; 23705, Pietro de Nyeto vs. Alonso de Larmes, 1475–1482, decision of the aldermen.
118. The consulted merchants were the beau monde of Bruges' commerce: Alberto Contarini, Tomasso Portinari, Christoforo de Migrono, Nicolas Betrani, Pierre de Cassel, Giovanni Spinola, Benique de Cassuia, Gomes de Sorye, Folco Portinari; SAG 23705, Pietro de Nyeto vs. Alonso de Larmes, 1475–1482, enquete par tourbe.
119. RAG 23705, Processen par Escript, Pietro de Nyeto vs. Alonso de Larmes, 1475–1482, decision of the aldermen.
120. Occasionally the Council of Flanders mentions all the evidence that was shown; RAG 2377, *Raad van Vlaanderen, Acten en Sententiën*, 1458–1459, fol. 233 r.
121. RAG 2409, *Raad van Vlaanderen, Acten en Sententiën*, 1478–1478, fol. 19 r., 72 r., 138 r.; RAG 2410, *Raad van Vlaanderen, Acten en Sententiën*, fol. 40 v., 165 v.

The Framework of the Aldermen

The aldermen of Bruges had a system. Twelve aldermen, twelve councillors and two burgomasters had to regulate the conflicts of a multitude of merchants. The state was still too underdeveloped to seek to actively intervene in commercial cases. Private conflict resolution had long been a favoured approach. Medieval merchants could resolve conflict perfectly well through their peers and Bruges provided the authority to respect a judgment. However, the lingering paradox remains between a commercial city that was renowned for its structured and surveyed commercial facilities and apparent leniency in legal affairs.

Bruges demonstrated its concern for justice in the procedures it applied. The *vierschaar* was too slow and the chamber procedure was not sufficiently detailed. The authority of a decision taken in the chamber procedure did not come close to what the *vierschaar* could provide. Although the problem would never be truly resolved, the initiatives the aldermen and litigants took are apparent. In each of the solutions, the aldermen relied on the networks that were present in Bruges. If both parties agreed, the case was solved through arbitration. Peers and confidants of the litigants would then treat the matter as having been conclusively dealt with. The aldermen surveyed the procedure and retook the case if the arbitration failed. However, the system of sureties provided the first line of defence. Sureties were made to ensure that parties stuck to the arbitration, that both parties would be faithful and respect the decision of the arbiters. Similarly, the aldermen often demanded sureties for a litigation procedure before their court. Arrested debtors and seized merchandise were released in exchange for a surety assuring a proper procedure. As such, the sureties trapped the debtor in a web of obligations, ensuring that the aldermen could do their work effectively.

Bruges leveraged its commercial character to enhance its judicial processes. The city's networks were distinctive, with various merchant firms holding significant interests, and hostellers, as commercial intermediaries, not only brokering deals but also playing a crucial role in maintaining oversight over merchants. The aldermen of Bruges, while typically adhering to a streamlined procedure, often departed from this in cases they deemed particularly significant. However, the primary aim of the legal framework was not to serve commerce, though this was sometimes an incidental outcome. Instead, the fundamental purpose of the aldermen's framework was to ensure the delivery of justice within the city.

Part II

Leverage: Group Strategies to Adapt the Framework

Introduction

One can only imagine the emotions that must have surged within Tommaso Portinari in the year 1473. During that period, one of his boldest investments took an unexpected and unfortunate turn. The Florentine merchant had entered into a lease agreement for the Burgundian Galleys, the San Giorgio and the San Mateo, with the Duke of Burgundy. These ships, conceived as symbols of prestige, were entrusted to the Italian in hopes of generating lucrative return.[1] Tommaso Portinari had employed them to transport valuable goods between Bruges, London and Italy, even embarking on a journey to the Eastern Mediterranean. However, in 1473, tragedy struck as one of the vessels, laden with precious cargo including spices, woollens, alum and two precious altarpieces, fell victim to an attack and was captured by Paul Beneke, a Danzig plunderer.[2] The ship was violently seized, resulting in the loss of several crew members, and it was eventually taken to the Baltic along with its valuable cargo.

This marked the catastrophic ruin of Portinari's investment. While he likely held some form of insurance, it is unlikely that it covered the immense value of the lost ship.[3] To compound matters, the shipper, Paul Beneke, had acted under the banner of the Hanse, although the organisation distanced itself from the incident. The Hanse was a coalition of cities and merchants bound by shared privileges. One of its primary functions was safeguarding merchants abroad, a role it adeptly fulfilled by the late fifteenth century. Before Portinari, the Hanse disavowed any responsibility in the case, and was ready to present itself as a formidable adversary in court.

Tommaso Portinari, however, was no ordinary individual. The Florentine had spent the past three decades in Bruges, arriving in the city as a young boy in the 1440s. Over time, he had steadily advanced his career within the Medici firm. By 1465, Portinari held the esteemed position of senior partner of the Medici branch in Bruges. By 1473, he had emerged as a key figure within the Florentine merchant community.[4] He had also earned the trust of Charles the Bold, the Duke of Burgundy. Therefore, Portinari was far from powerless; he promptly invoked his influential connections to ensure that the Hanse was held accountable for the actions of its associates. Duke Charles wrote a letter to the Hanseatic assembly, expressing his profound disappointment regarding the attack and demanding reparation on behalf of Portinari.[5] In the event his warnings were ignored, the Duke threatened to summon representatives of the Hanse to his court, the Great Council. At the 1473 Hanseatic Diet in Utrecht, the Hanseatic cities conveyed their sympathy for Tommaso Portinari but tried to dissociate themselves from the actions of Danzig.[6] Portinari deemed their explanation misguided and departed the Utrecht Diet without any prospects of seeing his damages covered.[7]

Upon returning to Bruges, Portinari initiated proceedings by issuing arrests. These arrests aimed to seize merchandise, compelling representatives of the Hanse, or in Portinari's view, the Hanse Kontor, to appear before the Great Council. Agents acting on behalf of the Duke seized Hanseatic assets in Bruges and beyond, ensnaring the organisation in a financial entanglement. The Hanseatic representatives swiftly protested to the Bruges aldermen, arguing against the unconventional approach.[8] As the Hanse was commercially vital for the city of Bruges, the aldermen listened. In an attempt to retain Hanseatic trade in the city, the Bruges aldermen negotiated with Portinari.[9] The negotiators offered to deliberate the matter within their own jurisdiction, provided Portinari relinquished his claim before the Great Council. This arrangement would spare Portinari protracted and costly proceedings before the Council, and in return, the Hanse vowed to respect the aldermen's decision.[10] However, once Portinari withdrew his case from the Great Council, the Hanseatic Kontor reneged on its commitment. The Bruges Kontor reverted to its conventional defence: the Kontor could not be held collectively liable for the actions of individual members.[11] Additionally, the Hanseatic negotiators hinted that unless Bruges shared the same stance, Hanseatic traders might explore alternative cities for their commerce. Bruges was coerced into ensuring protection for the Hanse Kontor against any potential future claims from Portinari.

Consequently, Bruges had no choice but to marginalise Portinari. His situation worsened as other investments similarly unravelled, and by 1477, the Medici firm severed ties with him. The Bruges branch disbanded, leaving Portinari saddled with insoluble assets. The 1480s saw Portinari ensnared in fierce battles with creditors, all while attempting to salvage his ailing investments.[12] Yet, a turning point arrived by 1492. Following the Flemish rebellion (1482–1492), all merchant communities, including the Hanseatic Kontor, abandoned Bruges for Antwerp. Unlike Bruges, Antwerp had not promised to safeguard the Hanse from Portinari's claims. Meanwhile, Portinari had cultivated amicable relations with the Burgundian court, managing to reopen his case before the Great Council. The Hanseatic Kontor was taken aback and argued that they no longer possessed members with knowledge of the case.[13] They attempted to delay proceedings, but the Great Council remained unyielding – the Hanseatic Kontor was compelled to attend the court. During the hearing, the Hanseatic Kontor maintained that it bore no responsibility for the actions of its subordinates. Nevertheless, Portinari persuaded the Council members that actions conducted in the name of a city, state, or league should be attributed to that entity. Portinari was not holding the Hanse liable for its subordinates; rather, he was holding the organisation responsible as the principle in the case.[14] This strategy proved effective, and in 1496, Portinari secured a judgment that offered the hope of partial reimbursement.[15]

In the interim, the Hanseatic Kontor had returned to Bruges. However, the Hanseatic negotiators made a resolution to the Portinari case a prerequisite for continuing trade within the city. The city marshalled support from influential figures to delay the judgment's execution. Eventually, an agreement was reached with Portinari's heirs to make a partial payment. Tommaso Portinari had ceded his claim to his relatives and relocated from Bruges to Florence, where he eventually passed away.

In the end, very few emerged victorious from this saga. Bruges sought to recoup a portion of its expenditure paid to the Portinari heirs through taxation, while the Portinari family received only a fraction of the sum lost, with none of their valuables restored. Bruges was compelled to bear the cost of a matter unrelated to its actions, motivated solely by the desire to retain Hanseatic merchants within its borders.

This case of Portinari serves as a vivid illustration of contrasting litigation strategies influenced by background and context. On one hand, the Hanseatic Kontor relied on its privileges, collective actions during assemblies, and its relation with Bruges. Throughout the course of the case, the Hanse successfully exerted pressure on the city by threatening to shift their trade elsewhere. Conversely, Portinari employed his intellect, cultivated ties with the Burgundian court, and displayed initiative in steering the case toward a favourable outcome. Both had a distinct litigation strategy based upon their different context and tools available to them. In the following chapter, I will explore how the context of merchants shaped merchants' litigation strategies, the communities they formed and how the communities influenced how merchants litigated in Bruges. These merchant communities represented the merchants of a certain nationality trading in Bruges, with privileges bestowing rights and protection, and the option to leverage Bruges into additional protection. The extent of leverage a merchant community held against Bruges played a pivotal role in litigation. Consequently, how a merchant community was shaped and which contextual factors aided them in their litigation, influenced the way they behaved legally in Flanders. The major indication of whether Bruges can be considered as a city of justice, was the ability of merchants to group together, to obtain rights that assured their property and livelihood in Flanders and defend these rights before a court. One of the most important conclusions arising from the Portinari case is that the aldermen could definitely succumb to pressure from a vital merchant community.

This part of the book is divided into three types of leverage, each represented by different forms of commerce. The first is the North Sea trade, dominated by Hanseatic, Scottish and English merchants, which was the most intensive. These merchants formed the largest communities and controlled crucial trade routes for Bruges. They employed this influence, with varying degrees of success, to pressure the Count of Flanders into granting privileges. The second category is the Iberian trade, represented by Castilian – often referred to as 'Spanish' in the sources – Portuguese, and Aragonese merchants. Politically supported and emerging as influential powers, these nations formed strong communities to protect their traders. The final trade stream is Italian commerce. While the concept of a unified Italy was anachronistic, Italian cities nevertheless established communities that extended beyond individual city-states. Notably, in 1493, they were granted a privilege 'for the Italians', though this was one of the few such privileges awarded to Italian cities. Unlike other groups, the Italians relied more on community-based protection than on formal privileges. Although the classification of these trade streams is somewhat artificial, it facilitates a comparative analysis of the varying strategies, leverage, and forms of protection employed by different merchant communities.

NOTES

1. Elder De Roover, 'La voyage de Girolamo Strozzi', 120–121.
2. Portinari claimed 6,540 Flemish pounds losses in cargo and an additional 4,200 lib gr. in damages; Von der Ropp, Hanserecesse II, vol. 7, pp. 115–117, n. 41; Wubs-Mrozewicz, 'Mercantile conflict resolution in practice', 11.
3. Elder de Roover, 'A prize of war', 3–12; Mozejko, 'Maritime Danzig', 107–108.
4. De Roover, 'Tommaso Portinari', dl. 2, 690–698; Boone, 'Apologie d'un banquier médiéval', 31–54; English translation: Boone, 'In defence of a medieval banker', 111–134.
5. Von der Ropp, Hanserecesse II, vol. 7, p.19, n. 29.
6. Von der Ropp, Hanserecesse II, vol. 7, p. 63, n. 35.
7. Von der Ropp, Hanserecesse II, vol. 2, p. 65, n. 35.; Elder De Roover, 'A Prize of War', 7.
8. Von der Ropp, Hanserecesse II, vol. 7, p.235, n. 134.
9. Mozejko, *Peter von Danzig*, 209–210; Meltzing, 'Tommaso Portinari', 111; Von Reumont, 'Di alcune relazioni', 40; Elder, 'A prize of war', 6; De Roover, *The Medici bank*, 347.
10. Von der Ropp, Hanserecesse II, vol. 7, p. 236, n. 134.
11. Von der Ropp, Hanserecesse II, vol. 7, p. 236, n. 134.
12. See, for example, a decision from the Great Council obliging Portinari to pay his debts: ARA, *Fonds Grote Raad*, 796.199, fol. 244 v.–245. See also the case against Jehan Listrossy for 4204 ducats of debt: SAB 165, *Civiele Sententiën Kamer*, 1487–1488, fol. 3 v.–5 r.; SAB, *Geluwenboek*, fol. 87 v.–88 r.
13. Schäfer, Hanserecesse III, vol. 3, 139, n. 175.
14. SAB, *Politieke Charters*, 1262.
15. SAB, *Politieke Charters*, 1262.

5

The Strategy of Economic Leverage: The Hanseatic, English and Scottish Communities

VITAL TRADE STREAMS

The Hanseatic, English and Scottish merchant communities made up the bulk of the international trade that came from the North Sea and arrived in Bruges. In comparison to Mediterranean trade, they were closely located to the city of Bruges and had an ancient tradition of sailing towards the commercial city.

German merchants from cities such as Cologne were among the first to undertake regular trade towards Bruges. By the fourteenth century, several cities and merchants had organised themselves in a loose organisation called the Hanse. These Hanseatic merchants comprised cities and merchants from present-day Netherlands to the Baltic area. They transported commodities such as grain, wood, furs and wax. Cities like Lübeck, Hamburg, Danzig and Konigsberg had acquired far-reaching autonomy to organise trade independently from their sovereign (the Holy Roman Emperor or the King of Poland).[1] By grouping together and bundling their demands, the cities formed an effective block against other trade partners and political authorities. Their representatives convened at the Hanseatic assemblies (*Hansetag*) where the cities addressed existing abuses, resolved issues, and laid out a common policy. Participation at these gatherings was voluntary and the towns that defined themselves as part of the network varied. At its height, the Hanse included seventy principal cities and 200 lesser cities, though this was just a snapshot.[2]

Once a city was part of the Hanse community, its merchants also enjoyed its privileges. When threatened, the merchants' block could be highly efficient.[3] Being a Hanseatic merchant in Bruges had both advantages and disadvantages. Besides reaping the fruits of the shared privileges, the Hanse demanded obedience to the Hanse Kontor from its merchants in a centre such as Bruges. A Kontor was a trading post the Hanse founded in a city that was no part of the Hanse, but offered lucrative prospects. There were four important Kontors: London, Bergen, Novgorod and Bruges. In contrast to the Hanse as an organisation of traders and cities, the Kontors entailed a formal organisation.[4] The *olderluden* (the Hanseatic aldermen) had oversight of the trade post, they issued ordinances, monitored the behaviour of merchants and corresponded with the Hanse meetings.

Among all trade posts, Bruges was the most vital for Hanseatic traders,[5] as it connected the Northern Hanseatic trade with the Southern Mediterranean. Likewise, Bruges was highly dependent on these Hanseatic merchants, which they called 'Easterlings'.[6] The Easterlings brought raw materials (wood, amber, fish) from the North in exchange for Flemish cloth or other commodities from the South. Several hostellers specialised in Hanseatic trade, making at least a part of the political elite dependent on the Hanseatic presence.[7]

However; during the fourteenth century, the population of Bruges, and with it Flanders, depended mainly on another commercial stream: the supply of English wool. Flemish cloth production relied heavily on the finest wool. The English 'lemster ore' and Cotswold sheep gave fine, short and curly-fibred wools suitable for the heavy quality broadcloth made in Flanders. These cloths gave long durability and great warmth.[8] The sheep were bred in a narrow area in Northern England and the best-quality wool needed extensive treatment.[9] The Flemish textile guilds acknowledged the quality and ordained that only English wool would suffice for the best garments.[10] This made Flanders particularly reliant on the English export.[11]

The English king was aware of this dependence and used Flemish wool hunger for political purposes. From 1066 onwards, France and England would be the usual suspects in violent upheavals in Western Europe. The Flemish counts participated in the longstanding conflict between England and France when Baldwin IX (1194–1205) allied himself in 1197 with the English king against France.[12] However, when the pro-English attitude wavered during the thirteenth century, the English king did not hesitate to pressure Flanders into doing his bidding by means of economic warfare. One of the most important conflicts was in 1270–1274, when the English king forbade the shipping of English wool to the County of Flanders. Flanders yielded to the English demands and from then on, the threat of an English wool-embargo hung over the Flemish like the sword of Damocles.[13]

In theory, the English had a good bargaining position when asking for trade privileges. Trade between England and Flanders flourished for most of the Middle Ages and the harbours of Southampton, Dover, Sandwich, and later on Calais were vital for the trade with Flanders. For most of the fourteenth and fifteenth centuries, Calais was a special English enclave surrounded by Burgundian possession. From this city, the English organised their wool export to Flanders.[14] The combination between closeness, vital commodity and royal influence made the Flemish negotiating position precarious.[15] This perspective seems to be shared by historians. The initiatives that the aldermen of the cities of Flanders undertook to convince the Flemish count to maintain good relations with England suggest the strong leverage the community had over Bruges.[16] If the count refused and chose confrontation with England, the Flemish cities were at least reluctant and could rebel outright in protest.

An alternative to the English wool supply was provided in the form of Scottish wool. Scottish wool was coarser than English wool, and exports of English wool surpassed those of Scottish wool more than five times.[17] However, despite the fact that English wool was the most sought after, the Scottish advantage was their steady supply stream and the fact that they were less prone to use wool as an economic weapon. While it is true that Scottish–Flemish relations were not always warm, the Scottish–French alliance proved to be far less of a hindrance to trade with the Low Countries than was the case for English relations. In addition, the Scottish trade was complementary to the Flemish. While the English merchants and their draperies presented direct competition for the Bruges market, the Scottish merchants were mostly suppliers of raw materials.[18] Wool, fish and hides were the main products Scottish sailors brought to the Low Countries until well into the fifteenth century.[19] This is also apparent in our court register: when Scottish goods were seized in medieval Bruges, such seizures almost always concerned cargoes of wool.[20] The textiles that the Scots did manufacture, were mainly of low value and no competition for the high-value textiles sold in Bruges. On the contrary, the cheaper textiles added a complementary value to the market.

Nevertheless, politics had the potential to ruin such commercial relations. These relations paralleled the stance Flanders adopted in the conflict between France and England that would dominate Western Europe for over a century. In this war, Flanders often found itself between the devil and the blue sea. Flanders was bound to the Kingdom of France and had to follow the kingdom in its wars with England. However, Flemish wealth, derived mainly from the big textile cities that relied on wool imports. Because the Scots depended mainly on France for their protection against England, it meant for Flanders that choosing one wool-exporter would be to lose another.[21] In order to counter this before it became too big an issue, the Flemish counts generally maintained a policy of neutrality towards Scotland. Illustrative in this case are the different letters Edward I sent to the Count of Flanders hoping to cut supply lines for the Scots. In 1305, the king asked the city of Bruges to exclude Scottish merchants from the privileges that were awarded and, similarly, a couple of years later he asked the Flemish Count, Robrecht of Bethune, to ban all Scottish merchandise from his lands. In both instances, he was to be disappointed.[22]

The Burgundian dukes would continue this policy of neutrality in the fifteenth century. Certainly, during the reign of Philip the Good (1419–1467), this was a bit odd. When in 1419 the French Dauphin ordered the murder of the Burgundian duke, his successor sided with the English and was thus formally an opponent of the Scottish king. The apparent friendly relations with opposing sides would not prove an unsurmountable obstacle. On the contrary, the growing political cohesion that the Valois dukes brought to the Low Countries encouraged good relations with Scotland, while Duke Philip the Good was probably playing a double game so England would not become too powerful.[23]

Each of these merchant communities was a commercial lifeline for the city of Bruges. These communities were aware of their importance and when political events or perceived malpractice occurred in the city, they refused to trade in the city and sought to embargo it into submission. As relations occasionally deteriorated, these communities requested additional rights in return for their re-entry to the city. In this way, the Hanseatic merchants received privileges in 1280, 1307, 1309, 1359–1360, 1392 and additional promises from the city in 1438 and 1457. The English merchant community received one important privilege in 1359, and the Scottish community received privileges in 1387, 1397, 1407 and a final large extension in 1427. It is the combination of economic importance for the Flemish economy, an effective embargo and a city of Bruges willing to do what it took that rendered these communities among the most privileged of Flanders.

THE STRATEGY OF PRIVILEGES

German merchants from Cologne received the first privileges in matters relating to debt settlements.[24] Before the foundation of the Hanse, these merchants appreciated the great value in Flanders and a trade settlement would follow in the 1250s. The trade settlements in Bergen, Novgorod and London, evolved to become enclaves where the merchants could store merchandise, find shelter and abide by their laws.[25] Bruges was the exception. The German merchants proposed to found a colony near Bruges in 1252 under the leadership of Lübeck. However, in the mid-thirteenth century, Bruges was vehemently trying to bind the small Zwin towns into accepting Bruges as a legal head. The foundation of another small town with its own rules, was probably not to the liking of the Flemish city. The German request was denied, but Countess Margaret and her son Guy of Dampierre did grant the *mercatores romani imperii* privileges in 1252.[26] The count granted reductions on toll tariffs, exemptions from trial by combat, the right of shipwreck and debts of third parties.[27] Demands for a legal enclave were denied, so the Easterlings had to live in the city of Bruges among the other merchants and citizens of Bruges.[28] Bruges would not concede this exception throughout its history.

Even after the proper foundation of a Kontor in 1347, when the Hanseatic merchants ordained that the *olderluden* would gather in the Carmelite monastery and issue ordinances. The Hanse merchants remained closely connected to the city of Bruges. The Easterlings had no option but to interact with the services provided by Bruges, the taxes Bruges' officials and the count levied, and the law that was used to regulate the city.[29] They were part of the social life of Bruges and had close relations with the rest of the city.[30] It would be a bold hypothesis to state that most problems would have been avoided if Bruges had given the Hanseatic merchants their enclave. The close connection between the merchants, the services provided in the city, Flemish/Burgundian officers and the local aldermen bench caused many problems in the eyes of the Hanse. The Easterlings continually struggled for better protection. While the German merchants never received this enclave, their demands came very close to setting one up in Bruges.

The subsequent privileges of the Hanse in 1280, 1307 and 1309, 1359–1360 and 1392 followed the pattern of years of dissatisfaction with the Bruges city council, who ignored previously granted privileges and the opportune moment to leave the city and embargoed it into better conditions. As the Count of Flanders was the only one to issue these privileges, it relied heavily on the influence Bruges possessed over the count. Hence it was the Hanse who pressurised Bruges, and then Bruges, in its turn, persuaded the count to grant additional rights. Such rights could be far-reaching. For example, in matters of taxes on wines, the Hanseatic merchants received several significant reductions or even exemptions. They also received the promise that the city would hold itself accountable for its money exchangers and compensate Hanseatic merchants if these money exchangers proved to be malicious. In addition, Hanseats could choose where they were buried, and they were not obliged to keep the staple for grain. Hanseats were free to transfer English cloth from one ship to another without punishment, and they were free to sell cloth without paying the usual tax – the 'hallegelde'. In addition, Easterlings could load and unload ships where and when they chose. Their shipmasters could dock their vessels at any place they believed to be suitable. When a shipmaster had been driven back by the wind after disembarking goods in Bruges, there was no obligation to pay any tolls, even if the ship was loaded again.

In matters of maritime plunder, the Hanseats received far-reaching concessions. If a 'robber', who had plundered Hanseatic vessels or merchants, was found in the County of Flanders, this person would be apprehended and was to remain in custody until a judgment was reached. The stolen goods, however, would be identified based on the markings on the goods and returned to the German merchants, without any form of trial.[31] In 1392, these clauses were even widened. The 1392 privileges declared that if a merchant in the County of Flanders suffered losses in life or goods, the aldermen would see that justice (according to the Hanseatic definition) prevailed. The duke assured that his officers would pursue cases of theft, damage and murder by Flemings, and if the aggressor was not a native, the duke would do whatever necessary to see justice done.[32] When a German merchant was robbed, the cities of Ghent, Bruges and Ypres would be held accountable for the return of the merchandise. If robbery occurred outside the lands of Flanders, the Duke promised that justice would be done.[33] Already in 1309, the Easterlings had amassed some advantages in regard to conflict resolution. When the goods were inspected and delivered, complaints before the aldermen in matters of cloth, wax and copper were impossible. When the goods were not inspected, complaints would only be considered within the lines of reason.[34] In contrast, Hanseatic merchants could claim 'disadvantage' before the aldermen. If a commercial deal did not work out as planned, the Easterlings could bring the case before the aldermen of Bruges.[35]

Similarly, the English obtained a very important privileges in 1359. Just as the Hanse had used moments of weakness on the part of the city of Bruges, the 1359 privilege of the English nation came at a time that the Count needed Bruges to rule the county and the city of Bruges needed the English merchants for its commerce. The English negotiators however succeeded in obtained very extensive privileges. The English merchants received far-reaching autonomy in the resolution of their internal disputes. A governor could regulate all internal affairs, except capital offences, which were reserved for the aldermen (in *vierschaar*). The English merchants were granted the right to choose the most profitable houses in which to conduct their commerce. If the inhabitants refused, they would be compelled by the aldermen to grant entry to the English.[36] The English could ask the aldermen to change the weights used in the city, and the aldermen and the merchants would choose the weighters together. These weighters would swear an oath and would be punished if they refused.[37]

The English were excluded from the right of shipwreck upon paying a reasonable price for the expenses of saving the merchandise.[38] It should be noted that they desired not to be arrested for acts of maritime plunder, but the stipulations went further. According to the 1359 privilege, nobody who committed acts of maritime plunder, past or present, could be prosecuted.[39] However, if an English merchant was robbed at sea, this should be addressed and compensated expeditiously. If these goods appeared in Bruges, and a merchant could prove that the goods were indeed his, the merchandise should be returned to the owner without the intervention of the aldermen.[40]

The English received a few other legal exceptions undermining the existing legal system. If there were complaints about the quality of wool, these complaints would not be brought before the Bruges court but would be handled by a commission of two 'good members of the city' and two merchants from England.[41] Furthermore, unanimity in this commission was not required; the decision took effect if three out of four agreed. It is hard to imagine how this commission could maintain the image of objectivity or how non-English inhabitants would even abide by the ruling. However, equality or objectivity was not the goal of the English merchants. If a debtor was detained by an English merchant, that person should remain in detention until the English merchant was repaid. Even procuring a surety that the debtor would faithfully abide by the decision of the aldermen would not suffice to secure the release of such a prisoner. The English on the other hand could handily use the debtors' prison to their advantage: English creditors only had to furnish proof of the debt by providing a debtor's note with the seal of the debtor.[42]

A recurring complaint from the Hanseatic, English and Scottish communities was the inadequate justice provided by the aldermen of Bruges, and how privileges might remedy this situation. Although it is hard to assess the veracity of these claims, the accusations do form a part of the general discourse among merchants and their mutual interest in forming their own legal entities in the city. However, the interesting contrast here is that the eventual goal of these privileges was an equitable system of justice but with some procedural advantages to their own community. Similarly, Scottish merchants received basic assurances in 1359 and 1387, and they further expanded on them in 1394.[43]

The 1394 privilege, in particular clause three, offered Scottish merchants a considerable advantage in relation to debt imprisonment. They could not simply be thrown into a debtors' prison. Instead, Scottish debtors would first have the chance to go to the city hall and provide a sufficient caution in order to be released again. Only if the aldermen were not present or the caution was not possible, would the merchant be incarcerated, while still being able to provide sureties in order to obtain a temporary release in the foreseeable future.[44] The clause drew a distinction between the bail posed when the merchant was already in prison, and the surety given when the merchants was apprehended. The standard procedure was to bring a merchant to the city prison and then it was up to the captured merchant to challenge the rightfulness of the imprisonment before the aldermen. The introduction of this clause not only gave the Scottish merchants a serious defence against arbitrary imprisonment, but it also gave them an advantage in debt settlements. These debtors still could be incarcerated if they proved to be defaulting debtors, but creditors would think twice before using this action. The clause shielded Scottish debtors from extra-judicial arrest for civil causes, as was the case for other merchant nations, although not all.

The privileges of 1407 and 1427 indicate how the objectives of the nation shifted.[45] There were no more clauses containing arrests or assurances on the status of a person; these privileges aimed at concrete advantages over other merchant nations. Both the 1407 and 1427 privileges were the result of a crisis where the Scots had lamented the maritime plunder en route to Flanders. In 1407, the privileges would receive liberties in the port of Sluis. The Scots acquired the right to dock their ships in the Zwin where they wanted, as long as it was in the accustomed places; they could dock their ships next to each other, but no more than four; and if they were to be driven back to the harbour by bad weather, the merchants could reorganise their merchandise in these ships without paying staple rights.[46]

In the subsequent years, the Scottish nation and the Hanse were again at loggerheads with each other as a result of mutual claims of privateering. In addition, the Burgundian duke had not been particularly helpful. In 1413, Scottish merchants had seized a ship from merchants from Mechelen, and when these merchants complained to Philip of Burgundy, then Count of Charolais, he gave the Mechelen merchants reprisal letters. The Mechelaars had *carte blanche* to avenge themselves upon other Scottish merchants. They duly did avenge the seizure and, in so doing, the *Mechelaars* infringed the privileges of the Scottish community. As was the case with several other nations, Scottish merchants could not be held accountable for a debt owed by third parties. Duke John the Fearless (1404–1419), had to intervene and release some of those arrested by the Mechelen merchants; among them Archibald, Earl of Douglas.[47] The problem with the Mechelaars kept festering and the duke eventually had to pronounce his verdict upon the matter on the 18 May 1416.[48] Despite a merchant truce in 1420, the Scots remained deeply dissatisfied as a result of the affair.[49] When Flemish merchants attacked and sacked ships in 1424, the Scottish King James I decided to impose drastic measures on Bruges and blockaded the Scottish trade on Flanders.[50] The royal pressure worked, and the 1427 privileges were a complete victory for the Scottish merchants.

In the context of the Anglo-Burgundian alliance, these privileges are remarkable to say the least. The Scottish king's tough stance, along with economic dependency on Scottish wool and the pressure the Flemish cities exerted on the Burgundian duke proved to be crucial.[51] The Scots obtained highly beneficial clauses for their privateering business and succeeded in fending off the abuses of Burgundian officials. The clauses open with a statement regarding recent experiences and the problems that arose when the property of Scottish merchants was seized. The duke and the Four Members of Flanders promised to satisfy all those who had suffered losses since the coronation of James I as king of Scotland. These losses were inflicted due to maritime plunder and the stance of Bruges in these international conflicts. Yet, while they affirmed that they would not damage any Scottish goods, the dukes also acknowledged that a cargo of captured English wool should remain in the hands of the Scottish nation.[52] The Scottish nation was allowed to bring their prizes safely into the city of Bruges while not being disturbed by the Burgundian officials,[53] and, in time of adversity, Scottish sailors would be able to use the ports of Bruges in order to resupply and refit damaged ships, again without being disturbed.[54] These clauses were formulated vaguely and though the privileges sometimes included only small additions, they were important. For example, in 1407 the Scottish nation had already discussed the right to sail back to the harbours of the Zwin area in the event of bad weather. In 1427 the phrase 'adversity or else' was added. The 'or else' was a meaningful addition and gave the Scottish merchants more space for interpretation.

THE STRATEGY OF DUCAL INTERVENTION?

The Scottish privileges of 1427 are even more astonishing if one considers that they were one of the last new charters that were granted by the Dukes of Burgundy. Duke Philip the Good would skilfully enlarge his political powerhouse. The County of Holland-Zeeland-Henegouwen, the Duchy of Brabant, the County of Namur and the Duchy of Luxembourg would fall into his lap through inheritance, marriage or war. Although the County of Flanders was still the wealthiest of his possessions by far, there was a larger project than just the Flemish cities. Since the cities could have less and less influence on policy, the scales were tilting in favour of the duke.

The waning power of the cities was demonstrated by the failed rebellions of Bruges in 1438 and Ghent in 1453, but also by the cities' increasing absence from commercial decisions.[55] Whereas privileges were granted in the name of name of both count and city in the fourteenth century, these charters were now only conferred by the count and, at best, confirmed by the city.[56] The division between city and state, in particular the appropriation of authority by the count, also increased the division between privileges and ordinances. Privileges were 'rights' or 'liberties' bestowed by the prince; ordinances were concessions given by the city. Merchants still looked to the city for privileges, but if the prince refused to bestow them, the merchants had to make do with smaller concessions from the city.[57]

When the cities' political pressure on the prince decreased, the prince was more reluctant to award privileges. New privileges became scarce from 1430 onwards. There are a number of reasons for this. First, the tone – and with it the legal value – of the privileges had changed. Take the Spanish privilege of 1428, for example. The Duke included a clause in this charter foreseeing the possibility of the privileges being revoked.[58] Previously, privileges were deemed 'forever'. Clauses explaining that the duke could undo an earlier decision, whenever it pleased him, were a major shift.[59] It went from privileges as rights to privileges as favours from the Duke.[60]

The Hanse complained loudly about this shift in attitude on several occasions. Of course, the Hanse had the most far-reaching privileges by the 1420s, but the Hanseats had grown suspicious of Burgundian ambitions.[61] The German merchants had asked for further assurances from the Count of Flanders in 1392, but in the later sessions of the Hansetage they lamented the Duke's bad practices. The latter sought to increase his revenues by extracting extra tolls regardless of Hansa's privileged position.[62] The fact was that the Hanse's rights could seriously disrupt existing relations. For example, in 1419–1421 a great famine threatened the county of Flanders. The Hanseatic merchants were exempt from stapling their grain and it could thus be sold wherever they pleased. In the famine, the Flemish cities believed such a staple was no longer feasible and forbade the export of grain and thus angered the Hanse which invoked its privileges.[63] This was a slight to the Hanseatic privileges, for which the Flemish cities excused themselves and explained that 'in times of sorrow, it is better to show compassion than to follow the letter of the law'.[64] For the Hanseatic merchants, this was confirmation of their suspicion that their rights were threatened and were seen as 'breakable'.[65]

The Hanseatic merchants reacted in the last blockade of the fifteenth century, between 1451–1457, by demanding favourable justice from Bruges. The Hanseats demanded that in cases of doubt regarding clauses in the privileges, the most beneficial interpretation would be applied to Hanse privileges. The Easterlings demanded that they would be able to complain before the Council of Flanders if Bruges threatened these privileges, and that all other claims from Hanseatic merchants should be handled before the Four Members of Flanders.[66] Before the Flemish courts of aldermen, Hanseatic law should triumph over local law.[67] In short, the Easterlings wanted to use the princely court to question Bruges' conduct, while at the same time seeking to be exempt from that same princely court in all other cases. The Flemish cities simply answered that if the Easterlings wanted their law, they should attempt it before the Duke of Burgundy's court.[68] Neither the duke nor the cities were keen on granting these legal concessions.[69] The Duke did not wish to extend the legal capabilities of the Four Members and the Four Members were reluctant to give the Council of Flanders jurisdiction in matters concerning Hanseats.[70] The Hanse did not receive any new privileges from the Duke and had be satisfied with additional promises from the city of Bruges. No procedural advantages were granted.[71]

By the fifteenth century, the strategy of relying on privileges was beginning to falter. This was partly due to the Duke of Burgundy, who held a stronger position than his predecessors and refused to grant or uphold far-reaching rights. Additionally, the city of Bruges itself increasingly disregarded the more inequitable clauses of these privileges. For example, the English privileges of 1359 were already forgotten fifteen years later. English and Flemish relations had deteriorated soon after the 1359 privileges. In 1369, when Louis of Male was without a male heir and chose the Valois Duke of Burgundy over the English crown prince, relations with

Flanders quickly deteriorated. Not only was the king of England disappointed that he lost the prospect of binding the wealthy County of Flanders to his domains, but the Valois Duke, Philip the Bold (1369–1404), was also a staunch supporter of the French royal house.[72] This anti-English policy in combination with rising inequality in the Low Countries was one of the causes of the Ghent War.[73] Although, the economic reliance on England remained, the negotiations with England did not result in further extensive privileges. When the English claimed in 1389 that the right to check all the vessels sailing towards Flanders was included in the previous agreements, no matter their nationality, the Flemish ambassadors responded that such a clause was ridiculous and would 'enslave them like no other nation'.[74] The English merchants had to rely on smaller trade treaties occasionally negotiated between the King of England and the Duke of Burgundy.[75] However, these treaties only assured the most basic clauses. These charters did not come close to the concessions granted in 1359, or even the other privileges merchants had received.

However, not all clauses of the 1359 privilege had disappeared. The English community still had a governor who was acknowledged by Bruges. The Bruges aldermen acknowledged the head of the English nation as governors in the fifteenth century and these governors occasionally defended the rights of the English. However, the nature of the conflicts between Flanders and England, and the role the governor had to fulfil for both the merchant community and his king, limited the way the governor could operate. The English had a governor who specialised in English commercial policy and seldom assisted English merchants in their legal actions before the Bruges court. The difference between both would have severe consequences for English litigation strategies. In this regard, the English governor stood in stark contrast to the Hanseatic and Scottish legal representatives.

THE STRATEGY OF LEGAL EXPERTISE

Being part of the Hanse meant that merchants benefited from the Hanseatic privileges, but also owed obedience to the *olderluden* (aldermen) of the nation.[76] Before 1441, these aldermen were elected on Pentecost and served for a term of one year.[77] After 1441, the cities decided to elect three aldermen on Saint John's eve (23 June) and at Christmas another three aldermen. In this way, there would always be experienced members in the aldermen ranks. Their function was simple: together with a larger council of eighteen men, the *olderluden* had to act for the common good of the Hanse.[78] This included issuing ordinances, disciplining their members and intervening in intra-nation conflicts.[79] However, before the Bruges aldermen court, we see these *olderluden* exercising their most important function: the defence of the Hanseatic privileges.[80] However, on a day-to-day basis, this defence was given to a legally trained specialist.

The *olderluden* of the Hanse were six merchants chosen every year. They lacked the continuity to build up significant experience in Bruges. That consistency was the Hanse's main legal asset: the Kontor Secretaries. The latter's function in the

Hanse Kontor was essential in the way the Hanse operated and, more importantly, litigated before the aldermen of Bruges. The secretaries occupied the same job for prolonged periods of time, making them the true representation of experience and continuity in Bruges for the Hanse. Thideman van den Berghe was secretary from 1383 until 1393, Gobelinus Marten from 1393 until 1438 and Goswin von Coesfeld from at least 1441 until 1471.[81] Multiple secretaries were active at the same time; some had their families in Bruges, and they had a fixed Residence of the Secretary in Bruges.[82] The ordinances of the *olderluden* were published at the secretary's house, and before the foundation of the Oosterlingen house in 1478, the secretary's house was the centre of Hanseatic activity, in addition to the Carmelite church.[83] In addition, he was fully immersed in the daily life of Bruges and had a good knowledge of the local language.

It is hard to overestimate the Kontor secretaries' influence on the Hanse kontor. Their task was not limited to correspondence or the Hanseatic archive's organisation.[84] The secretaries were the key players in understanding how the Hanse defended its rights on a daily basis: they were highly influential figures who were the essential bridge between the town council and the German merchants.[85] Of course, formally, the secretary owed obedience to the *olderluden*, but whereas the latter were merchants, the secretary specialised in the problems of the Kontor, knew the sensitivities of both Bruges and the Hanse, and mastered both languages.[86] Most secretaries who were active in Bruges had enjoyed a legal education. Gobelinus Martens was the first to be described as *magister*, but his successors Johannes Swin and Goswin von Coesfeld were always addressed and described as *magister*, indicating legal training at a university.[87]

The secretary maintained correspondence with the aldermen of Bruges and was part of embassies to the Duke. Goswin bestowed diplomatic gifts and was always the legal representative of the Hansekontor for the entire Burgundian dominions.[88] He was apparently also the intermediary through whom the Four Members could address the grievances of the German merchants. For example, he addressed the Hansetage in Lübeck in 1469, claiming that the Four Members explained the violations of their privileges because the German merchants were not holding their staple as they should.[89] Although the *olderluden* held formal power, the secretary would come to be the face of the Hanseatic Kontor.

The Scottish merchants opted for a different litigation strategy than the Hanseatic nation. The Scottish nation relied on the Conservator of the Privileges as an asset to their litigation strategy. He would protect the Scots against the threats other merchant nations posed and was efficient in this role. However, he did not have tight control on the nation and it is obvious that merchants could still operate independently and through their own (hosteller) networks. Furthermore, the economic importance of the Scottish nation meant that they could count on some goodwill from the aldermen. This was nevertheless not unlimited, and the limits revealed themselves most clearly when relations were tested. The Scots used conservators such as Stevin Anguys and Anselm Adornes, who litigated on behalf of Scottish merchants in need and had a good knowledge of the Flemish judicial system.[90]

Anselm Adornes was a former aldermen and Stevin was described by the Bruges aldermen as a 'master', which hints at some legal training.[91] In addition, Stevin Anguys continued his legal activities in his own name after the Scottish nation took its leave in 1466, indicating that the Conservator of the Privileges was not necessarily Scottish, but was someone with a legal training in the law and usages of the Low Countries, rather than in Scots law.[92] Scotsmen did not solely rely on this Scottish Conservator. Other nations, like the Hanse, were keen on keeping quarrels inside the nation and were aggressive during disputes outside the nation. In comparison, the Conservator of the Privileges did not wield the same authority. For daily litigation or small-scale cases, the main Scottish solace seemed to be the hosteller families such as the Metteneye and Laris.[93] These were two influential families of late medieval Bruges, who tailored their services towards Scottish merchants. As much as this was the case for the Conservator, these hostellers were clearly the backbone of the Scottish defence strategy.[94] They supplemented the litigation of the Conservator. Certainly, in the case of the Laris, a firm knowledge of Scots Law can be presumed. Members of the family Laris were both found litigating before the Burgh Court of Aberdeen, and even before the Council of Lords.[95] The Burgh court of Aberdeen was a logical consequence of the trade in which the Laris family engaged. When the Laris traded in Aberdeen, that city would also be the competent court. However, the fact that these citizens of Bruges were found before even higher courts suggests some insight into how the Scottish legal system worked.[96]

In a 1465 case, Scottish merchants were accused by Hanseatic merchants of an illegal arrest. A Scottish merchant, Sanders Patrixs, was believed to have cargo with Hanseatic markings in his possession. The Hanseatic nation made a quick call and seized the goods from Sanders without the intervention of the aldermen, as the Hanseatic privileges allowed. Except for the markings, there was little proof that the goods were indeed stolen from the merchants. Stevin Anguys brought the case to the Bruges court and pleaded that the Hanseatic merchants had apprehended the goods illegally. In turn, the Hanseatic merchants were defended by Claeys van Attendare, a Kontor Secretary, from the German Hanse. The Kontor Secretary gave a stout defence, arguing that these arrests were legal, because as noted above the Hanseatic merchants had the privilege that if their goods with Hanseatic markings were stolen on the sea and found their way into Flanders, they were to be transferred to the Hanseatic merchants. This was even the case, argued van Attendare, if the goods were bought and not stolen.[97]

This privilege was a major problem for the Conservator, because even if he stated that the Scots had bought the goods, he would have to return them. The Hanse had a reputation of getting what it wanted. The Conservator pleaded for a third option and, while he stressed that the Scottish nation handled this in good faith, he believed that the aldermen should be able to grant him the opportunity to stand surety for the goods, have them in Scottish hands, but at the same time still be able to pursue justice before the aldermen court.[98] In doing so, he adapted to the vulnerabilities of the aldermen. By allowing bail, they were assured that commerce would not be disrupted and that the proceedings would be respected. This was a sensitive spot for the aldermen, certainly when we consider that the Hanse tended to evade the Bruges' court when it suited them. The aldermen agreed and stated that both sides should make an inventory of the goods, bring them for survey before the aldermen and after all parties agreed upon the value, provide sureties for the amount. The Scottish merchants were however allowed to sell the goods as long as their sureties assured that the litigation, for the agreed amount, would remain in place.[99] This solution was typical of the case-law of the aldermen, and it represented a major victory for Conservator. In any other case, the German Hanse would have received their goods and the Scottish merchants would quickly find themselves in defiance of the Hanse's further litigation. Unfortunately, we do not know how the case ended.

A perfect illustration of the value of this Conservator was when the Scottish nation encountered Jan van Boschuysen and they were unable to use a Conservator. Jan van Boschuysen was a Burgundian official who rose to prominence in the late 1460s and early 1470s as a trusted friend and advisor of duke Charles of Burgundy.[100] In this position he wielded significant informal power. In 1469, van Boschuysen arrested a Scottish ship as a countermeasure against Scottish privateering that had harmed his own possessions. Although it was unlikely that he had reprisal letters, or that the merchants whose ship and goods were arrested were the actual maritime predators, Van Boschuysen arrested the Scottish merchants anyway. For the Scottish merchants, the problem was evident: obtaining justice from a man this powerful would not be easy. They also had an additional problem. The Scots had left Bruges in 1466, and there were no signs of a working Scottish presence in Bruges. They were negotiating with Bruges for an eventual return, but at that moment there was no Scottish community in Bruges, and thus no Conservator protecting the merchant community. The aldermen had to intervene. On 30 May, they had sent the Burgomaster of the Commune and the cities' legal specialist to speak 'favourably for the Scottish nation' with Jan van Boschuysen.[101] When the Scottish nation tried to make their case before the Duke of Burgundy in August 1470, the aldermen sent their legal assistant (*pensionaris*), Antheunis Louf, with them as support.[102] Eventually, the parties agreed to bring the case before the aldermen. The aldermen thus succeeded in bringing reprisals that had taken place in Zeeland before their own court.

However, the aldermen would not prove to be resistant to the strategies of Jan van Boschuysen. Jan van Boschuysen came to court and immediately reminded the Scottish merchants of their promise, or concession, that they would reimburse his travel costs relating to the case. This promise had been made to convince Jan van Boschuysen to take a legal way out of the conflict, but now, when only little progress had been made, the Scottish merchants proved to be more hesitant. The aldermen concluded that the Scottish merchants should uphold their promise, regardless of the progress of the case.[103] The further dealings of the case progressed only very slowly. First, van Boschuysen appeared before the court, and confessed that he had taken these ships, but also indicated that he had ample reason to do so. However, because of the difficulty of the case he wished to state his arguments on paper and asked for extra time in order to do so.[104] The aldermen granted van Boschuysen this extra time, but he failed to appear at the following three court sessions.[105]

The court register does not state how the case was resolved, but the vulnerable situation of the Scots was evident. Even with the backing of Bruges, it proved difficult to resolve the case quickly. The aldermen of Bruges wished to help these merchants, and clearly acted on their behalf, but were limited both by the influential powers of the Burgundian official and, more importantly, by their own court system. Jan van Boschuysen used the absence of a legal specialist defending the Scottish merchants fully to his own advantage.

The absence of a legal specialist to assist with their cases was keenly felt by the English. The effectiveness of the English governor was in stark contrast to their privileges and economic leverage. Although he was certainly present, he was also ignored by the aldermen of Bruges.[106] In 1458, the governor, William Overey, had arrested the English merchant William Charrety. The latter had visited the Antwerp Market, contrary to the ordinances promulgated by Overey.[107] Charrety, however, refused to remain imprisoned and pay the fines that the governor determined. The governor brought the case to the aldermen of Bruges. There, William Overey explained the situation and asked the aldermen to confirm his decision. However, Charrety claimed that he was unaware of the ordinance that forbade his passage to Antwerp and was therefore not bound by it. To strengthen his case, he offered to swear an oath.[108] Although the aldermen acknowledged that it was the governor's task to discipline recalcitrant merchants, they nevertheless allowed Charrety to swear his oath and obtain his release. In a context where Bruges was losing commerce to Antwerp, it is difficult to understand why the aldermen went against the governor.

Despite controlling the vital wool supply, they were also a significant political adversary with whom the Duke of Burgundy occasionally engaged in conflict. As a result, the English community had to renegotiate the clauses that regulated their presence in the Burgundian dominions. The English governor was caught up in this system and had to execute the orders of the crown. Compared to the Hanseatic and Scottish communities, the English had a weaker hold on the merchant community and were less involved in their daily affairs. Unlike the Hanseatic and Scottish legal representatives who defended the merchants from their community, the English had to defend themselves. The active defence of the Hanseatic and Scottish merchants highlights two aspects. To begin with, the community could not rely solely on the privileges they obtained through their economic leverage. They had to actively pursue a policy to guard and defend the clauses written in them. The legal representatives who appeared in the fifteenth century indicate this change in strategy. The Burgundian Dukes frowned upon the more inequitable clauses in privileges, and they were still difficult to enforce. However, merchant communities gained a competitive advantage over others by using legal representatives such as Kontor Secretaries, Conservators or hostellers. These trained legal specialists knew the system and used it, without altering it. Likewise, the attitude of Bruges underscores its ambition as a city of justice. The most effective strategy was not underscoring the privileges and embargoing the city of Bruges into further concessions. The merchant communities could defend themselves through these legal representatives and did so with great effect before the aldermen of Bruges. Nonetheless, the political and economic context remained crucial. The aldermen treated different communities differently. Those with significant economic leverage could still exert pressure on the city.

NOTES

1. Jahnke, 'Lübeck', 231–247.
2. Paravicini, 'De Hanze als Europees verschijnsel', 12; Frankot, 'Der ehrbaren Hanse-Städte', 109–128; Weststrate, '"Des kopmans Hense ende vriheden"', 29; Boestad, '*Pour le profit du commun marchand*'; Boestad, 'Legitimizing interurban cooperation in the Middle Ages', 29–30.
3. Dollinger, *La Hanse*, 133–140; Friedland, *Die Hanse*, 95–107; Dollinger and Meijers, *De Hanze*, 133–140; Graichen, Hammel-Kiesow, Hesse, *Die deutsche Hanse*, 247–256; Wubs-Mrozewicz, 'The Hanse', 5–6.
4. Burkhardt, 'Kontors and outposts', 127–161; Schubert, 'Novgorod, Brügge, Bergen und London', 19–27; Burkhardt, 'The German Hanse', 60–61; Wubs-Mrozewicz, 'The medieval Hanse', 219.
5. Beuken, *De Hanze en Vlaanderen*, 14.
6. Jahnke, '"Homines Imperii"', 1–57.
7. Greve, 'Hoteliers en Hanzekooplieden in Brugge', 101; Greve, 'Die Bedeutung der Brügger Hosteliers', 259–296; Greve, 'Brügger Hosteliers', 151–161.
8. Rose, *The wealth of England*, 160.
9. For the process of wool making: Munro, 'Spanish Merino wool and the Nouvelles Draperies', 433–435.
10. Munro, 'Spanish Merino wools and the Nouvelles draperies', 449.
11. Nicholas, *Medieval Flanders*, 289–292.
12. Dept, *Les influences anglaise et française*, 155–173.
13. Berben, 'Une guerre économique au Moyen Age', 14–17; Wyffels, 'De Vlaamse handel op Engeland', 205–213; Munro, *Wool, Cloth and gold*, 5–6.
14. Rose, *Calais*, 39–40.
15. Sutton, *The Mercery of London*, 237.
16. Dumolyn, Ryckbosh, and Speecke, 'Did inequality produce medieval revolt?' 383.
17. Rorke, 'English and Scottish overseas trade', 269.
18. Munro, 'Three centuries of luxury textile consumption', 3–4.
19. Exports in wool, hide, cloth and freshwater salmon trades would only stagnate or even decline in the sixteenth century; Rorke, 'The Scottish herring trade', 154.
20. See for example, SAB 157, *Civiele Sententiën*, 1447–1453, fol. 38 r.
21. Bonner, 'Scotland's "Auld Alliance"', 6.
22. Finlayson, 'The Scottish nation in Bruges', 49–50; Speecke, 'Isti ponetur', 36.
23. Ditchburn, 'Scotland, France, and the Auld Alliance', 81–100; Stevenson, 'The Flemish dimension', 28–42.
24. In 1198 the merchants from Cologne already made a short deal with Bruges concerning the debt settlement of their merchants; ADNB 504/1197.

25. Yet even those Kontoren were obliged to interact with the communities in place; Burkhardt, 'Policy, Business, Privacy', 138; 143–147; Weststrate, 'Des kopmans Hense ende vriheden', 25. Each of the trade settlements had to abide by both the Hanseatic and the local laws: Jörn, 'Die Herausbildung der Kontorordnungen', 217–235; Wubs-Mrozewicz, *Traders, ties and tensions*, 119.
26. In fact, the German merchants received three privileges giving them basic rights such as an exemption from the judicial duel, toll exemptions or collective liability. The request was denied because the cities of Lübeck and Hamburg refused to give similar privileges to Flemish merchants; Privileges for merchants from Lubeck and Gotland: ADNB 504/1252 (1064, ter, quater), Privileges for Cologne, Munster and other cities from the Holy Roman Empire: ADNB 504/1252 (1069); Cordes, 'Litigating abroad', 281–299; Henn, 'Über die Anfänge des Brügger Hansekontors', 43–66; Stein, *Privilegien der deutschen Hanse*, 86; Henn, 'Het ontstaan van de Hanze', 19; Gilliodts-Van Severen, *Coutumes des petites villes*, 174–175. See on the judicial duel: UAG.HS. 3800. Denys Heyman, *Juridische tractaten en teksten in het Nederlands betreffende Gent*, fol. 1 r.–2 r.
27. This right entailed that all things washed ashore from the sea belonged to the prince; Levy-Bruhl, 'Droit de naufrage', 35.
28. Murray, 'Bruges as Hansestadt', 183.
29. Henn, 'Das Brügger Kontor', 216–222.
30. Wubs-Mrozewicz, 'De kantoren van de hanze', 92.
31. Gilliodts-Van Severen, *Inventaire des chartes*, vol. 2, 53, art. 44.
32. Gilliodts-Van Severen, *Inventaire des chartes*, vol. 3, 225, art. 2; Koppmann, Hanserecesse I, vol. 4, 37–38, n. 39.
33. Koppmann, Hanserecesse I, vol. 4, 37–38, n. 39.
34. Höhlbaum, *Hansisches Urkundenbuch*, vol. II, 67, art. 11.
35. Höhlbaum, *Hansische Urkundenbuch*, vol. II, 67.
36. SAB 96, *Oude Wittenboek*, fol. 18 r. Gilliodts-Van Severen, *Cartulaire de l'estaple*, vol. 1, 228; Sutton and Visser, 'The Bruges privileges, 1359', 197. In the Brabantine privileges, the English would only have 'suitable houses'.
37. SAB 96, *Oude Wittenboek*, fol. 18 r.; Gilliodts-Van Severen, *Cartulaire de l'ancien estaple*, vol. 1, §3 and §4, pp. 226–227; Sutton and Visser, 'The Bruges privileges, 1359', § 5 and § 6, p. 196.
38. SAB 96, *Oude Wittenboek*, fol. 18 r.; Gilliodts-Van Severen, *Cartulaire de l'ancien estaple*, vol. 1, §24 p. 231; Sutton and Visser, 'The Bruges privileges, 1359', §25, p. 201.
39. SAB 96, *Oude Wittenboek*, fol. 18r.; Gilliodts-Van Severen, *Cartulaire de l'ancien estaple*, vol. 1, §15, 228; Sutton and Visser, 'The Bruges privileges, 1359', § 17, p. 199.
40. SAB 96, *Oude Wittenboek*, fol. 18 r.; Gilliodts-Van Severen, *Cartulaire de l'ancien estaple*, vol. 1, §27, 230; Sutton and Visser, 'The Bruges privileges, 1359', §19, 199.
41. SAB 96, *Oude Wittenboek*, fol. 18 r. Gilliodts-Van Severen, *Cartulaire de l'ancien estaple*, vol. 1, 228; Sutton and Visser, 'The Bruges privileges, 1359', §10, p. 197.
42. SAB 96, *Oude Wittenboek*, fol. 18 r.; Gilliodts-Van Severen, *Cartulaire de l'ancien estaple*, vol. 1, §13, p. 229; Sutton and Visser, 'The Bruges privileges, 1359', §15, p. 199.
43. ADNB, 513/8621.
44. SAB 96, *Ouden Wittenboek*, fol. 44 r.; Gilliodts-Van Severen, *Inventaire des chartes*, vol. 5, 802; Bonenfant, Bartier and Van Nieuwenhuizen, *Ordonnances de Philippe le Hardi*, 53.
45. The previous rights were confirmed by the duke in a separate charter in May 1407; Cauchies, *Ordonnances de Jean sans peur*, 89–90; SAB 96, *Oude Wittenboek*, fol. 183 r.–v.

46. But still the tonlieu; SAB 96, *Oude Wittenoek*, fol. 183 v.–184 r.; Gilliodts-Van Severen, *Cartulaire*, vol. I, 448–451; Cauchies, *Ordonnances de Jean sans peur*, 84.
47. SAB 96, *Groenenboek* A, fol. 72 r.–73 r.
48. SAB 96, *Groenenboek* A, fol. 96 r.–97 v.
49. RAG 2963/71, Varia D, *Afschrift van een handelstraktaat.*
50. On 4 April 1406, the King of Scotland died. However, his successor, James I, had been seized by the English while his ship was sailing to France. He would remain a hostage until 1424; McKelvie, 'The royal prisoner', 158–173; Blockmans, *Handelingen van de leden*, n. 137, p. 201.
51. Blockmans, *Handelingen van de leden* vol. I, n. 238, 242, 273, pp. 286–287, 293–294, 326–327.
52. SAB 96, *Ouden Wittenboek*, fol. 186 r.
53. Promises were made, for example, that there would be no new levies on their good at Damme; SAB 95, *Ouden Wittenboek*, fol. 186 r.
54. SAB 96, *Ouden Wittenboek,* fol. 186 r.
55. Dumolyn, *De Brugse Opstand*; Haemers, *De Gentse opstand.*
56. The same goes for formal political treaties. In 1420 the treaty of Troyes was proclaimed with the approval of the people, personified by the Four Members. In 1424, the duke stated that it always had been within the power of the Count of Flanders to conclude such treaties; Braekevelt, 'Un prince de justice', 276–277; Godding, *La législation ducale.*
57. Braekevelt, 'Entre profit et dommage', 124–125.
58. Gilliodts-Van Severen, *Inventaire des Chartes*, vol. 2, 496–499; Gilliodts-Van Severen, *Cartulaire de l'ancien consulat*, p. 23.
59. Gilliodts-Van Severen, *Inventaire des chartes*, 499; SAB, *Spaans Consulaat*, nr 4.
60. In 1392, the Hanseatic merchants made sure that it was included that they could use these privileges for all eternity; Bonenfant, *Ordonnances de Margheret de Male*, 478.
61. Dumolyn, *De Brugse Opstand*, 267–295; Fris, *Schets van den economischen* toestand, 32–61.
62. Although in some cases the Hanse believed that the city of Bruges should do something against the tolls the French King demanded at Tournay (Doornik); Blockmans, *Handelingen van de Leden*, vol. 2, n. 1025, p. 1056.
63. Koppmann, Hanserecesse, I, 7, 261–263, n. 437.
64. Von der Ropp, Hanserecesse, II, 1, 335.
65. They claimed that the Bruges city council saw the privileges 'as breakable' and as a consequence, they had large expenses in litigating before the court; Von der Ropp, Hanserecesse, II, 1, 66. In the context of the grain transport the Germans received the answer that . . . *umme dat noed alle recht unde privilegien brekende were* . . .; Von der Ropp, Hanserecesse, II, 7, 264, n. 438.
66. Von der Ropp, Hanserecesse II, vol. 4, 113 n. 162.
67. Von der Ropp, Hanserecesse II, 4, n. 162, pp. 112–113, art. 4, 5, 7.
68. Von der Ropp, Hanserecesse II, vol. 4, 115.
69. Von der Ropp, Hanserecesse II, vol. 4, p. 152, n. 211.
70. Von der Ropp, Hanserecesse II, vol. 4, p. 312, n. 444, art. 5. On the matter of the Council of Flanders they would allow compromise solution in the form of an informal and quick procedure whereas the Council members would judge these ducal officers. This was, however, also in their favour, although the Four Members promised to give the cases back to the Council; Von der Ropp, Hanserecesse II, vol. 4, p. 313, n. 444, art. 9.

71. Gilliodts-Van Severen, *Inventaire des chartes*, vol. 5, 399–401.
72. Although he would not pursue a clear anti-English policy as Count of Flanders, he had participated in the campaigns against chevauchées of the English, making pro-English sympathies unlikely on his part.
73. Demuynck, 'De Gentse oorlog 1379–1385', 304–318; Mertens, 'Twee weversopstanden te Brugge', 5–20; Dumolyn, Speecke, and Ryckbosch, 'Did inequality produce medieval revolt?', 376–379.
74. Prevenier, *Handelingen van de leden*, 433.
75. See, for example, the peace of 1439: ADNB 572/1439 (15729); National Archives Kew, Chancery Miscellania, C 47/130/9/nr. 17; Edition in Thielemans, *Bourgogne et Angleterre*, 443–453. This was a separate peace with Flanders. The Duke of Burgundy would conclude peace in 1443: ADNB 306/1443 (15780).
76. Schubert, 'Novgorod, Brügge, Bergen, Londen. Kontore die Hanse', 5, 22; Koppmann, Hanserecesse I, vol. 1, p. 74–76, nr. 143.
77. Von der Ropp, Hanserecesse II, vol. 2, 361–2; Wubs-Mrozewicz, 'De kantoren van de Hanze', 101–102.
78. Von de Ropp, Hanserecesse II, vol. 2, 362; Koppmann, *Leitfaden für die Alterleute*, 11–13.
79. The law that was applied seems to be specific law of the 'coopman'. This is a reference to specific customs, rather than a body of law. It diverged on some points with the Bruges law; Dierck, 'Hansische Älterleute', 75.
80. Dierick, 'Hansische Älterleute und die Brügger Führungsschicht', 80.
81. Dierck, 'Hansische älterleute', 79. Similar clerks were also present in London. Further investigation will show whether they had a similar function; Von der Ropp, Hanserecesse II, vol. 7, 154. n. 184; Manger, 'Behind the scenes', 582.
82. From 1451 on the Hanseatic merchants possessed a house. It is not certain, however, that this was the domus Osterlingorum from the 1470s; L. Devlieger, 'Het Oosterlingenhuis te Brugge', 15–16.
83. Stein, *Hansische Urkundenbuch*, vol. VIII, 405, n. 630.
84. Wubs-Mrozewics, *Traders, ties and tensions*, 82–90.
85. Although we already see from the early fifteenth century onwards, that these secretaries played a vital part as being the node between the Bruges Kontor and the representatives at the Hansetage; Von der Ropp, Hanserecesse II, vol. 2, 496, n. 594.
86. Dierick, 'Die Hansische Älterleute', 79.
87. See for an overview in Leloux, 'Zur Sprache', 16.
88. Goswin von Coesfeld to the duke; Von der Ropp, Hanserecesse II, vol. 3, 250, 252; Wine: Von der Ropp, Hanserecesse II, vol. 3, 300. In 1451 he was sent to the Flemish cities in order to proclaim peace and to provide a concept treaty; Von der Ropp, Hanserecesse II, vol. 4, 7.
89. Von der Ropp, Hanserecesse II, vol. 7, p. 164, n. 185.
90. SAB 157, *Civiele Sententiën*, 1465–1469, fol. 125 v.
91. Macquarrie, 'Anselm Adornes of Bruges', 15; Macquarrie, 'Anselm Adornes of Bruges', 15–22; SAB 157, *Civiele Sententiën*, 1465–1469, fol. 226 v.
92. SAB 157, *Civiele Sententiën*, 1465–1469, fol. 82 v.
93. SAB 157, *Civiele Sententiën*, 1453–1461, fol. 17 v., 21 v.; SAB 157, *Civiele Sententiën*, 1447–1453, fol. 313 v.
94. Remarkably, the conservator was absent prior to 1465.

95. CAA, Council, Baillie and Guild court registers 1 April 1448–18 July 1468, 441, 473; CAA, Council, Baillie and Guild court registers from 3 October 1468 to 30 December 1486, vol. 6, 185, 286, 374, 640, 644, 677, 680; CAA, Council, Baillie and Guild court registers from 3 October 1468 to 30 December 1486, 312.
96. Even though they still worked with a procurator, it might be suspected that a procurator described as 'Franklin Sersanders' was also of Flemish descent, *Acts of the Lords of Council,* vol. 1, 77; 87; SAB 157, *Civiele Sententiën*, 1447–1453, fol. 47 r.
97. SAB 157, *Civiele Sententiën*, 1465–1469, fol. 60 v.
98. SAB 157, *Civiele Sententiën*, 1465–1469, fol. 60 v.
99. SAB 157, *Civiele Sententiën*, 1465–1469, fol. 60 v.
100. Brand, 'Floris en Jan van Boschuijsen', 103–104.
101. SAB 216, *Stadsrekeningen Brugge*, 1469–1470, fol. 65 v.
102. SAB 216, *Stadsrekeningen Brugge*, 1469–1470, fol. 66 r.
103. SAB 157, *Civiele Sententiën*, 1469–1471, fol. 114 v.
104. Postponement: SAB 157, *Civiele Sententiën*, 1469–1471, fol. 128 v.
105. SAB 157, *Civiele Sententiën*, 1469–1471, fol. 131 v.; twice: SAB 157, *Civiele Sententiën*, 1469–1471, fol. 132 r.
106. SAB 96, *Groenenboek ongecotteerd*, 375 r.
107. The Sinxen Markt ran from about 25 April to 13 June.
108. SAB 96, *Groenenboek ongecotteerd*, 375 r.; SAB 157, *Civiele Sententiën*, 214 r.

6

The Strategy of Political Leverage: The Iberian Communities

The economic importance of the Iberian peninsula for Bruges is undeniable.[1] Iberian merchants from Castile, Aragon, Navarre and Portugal appear in the sources from the 1230s, but may well have been trading prior to this date.[2] In the fifteenth century, Atlantic trade was becoming even more essential to Bruges.[3] The Castilians – commonly denominated in Bruges as Spanish – developed a highly valued merino-wool trade in addition to their already existing trade in agricultural products; and, during the fifteenth century, the Portuguese added African products to the international market of Bruges.[4]

The Spanish trade was valuable and in the same way as with the Hanseatic, English and Scottish communities, it resulted in privileges.[5] Bruges would have been eager to maintain good relations with these merchants. However, it is often overlooked that the Spanish merchant community had to request the observance of their rights through their nation, an institution established by the Spanish king and operating with his consent. As with the other nations, the observance of their privileges was not evident. Economic leverage alone proved insufficient, and it cannot be assumed that preferential treatment was granted to all as a matter of course. However, in contrast to the Hanseatic merchants, they could rely on influential – royal – connections to help them. The merchant communities of the Iberian Peninsula, including those of Castile, Portugal, and Aragon, provide an interesting comparison in this regard.[6] The Portuguese and Spanish trades, in particular, were becoming increasingly important. Both had powerful kings who were willing to negotiate better privileges for their merchants, and both were among the last to obtain such privileges from the Duke of Burgundy.[7] The biggest difference, however, was how these Iberian communities were treated by the aldermen of Bruges, and how they operated in the presence of these same aldermen.

In this chapter, I will examine how political influence led to a position of privilege. To achieve this, I will use the term 'privileged' in two different senses. The first is the denotation (objective) of charters granting rights to a merchant community. The second is the connotation (subjective) of having more benefits than another. This can find practical expression in formal rights as well as in informal advantages. Privileges were merely an indication, and being truly privileged is revealed in the litigation recorded in the registers.

THE CASTILIAN COMMUNITY

The community that called itself the 'Spanish nation' was well represented in Bruges, not least because these merchants, styling themselves as Spanish, came from several areas in possession of the Castilian king, of which the coastal area in the North of present-day Spain (*Vizcaya* or Biscay) had the oldest tradition of sailing to Bruges.[8] However, the economic influence of the Spanish merchants was less significant than that of Bruges' largest trading partner, the Hanseatic community. They offered fewer essential commodities for Bruges, focusing primarily on agricultural products such as fruits. It was only in the fifteenth century that the Castilians began to gain prominence through the merino-wool trade. This high-quality wool approached the prestige of the preferred English varieties and became a valuable addition to the existing wool market.[9] Nevertheless, before they could fully exploit this crucial trade flow, the Spaniards employed a shrewd strategy. In securing each of the three major privileges granted to them in the thirteenth and fourteenth centuries, they skilfully leveraged political developments within the County of Flanders.

Spanish merchants received their first concession in 1280 during the political upheavals of Flanders.[10] During these troubles, the Germans had moved to Aardenburg as a protest against the prevailing political instability. The Spanish merchants were able to follow in the wake of the complaints the German merchants made. The Spanish followed suit and used their collective power against the city. The Flemish count was also at loggerheads with Bruges and granted both the German and Spanish merchants' privileges in Aardenburg. Although the Spanish merchants did not possess a similar level of collective power, they were able to obtain their first privileges by using the political context. When the German merchants returned to Bruges, the city promised that the charters of Aardenburg would also be valid in Bruges.[11] While it is likely that the Spanish received a similar promise, it is not entirely certain.[12]

In 1343 the Spanish received a second and even more extensive charter, albeit from a somewhat questionable authority. The communities had received these privileges at a time of great turmoil in the County of Flanders. After the insurrection headed by James of Artevelde in 1337, the Flemish count Louis of Nevers had fled Flanders and left the County leaderless. In the meantime, the three rebellious cities of Ghent, Bruges and Ypres governed the county with a strawman Simon de Mirabello as *Ruwaard*, or placeholder for the Count. The actual power lay with James of Artevelde and his faction.[13] Although the privileges granted to the Spanish nation were given in the name of Simon de Mirabello, they were made with the authorisation, and most likely at the instigation of the three big cities of Flanders.

In contrast to the 1280 privileges, which only guaranteed basic clauses like safe trade and protection from arrests for the debts of third parties, the Spaniards demanded far-reaching concessions from the rebels. By promising that Spanish ships would continue to come to Bruges, the merchants received liberties that granted them the right to load and unload their ships as they pleased.[14] In addition, the Spaniards would be exempt from the right of shipwreck, the toll of Damme and some of the expenses the Bruges brokers or hostellers charged.[15] The latter group grew from being innkeepers to the essential brokers of the Bruges commercial world. Their remuneration was fixed by charter and was not easily altered. As inflation hit them hard, these hostellers occasionally sought new ways of supplementing their income. These new 'charges' caused much vexation to international merchants, and merchant communities therefore also sought to have the (ambitious) clause of being free from 'all new customs'.[16] Fortunately for the Spanish merchants, once order had been restored in the County of Flanders, the new Count of Flanders, Louis of Male, chose to ratify these privileges and thus ensure Spanish trade in the Low Countries.[17] By using the rebellion to their advantage, the Spanish merchants now possessed prestigious privileges without having had to confront the Count of Flanders too much.

The same was true for the third charter in 1366.[18] The main objective here was to be placed on a more or less equal footing to the clauses the Hanseatic merchants had received in 1359, granting the Spaniards reductions on tolls when entering the harbour, in ballasting and the crane. The Spanish merchants received the much sought-after clause that Bruges should be considered liable for the money changers of the city.[19] If a money changer went bankrupt, the city would pay on his behalf. In addition, the brokers had to keep their word and would be sanctioned by the aldermen if they made a deal and changed the terms later. They had to pay the agreed price and could not change it afterwards. In addition, the buyers had to pay for the entire cargo once they had seen it, while the shippers sailing between Sluis and Bruges would be held responsible for any damage to the merchandise.[20] Lastly if debtors were to try to flee from their obligations, the Spaniards would be protected by the aldermen as if they were citizens.[21] In the fourteenth century, the privileges the Spanish merchants received guaranteed that trade was properly conducted and ensured their competitive position vis-à-vis both the Hanse merchants, who had exemptions from several tolls, and others, who did not.

The tone of the Spanish privileges was to change in the fifteenth century. Whereas at first privileges gave basic protection to the merchants involved in the Atlantic trade, the privileges the Spanish acquired in 1428 were the result of a hard bargain with the Burgundian duke. The arena of power had changed, and Spanish merchants felt that their trade was better guaranteed if they clustered together. The Spanish organised themselves into a merchant community eager and ready to defend its rights.

Though there might also be a link with the growing importance of the Spanish trade, there was certainly a concrete threat that spurred the nation into action.[22] During the 1420s, a diplomatic dispute arose between the Spanish merchants, Flemish merchants and Hanseatic merchants which had led to mutual plundering, letters of reprisal and much economic damage to the city of Bruges.[23] Duke Philip the Good demanded an additional tax from Spanish merchants as compensation for the plundering. The Spanish monarch issued several letters of reprisal against

Flemish merchants.[24] In addition, the Spanish king had ordered that all Spanish merchants should sail back to their homeland and leave Bruges to its fate.[25] The Four Members requested that the Duke abolish the tax he had imposed on Spanish imports and urged him to suspend all reprisal letters for the next three years.[26]

The Spanish were nevertheless determined to drive a harder bargain and wanted new privileges.[27] With the help of the Four Members, the Spanish found a compromise that suited them.[28] The merchant community from Castile already existed, but with these privileges, the Castilian merchants now also enjoyed the formal recognition that they were a nation with consular jurisdiction. The Spanish were granted the right of electing one or two consuls and of organising the latter's office as they saw fit. They could organise meetings, issue ordinances, and organise the Spanish trade in the way that was most profitable to them. In addition to the increased organisational competence, the consuls could also pronounce upon civil cases between Spaniards. However, the consuls could neither intervene in a case that questioned the rights of the duke, nor in one that involved merchants who did not belong to the nation. In all other cases, the merchants of Spain had the option to seek recourse before the aldermen of Bruges when they did not agree with a consular ruling.[29] Consular jurisdiction was thus officially established for civil cases, albeit with certain limitations. All criminal offences, including those committed in Spain, were to be handled by comital officers.[30]

In addition, the duke promised not to issue any reprisal letters against (alleged) cases of maritime violence on any of the subjects of the County of Flanders.[31] These letters were given to unfortunate merchants to compensate themselves by arbitrarily seizing the merchandise of compatriots of the wrongdoer. The duke proclaimed that innocent Spanish merchants were not subject to such letters.[32] At first sight, this might seem a considerable concession, but it was an articulation of the clause that merchants were not liable for the debts of third parties, one of the most standard clauses of a privilege.[33] More significant was the concession that if Spaniards were victims of maritime violence and the goods were found in some way, the unfortunate merchant would enjoy the same rights as citizens of Bruges.[34] This implied that the Spanish would be able to retrieve the goods and claim them before the aldermen's bench. This was a substantial advantage over other merchants, though it still fell short of the one given to the Hanseatic merchants who could retrieve the merchandise without the intervention of the aldermen.

Spanish merchants also had to make concessions. The nation of Spain was expected to help Bruges maintain justice in the city. If a factor or representative refused to be accountable for the action of his master or partner, the nation would be responsible for reporting the letters to the master or partner living in Spain in such a way that the debts were satisfied.[35] However, if the factor or partner still had possession of the goods of a debtor, the latter was still liable to arrest.[36]

The Spanish merchant community had received a consulate that was recognised by Bruges. These consuls not only arbitrated between two compatriots, they also actively protected trade conditions for Spanish merchants. When, for example, the hosteller and broker Vincent Heyns was likely to go bankrupt, the Spanish consuls, in name of the nation, litigated against Vincent Heyns. The Spanish consuls made him provide guarantees so that when he defaulted, these guarantors would intervene and compensate the merchants.[37] Ten days later, the nation would repeat this pattern in relation to Absalon van Munten, who was to provide sureties so as not to damage the nation. The sureties were made in the presence of, and accepted by, the consuls.[38] These sureties were a long-term promise (five years) not to damage the Spanish nation.[39] When in 1449 the leaseholders of the Bruges cloth hall (*lakenhalle*) complained that the Spanish were evading their commissions by selling draperies outside of Bruges, the nation took prompt action against the leaseholder who had already taken steps in recovering the – according to the leaseholders – rightful levies.[40] The Spanish consuls sued the leaseholders before the aldermen court. The latter defended themselves by stating that the Spanish evaded their duties through hostellers in Ypres, Kortrijk and elsewhere, but after the aldermen interviewed some former leaseholders about the customs of the drapery hall, they decided that the actions of the Spanish nation were not an infringement of the leaseholders' rights.[41] In case of doubt, the Spanish had to swear an oath that it concerned their own cloth, that the cloth was delivered and that the merchandise was taken at their own risk.[42] In a similar fashion shippers travelling from the docks in Sluis to the markets of Bruges, often attempted to raise their revenue and saw themselves – on several occasions – blocked by the Spanish nation.[43]

The Spanish nation pursued an aggressive litigation strategy based on its collective power. The community enjoyed the political support of the Castilian king or queen, who intervened on their behalf, appointed consuls, and actively stimulated the nation.[44]

The consulate was established in 1428. In 1441, the Spanish merchants gathered at the chapel of the Franciscans and proclaimed their statutes. These were agreed in a spirit of unity and solidarity towards each other. Financial contributions were levied, all merchants had to help in cases of shipwreck and all merchants could be called upon when the Spanish needed testimonies in court.[45] However, it was also established that the nation would act as one if someone from another nation were to 'dishonour' the Spanish nation.[46]

The major paradox of the Spanish nation was that this coherence had its limits. Although the Spanish proved to be one of the most coherent communities, the community eventually split up. The nation was nominally under the control of the mercantile court in Burgos, and the control might not have been to the liking to all merchants.[47] Although it is unlikely that this court interfered on a daily basis in the affairs of Spanish merchants in Bruges, we must remember that the Castilian possessions were far from a unified state.[48] Shippers from the coastal region *Vizcaya* were particularly unhappy with the dominant attitude of the 'inland' merchants from Burgos. Discussion arose, and the Castilian king divided the nation in 1455. Bruges acknowledged the division but did not grant any privileges to the merchants from Biscay.[49] The result was that the Biscayan merchants were seriously disadvantaged and in fact lost their privileges. When the Biscayans invoked these charters in 1483, the aldermen of Bruges refused.[50] It would take until 1493 for the Biscayans to regain a number of their rights.[51] However, the fact there were two nations subject to the same monarch also provided opportunities for insightful merchants to change the statutes of the nations. The Spanish king had left the membership of the nations optional and not compulsory.[52] This loophole was closed in 1494 when, at the request of the Spanish – Castilian – nation, the Bruges aldermen made it impossible to escape consular jurisdiction by simply moving to another nation.[53]

The Spanish nation proved to be a tough competitor and not shy in defending its rights. Litigating as a collective entity allowed it to achieve significant results. The Spanish merchants relied on each other, defended their rights as a group, and used this to pressure the aldermen to at least give them due diligence. Nevertheless, their statute had to be actively defended, and, in this defence, various cracks appeared.[54]

THE PORTUGUESE COMMUNITY

The mercantile landscape shifted in the fifteenth century. In the fourteenth century, the main competitors had been the Hanseatic merchants, and the Spanish tried to match their privileges accordingly. However, at the end of the fourteenth century, Portuguese merchants were becoming more prominent. In the fourteenth century, there had been occasional Portuguese trade in Bruges, but from the fifteenth century on, both king and country were committing themselves more and more to the Atlantic trade.[55]

Before the mid-fifteenth century, the main Portuguese exports were agricultural products such as dried fruit, wine and cork.[56] It was only in their search for new, more lucrative alternatives that the Portuguese crown built a commercial empire in the Azores, Madeira and had important relations with African powers. From the middle of the fifteenth century, Portuguese merchants were important distributors of sugar, gold and ivory; all high-priced commodities in Bruges.[57] The Portuguese merchants were a rather small group who traded primarily in luxuries. As Bruges was a centre of luxuries, their trade was especially appreciated.

The first privileges the Portuguese received were only mildly interesting. They first received safe conduct in 1384 and 1386, a grant bestowed on all merchants except the English.[58] In 1387 this safe conduct was extended, so the Portuguese would enjoy the same rights regarding access to the Zwin as other nations.[59] The duke granted their first major privileges in 1411. On 25 March 1411, the Portuguese had concluded an accord with the Dominicans of Bruges to use one of the latter's chapels for their members.[60] These concessions regulated the presence of the Portuguese and were largely in line with the privileges received by other nations. They gained assurances on free trade, weights and the good conduct of officials.[61] The water bailiff, the comital officer with jurisdiction over the sea, could no longer just imprison merchants, except for cases involving life and limb. Moreover, the right on shipwrecks, and most other extra fees for docking and entering the harbour did not apply to the Portuguese.[62] If any comital officers were to infringe one of the clauses, they were to repay (reasonable) damages after each disputing party had told its side of the story.[63] In short, the Portuguese gained all the specific rights and liberties which had already been granted to the Spanish since the fourteenth century.[64] The merchants were free to leave the country, they could carry certain weapons from their ships to their hostels,[65] and they could load and unload their vessels when they wanted.[66] And, as was the case with the Spanish privileges, Bruges was liable for the money changers.[67] It seems that the Portuguese nation modelled itself on the Castilians.

Although the Portuguese privileges were inspired by the charters of their Spanish colleagues, each community adopted a different litigation strategy. For example, the 1411 privileges contained some clauses specific to the Portuguese trade. The Portuguese merchants could sell their wine on their ships or on the docks. They were not excluded explicitly from the excises, but the Portuguese could circumvent the excises. The Portuguese had considerable trouble with the shippers who organised the transport from the big ships in Sluis to the Bruges market. The privileges stated that if these shippers ate Portuguese fruit or drank their wine, they would have to pay for it.[68] The Portuguese had an even more far-reaching clause. After hostellers or brokers inspected the goods, bought them and brought them into their hostels, there could no longer be any discussion about the quality of the goods.[69] In a mainly fruit-oriented trade, this clause was of paramount importance, especially because in some cases buyers would simply inspect the fruit on delivery. With these clauses, the Portuguese could still enforce the sale regardless of the quality of the fruit.[70] Nevertheless, such clauses did not mean that these Portuguese merchants could act fraudulently. When suspicion arose in the case of the merchants Álvaro de Communs and João Vaaz, they had to swear that the fruit they had sold was merchandise of fine quality and the buyer was not purposely deceived.[71]

The Portuguese had used the Castilian privileges as their example and demanded the same tax reductions as their economic competitors. With those privileges, the Portuguese attempted to be on a par with the Spanish merchants, and since the Spanish received privileges in 1428, the Portuguese tried the same thing in 1438. In 1411 a chief (*chef*) was nominated, but could only decide on quarrels between shipmasters and sailors.[72] This limitation was lifted in 1438 when, in addition to a confirmation, the Portuguese received a small charter from the Duke of Burgundy.[73]

The charter itself contains two clauses, but their implications were vague for the present-day reader and possibly for contemporaries. In the first clause, the duke grants the Portuguese consuls the right not only to organise their merchant community, but also authority in all civil matters concerning two Portuguese merchants.[74] This is a similar privilege to what the Spanish had enjoyed since 1428, albeit with some small differences. In contrast to the Spanish privileges, this privilege laid out which law applied and when it could be used. The Portuguese consuls could not decide on criminal matters, and act only in civil disputes. However, neither the princely officers nor the aldermen of Bruges had a right to evoke cases before their court on matters between Portuguese merchants. However, should one of these merchants feel aggrieved, then he could bring his case before the aldermen of Bruges. So rather than a concession for the Portuguese merchants, it was presented as one where the aldermen of Bruges would not entirely lose their authority when dealing with Portuguese merchants.[75] In addition, if one of the two parties did not belong to the Portuguese nation, they were not allowed to pursue their case before the Portuguese consular court.[76]

The privileges only indicate that they should apply the law of the 'country'.[77] Most likely, the consuls decided between members of their nation according to their customs, but the 'law of the country' is a reference to Flemish/Bruges customary law. Unfortunately, we have no legal records from the Portuguese consuls. We know very little about their practice. However, once a decision was appealed, it was not checked according to the law of Portugal, but according to the law of Bruges. Even in the most far-reaching privilege, the aldermen of Bruges maintained the primacy of Flemish law over foreign law.

The legal practice is even more confusing. When a Portuguese merchant chose to bring his case before the aldermen, the court often behaved in an uncharacteristic way. At first glance, the aldermen were reluctant in relation to appeals against the Portuguese consulate. For example, in 1458 a case was started between Rodrigo Eanes, a Portuguese shipmaster in the service of the King of Portugal, and João Lopez (Jehan Louppes) from Lisbon. The latter had used the services of a royal ship to transfer wine barrels from Portugal to Damme.[78] Each claimed that the other party's obligations were unfulfilled: Rodrigo Eanes claimed that Lopez should pay for the voyage, while Lopez believed that the voyage was unsatisfactory. During the trip, Lopez had suffered damage and, once he was in Bruges, he had even seized some wine barrels in possession of the shipmaster.[79] Since both were Portuguese merchants, they had to appear – according to their privileges – before the Portuguese court.[80] The consuls ruled in favour of Rodrigo Eanes, allowing João Lopez to appeal his case before the aldermen.[81] The latter did so, though the aldermen did not rule in his favour. The review effected by the aldermen consisted of two steps. They first asked the consuls the reasons behind their decision, and in the second instance asked Lopez to defend his decision for an appeal. Whereas the consuls had to explain how they came to this judgment, it was up to Lopez to explain why this decision flawed.[82] In this way, the aldermen made appealing more difficult. Perhaps the Bruges aldermen introduced this principle to favour the Portuguese nation.

Although the privileges still granted Portuguese merchants the right to appeal, the way the aldermen of Bruges treated these cases rendered it extremely hard to actually do so. If Portuguese merchants appealed, they were not only expected to plead the case, but also had to prove that the decision of the consuls was malicious. Nevertheless, a certain degree of ambiguity would remain. For example, when Rui Massado appealed against his judgment before the aldermen, he was promptly imprisoned by his adversary.[83] Submitting an appeal was not a cause for imprisonment, so the aldermen intervened and demanded that both Massado and his counterparty, Fernando de Loys, assure they would adhere to their decision.

In 1465, the aldermen decided that the case between Álvaro Dinis and Fernande Álvaro – as it stood – should be dealt with before the consuls of the Portuguese merchants, according to their privileges.[84] João Vasques received an even more sterne warning. If he 'annoyed' the Portuguese consuls any more with his appeals, he would be 'corrected through a banishment or otherwise'.[85] Appeals were certainly allowed, but both aldermen and Portuguese consuls probably avoided them as much as possible. João Vasquez was far from a nobody.[86] He was the secretary of Isabella of Portugal, the duchess of Burgundy and the younger sister of Henry the Navigator. Portuguese like João Vasquez represented a different breed of merchants operating in Bruges.[87]

The Portuguese presence in Bruges was smaller than that of the Castilians. Unlike the Castilian nation, there are few instances of collective legal actions brought by the Portuguese community before the Bruges aldermen. However, the Portuguese merchants who were present appear to have navigated the local legal and commercial environment quite effectively. Rather than relying on national unity in legal matters, it seems that the Portuguese may have placed greater trust in the strength of their individual connections.[88] One such, was the connection with Isabella of Portugal. In addition, the Portuguese king had a factor in Bruges, who represented the royal monopoly on the African trade and was increasingly becoming a political power to be reckoned with alongside the nation.[89] Some of the Portuguese merchants even had a close connection to the Burgundian court.[90]

Before the aldermen of Bruges, they could use the help of hostellers though this was not always necessary.[91] The legal practice of the aldermen suggests that the Portuguese regularly opted for arbitration. In such cases, the decision would not come from the aldermen, but from other merchants, often members of their network, while still being sanctioned by the aldermen. Or for more sensitive cases, we see the Portuguese using submissions. This form of conflict resolution came close to arbitration, but instead of being exercised by international merchants or hostellers, it was exercised by representatives from the city magistrates. The Bruges aldermen used this method only rarely, and most submissions were reserved for citizens.[92] The fact that the Portuguese engaged in this form of conflict resolution is indicative of their importance to Bruges.

It seems that, while some cases were still being solved through normal litigation, the Portuguese benefited more than other communities from the informal means of conflict resolution. Why the aldermen allowed this is harder to explain. The Portuguese trade may not have been essential, but their luxuries were certainly appreciated, and perhaps valued more than other more mundane commodities. Add to this the combination of a trade exercised by a handful of merchants who were often well connected to both the Portuguese and Burgundian courts, and one can imagine that the aldermen of Bruges may have been very wary when dealing with these Portuguese conflicts.

This stance is probably best explained in a case that was brought before the Portuguese consuls in 1455. The Genoese merchant Desiderius de Viealde had used the shipping services of the Portuguese Gil Rodrigues.[93] The ship was, however, attacked by English maritime plunderers who seized part of the cargo belonging to Desiderius. The cargo belonging to other Portuguese merchants was left alone. The English were at war with Genoa and not Portugal. However, once the vessel arrived in Bruges, the Genoese merchant believed that his losses should be shared with the other Portuguese.[94] The Italian immediately seized a part of the remaining cargo and sold it to another Portuguese merchant, Pedro Dinis.[95]

The case was brought before the Portuguese consuls who realised that they were dealing with a complicated case and proposed that the parties submit themselves to arbitration.[96] They appointed the Florentine merchants Jacopo Strozzi, Rinieri da Ricasoli, Paolo Strozzi, and the Venetian Michele Quirino. The arbiters could not resolve the parties' dispute and the consuls took it upon themselves to decide the case. The consuls interviewed some witnesses who were present on the ship at the moment it had been seized and decided that Pedro Dinis had to give back the fruit that Desiderius had bought.[97]

Pedro Dinis immediately appealed the decision before the aldermen and the aldermen asked him why the decision of the consuls had aggrieved him.[98] According to Dinis, there were some serious shortcomings from the consuls. He claimed that he was not fully heard by them, and even alleged that one of the consuls had not been present, but both still signed the eventual decision, implying that it was not a fair trial. The real quandary emerged when he claimed that the fruit that he had seized and which the other merchants reclaimed, was not seized in the name of Desiderius, but of a citizen of Bruges, Maarten Lem.[99] The aldermen proposed a submission. The obvious advantage of a submission was that the aldermen could be more flexible in procedural matters.[100] They therefore did not alter the judgment of the consuls by allowing an appeal but altered it to an informal form of conflict resolution. By so doing, they could minimise the damage done to the consuls while at the same time the aldermen had the chance to thoroughly investigate whether their citizen might possibly have been harmed. The potential lack of justice may have prompted the aldermen to act. However, they did so without aggravating the Portuguese nation.[101]

The biggest contrast may have been between the Spanish nation, who had to fight for its cases before the aldermen of Bruges, and the Portuguese, who showed few signs of internal coherence and received quite different treatment from the aldermen of Bruges. Submissions for non-citizens were rare. It was a tool the aldermen of Bruges used to deal with speed and informality. For the aldermen of Bruges, the Portuguese nation differed from most other communities. It was relatively small, probably never exceeding thirty members, though they were often well-connected.[102] In addition, the political influence afforded by the presence of Isabella of Portugal, duchess of Burgundy, can be felt, and the Portuguese royal monopoly on certain luxuries made clear to the aldermen that they needed to treat these cases with diligence.[103] The privileges the Portuguese received were inspired by the Spanish, but also contained clauses specific to the Portuguese trade. The Portuguese consular jurisdiction was established by charter, but only in a vague and nebulous way. It gave the Portuguese clear authority in private matters. Appeals were possible, and the aldermen could intervene and did so sporadically. When a citizen of Bruges appeared before the consuls, the aldermen referred the case to their court.[104] Bruges still drew a critical line. However, consciously or unconsciously, in all other matters the aldermen seem to have given the Portuguese a considerable advantage.

THE ARAGONESE COMMUNITY

Both political and economic leverage were at play with the Portuguese and Castilian merchants in Bruges. However, they were not the first Iberian merchants to be granted significant rights in the city. In the fourteenth century, the Aragonese nation was the first to receive privileges and establish a consulate in Bruges. These subjects of the Aragonese crown, often referred to as Catalans, hailed from the territories of Aragon, Valencia, Mallorca, and the County of Barcelona. During this period, Genoese and Venetian galleys sailing to Sluis frequently made stops in Barcelona and Valencia.[105] Organising their trade from the ports of Barcelona, Valencia and Mallorca, the Catalans brought nuts, dried fruit, paper, sugar and spices, as well as leather, cotton and wool to Bruges in return for the highly valued Flemish cloth.[106] In the fifteenth century, precious alum was needed for the cloth industry, and ceramics were added to this. In addition, like the Italian merchants, the Catalans were involved in the world of finance as money changers and bankers.[107]

Politically, the Kingdom of Aragon was a major player in the Mediterranean. In the early fifteenth century, the Aragonese King Alfonso V the Magnanimous (1416–1458) became one of the most ambitious princes of the renaissance.[108] He oversaw the arrangement of new economic ties with the East for his Kingdom of Aragon, but also launched a daring expedition to Southern Italy to claim the crown of Naples. However, in 1443, the Burgundian duke supported Alfonso's rival and ordered the collective arrest of Catalan merchandise in Flanders. Although relations would soon be restored, the clear disregard of the Aragonese privileges is puzzling.[109]

How is it possible that a large economic trade partner, rich in privileges, was so quickly faced with serious arrests? As we have seen, the same thing happened to the Castilian merchants in 1421–1428, but this was met with grave repercussions and threats from the Castilian king. In contrast to the Spanish, the Aragonese would not receive any new charters. The nation of Aragon provides the necessary correction to the thesis of how politics influenced the position of the merchant in Bruges. Although in the first half of the fifteenth century Aragonese merchants certainly had significant political power negotiating with the Duke of Burgundy, both in terms of war and peace, they lacked protection against the rare collective arrests.

Interestingly enough, while the organisation of the Catalan consulate is well documented, its activity is not. Much of what we know about Catalan organisation derives from the *Llibre del consulat*. The Catalans were the first to found a consulate in 1330. Without naming it such, they already determined that all civil matters between their merchants should be dealt with by their legal heads or *sobrepotestas*. These two consuls were elected among the members and served for four months, later six.[110] The task of the consul was to be aware of quarrels between the merchants and to settle them as fast as possible. The consuls could reprimand merchants who disrespected a resolution, and they could even threaten these merchants with expulsion from the nation.[111] However, as the 1330 ordinance stated, the jurisdiction of the consul was limited by the customs already in existence in Bruges.[112]

The ordinances that followed fixed the boundaries and regulations in detail.[113] The nation was based on consensual membership. Although only merchants could become members, they were free to join the nation or not. If they paid a membership fee and attended the masses at the Carmelite church on the first Sunday of each month, they could enjoy the advantages of being part of this.[114] Of course, Catalans entering the nation were bound to swear and obey these statutes, yet it was stressed several times that these statutes were accepted by the community because of the common good of these merchants.[115]

The regulations of the nation give the impression of a vibrant merchant community. It was also one with a working consulate. Next to the consuls, the Catalans were under the jurisdiction of the consulate of the sea in Barcelona.[116] However, the consuls in Bruges could resolve internal quarrels without much interference. In 1389, the regulation expressed that all Catalan merchants, punishable by fine or expulsion, should bring all matters below 10 lib. gr. to the consuls. The consuls had to decide within eight days, and they even claimed some authority over strangers 'harming' the nation.[117] In 1396, this was amended. As the ordinance indicates, merchants had complained about the duration of the term in office of the consuls and their lack of expertise. Therefore, as the ordinance proclaimed, the consuls – who still heard and saw the question – could from now on appoint arbiters to decide together with the consuls and come to the most equitable solution.[118] Of course, such an intervention envisioned ending a dispute without further options of appeal. The consuls were still the main players in the nation, but the act of adding arbiters might also have been a sign of the deteriorating authority of the consuls themselves.[119]

The ordinances also specify the usage of the seal, the demands of religious life and contributions to a fund for the jettison of cargo.[120] In 1389, the Aragonese added to their own ordinances a privilege from the duke. This privilege was aimed at sailors from Catalonia. Captains had been given the power to decide upon the quarrels of their sailors, and for any of their debts. Therefore, captains had to give their permission before hostellers could negotiate with their sailors.[121] Sailors enjoyed the right of portage, a small supply of merchandise that was excluded from normal tolls.[122] In addition, the Catalans were granted a house to staple their goods.[123] Furthermore, in the fifty days their galleys were present in Bruges, merchants were not to be halted when they tried to unload their merchandise and they could sell their merchandise outside of the cloth hall, thus evading the excises (*hallegeld*) to be paid.[124]

In the fifteenth century, there is one big difference to be noted between the Catalans and the Portuguese and Spanish. The Catalan nation issued these ordinances on its own authority and did not receive prior recognition from the Count of Flanders. Whereas the Spanish and Portuguese, respectively in 1428 and 1438, received privileges granting formal jurisdiction to the Spanish consuls and bringing their court within the general framework of medieval Bruges, the Catalans lacked such privileges. The privileges the Catalans received, in 1414 and 1419, were brief and the clauses were poorly observed. The Aragonese merchants received the assurance that they could enter the county and conduct trade as they saw profitable, leave the county unhindered within forty days in case of war or other upheaval and that these merchants would not be arrested for debts that were not their own.[125] In 1419, the new Duke Philip the Good confirmed these clauses without any alterations.[126] As we have seen, Philip the Good did not respect them in 1443, when he ordered the arrest of all Catalan merchandise. Only in the 1490s, would the Aragonese receive extensive privileges from Bruges, after the city had lost its status as a commercial powerhouse.[127]

A possible explanation is the decline of the merchant community itself. While in the fourteenth century it was claimed that hundreds of Catalan merchants traded in Bruges, by the first half of the fifteenth century their numbers had dwindled to a dozen, and by mid-century, only around five merchants remained.[128] It is not the place here to speculate as to why the Catalan trade in Bruges deteriorated so drastically. There seems to be a discrepancy between the political rise and economic demise of the crown of Aragon. The exploits of Alphonso the Magnanimous created many enemies resulting in constant harassment of the Catalan trade. In addition, Italian shipping passed through ports like Valencia, allowing for a more passive Catalan trade. Furthermore, surging Castilian merino-wool exports proved to be a tough competitor for the export of Catalan wool.[129] Be that as it may, we do know that by 1450 the Catalan trade in Bruges was in the hands of a handful of merchants.[130] The trade structure was of course somewhat different to that of Portugal and Spain, but still, the absence of a certain mass of merchants impacted their leverage over the aldermen of Bruges.[131]

The ordinances clearly stated that there should be two yearly elected consuls. They do not appear in the court proceedings between 1447–1470. That should not come as a big surprise. When there are were five merchants present in the city, the collective action a nation could take was negligible. The merchants who were present, however, would quickly adapt to this situation and become frequent litigators in their own right. During this period, only a handful of merchants appear in the sources.

The apparent absence of merchants was not the end of the Catalan nation. The few members still present, simply made it work for them. The Catalan merchant Saldone Ferrier, for example, used the nation as a cover for his arrests. It was unclear what he arrested, but he made the arrest claiming that the money – a handsome 47 lib. gr. – belonged to the Catalan nation and made a surety before the aldermen, as was the custom, in case anyone should protest and claim otherwise.[132]

On 6 August 1453, another Catalan merchant – Francois Pimenes – would protest against the arrest and claim that the money belonged to other private merchants. The Bruges aldermen demanded that each party prove their case.[133]

Francois Pimenes claimed that Saldone Ferrier had seized the money under a false pretext. In effect, the money was disputed between Saldone Ferrier and four other merchants; at that time the only Catalans present in Bruges. As the others had left, Saldone had transferred the money into the funds of the nation under the pretext that it was to fund the tax for cases of General Average (*avaria*), the common contribution against jettison. All merchants had to pay this tax, and it could be levied on the merchandise of the merchants. However, when he was the only merchant in Bruges, Ferrier claimed that the nation still owed him money as an outstanding loan. According to Pimenes, Saldone Ferrier reasoned that the money, now in the funds of the nation, belonged to him.[134] Thus, Ferrier had used a ruse so the other merchants would lose their claim to it. In addition, Pimenes continued, the rest of the freight money could not be used to pay outstanding loans, but had to be transferred to the service of the chapel at the Carmelites.[135] In the six months the aldermen had given him to prove his point, Francois Pimenes even procured letters from the Aragonese king stating that the freight money could not be used in such a fashion.[136] The aldermen agreed with Francois Pimenes, decided to annul the arrest Ferrier had made and ordered that the money be transferred to the chapel of the Carmelites.[137] Saldone Ferrier did not win this case, yet his ruse was not foolish either. The other Catalan merchants could not undo his arrests on behalf of the freight money, they could only change its ultimate destination. Saldone used the absence of the other Catalan merchants to his advantage, he used the Bruges aldermen to gain a form of legitimacy, and he almost succeeded in doing so. Unfortunately for him, one of the Catalan merchants, Francois Pimenes, came back and protested the scheme. Had this not happened, the money would have been his.

Saldone Ferrier certainly did not win every case he started. However, he was duly aware of the customs of the Bruges aldermen and not shy of using them to further his proceedings. Even when Saldone found himself in a perilous situation, he still managed to confuse the aldermen by claiming Flemish customs. For example, when the Aragonese merchant wanted to refute a claim by providing his oath, he claimed he could do so according to the laws and customs of Bruges. His opponents however refuted this, and the aldermen had to investigate the matter in depth in order to check whether or not Saldone Ferrier was correct.[138] He lost the case and was even briefly imprisoned. Two important hostellers, Zegher Parmentier and Gérard Plouvier, stood surety for his release.[139]

Tellingly, very few Aragonese connections helped the man.[140] When the Spanish merchants asked to unload their armed fleet, the Spaniards asked the aldermen of Bruges in the name of the nation. Saldone Ferrier could not rely on the nation's support.[141] Despite the power of the Aragonese king, the man had to fend for himself. His cases mostly span a couple of years, during which he relied extensively on the aldermen as mediators, but also on his networks in Bruges. He would use arbitration procedures to his advantage and was acquainted with the Bruges legal system.[142] For example, he would use the higher courts of the Burgundian Netherlands to his advantage. In 1461 he brokered a deal with the aldermen when he initiated an appeal before the Council of Flanders.[143] A couple of years later he would successfully compel the aldermen to pay 48 lib gr. through the Great Council.[144] The aldermen would come to the same conclusion in October 1466. The aldermen had brokered a deal with Saldone Ferrier in which they would pay him 281 lb. par (40 groats the pound), so he would renounce his case before the Great Council. They did this, so they claim not because of the appeal, but to avoid 'further involvement and costs in this case'.[145] The parties came to an agreement that was mutually beneficial. Saldone Ferrier received a handsome payment and the aldermen of Bruges were spared from the legal proceedings before the Great Council.[146]

The Aragonese merchants demonstrate a third form of leverage distinct from that of the Castilian and Portuguese communities, who utilised both political and economic influence over Bruges. In contrast, the Aragonese relied on their personal resourcefulness. It is not our intention to determine which strategy was most effective, as the context largely dictated whether and how a merchant community could exert pressure on Bruges. Spanish merchants as a whole wielded significant influence due to the importance of their trade, and the Portuguese nation was particularly privileged in Bruges. They secured both privileges and privileged treatment, thanks to the personal and ducal connections of the Portuguese, combined with their relatively small number. This led the Bruges' aldermen to act with caution. Nevertheless, the aldermen never gave the Portuguese full independence in Bruges. Despite the favourable rights granted to the Portuguese, the aldermen ultimately maintained their authority as the primary guarantors of justice. Thus, even when significant political and economic leverage was at play, the aldermen of Bruges remained central to the equation.

NOTES

1. Casado Alonso, 'Brugge', 53.
2. Orella Unzué, 'Relaciones mercantiles', 135–136.
3. De Clercq et al. 'Ballasting the Hanse', 728.
4. Dumolyn et al., 'Production, markets and socio-economic structures', 199–205; Abraham-Thisse, 'Les relations hispano-hanséates', 144; Bonduel, 'Late medieval Bruges', 131–137.
5. Maréchal, 'La colonie espagnole', 12–13; Casado Alonso, 'La nation', 64; or how the judicial framework also benefited trade: Miranda, 'Conflict management', 11–36; Verlinden, 'A propos de la politique économique', 685.
6. See for Portugal: de Oliveira Marques, 'Notas', 439–476; Paviot, 'Les Portugais', 1–122; Verissimo Serrão, 'Le Portugal', 231–240. See for Spain: Casado Alonso, 'La nation et le quartier', 64; Fagel, 'Spanish merchants', 87–104. See for the sixteenth century: Sicking, 'Les marchands espagnols', 257–261. An exception for Antwerp: G. Martyn, 'De Portuguese natie', 74–87.

7. The privileges they received in 1421, 1469 were only confirmations and even limited certain rights of these merchants: Braamcamp Freire, *Noticias da feitoria de Flandres,* 133, 147–149.
8. Brown, 'Cities, nations and divine service', 168–169.
9. Munro, 'Spanish Merino wool', 433–435. Fagel, *De Hispano-Vlaamse Wereld,* 128–135; Philips, 'Local integration', 34.
10. Höhlbaum, *Hansische Urkundenbuch,* vol. I, 295, 862; Bervoets, Dumolyn, 'Urban protest', 97.
11. The Germans also complained about tolls and mint policies; Beuken, *De Hanze en Vlaanderen,* 60–62.
12. Maréchal seems to accept this, but does not provide any evidence; Maréchal, 'La colonie Espagnole', 12–13.
13. Kusman, 'Jean de Mirabello', 902.
14. SAB 96, *Groenenboek* C, fol. 82 v.–84 r.; Gilliodts-Van Severen, *Consulat d'Espange,* p. 9–10, art. 9, 10, 11, 14.
15. Gilliodts-Van Severen, *Consulat d'Espagne,* 8–10, privilege from 1343, Art. 3, 5, 6, 7, 8.
16. Gilliodts-Van Severen, *Consulat d'Espagne,* p. 11 art. 12; Gilliodts-Van Severen, *Inventaire des chartes,* vol. 2, 130, n. 564, art. 3 and 12.
17. SAB, Politieke Charters, 564; Perroy, 'Louis de Male', 305–317.
18. SAB, Politieke Charters, 564; CAB 96, *Wittenboek,* fol. 52 r.–v.; Gilliodts-Van Severen, *Cartulaire,* 132–139.
19. Gilliodts-Van Severen, *Inventaire des chartes,* vol. 2, p. 138, n. 564, art. 41 and 48. See on these money changers/early bankers: De Roover, *Money, banking and credit,* 185, 236; De Roover, 'New interpretations', 213, 219.
20. Gilliodts-Van Severen, *Inventaire des chartes,* vol. 2, pp. 137–138, art. 37, 38, 47.
21. Gilliodts-Van Severen, *Inventaire des chartes,* vol. 2, p. 138 art. 46. See for similar clauses in the Portuguese privileges in 1411; Gauchies, *Ordonnances de Jean sans Peur,* 259, art. 46.
22. Casado Alonso, 'La nation et le quartier des Castillans de Bruges', 65–66.
23. The problems were already present from 1419 and escalated in 1426; Blockmans, *Handelingen van de Leden,* 1419–1438, p. 320, n. 266; Verlinden, 'A propos de la politique économique', 691.
24. De Clercq et al. 'Aragonese tiles', 166–168.
25. The duke had levied the twentieth penny on all incoming merchandise from the Spaniards; Blockmans, *Handelingen van de Leden,* 1419–1438, 326, n. 272.
26. SAB 96, *Groenenboek* C, fol. 171 r.–172 r.; Blockmans, *Handelingen van de Leden,* 1419–1438, 327, n. 274.
27. Blockmans, *Handelingen van de Leden,* 1419–1438, p. 329, n. 277; p. 331, n. 279; 333 n 282; p. 346, n. 295; p. 348, n. 297; p. 364, n. 309; p. 365, n. 310; p. 371, n. 313; SAB 216, *Stadsrekeningen Brugge,* 1427–1428, fol. 59 r.
28. Blockmans, *Handelingen van de leden,* 1419–1438, 408, n. 351.
29. Gilliodts-Van Severen, *Inventaire des chartes,* vol. 4, 497.
30. The Spanish frequently came into contact with the authorities of Bruges. See, for example, Jehan Pardo who was arrested by the schout for abducting a girl of fifteen or sixteen; ARA, CC, 13775, *Accounts of the city bailiff of Bruges,* Joos van Varsenare, fol. 12 v; Gilliodts-Van Severen, *Inventaire des chartes,* vol. 4, 498; SAB, *Spaans Consulaat,* nr. 4.
31. SAB, *Politieke Charters,* 1039.

32. Gilliodts-Van Severen, *Inventaire des chartes*, vol. 4,497.
33. And already in the possession of the Spanish since 1343; Gilliodts-Van Severen, *Inventaire des chartes*, vol. 2, p. 130.
34. Gilliodts-Van Severen, *Inventaire des chartes*, vol. 4, 498; SAB, *Spaans consulaat*, nr. 4.
35. The accountability of partners or masters was always a difficult case. The Hanseatic merchants excluded this specifically. In most cases, it depended on the practice of the aldermen who considered cases.
36. Gilliodts-Van Severen, *Inventaire des chartes*, vol. 4, 498; SAB, *Spaans Consulaat*, nr. 4.
37. SAB 165, *Memoriaal van de Kamer*, 1478–1479, fol. 13 v.
38. SAB 165, *Memoriaal van de Kamer*, 1478–1479; fol. 14 r.
39. SAB 165, *Memoriaal van de Kamer*, 1478–1479, fol. 14 r.
40. Cloths could only be sold in a select number of 'halls'. Here, the marketing was supervised, and the leaseholders had a small fee from merchant who wanted to sell their cloths; Munro, 'The abortive staple', 1158.
41. SAB 157, *Civiele Sententiën*, 1447–1453, fol. 96 v.
42. SAB 157, *Civiele Sententiën*, 1453–1461, fol. 59 r.
43. SAB 157, *Civiele Sententiën*, 1447–1453, fol. 40 v.; SAB, *Spaans Consulaat*, nr. 17.
44. The consuls of the Spanish nation had close ties with the crown; Casado Alonso, 'La colonie des marchands', 235.
45. SAB, *Spaans Consulaat*, nr. 25, art. 4, 7, 10, 11.
46. SAB, *Spaans Consulaat*, nr. 25, art. 13.
47. I will discuss the relation between mercantile 'home' courts and Bruges in the chapter on the Italians. See on Burgos: Vandewalle, 'El consulado de Burgos', 204–205; Gonzalez Arce, 'La Universidad', 170; Fagel, *De Hispano-Vlaamse Wereld*, 13.
48. Flórez, 'Vicissitudes of commercial trading', 33–53.
49. SAB 157, *Civiele Sententiën*, 1453–1461, fol. 123 r.; Giliodts-Van Severen, *Consulat d'Espagne*, 75; SAB, *Spaans Consulaat*, nr. 20; Gilliodts-Van Severen, *Constulat d'Espagne*, 70.
50. Rijksarchief Gent, *Raad van Vlaanderen, Interlocutoire Sententiën*, 1483–1485, fol. 219 v.
51. SAB 96, *Groenenboek B*, fol. 147 v.; Gilliodts-Van Severen, *Consulat d'Espagne*, 161, art. 47.
52. SAB, *Spaans Consulaat*, nr. 20; Gilliodts-Van Severen, *Constulat d'Espagne*, 70.
53. Gilliodts-Van Severen, *Consulat D'Espagne*, 175, art. 10.
54. SAB, *Spaans Consulaat*, nr. 23; Gilliodts-Van Severen, *Consulat d'Espagne*, 84–86.
55. Aguiar Andrade, Miranda, 'Lisbon', 340; Elbl, 'Croscultural trade', 198–199; Verlinden, 'Henri le Navigateur', 423–435.
56. Which does not mean that one of these merchants could not grow wealthy from this trade; Miranda, 'Portugal', 75; Miranda, 'Portuguese traders', 122–123; Barros and Miranda, 'To make good peace or total war', 305–308; Gilliodts-Van Severen, *Inventaire des Chartes*, vol. 1, p. 20; Miranda, 'Urban Economy', 181.
57. Everaert, 'The Flemish Sugar', 257–258; Strubbe, 'Aantekeningen over de ivoorhandel', 226–230; van Houtte, 'Portugal en de Brugse handel', 35; 40; Miranda, 'Before the empire', 76–77; Russel-Wood, *The Portuguese Empire*, 9.
58. Bonenfant, *Ordonnances de Philips le Hardi*, 201–202, 243–244; Paviot, *Bourgogne et Portugal*, 57, 137–138; SAB, *Politieke Charters*, 663.
59. SAB, *Politieke Charters*, 688.

60. It is also possible that it was issued on 25 March 1410 since the document does not mention whether it was done before or after Easter; Braamcamp Freire, *Noticias*, 128. See for the privilege: ADNB 1602, fol. 211 r.–213 r.; SAB 96, *Ouden Wittenboek*, 94 r.–95 v.; FA 1070, Privilegiekamer, Vreemde natiën, Natie van Portugal, 1411–1650, 11 r.–24 r.; Gilliodts-Van Severen, Cartulaire, vol. I, 482–491; Cauchies, *Ordonnances de Jean sans Peur*, 253–259.
61. Cauchies, *Ordonnances de Jean sans Peur*, 254, 257, art. 1, 5, 9, 36.
62. Ibid. 255, art. 6, 7, 8, 42.
63. Ibid. 257, art. 42.
64. Ibid. 255–256, art. 2, 5, 11, 12, 14.
65. Swords and other 'suitable weaponry'; Cauchies, *Ordonnances de Jean sans Peur*, 255, art. 10.
66. Ibid. 255, art. 15–22.
67. Ibid. 259, art. 48
68. Ibid. 257; art. 34 and 35.
69. Ibid. 258, art. 38.
70. SAB 157, *Civiele Sententiën*, 1465–1469, fol. 3 v.
71. SAB 157, *Civiele Sententiën*, 1465–1469, fol. 50 r.
72. Cauchies, *Ordonnances de Jan sans Peur*, 254, art. 3.
73. SAB 157, *Oude Wittenboek*, fol. 98 v.–99 r.; FA 1070, Privilegiekamer, Vreemde natiën, Natie van Portugal, 1411–1650, fol. 7 r.–9 v.; Gilliodts-Van Severen, *Cartulaire*, vol. I, 615–617.
74. As was the case in the Castilian privileges; SAB 96, *Ouden Wittenboek*, fol. 99 r.; Paviot, *Portugal et Bourgogne*, 58.
75. SAB 96, *Oude Wittenboek*, fol. 98 v.
76. SAB 96, *Oude Wittenboek*, fol. 98 v.
77. SAB 96, *Oude Wittenboek*, fol. 98 v.
78. Damme had the staple on wine in the middle ages; Rose, *The wine trade*, 90; Craeybeckx, 'De wijnvaart tussen West-Frankrijk en de Nederlanden', 141–142.
79. The decision is unclear as to what these expenses were. Maybe this was a general payment for the cargo, but it is more likely a case of jettison where the expenses would be shared. João would have refused this, but it is also possible that he suspected other fraudulent behaviour; SAB 157, *Civiele Sententiën*, 1453–1461, fol. 213 v.
80. SAB 157, *Civiele Sententiën*, 1453–1461, fol. 213 v.
81. SAB 157, *Civiele Sententiën*, 1453–1461, fol. 213 v.
82. SAB 157, *Civiele Sententiën*, 1453–1461, fol. 213 v.
83. This was possible because the previous decision had made him a debtor in the legal sense. In late medieval Bruges, foreign debtors could be imprisoned as soon as a creditor wished to call in a debt. Citizens could not be imprisoned that quickly.
84. SAB 157, *Civiele Sententiën*, 1465–1469, fol. 68 r.
85. The aldermen of Bruges banished people out of the County of Flanders; SAB 157, *Civiele Sententiën*, 1465–1469, fol. 83 v.
86. He also stood surety several times for Portuguese merchants who had infringed the staple regulations; an indication of a certain prestige and wealth. SAB 216, *Stadsrekeningen Brugge*, 1455–1456, fol. 15 r.
87. Eventually, he was appointed *maître d'hôtel* in the autumn of the Duchess' life; Sommé, *Isabelle de Portugal*, 211, 326–327; Sommé, 'Les portugais dans l'entourage', 326; Paviot, *Portugal et* Bourgogne, 125–127.

88. Miranda, 'Network takers', 184–185.
89. Although we should not overstate this. The feitor was a representative of the royal trading interest. Although the office of feitor and consul could be combined, it is unlikely that they controlled the nation on behalf of the king; Elbl, 'Nation, bolsa and factory', 3; Sommé; 'Isabelle de Portugal', 261–280; Sicking, 'Funduq, Fondaco, Feitoria', 201–202.
90. There were some ancient contacts between Flanders and Portugal. Mathilde of Portugal was the wife of the Count Philip of Alsace, Ferrand of Portugal was the husband of count Johanna of Constantinople; Van Houtte, 'De politieke en dynastieke banden', 12; 23.
91. SAB 157, *Civiele Sententiën*, 1453–1461, fol. 61 r.–62 v.
92. It should be noted that the Portuguese were well-integrated. Several became Bruges citizens; Miranda, 'Commerce, conflits et justice', 6.
93. Gil Roderigues was probably closely aligned with the shipping services from the Portuguese crown; Miranda, 'Portugal and the Medieval Atlantic', 239–240.
94. This principle is called General Average in which in a case of jettison the unfortunate merchants would see their losses (partially) reimbursed by the merchants whose merchandise was saved. See Dreijer, 'Maritime averages and the complexity of risk management', 31–54.
95. SAB 157, *Civiele Sententiën*, 1453–1461, fol. 68 r.
96. As the merchandise was sold to another Portuguese merchant, Piero Denis, the latter could litigate on his behalf for the Portuguese consuls. As discussed, the Portuguese privileges explicitly forbade non-Portuguese to appear before the consuls. However, actual practice may have been different.
97. Desiderius had first seized these goods.
98. SAB 157, *Civiele Sententiën*, 1453–1461, fol. 68 r.
99. Who was in his turn also highly involved in the Portuguese trade; SAB 157, *Civiele Sententiën*, 1465–1469, fol. 91 v.–93 v.
100. SAB 157, *Civiele Sententiën*, 1453–1461, fol. 68 v.
101. SAB 157, *Civiele Sententiën*, 1453–1461, fol. 68 v.
102. Marques, 'Notas para a História da Feitoria Portuguesa', 455; 458.
103. This changed in the sixteenth century when the Spanish crown came into the hands of successors of the duchy of Burgundy; Dreijer, 'Identity, conflict and commercial law', 118–138.
104. SAB 96, *Groenenboek* A, fol. 295 v.
105. Pifarré Torres, *El Comerç internacional de Barcelona*, 31–33.
106. Hinjosa Montalvo, 'De Valencia a Portugal y Flandres', 149–168.
107. Vandewalle, 'Brujas, centro del comercio internacional', 293, 296.; Coll Conesa, 'El comercio de la cerámica', 317–318.
108. Hollingsworth, *Princes of the renaissance*, 26–60.
109. De Clercq et al. 'Aragonese tiles', 166–168; C. Marinesco, 'Les affaires commerciales', 33–48.
110. *Llibre del* consulat, 446.
111. In 1330, the consuls had the barema on 20 florins, *Llibre del consulat*, 447.
112. *Llibre del consulat*, 446.
113. 1330, confirmed in 1355, additional fol. I to II 1389, 1392, 1394, 1396, 1401, 1409, 1419, 1426, 1427, 1430, 1441, 1455, 1488, 1532.
114. *Llibre del consulat*, 461.

115. *Llibre del consulat*, 461.
116. Vandewalle, 'Brujas, centro del commercio', 294–295.
117. *Llibre del consulat*; 459–460.
118. *Llibre del consulat*, 462–463.
119. This is also hinted in the ordinance of 1396; *Llibre del consulat*, 463.
120. Also present in the Spanish nation: see Dreijer, *The power and pains of polysemy*, 215–254.
121. Gilliodts-Van Severen, *Consulat d'Espagne*, 19.
122. See for a list on the rights each nation had on the droit de portage: SAB 522, *Waterrecht, Stapel van Sluis*, fol.; 11 r.–12 r.; The Catalans on SAB 522, *Waterrecht, Stapel van Sluis*, fol. 11 r.
123. Gilliodts-Van Severen, *Consulat d'Espagne*, p. 20.
124. Which was very similar to the free conduct the Venetian fleets received.
125. Cauchies, *Ordonnances de Jean sans Peur*, 297–8; SAB 96, *Ouden Wittenboek* 46 v.
126. SAB 96, *Ouden Wittenboek*, 46 v.
127. Gilliodts-Van Severen, Consulat D'Espagne, 163–167.
128. Desportes Bielsa, 'El consulado catalán', nr. 1382.
129. Hinojosa Montalvo, 'De Valencia a Portugal y Flandes', 160–168; Hinjosa Montalvo, 'Los intercambios mercantiles', 303–304; Del Treppo, *I mercanti catalani*, 142–147.
130. Teresa Ferrer, 'Catalan commerce', 32–33.
131. Around four years' work for a master stone mason; Ortega Villoslada, 'Mallorca y el commercio atlántico', 72.
132. SAB 157, *Civiele Sententiën*, 1447–1453, fol. 311 v.
133. SAB 157, *Civiele Sententiën*, 1447–1453, fol. 330 r.; SAB 157, *Civiele Sententiën*, 1453–1461, fol. 3 v.–4 r.
134. SAB 157, *Civiele Sententiën*, 1447–1453, fol. 70 r.
135. SAB 157, *Civiele Sententiën*, 1447–1453, fol. 70 r. see their statutes: *Llibre de consulat*, 474.
136. SAB 157, *Civiele Sententiën*, 1453–1461, fol. 70 r.
137. SAB 157, *Civiele Sententiën*, 1453–1461, fol. 70 r.–v.; SAB 157, *Civiele Sententiën*, 1453–1461, fol. 72 v.
138. SAB 157, *Civiele Sententiën*, 1453–1461, fol. 272 r.
139. SAB 157, *Civiele Sententiën*, 1453–1461, fol. 274 v., 339 v., 364 v.
140. In 1452, he would act as a surety to a state-owned ship; SAB 157, *Civiele Sententiën*, 1447–1453, fol. 300 v.–301 r.
141. See for the Spanish request: SAB 157, *Civiele Sententiën*, 1453–1461, 271 v. See, for example, a request from Saldone Ferrier and another Catalan merchant asking the Bruges aldermen whether their ship – then at Blankenberghe – could safely dock and unload its cargo; SAB 157, *Civiele Sententiën*, 1447–1453, fol. 317 v.
142. SAB 157, *Civiele Sententiën*, 1453–1461, fol. 372 r.; SAB 157, *Civiele Sententiën*, 1453–1461, fol. 361 v.
143. SAB 157, *Civiele Sententiën*, 1453–1461, fol. 364 v.
144. SAB 157, *Civiele Sententiën*, 1465–1469, fol. 23 v.
145. SAB 157, *Civiele Sententiën*, 1465–1469, fol. 57 v.
146. SAB 216, *Stadsrekeningen Brugge*, 1466–1467, fol. 27 r.

7

Strategies without Privileges: The Italian Communities

The verdict of historians on Bruges' attitude towards the Italian nations has been highly positive.[1] Merchants from Venice, Genoa, Florence, Lucca and Milan were very welcome in Bruges. They were allowed to organise themselves in nations, to organise justice as they saw fit, and to organise their communal life as they pleased. According to Jean-Marie Yante, these nations possessed consulates who could judge cases between their litigants.[2] While there is a persistent view that Italian merchants were favoured, at the same time there is the lingering paradox they had little political leverage over Bruges.[3] As we have seen in the Portuguese and Spanish cases, the king was actively involved in procuring additional rights for their merchants. This was not the case for the Italians. Although the duke could consider a state like Milan as an esteemed ally, most of the cities on the Italian peninsula lacked the political leverage possessed by monarchies like France, Castile or England. The Italian city states were divided and their merchant communities were rather small. If one Italian community refused to trade on Bruges, another would step into the vacuum. Despite their differences, the Italians were a rich group of individuals with connections to the Burgundian court. How did the traders from the various Italian cities defend themselves in Bruges?

In the twelfth and thirteenth centuries, commercial contacts between the Northern European economy and the Italian peninsula took place through an international system of fairs. These Champagne fairs were the connection between woollen products, particularly high-quality draperies, from the Low Countries and Levantine products imported by the Italians. Initially, communications ran through transcontinental routes via the Alps. Once the Italians started to use a direct seaborne passage via the Atlantic in the early fourteenth century, they had direct access to the Bruges market.[4]

The Italians dominated parts of Bruges' commercial life with their spice trade and other oriental products, advanced financial techniques, and crucial alum.[5] The latter was a mineral used for fixing colours to Flemish cloth.[6] These Pisans, Genoese and Venetians provided banking services and became the essential go-between in the trade in oriental luxuries, and they possessed enormous wealth. Some Italian families emerged as the moneylenders of dukes and kings. In the Burgundian Netherlands, the dukes used the Italian lenders so they could continue their conspicuous consumption.[7] These Italian banking families used their financial power and their access to luxurious commodities to win the favour of the Burgundian dukes or other princes, and received occasional benefits from the prince.[8] Families like the Rapondi, Arnolfini and Portinari became close allies of the Burgundian state. They provided the duke with credit, works of art and prestige.[9] The duke repaid them handsomely with titles, influence and the occasional personal privilege. However, these benefits were strictly personal. The dukes granted concessions based on individual merit and their value to the duke.

The apparent paradox between being important and not having important privileges has largely been ignored by historians. Laura Galoppini, for example, has claimed that one of the main objectives of these communities was the formal recognition of these nations by the local authorities.[10] If this was their objective, why did the Italians fail so miserably in Bruges? Without privileges, how did these merchants organise themselves, and how did they try to protect themselves against external threats?

Not all Italian nations were alike, and the state structure back home influenced the way merchants traded. Yet they were all confronted by the same problem. The Italians had no privileges like the Iberians and certainly not like the Hanseatic and Scottish merchants.

Venice possessed the strongest political and economic leverage. It possessed some privileges, though they did not apply to all merchants. Again, the Venetian state illustrates the conditionality of these privileges. As the Venetians failed to procure privileges for their entire merchants' community, we have to wonder how other communities like Genoa, Lucca and Florence operated in Bruges. After deconstructing the idea of 'Italian nations' and certainly their 'consulates', I will illustrate how the omission of a consulate does not equal vulnerability but was just another way of coping with the context of Bruges. It is only when economic or political leverage is absent that we can also see how these merchants had to operate in late medieval Bruges. The Italians could rely on very few privileges, and yet they were successful.

THE STRATEGY OF DIPLOMACY

Venice was one of the first Italian cities to solicit for privileges in Flanders. The Venetian city-state had grown from a Byzantine satellite state into a mercantile superpower in its own right.[11] The Venetians had invested heavily in Byzantine and Crusade politics and were awarded trade privileges, exemptions and concessions in the East. In the fifteenth century, the longstanding rivalry between other commercial centres such as Pisa and Genoa ended with uncontested Venetian control of the Levantine trade.

The way the city of Venice operated gave its merchants certain advantages. In Venice, the merchant nobility had consolidated its power and had built a bureaucratic system based on written law enforced by councils.[12] According to Elisabeth Crouzet-Pavan, it was the unique challenge of building a city in a lagoon that demanded a highly centralised state with relative stability to prosper.[13] Since the political and commercial elite overlapped, the establishment of staple rights, the organisation of protective convoys and obtaining exceptional trade privileges made Venetian commerce more secure – and thus profitable – than that of other city-states.[14]

The galley system was Venice's strongest bargaining chip. These galleys were the largest ships with multiple decks engaged in the well-established routes by the state.[15] The trade in the Eastern Mediterranean was a perilous undertaking, and commercial success depended on several factors such as piracy, bribes paid to officials, shipwrecks and storms. Such dangers were equally present on the route to Flanders. The Venetian state was keen to address these risks, organise convoys and allow Venetian merchants to share the investment.[16] Between 1384 and 1453, the Venetian state outfitted each year four or five state galleys and other ships for voyages to Flanders and England.[17] These were outfitted by the state, but farmed by private individuals who could buy a share to transport commodities to Bruges. Several control mechanisms were present: merchants' accounts were verified and transgressors were reprimanded through administrative controls and legal sanctions.[18] By allowing merchants to rent a space on the state-owned-galleys, the risk would be spread for both investors and the city. In this way, the fleet secured trade for these merchants.[19]

For Venice, the Flemish route was one of the longest and most intensive of the four itineraries. After leaving Venice, the fleet would first touch Manfredonia, Brindisi and Otranto in Puglia (Naples), after which it sailed to Sicily to trade for sugar. The fleet would continue to the African coast via Tripoli, Tunis, Algiers, Oran and Tangiers, trading in inland African commodities such as ivory, dried fruit and gold powder. After passing the Moroccan coast, the fleet followed the Portuguese, Spanish and French coasts to Flanders to buy Flemish cloths and trade with the Hanseatic merchants. On their return voyage to Venice, the galleys frequented the ports of Lisbon, Cadiz, Alicante and Barcelona.[20] Between 1410 and 1438, the route would have taken shape by following the Adriatic coast and turning off towards Messina, following Palermo to continue to Mallorca for the necessary sugar and then passing through Cadiz, Malaga and Sevilla for short periods along the Spanish coast. After this route, the fleet would speed up and part for London and Flanders, where it split up.[21] The Venetian Senate stipulated these journeys, but there still was some room for the captains to search for the most profitable spaces or to deviate from specific ports when they were considered perilous.[22]

The fleet's arrival in Bruges was a much-anticipated event that was considered as a boost to commercial activity. For example, money changers knew that with the arrival of the Venetian fleet, considerable commercial activity would take place, and thus money would be scarce, making for profitable exchange rates.[23] Venice knew how important it was for Bruges, the captains knew the fleet's importance, and the aldermen knew how important the fleet's arrival was for their commercial year. The collective seafaring system allowed Venice to present a more unified negotiating partner than other cities.

Some historians have observed a structural difference between the Venetians and the other nations. The Venetians did not establish highly respected merchant firms, such as the Frescobaldi and Medici (Florence), Arnolfini and Rapondi

(Lucca), and the Spinola and the Adorno (Genoa).[24] The registers of civil justice were bursting with these Italian personalities while the Venetians figure only rarely.[25] As a result, historians believe that the Venetian merchants were able to create a private form of conflict resolution that bypassed the city administration.[26] The argument of this chapter is to show that, although many Italian merchants were ambitious to establish a form of 'Italian/consular' conflict resolution, the aldermen of Bruges always had the final say on matters occurring in Bruges.

Even Venice, despite its considerable commercial leverage, did not secure privileges that exempted it from Bruges' jurisdiction. In fact, during the fifteenth century, Bruges tended to restrict rather than expand the liberties granted to the Venetians. Furthermore, the state-organised fleet was not the only Venetian presence in Bruges. While the fleet undoubtedly held the greatest influence, it is important to recognise that private voyages continued to constitute a significant portion of Venetian trade with the Low Countries.[27] The clauses the Venetians received were only applicable to the fleet, not the individual merchants. Hence, the way Bruges behaved towards these merchants, was not based on nationality, but functionality.

The importance of the Venetian fleet resonates in the first Venetian privileges. In 1319, Venice sent ambassadors to Brabant and Flanders with a proposed list of clauses they wanted in their privileges.[28] In 1322, the Count of Flanders and the aldermen of Bruges conceded and accepted all their clauses.[29] The privileges the Venetians received were unprecedented. Venetian merchants received the right to set up consular jurisdiction over all Venetians in Bruges, they were immune from debt imprisonment without a writ from the aldermen, and they received extensive advantages on the Bruges market: Venetians could freely sell and buy on the Bruges market within forty days of the arrival of the merchandise. In addition, the privileges granted unrestricted access to the Flemish hinterland, something that was normally restricted, and assurances were given on the weight and measures that were used.[30]

The promise of a staple had its effects. By promising to dock at one port, Bruges would make a huge economic gain. The Venetians were well aware of their importance, and played Bruges and Antwerp off against each other.[31] The phrasing of the clauses suggests that the Flemings accepted all Venetian demands without making any alterations, a decision they would regret. The privileges undermined several urban monopolies. To begin with, unrestricted access to the Flemish hinterland undermined the staple rights and all sellers and buyers in Bruges. In addition, the clause on the consular court omitted to state that the consul was only competent over the internal conflicts of Venetians. By the letter, the consular court could be involved in all cases that involved Venetians. In cases of conflict between a citizen and a Venetian, the consuls could be regarded as competent judges. This privilege effectively undermined the jurisdiction of the aldermen entirely. It is unlikely that the aldermen intended for the Venetians to have the authority to adjudicate disputes involving local citizens as well.[32]

Unfortunately for the Venetians, the 1322 clauses were short-lived. When a rebellion broke out in 1323, the guilds tried to protect their commercial rights.[33]

The Venetians' exemptions from tolls and lack of accountability towards the communal leaders were probably not very popular. Although the roots of the unrest lay deeper than just the Venetian privileges, these privileges disappeared from sight. There are no traces of the 1322 privilege in the Bruges registers, only in the Venetian archive.[34] After the rebellion ended in Flanders, the Venetians received new clauses in 1332, though this charter was considerably less favourable. They still enjoyed concessions on arrest, weighters, and some safeguards on their persons and property. However, the Venetians did not have complete freedom of trade and, although the consul is mentioned, his rights in the Venetian community were not confirmed.[35]

Together with the other – influential – nations, the Venetians received new privileges in 1358. However, while the Hanseatic, Scottish and English nations were granted extensive rights concerning personal security, tolls and protection from maritime plunder, the privileges of the Venetians present a more mixed picture. Their rights were restricted to the period when the Venetian fleet docked in Sluis. Therefore, the privileges only applied to the sailors and merchants accompanying the official fleet. As some requests were extensive, this is an important nuance. For instance, any Venetian arrested for debt imprisonment would not be sent to prison but straight to the aldermen, who would decide immediately upon the matter.[36] Also, when the Venetian galleys arrived, its merchants were granted a term of forty-five days during which they would be free to sell as they pleased, with no other charges than the accustomed ones. This one is similar to the 1322 privileges with important alterations: in 1358 there is an essential link with the fleet. It is easy to see why. The economic importance of the fleet made Bruges lenient, but only for a limited amount of time. The fact that sailors could not be burdened during these forty-five days was an effective clause against new tolls or other imports, but it was also vague and it is doubtful that toll collectors would apply the clauses meticulously for all Venetians. If the galleys, and with them state-sponsored commerce, disappeared so would the privileges of these merchants. Although the privilege was not as far-reaching as it had been in 1322, it still contained considerable grants.[37]

The Venetians remained divided between their fleet and the larger merchant community. The 1406 privileges increased the authority of the captain and granted him more power to arbitrate conflicts concerning his crew. The captain was a state official and a critical element in the excellent organisation of the fleet. He was both an experienced sailor and a commercial expert. He was responsible for the safest commercial routes, evading pirates and wreckage, and he had to take the commercial success of the fleet into account. His function also extended to shortening or prolonging the presence of the fleet at a given time and place. The fleet could not hibernate in the Low Countries and had to leave the North Sea before the end of the summer. Time was scarce and commercial gain had to be made fast. The decision, and thus at least a part of the responsibility, rested with the captain in accordance with representatives of the Venetian communities in London and Bruges.[38] By giving captains the right to sanction their sailors, the water bailiff and the bailiff of Sluis lost authority over these cases.[39] However, they had no say over the larger merchant community, and had to work together with the consuls.

In addition, the sailors were protected by a ban on credit operations for subsistence commodities with hostellers without the captain's authorisation. In brief, the captain would arbitrate in all matters of debt, revolt, fights and all possible debates that might arise between his sailors. They could do this explicitly according to their insight and the rules of the country from which they came.[40] However, the right for sailors to carry untaxed small commodities, like a barrel of wine, to Bruges would still provoke many conflicts.[41]

The Venetian effort in relation to safe conduct is indicative of its position. The fleet sailed annually and, each year, the Venetians were keen on gaining formal assurances from the Count of Flanders that they would go unharmed. Certainly, in the fourteenth and early fifteenth century, the Venetian consul regularly presented gifts to ease the issuing of safe conduct. Obviously, such safe conduct was strictly associated with the fleet.[42]

By the mid-fifteenth century, there were other lucrative destinations such as Antwerp, Middelburg and London, and the Venetian captains were given the liberty to choose their port of destination.[43] Bruges was still very keen to have the Venetian fleet dock at Sluis, but the Venetians lost most of their leverage over the Burgundian duke.[44] This is also particularly apparent in their rights. In 1450, for example, the Venetians received a new safe conduct from the Burgundian duke. In this safe conduct, the Venetians received additional rights for their promises to keep sailing to Bruges.[45] Although the time limit for Venetian grants was no longer contingent on the fleet, the captain lost his right to consider cases of debt, riot or fights among his sailors.[46] Such cases should be dealt with by the law of the area where the Venetians docked, or in other words, the bailiff regained the jurisdiction to consider these cases. So, instead of an evolution towards more rights, the Venetians became more reliant on the duke.

This is in contrast with the privileges the Venetians enjoyed in the East. The Venetians are famed for the extensive privileges they received in *Romania*, the Crusader states and Alexandria.[47] Here the Venetians organised their trade through a network of islands and ports, assuring access to the lanes, supply and shelter.[48] This network was the reason why the Venetians gained a dominant foothold in the Levantine trade.[49] In Flanders, however, the Venetian nation never attained the rights and protections granted to their colleagues in the East. For example, in the Eastern territories, a recurring demand was the application of Venetian criminal law to their merchants.[50] In the Burgundian principalities, such a thing was actively blocked by both Bruges and the Burgundian duke. In matters of criminal law, very few advantages were given to merchant communities. Initially, small offences could be handled by the Venetian captain but even these rights were cancelled in 1450 when the duke handed back all cases of debts, riots and fights between sailors to the different bailiffs in Sluis.[51] In addition, the rights the Senate procured were only for the galleys sailing to Bruges.[52]

The galleys were only part of the Venetian trade in Bruges. Alongside the captains of the galleys, the Venetian merchants had to obey the Venetian consuls in Bruges. The latter also worked for the Venetian state with a distinct task from the captain.[53] For example, in 1411 the Venetian Senate informed the consuls in Bruges that they should obtain the customary safe conduct from the authorities in Bruges and that any costs could be levied from the other merchants in Bruges.[54] In 1475, the Venetian Senate ordered the consuls to make a list of all unjustified profits. If the consuls refused, the senate would fine them 500 ducats.[55] The consuls also represented the Venetian merchant community and intervened multiple times on their behalf for the aldermen of Bruges. For example, when in 1448 the water bailiff prosecuted a member of a galley crew for trespassing the staple laws, he was condemned to pay 25 lib. par. Thanks to the intervention of a Venetian consul, the aldermen indicated that they and the water bailiff relinquished his claim after a fine.[56]

The consuls were certainly respected before the aldermen of Bruges. As representatives of Venice, they enjoyed Venetian leverage and demanded some unusual requests. For example, there are occasions when the aldermen of Bruges remanded a case back to Venice, and even in rare cases, some Venetian customs were allowed.[57] However, as the privileges also indicate, this divergence remains between the consul and the captain, and the fleet and the larger Venetian community. Three cases from 1467 will illustrate this relationship between Bruges and Venice.

The first example is that of one of the Venetian captains appearing before the aldermen. In 1467, three captains of galleys, Marin Bousy, Domenico de Pireto and Donato Remundo appeared before the Bruges court when the Bruges citizens Guillaume le Fevre, Jan Dhont, Cornille vande Velde and Jan Losschaert refused to pay for a delivered cargo of gallnut. The defenders acknowledged the existence of the transaction, but claimed that the transaction was done in good faith while the merchandise was not of reasonable quality (hence the Flemish had not checked the merchandise before the sale). After the Flemish buyers discovered that these were fraudulent products, they refused to pay and submitted a counterclaim for fraudulent merchandise.[58] The aldermen listened to both parties but immediately demanded further investigation. The aldermen appointed three established merchants, Nicholas de Poge (or Niccolo Di Poggio) (Lucca, but also a citizen), Franchois Betrain (Aragon) and Jacopo Doria (Genoa) to investigate the merchandise more closely and determine whether or not it was indeed fraudulent.[59] These commissioners reported back, and the aldermen decided, based on the commissioners' advice, that the initial agreement would stand: the merchandise was not fraudulent enough, and the defendants had to pay for the wares.[60] Nevertheless, the Flemish buyers refused to abide by this judgment. They arrested the captains to pressure them into providing guarantors promising that if the merchandise was sold they would be liable for any claims arising out of the poor quality of the goods.[61] Again, the Venetians went to the aldermen of Bruges and demanded their immediate release without giving any sureties. The aldermen agreed: there was no evident debt, and since the entire undertaking was meant to provide sureties, no sureties were given.[62]

The consuls, on the other hand, had to fight a bit more arduously. Two days later, the consuls Alberto Contarini and Piero Sorance represented the nation of Venice in a case against the Florentine merchant Piero Bandini. The Florentine had arrested several spices (pepper and cloves) from the merchant Ludovico Baseo from Venice. However, Contarini and Sorance claimed that the goods came from the estate of Marco Morosini and that the arrest should therefore be nullified. The aldermen decided that both should prove their claims. While Piero Bandini had to prove that he had arrested the merchandise of Ludovico Baseo with a just cause, the nation's representatives had to prove that it was detained from Morosini's estate.[63] Eventually, Piero Bandini received the goods to be used – under surety – until the heirs of Marco Morosini turned up and proved that the goods were theirs.[64] Later on, the same discussion arose when Piero Bandini arrested some alum. Again, the Venetian consuls intervened.[65] The Venetian consuls were prepared to defend the interests of their members, although not all members of the nation were entirely satisfied with the consuls' authority.

An internal dispute among Venetians in the same year, 1467, illustrates this apparent inability of the Venetian consuls to exert authority over all Venetian merchants. The Venetians Jacopo Balbi and Leonardo Boudumeris claimed compensation from Venetian captain Piero Morosini, probably a relative of the previously mentioned Marco. Piero Morosini had bought a carrack, a large boat, from Natalo Salomon, only to discover that the latter was suspected of deceiving his creditors. Salomon had probably sold the ship due to an expensive claim for damages that hung over his head. A previous voyage of Salomon had gone wrong, as most of the 19,000 bales of wool that he was transporting had perished. To outrun his creditors, he sold most of his possessions, including a boat to Morosini. His creditors, Jacopo and Leonardo, were not so easily deceived. They took the carrack anyway and ignored the fact that it had changed ownership. The creditors summoned Piero Morosini before the aldermen's court and stated that the carrack should be used to recover their losses.[66]

Piero Morosini had a different opinion on the matter. He claimed that he had faithfully bought the carrack 'for everyone to witness', and even more, the previous owner, Natalo Salomon, had remained in Sluis for six months to answer to everyone who might have a claim against him.[67] In addition, he accused the arrestors of malicious intent because they decided to make the arrest when he had resupplied the vessel, outfitted it and was ready to disembark. They waited for the most lucrative moment. Morosini played the aldermen brilliantly. Although initially, the arrestors might have been able to claim damages resulting from the conduct of the shipmaster, in this case, the aldermen of Bruges agreed with the captain of the carrack and declared the arrest null and void.[68] Although never stated, the fact that he came from a prominent family highly involved in the Venetian fleets may have helped.

The evidential basis of the Venetian litigation record is rather limited. It may have been luck that the Venetian captains won their cases, while the Venetian consuls lost theirs. Be that as it may, there are indications that the presence and the economic leverage of the fleet split the nation in two. On one side, was the fleet. Bruges did everything to have the fleet docking at Sluis and selling its merchandise in Bruges. On the other side, were all the other Venetian merchants. The Venetian consul was a representative of the Venetian state and operated in Bruges to help with the organisation of the fleet, keep the Venetian merchants in check, and settle their disputes. The captain, consul and Venetian state were certainly respected. The Venetian merchants operating for longer periods in the city nevertheless showed the same patterns as other Italians.[69] They knew the Bruges system and could operate within it quite effectively.[70] In contrast to the assumption of a favoured nation, the Venetians presented a complicated structure that could only partially translate its economic and political leverage. If a nation like Venice, with so much leverage over Bruges, did not succeed in getting their privileges respected, how did the other Italians fare?

THE STRATEGY OF CONSULS

The Venetian fleet system gave the city-state great leverage over Bruges. Until the end, Bruges was determined to have the Venetian fleet stop at Sluis and transport its goods to Bruges. No other Italian nation would receive such concessions from Bruges or the Burgundian duke. Still, the other merchant communities sought to make the best of their situation and protect their merchants.

While cities like Genoa and Florence organised the occasional fleet to Flanders, they would never receive the same privileges as Venice.[71] Even the ancient tradition of sailing to Bruges, as was the case for Genoa, did not convince the aldermen of Bruges – nor the Count of Flanders – to bestow far-reaching concessions to lure them to their Bruges market. While the Brabantine duke had already bestowed the Genoese privileges in 1315, the Count of Flanders waited until 1395 for the first concessions. Even then, the privileges were hardly comparable to the previous Brabantine clauses of 1315. In Antwerp, the Genoese had safe conduct to the Antwerp market, regulating the modalities of trade, protection from incarceration and the tolls that should be paid, and promising reasonable housing for an affordable price.[72] In Bruges, the Genoese merchants had to content themselves with some basic assurances regarding their liability for debt arrest, and that the shipmaster would judge upon the petty conflicts happening on his ship.[73] Neither the aldermen nor the count had given the charter out of free will: a secession in 1394 out of Bruges over existing malpractice was necessary before the Genoese merchants enjoyed these privileges.[74] The conditionality is remarkable: they were only to enjoy the privileges as long as they stayed in Bruges.

To make matters worse, the charter would be poorly observed. In 1409, the Genoese merchants only barely escaped a collective arrest from the Burgundian duke.[75] Unhappy with their current situation, the Genoese petitioned for new – more extensive – privileges.[76] First, the Genoese threatened to leave the County of Flanders again, but they quickly found that the carrot worked better than the stick. The duke required money and, for a not insignificant compensation, he happily obliged the Four Members and the Genoese by granting privileges in 1411.[77]

The duke granted the captains jurisdiction to manage petty crimes on their ships, and exempted them from the right of shipwreck.[78] The Genoese merchants would be free to travel the streets and port of Sluis, by both night and day, while carrying the same weapons as those borne by the citizens of Mude and Sluis.[79] Nobody from the Genoese nation could be incarcerated, except for criminal offences, without first having the opportunity to provide a surety. In addition, no arrest could be made on ships that were still anchored while they had the prospect of a favourable wind to leave.[80] Furthermore, the water bailiff could not pursue merchants for actions that had taken place outside of the County of Flanders, and merchants could not be held liable for actions outside the County of Flanders, making plunder claims against the Genoese nation quite onerous.

Generous as the privileges were, they came at a price. To achieve these clauses, the Genoese brokers had to finance the costly policies of John the Fearless. Once the Burgundian duke died, his successor Philip of Burgundy, stalled on confirming these privileges. In 1429, doubts arose about whether the privileges were legally valid. Apparently, they had not been published in Bruges, Sluis or Muide, and, thus, they were not properly recorded.[81] It would take until 1434, and an additional 800 écu, to settle the matter. However, the privileges were now slightly amended.[82] The Genoese sailors saw a reduction in their privileges. The shipmasters forfeited their authority over petty crimes committed by their sailors when Flemish individuals were involved in the dispute. Furthermore, the Genoese lost the right to bear arms at night in an effort to reduce violent altercations between merchants.[83] Although their fundamental rights were untouched, it is clear there is a small difference in context.

Even more significant is that while Genoese could negotiate with the duke, the formal recognition of the Genoese consul remained absent. The Castilians and Portuguese received the acknowledgement of their consuls in 1428 and 1438. These Portuguese and Castilian privileges incorporated the consuls into the judicial framework of Bruges, but apparently the Genoese, together with all Italians, preferred not to formalise their consulates.

Most Italian merchant communities had consuls, and they do appear in the sources.[84] There is nevertheless a key difference. Whereas the Spanish had a recognised court in Bruges treating all Spanish matters at first instance, the Bruges aldermen did not recognise the Italian consuls as a formal court. The Italian consuls were only recognised by their city of origin. Furthermore, only the Venetian consuls consistently appeared before the aldermen in their official capacity as consuls. In contrast, Florentine, Lucchese, and Genoese consuls frequently appeared alongside other merchants and never as formal representatives of their entire nation, as was the case with the Venetian and Spanish consuls.[85] How can we explain this difference?

Italian cities like Lucca issued ordinances to control and structure their merchants in a foreign country. By so doing, the city would organise the nation according to the insights of the mother town.[86] The Count of Flanders had not issued extensive self-governing rights, but Bruges did not attempt to prevent these merchants from organising themselves. While the consuls could not count on the aldermen of Bruges to enforce a decision, these consuls had some tools to make merchants abide by their judgment. However, they always had to respect the authority of the aldermen and not the other way around.

Be that as it may, the Italian communities also indicate the level of organisation that was possible without the duke's sanction. Take the city of Lucca. The city, in the form of a council of fifty, established Bruges' Lucchese nation in 1369.[87] The merchant community was to have its own consul(s) who represented the Lucchese merchants and who had to judge on both civil and small criminal matters between them.[88] Lucca's statutes allowed these merchants to group and settle differences among themselves, albeit without a formal process.[89] However, the consuls' authority and their compliance with the law derived from the city of Lucca, not Bruges. The consul could demand merchants' ledgers or even appoint arbiters, but the enforceability of his decisions depended on the authority of the consul.[90]

This lack of formal authority is exemplified in the judgments which have been preserved from the Lucchese nation. For example, in 1397, Niccolò – Claes – Barbagialla tried to resolve a case by using the Bruges aldermen to his advantage. The latter was also a citizen of Bruges and demonstrated his familiarity with the legal system.[91] On the basis of Bruges customs, he attempted to obtain three-quarters of the inheritance of the Lucchese Piero Brunelli, which according to him, should come to him through his wife.[92] Interestingly enough, Niccolò made the mistake of claiming this Bruges custom for the possessions in both Bruges and in Lucca. Whereas he could inherit in Bruges through his wife, this was not the custom in Lucca. Nevertheless, the aldermen supported him, although the applicability of Bruges law on Lucchese territory is doubtful. The consuls disagreed with the interpretation of the aldermen, and after consulting legal specialists, the consuls believed that the Lucchese law should be applied to the possessions in Lucca.[93] Dissatisfied with this outcome, the Bruges aldermen threatened to arrest the Lucchese merchandise in the city. The Lucchese nation answered by proposing an arbitration by jurists and petitioning the Duke of Burgundy, and its powerful Lucchese courtier Dino Rapondi. Since no collective arrests followed, the aldermen probably moderated their stance.[94] The consuls never questioned the primacy of the Bruges law in matters of inheritance in Flanders. Even if both were Lucchese, the consuls avoided a confrontation. It was when the aldermen went beyond their own jurisdiction, that the consuls protested.

This avoidance of confrontation was even more apparent in the 1478 statute. Therein, the city of Lucca confirmed the 1369 charter, and clarified the Lucchese position in Bruges. The charter determined that the nation would have one consul and two councillors with a mandate of one year. Merchants were subjected to the judgment of the consul (*allo arbitrio del console*), whose job it was to bring conflicts to a swift conclusion and, importantly, bring the parties to agreement. In doing so, the Lucchese had to respect the authority of the County of Flanders and not infringe it.[95] The 1369 statute had granted the consul authority over criminal matters, but by the late 1400s this authority had become increasingly impractical, as princely officers were evidently unwilling to acknowledge the consul's jurisdiction in such cases. As previously noted, the duke had curtailed these rights in all other privileges as well. Criminal arrests, being financially lucrative, had become a matter of economic interest for the ducal administration.

The Lucchese consuls had to discipline their members through fines and exclusion to keep discontent out of the community.[96] All arriving merchants in Bruges had to make themselves known before the consul. The lodge at the bourse was a centre for the community; everyone had to be present at the chapel on the *Sancta Croce alli Augustini*.[97] This community was the only way to enforce decisions. The 1478 statute demanded that all the Lucchese would first present their complaints before this consul before proceeding to another court. The charter stated this for the 'complaints of merchandise, money or any other cause' between one Lucchese and another for the same nation.[98] If merchants ignored these clauses, they would have to pay a fine, and in severe cases, they were excluded from the nation and any dealings with compatriots.[99]

Of course, the economic or political leverage that Lucca imposed was not extensive, but other far more important cities had to abide by the same rules. The Florentines, for example, had to rely on roughly the same system of statutes from the mother city to organise the Florentine merchant community. Such a stance can only be partially explained by the lack of economic leverage. Instead, we must consider the alternative of a system that was not reliant on Flemish privileges.

THE STRATEGY OF COMMUNITY

In the fifteenth century, Florence was a republic dominated by the Medici.[100] Florentine seaborne trade with Flanders began as a state experiment in 1425.[101] From the Porto Pisano, each year Florentine galleys sailed to Flanders and England until the system faltered from the 1460s onwards and was aborted in 1478.[102] It is illustrative that the organisation of these galleys was entrusted to the *Consoli di mare*. In this council, six annually elected councillors were responsible for outfitting the galleys, administering justice for what happened on these galleys, and fining perpetrators.[103] The council possessed complete jurisdiction over claims arising from handling the galley system.[104]

All merchants had to swear that they would respect the 1427 statutes. If not, they would be barred from the Florentine consular house in Bruges (the *loggia*) and they were also barred from making transactions with their compatriots.[105] The Florentine *loggia* occupied a prominent position at the Bruges bourse, the economic heart of Bruges making it one of the keystones of Italian commerce. If merchants disrespected their consuls, behaved in an insolent manner or refused to obey the consular statutes, they were not to receive any benefits from the nation.[106] Similarly to the Lucchese, the statutes made the consul competent in all civil matters between Florentines without any possibility of appeal. Florentine merchants had to bring their case to the consuls and their councillors. If merchants refused to obey a consul or did not wish to bring the case to the consul, they could be forced to arbitrate the conflict without ever running into the aldermen or another court in Flanders.[107] Be that as it may, the biggest difference was that the Florentine nation depended on its legal system, and its commercial court, the *Mercanzia*, instead of the aldermen of Bruges. While there were certainly Florentine consuls, the Florentines tried to keep cases within their own sphere of influence.[108]

However, a close connection between Bruges and the *Mercanzia* in Florence also gave way to some tensions.[109] Besides the impracticality of having to judge matters across Europe, the bigger question was the extent to which these decisions were legally valid in Bruges.[110] In 1474–1475 the *Mercanzia* decided upon a dispute that originated in Flanders between Piero Bandini and Giovanni Cambi, both Florentine merchants.[111] Once the decision came to the attention of the aldermen, they disagreed and compelled the parties to abide by a commission to investigate the matter in full.[112] The eventual decision was certified by a notary. This indicates three things. First, it was highly unusual to have decisions of the *Mercanzia* deciding matters in Bruges. Second, the Bruges aldermen sought to review the decision themselves. Ultimately, it was ratified through a notary. By so doing, the aldermen never annulled the decision of the *Mercanzia*, probably so the prerogatives of the city of Florence would not be infringed too much. Third, the verification this commission made was whether the decision of the *Mercanzia* was in line with Bruges customs.[113]

In regard to Florentine law, a fascinating case appeared in 1480 before the aldermen between Giovanni di Benedicto da Pasano, a creditor of the Pazzi, and Piero Antonio Bandini who worked for the Pazzi firm. The Pazzi had long been one of the leading banking firms in Florence until their story came to a bitter end in 1478. A failed coup to seize power from the dominant family of Lorenzo di Medici discredited the entire family and in a quick sequence of events the most important conspirators were executed and all their valuables forfeited.[114] As the Florentine state confiscated all belongings of an international banking family, representatives were sent to confiscate the goods in Bruges. For unknown reasons, the expropriation never materialised. Nevertheless, the banking firm was in danger and Da Pasano, one of the firm's creditors, believed in 1480 that he should have a claim on all the valuables of the firm in Bruges.[115]

Many arguments were put to the aldermen of Bruges. The relevant one here is whether or not the Florentine decisions concerning the confiscation of the Pazzi's had any value in Bruges. Da Pasano believed so. He claimed that as the Pazzi were Florentines, and their representative in Bruges, Piero Bandini, was a Florentine, even a consul for some time, Bandini had sworn to uphold the Florentine statutes, and should also respect decisions made in Florence.[116] Bandini on the other hand, maintained that such a significant issue had no applicability out of the jurisdiction of Florence (*hors de la jurisdiction et seignorie de Florence*).[117] However, the aldermen's decision ultimately mattered. The aldermen dismissed the claim of Da Pasano, stated that he should leave Piero Bandini in peace, and seek redress from the firm's principal, Guilelmo Pazzi, who operated Rome.[118] The Bruges aldermen were clear. There were no obligations arising from the fact that someone was a Florentine or belonged to the Florentine nation, only from contractual agreements.[119] The aldermen did not deny that Florentines should abide by the statutes they swore to uphold, but the prevalence of Florentine law was questionable to say the least.[120]

The key takeaway from this episode is the alternative structure the Florentines created in Bruges. The Italian communities would never acquire legal enclaves in Bruges. Although the Florentines, Lucchese, Genoese and even the Venetians relied on their mother cities to organise the nations and accept recourse from Bruges, this structure had disadvantages. Control from afar was more difficult, and in addition, the consular courts were not recognised by Bruges. The consuls could not count upon the aldermen to enforce their verdicts. Two aspects are indicative in this respect. To begin with, there were no appeals from the level of the community to the higher level; the aldermen regarded these as failed arbitrations. Second, there were plenty of cases where merchants from the same nation litigated against each other. The Florentine republic could claim competence in all quarrels arising between two Florentines. If merchants chose to disregard this, the consuls could only achieve enforcement through private conflict resolution and not through the aldermen.

The groups of merchants worked on a consensual basis. By becoming a member, they promised to keep their disputes within the community. Benefits came with membership of the community, and protection was organised against the outside world.[121] As was the case for Florence, the Florentines valued their legal system to such an extent that they did not want to compromise it.[122] In the Italian cities themselves, authority and law were also not exercised by one central authority but by a polycentric network of influential people working to control both the city's space and its moral space in the matter of authority.[123] The consul and his court provided some sense of familiarity, and undboubtedly one of the main functions of the consul to operate as a middleman between the city and the merchant.[124] However, the consul's authority was limited. If a merchant decided to litigate before the aldermen of Bruges, the merchant community could not intervene before the aldermen and demand that the case be returned to them. The consul could supplement the aldermen's jurisdiction, but never touch the aldermen's prerogatives.

Yet, the Florentine community still operated with a level of efficacy. The key to this was the unity of the nation.[125] The consuls could enforce this unity through the punitive measures in their statutes. These statutes envisioned punishing 'antisocial' behaviour. However, it seems that a positive sense of community cannot be ignored. For most of the fourteenth and fifteenth centuries, most merchant communities based themselves around places of worship where the nation maintained chapels, dedicated masses and celebrated their patrons. Although, the consuls punished non-attendance during these community events, there were evident benefits for the merchants in the community to partake to the collective identity.[126]

The Florentine nation offered the added advantage of a network. For example, Florentines frequently backed each other for guarantees. They stood surety before each other according to a reciprocity principle where they protected each other from external threats. For example, when Thomas de Marquil arrested Antonio Francesco, the latter was bailed out of prison by Angelo Tani of the Medici firm, Bernardo Cambi and Piero da Rabata of the Cambi firm and Bernardo de Bardi of the Bardi firm.[127] The Florentine nation did control internal problems, but when faced with an external threat, it still could unite to face them.[128]

The latter was a consequence of the economic relations in Bruges. Although the sale of merchandise could only pass through hostellers, the Florentines frequently relied upon each other for banking and assurance purposes. Although mutual commercial relations could lead to conflicts that were not limited to the nation alone, they also fostered strong ties within the nation itself. It should be noted that most commercial transactions had a positive outcome. The sheer number of transactions registered in the account books of Cambi, Da Rabata and Strozzi indicate how distorted views on Florentine relations can be when looking only at the failed partnerships and conflicts registered in the aldermen registers.[129] If we take, for example, the Salviati and Da Rabata firm registers, we can see most other merchants appearing in these ledgers.[130] Nevertheless, their relations also stretch further, and for example, for the Strozzi, other merchants such as the Genoese Lomellini and Gentili were frequent partners.[131] The Lucchese Arnolfini and even the Catalans, such as Piero Pierandrea (Piere de Perandre), had considerable accounts with each other.[132] But in reality, most of the Bruges' *bon ton* made their appearance at least once in these ledgers.[133]

As Jim Bolton and Francesco Guidi-Bruscoli have pointed out, the client networks relied heavily on trust, and these bankers were more than ready to change them for trusted and treasured clients.[134] The trust and reciprocity that was common in the interactions of these banking firms, was transplanted to their litigation strategies.[135] It is this system of trust that is also reflected in the registers of the aldermen. Unlike other merchant communities, the Florentines were frequent users of the Bruges aldermen and relied on their own networks and a certain knowledge of the Bruges legal system to make it work in their favour. This illustrates that merchant communities did not necessarily have to rely on privileges or external pressure to navigate the Bruges legal system. Knowledge, networks, and a strong and cohesive community could take a merchant a long way in medieval Bruges.

In conclusion, the Italians lacked political leverage over the Duke of Burgundy to negotiate for a better position. They lacked the unity to form an economic block to pressurise Bruges. Venice used its collective bargaining power to negotiate the best privileges possible in the fourteenth century. In the fifteenth century, Venice provides a good illustration as to how the context mattered. Concessions were reversed, adapted and modified to the new existing situation where ducal officers held most of the cards. However, the Italians also illustrated that litigation strategies did not depend on the privileges they received. Venetian captains showed that favour on the part of the aldermen could help a merchant. The Florentines, however, illustrate how an alternative system in Bruges was possible. The Italian way of conflict resolution was different and yet very similar to other communities. The Italians organised their consuls and respective courts through their mother cities. However, they still had to respect Bruges law. The statutes issued by their cities already made it clear that respect for the Bruges aldermen had precedence. However, conflicts that did not touch the prerogatives of the aldermen, could be perfectly decided within the authority of the respective consuls. These consuls tried to decide matters, and when this was not possible, they proved to be exceptionally apt for the Bruges court. Bruges was a network like no other. It provided a network of hostellers and services that the Italians could opt into, but it was also a network of peers. The Florentines who operated before the aldermen court of Bruges used this network. It is this network that explains the preference of the Italians for arbitration, not the applicability of their own law.

LEVERAGE ON BRUGES

There is one constant factor amongst the various merchant communities: Bruges was extremely reluctant to relinquish any of its legal authority. Several communities attempted to establish a legal enclave, but in each case, the aldermen stubbornly resisted these demands. Even during the 1457 negotiations, when the Hanseatic merchants requested a separate legal regime and Bruges was pleading for the return of the Hanseatic merchants, they were unable to grant this concession. While several merchant communities could pressure Bruges and the Count of Flanders into granting them additional privileges, the procedural advantages some communities acquired were rather modest. In this respect, it is illustrative that several communities relied on their legal experts to litigate on their behalf. The Hanseatic merchants had the Kontor Secretary, who defended the merchants from his Kontor; the Scots had the Conservator of privileges, who was probably skilled in Flemish law; and the Spanish could rely on their nation. In addition, almost all merchant communities could call upon the help of both legal experts in Bruges or the hostellers, providing several functions for these merchants. In all cases, it may be clear that knowledge of the Bruges system and how the aldermen behaved were essential to litigate successfully before the Bruges court.

For the aldermen, it was important to remain the ultimate source of conflict resolution in spite of the privileges. They certainly allowed fewer procedural forms in terms of arbitration or consular courts, but in each case, the aldermen still had the final say. The formally acknowledged courts of the Scots, Spanish and Portuguese had the right to appeal their decisions before the aldermen of Bruges. Hence, when inequitable decisions were made, the aldermen could still intervene. A similar situation existed for the Italian merchants. Although the Italian consuls were not formally acknowledged as a court in Bruges, they were still respected by the aldermen, intervened on behalf of merchants and forged networks. However, if a merchant had a problem with their merchant community, they could still resort to the aldermen of Bruges.

Context still mattered in this regard. The Hanseatic community was very successful in keeping conflicts within the community. Likewise, the Portuguese community had a formal right of appeal, yet the aldermen did their best not to hinder the nation. Bruges was an economic city, and at times this economic position was very precarious. Some nations could form a bloc and pressurise Bruges to deviate from its earlier rule. So, whilst Bruges maintained a theoretical desire for justice, the situation on the ground could be heavily influenced. The strongest communities could push Bruges into inequitable situations. This happened to Portinari when he trusted Bruges to solve his conflict on the Burgundian Galley. When the Hanseatic Kontor threatened to leave the city, there was very little Bruges could do.

In practice, this must have resulted in several unjust decisions on the part of the aldermen. Some communities were better protected than others. Yet, all communities had some link to the aldermen court for their protection. The question is what happened when merchants sought alternatives to the aldermen. What happened when they litigated before the princely courts that emerged during the fifteenth century?

NOTES

1. Stabel, 'De gewenste vreemdeling', 210.
2. Yante, 'Commerce et marchands Italiens', 92.
3. Mainly in the older literature, the Italians were lauded for their commercial spirit; Lopez, 'Le marchand génois', 509; 512; Petti Balbi, 'Brugge, Haven van de Italianen', 58–59.
4. Lopez, 'Majorcans and Genoese', 1166; Doehaerd, 'Les galères génoises', 10, 32.
5. Lane, 'Double entry bookkeeping', 177.
6. Unger, 'Rekening van den invoer van aluin', 75–88; Cannelloni, 'Il commercio dell'allume', 520; Liagre, 'Le commerce de l'alun', 177–179; Delumeau, *L'alun de Rome,* 32–45 and 219–242.
7. Haemers and Lambert, 'Pouvoir et argent', 48–52; Lambert, 'The political side', 103–112.
8. Lambert, '"Se fist riche par draps de soye"', 95–96.
9. Boone 'Les ducs Valois de Bourgogne', 108; Lambert, *The city, the duke and their banker*, 113–120; Galoppini, 'Gli Arnolfini a Bruges nel quattrocento', 277–280; Walsh, *Charles the Bold and Italy*, 145–178; Veratelli, *A la mode Italienne,* 90–130. See Bernardo Cambi supplying a rich 'fleur de lis' tapestry to the duke; ADNB 17742, *Lettres missives et dêpêches*, Cambi; or Giovanni Arnolfini as supplier of the court: ADNB 17675, *Lettres missives et dêpêches*, Arnulphin.
10. Galoppini, '"Nationes" toscane', 150.
11. This was the situation until the Venetian Senate decided to conquer terra firma. By the fifteenth century, the Italian state ruled a large part of Northern Italy, several cities in the Balkans and several Mediterranean islands.
12. Ruggiero, 'Law and punishment', 243.

13. Crouzet-Pavan, *Venise*, 21–26; Crouzet-Pavan, *Venise triomphante*, 122; Crouzet-Pavan, *Venice triumphants*, 46–56; Crouzet-Pavan, 'Venice and its surroundings', 36, 46; Crouzet-Pavan, *Les villes vivantes*, 219–229.
14. See also how Venetian legislation intervened in the *commenda* (colleganze) and made the structure largely obsolete; Lane, 'Investment and usury in medieval Venice', 7.
15. Gluzman, *Venetian shipping*, 217–223; Lane, 'Fleets and Fairs', 651–663.
16. Even foreigners could partake, but they had to pay a 25 per cent penalty; Venetian State papers, 66, nr. 265.
17. Fryde, 'Italian maritime trade', 311; Rawlinson, 'The Flanders galley', 145–168.
18. De Lara, 'The secret of Venetian success', 249; 278.
19. Doumerc, Stöckly, 'L'évolution du capitalisme marchand', 135; Pezzolo, 'The Venetian Economy', 259; de Larivière and Doumerc, 'Le rôle du patriciat', 57–84.
20. Montemezzo, 'Galley routes', 155–156; Daru, *Histoire de la république de Venise*, vol. III, 47–50.
21. Stöckly, *Le système de l'Incanto*, 159.
22. Gilliodts-Van Severen, *Cartulaire de l'ancienne staple de Bruges*, vol. I, 341; Brown, ed. *Calendar of State Papers*, 145.
23. De Roover, *The Bruges money market*, 54.
24. Stabel, 'Venice and the Low Countries', 35.
25. In the 1460s, members of the Dandolo-clan were very present in Bruges; SAB 157, *Civiele Sententiën*, 1465–1469, fol. 37 v.; SAB 157, *Civiele Sententiën*, 1469–1471, fol. 47 r.
26. Stabel, 'Venice and the Low Countries', 35–40; De Lara, *The secret of Venetian success*, 259–260; Fusaro, 'Cooperating mercantile networks', 708; Cecchini and L. Pezzolo, 'Merchants and institutions', 93–94; Burke, 'Early modern Venice', 393–394.
27. De Larivière, 'Entre gestion privée et contrôle public', 59; Fusaro, *Political economies of empire*, 36.
28. ASV, *Commemodandi*, vol. 2, fol. 65 v.; After 1317 and 1318 private operators used the state-owned galleys rent free under the command of Gabriello Dandolo, who also tried to negotiate privileges in Bruges; Lane, 'Venetian merchant galleys', 192.
29. See for letters sent by the Duke of Brabant and the city of Antwerp also confessing that they would grant the same liberties in 1325; ASV, *Comm.*, vol. 2, fol. 159 v.–160 r.
30. ASV, *Comm.*, vol. 2, fol. 121 r., nr. 302; Predelli, *I Libri commemoriali* 241; Cessi, 'Le relazioni commerciali', 27–28.
31. In 1319 the Senate had sent an ambassador to Flanders in order to obtain these extensive rights. If they were not granted, he could go to Antwerp, where they were had been received the previous year; *Venetian State papers*, p. 4, nr. 12. De Roover, *Money, banking and credit*, 15. See on ambassadors: Spitzbarth, *Ambassades et ambassadeurs*, 61–62.
32. ASV, *Comm*, n. 302, fol. 121 v.
33. Haemers and Dumolyn, 'Pattern of Urban Rebellions', 377; Sabbe, *Vlaanderen in opstand 1323–1328*, 18–29.
34. Schouteet, *Regesten op de oorkonden*, 138–144.
35. ASV 40, Senato, Deliberazioni. Misti Registro 15, fol. 5 r.
36. A similar clause was granted to the Scottish merchant in 1392; SAB 96, *Oude Wittenboek*, fol. 42 v.

37. The 1332 privileges were also confirmed; Louis de Male in 1357: ASV, *Comm.*, vol. 5, fol. 89 r.; Louis de Male and Guillaume of Namur in 1378: ASV, *Comm*, vol. 7, fol. 203 v. and 204 r.; Filip the Bold in 1395: ASV, *Comm*, vol. 9, fol. 17 r.–17 v.
38. Stabel, 'Venice and the Low Countries', 31–32.
39. The galleys were seen as beyond their jurisdiction. In 1423 a Venetian captain was arrested because the bailiff of Sluis accused him of taking a sailor on his ship so he would escape justice; ARA, CC, 13935, *Account of the Bailiff of Sluis,* Jan de Baenst, May 1423–September 1423, fol. 6 v.
40. SAB 96, *Ouden Wittenboek*, fol. 46 r.; Cauchies, *Ordonnances de Jean sans Peur*, 40–41.
41. This was called the right of portage. Bruges would frequently argue with Sluis over this right and how far these sailors could also sell their goods in Bruges; SAB, *Political Charters*, 945; SAB 157, *Civiele Sententiën*, 1465–1469, fol. 23 r. See Lambert, 'Merchants on the margins', 243.
42. In this regard, there is some confusion between safe conduct and privileges. As the privileges only applied to the Venetian Fleet, they were often issued as safe conduct although they are incomparable with for example the English safe conduct: ASV, *Comm*, vol. 6, fol. 6 r.
43. Venetian State papers 74, nr. 298; ASV, Senato, Senato Mar, vol. IV, fol. 10.
44. See, for example, a complaint of the aldermen of Bruges to Venetian authorities that their fleet had skipped Bruges in 1461; ASV, *Comm.*, vol. 15, fol. 76 r. See for a formal apology and request that the galleys returned from Sluis in 1461; ASV, *Comm.*, vol. 15, 76 v. See for Bruges giving reductions on the Venetian excises; SAB 216, *Stadsrekeningen Brugge*, 1450–1451, fol. 41 r. See later instances: SAB 96, *Rodenboek*, fol. 247 r.–248 v.
45. See for example SAB 96, *Rodenboek* A., fol. 248 r.–v.
46. SAB 96, *Oude Wittenboek*, fol. 99 v. Confirmed and even made more stringent in 1467; SAB 96, *Rodenboek* A, 259 r.–260 v.
47. Wansbrough, 'Venice and Florence', 490–492.
48. Arbel, 'Venice's maritime empire', 137.
49. Ashtor, 'The Venetian supremacy', 16, 30, 48–50.
50. Ortalli, 'Il ruolo degli statuti', 205; Moukarzel, 'The latin traders in Egypt', 341–342.
51. SAB 96, *Oude Wittenboek*, fol. 99 v. Confirmed and made even more stringent in 1467; SAB 96, *Rodenboek* A, 259 r.–260 v.
52. Venetian State papers, 18, nr. 51.
53. Venetian state paper, 13, nr. 46.
54. Venetian state paper, 53, nr. 188. In 1419: Venetian State Papers, 60, nr. 223; Venetian State Papers, 73–74, nr. 297.
55. Venetian State papers, 133, nr. 447.
56. SAB 157, *Civiele Sentenien*, 1447–1453, fol. 73 r.
57. See for a case referred back to Venice in 1362: ASV, *Comm.*, vol. 6, 132 r.
58. SAB 157, *Civiele Sententiën*, 1465–1469, fol. 80 v.
59. However, if they could agree between both parties, the aldermen would accept this, but it was not the prime goal; SAB 157, *Civiele Sententiën*, 1465–1469, 81 r.
60. SAB 157, *Civiele Sententiën*, 1465–1469, fol. 81 r.
61. SAB 157, *Civiele Sententiën*, 1465–1469, fol. 82 v.
62. SAB 157, *Civiele Sententiën*, 1465–1469, fol. 82 v.
63. SAB 157, *Civiele Sententiën*, 1465–1469, fol. 81 r.
64. SAB 157, *Civiele Sententiën*, 1465–1469, fol. 82 v.
65. SAB 157, *Civiele Sententiën*, 1465–1469, fol. 83 r.

66. SAB 157, *Civiele Sententiën*, 1465–1469, fol. 87 r.
67. SAB 157, *Civiele Sententiën*, 1465–1469, fol. 87 r.–v.
68. The aldermen maintained the action these arrestors had on Nadal Salomon. If the creditors could arrest the latter or his possessions, they could bring it before the aldermen; SAB 157, *Civiele Sententiën*, 1465–1469, fol. 87 v.
69. RAG 2383, *Raad van Vlaanderen, Acten en Sententiën*, 1461–1462, fol. 265 v., 317 v., 336 v.; RAG 2384, *Raad van Vlaanderen, Acten en Sententiën*, 1462–1462, fol. 41 r., 230 v.; RAG 2385, *Raad van Vlaanderen, Acten en Sententiën*, 1462–1463, fol. 238 r.; RAG 2387, *Raad van Vlaanderen, Acten en Sententiën*, 1464–1464, fol. 100 v., 143 r.; RAG 2389, *Raad van Vlaanderen, Acten en Sententiën*, 1465–1465, fol. 24 r.
70. See, for example, the case of Niccolo Pizani against Bonnore Olivier: SAB 96, *Rodenboek*, fol. 197 v.–199 r.
71. Petti-Babli, 'Flottes publiques et flottes privées', 216; 220–221.
72. Documenti, n. III, 374; 374–377 and 378.
73. Documenti, n. III, 385–388.
74. Documenti, n. III 378; Finot, *Etude historique sur les relations*, 45–47.
75. Braekevelt, 'Entre dommage et profit', 120; Zoete, *Handelingen van de leden*, p. 401, nr. 280–286
76. Zoete, *Handelingen van de Leden*, n. 285, p. 409.
77. Cauchies, *Ordonnances de Jean sans Peur*, 320; Braekevelt, 'Entre profit et dommage', 122; Schnerb, 'Un aspect de la politique financière de Jean sans Peur: la question des dépenses de la guerre', *Publication du Centre européen d'études bourguignonnes* 27 (1987), 117 and 124–125.
78. Cauchies, *Ordonnances de Jean sans Peur*, 320–321, art. 1, 2.
79. Cauchies, *Ordonnances de Jean sans Peur*, 321, art. 7.
80. Unless it was for a known debt; Cauchies, *Ordonnances de Jean sans Peur*, 321–322, art. 5 and 9
81. See for this: Braekevelt, 'Entre profit et dommage', 125; RAG 7508, *Raad van Vlaanderen*, fol. 148 v.–150 v.
82. ADNB, 1605, Registre des chartes, fol. 64 r.–70 r.; Braekevelt, 'Entre profit et dommage', 126.
83. Braekevelt, 'Entre profit et dommage', 126.
84. CAB 157, *Civiele Sententiën*, 1447–1453, fol. 302 v.
85. CAB 157, *Civiele Sententiën*, 1453–1461, fol. 331 r.
86. De Maddalena, 'Per la stoia delle "colonie" mercantile', 567.
87. In 1369 the Lucchese received their independence from Pisa. De Roover suspects that the Luccesse from Bruges generously contributed to the payment for their declaration of independence and were rewarded with their own nation; De Roover, 'La communauté des marchands Lucquois', 41; Meek, *Lucca*, 29–30; 41–42.
88. Romiti, *Riformagioni della repubblica*, 138.
89. Ibid. 138.
90. Lazzereschi, *Libro della comunità*, 14–16, 28, 66, 68, 209, 211.
91. *Clais Barbagialla da Luca, Brugese di Brugia*; De Roover, 'La communauté des marchands Luquois', 60–61; Lazzereschi, *Il libro della comunità*, 124.
92. Ibid. 188.
93. Ibid. 188; 202–203.
94. Ibid. 210–211.

95. Simonetti and Tangheroni, *Lucca*, 119. However, in the 1369 stipulations, the Luccesse also claimed authority in criminal matters, but this seemed not to be feasible without encroaching on the authority of the Count; De Roover, 'La communauté des marchands Luquois', 55. See also Galoppini, 'Lucchesi e uomini di comunitá', 47; 59–60.
96. For example, it was forbidden to arrest and throw a compatriot in the Bruges prison without prior consent; Lazzereschi, *il libro della comunità*, 6–7. Francesco Panichi was even condemned to pay 60 florins for arresting someone on the threshold of the Lucchese nation; Lazzereschi, *Il libro della comunità*, 114.
97. Simonetti and Tangheroni, *Lucca*, 118.
98. Simonetti and Tangheroni, *Lucca*, 119.
99. Although they could receive permission from the consuls to proceed before the aldermen, it was instead a matter of not infringing on the consuls' authority; Lazzereschi, *Il libro della comunità*, 204.
100. Florence was still a republic in which the Medici dominated, although without complete control. Scions such as Cosimo and Lorenzo de Medici wielded considerable political influence and prestige, but were not always able to push their vision through; Rubinstein, *The government of Florence*, 149, 156.
101. The first voyage was to the orient: Sapori, 'I primi viaggi', 82.
102. Watson, 'The structure of the Florentine galley trade', 1074.
103. Müller, *Docimenti sulle relazioni*, 280; Plebani, *I consolu del marie di Firenze*, 54–61.
104. Three out of the six consuls who resided in the port of Pisa were, in their turn, responsible both for the defence of the city and all quarrels between foreign merchants in Pisa; State Archives, Florence. *Provisioni*, 1448, 139, fol 3 r and Provvisioni 1428, 120, fol. 44 v.; Mallett, 'The sea consuls of Florence', 160.
105. Masi, *Statuti delle colonie Fiorentine all'estero*, 6, art. 6 and 10, art. 11; the Luccesse also used this mechanism of exclusion as a means to discipline their merchants; Lazzereschi, *Il libro della comunita*, pp. 45–50.
106. Masi, *Statuti delle colonie Fiorentine all'estero*, 9–10, art. 9–11.
107. There was also a 10 lib gr. fine for ignoring the judgment of arbiters and a 25 lib. gr. fine for petitioning another Flemish court; Masi, *Statuti delle colonie Fiorentine all'estero*, 7–8, art. 2, 3 and 5; Galoppini, '"nations" toscane nelle fiandre', 154.
108. Quertier, 'Les Florentins', 461–472; Masi, 'Prefazione', XVI–XVIII.
109. The Mercanzia remains understudied. We have taken some samples of the Mercanzia registers in Florence but could find no cases from Bruges. More research is needed to give a final answer to this question: ASF, *Sentenze de' Sei e dell' Ufficinte*, 7235, 7238; and ASF, *Deliberazioni dell'Ufficinte forestiero*, 313.
110. We searched the normal registers, but cases regarding foreign problems are most likely to be found in the Ufficinte forestiero; ASF, *Atti in cause ordinarie*, 1482, fol. 205 v.–209 r.; 1486, fol. 362 r.–365 v.
111. SNSP, *Diplomatico*, 271; ASF, *Deliberazioni dell'Ufficinte forestiero*, 314, 17 mars 1474.
112. The notarial document refers to officials. These were probably aldermen. Johannes vanden Beurze was registered as a witness of the document; SNSP, *Diplomatico*, 271.
113. SNSP, Diplomatico, 271.
114. Martines, *April blood*; Daniels, *De Verschwörung der Pazzi*, 135–140; The Pazzi firm in Florence ceased to exist, but the firms in Rome and elsewhere continued their activities.
115. Da Pasano claimed that more than three hundred creditors were left behind; ASF, Carte Strozziane, serie II, 21bis, fol. 34 v.–35 r.

116. ASF, Carte Strozziane, serie II, 21bis, fol. 40 r.–41 r.; 73 r.–v.; 89 r.–v.
117. ASF, Carte Strozziane, serie II, 21bis, fol. 57 r.–60 r.; 78 r.–v.
118. Which should not have been strange to the Italians as it was according to *locus regit actum*; Ancel, *Elements d'histoire du droit*, 105. ASF, Carte Strozziane, serie II, 21bis, fol. 97 r.
119. ASF, Carte Strozziane, serie II, 21bis, fol. 98 r.
120. ASF, Carte Strozziane, serie II, 21bis, 101 v.
121. Michienzi, 'La "nation"', 300–301.
122. Petti Balbi, 'Le nationes italiane all'estero', 397–423.
123. See for example: Caravaggi, 'Tra dialogo e conflitto', 677–712; Caravaggi, 'Keeping the peace', 178–191; Acheri, *The law of Late Medieval*, 155–158; 179–182.
124. Petti Balbi, *Negoziarti fuori patria*, 5.
125. Galoppini, *Mercanti toscani e Bruges*, 124.
126. See for example: Leloux, 'Kirche und Caritas', 36–37; Vermaseren, 'De Carmel van Brugge', 19–31.
127. SAB 157, *Civiele Sententiën*, 1447–1453, fol. 66 r.
128. See, for example, a case between Tommaso Portinari and Jeronimo Frescobali. Piero Bandini was the surety of Frescobaldi: SAB 165, *Civiele Sententiën Kamer*, 1474–1475, fol. 27 r.–28 v., 29 v.–30 r., 57 r., 64 r. Of course, such networks of sureties were not the sole property of the Florentine community and merchants still gave sureties according to their commercial partners and interests. For example, in 1459 the Florentine Renaldo Baroncelli, Genoese Francesco Guinigi and Venetian Francesco Dandulo gave sureties for the Florentine Guillaume Berti, who was taken prisoner by another Florentine Rinieri da Ricasoli; SAB 157, *Civiele Sententiën*, 1453–1461, fol. 273 v.
129. Of course, as De Roover has already mentioned, almost all merchants in Bruges had accounts with each other; De Roover, 'Le contrat de change', 115.
130. These were mainly letters of exchange; Scuola Normale Superiore Pisa *Libri di commercio*, 24, fol. 104 r.; 134 r.; 106 r. 179 r.; 185 r.; 187 r.; 258 r.; 333 r.; SNSP, *Libri di commercio*, 25, fol. 33 r.; 50 r.; 65 r.; 92 r; 147 r., 189 r.; 199 r.; 265 r.; 273 r.; 299 r.; 349 r.; 364 r.
131. Lommelini: SNSP, *Libri di Commercio*, 24, fol. 212 r., 238 r., 277 r.; SNSP, *Libri di Commercio*, 25, fol. 59 r.; 65 r.; 149 r.; 202 r.; Gentili: SNSP, *Libri di Commercio*, 24, fol. 100 r., 249 r., 142r.; SNSP, *Libri di Commercio*, 25, fol. 70 r., 71 r., 176 r., 220 r.
132. Arnolfini: SNSP, *Libri di Commercio*, 24, fol. 106 r.; 187 r. PSNS, *Libri di Commercio*, 25, fol. 59 r., 184 r., 230 r. Perandrea: SNSP, *Libri di Commercio*, 24, fol. 100 r., 249 r., 142r.; SNSP, *Libri di Commercio*, 25, fol. 65 r.
133. BNCF, Ginori Conti 7, Cambi, 1455–1460; BNCF, Ginori Conti, Cambi 8, 1435–1457; BNCF, Ginori Conti, Cambi, 1470–1490; Pisa, Scuola Normale Superiore, *Libri di commercio*, 24; ASF, Carte Strozziane, V, 14. See also the (badly damaged) 1305 accounts of the Fini in Bruges indicating a close relationship with Count Thomas of Flanders: RAG 3117, Varia D, *Verschillende documenten m.b.t. Italiaanse handelaars*.
134. Bolton and Guidi-Bruscoli, 'Your flexible friend', 889.
135. Bolton and Bruscoli, 'Your flexible friend', 879.

Part III

Litigation: Individual Strategies Adapting the Framework

Introduction

In 1474, a Bruges' clerk wrote the opening of Justinian Institutiones 'The imperial majesty should not only be made glorious by arms, but also strengthened by laws' as a *probatio pennae* on the register of decisions of the aldermen.[1] I can only wonder what was on the mind of the secretary when he was testing his pen in preparation to the court procedure before the aldermen. Was it an allusion to the state of affairs of the bellicose Duke Charles the Bold? Was it a reference to the newly founded parliament of Malines? Did he see the proceedings of the aldermen as the source of justice?[2]

The 1470s were a troubling time for Bruges. Appeals before the regional court of Flanders, the Council of Flanders, reached an all-time high. In 1473, Charles the Bold, Duke of Burgundy, established a new Parliament in Malines and forbade Flemish subjects from interacting with the Parliament of Paris. This was a clear attempt to assert judicial independence. The cities lost their right of recourse to the Parliament of Paris, ending a long tradition of appealing to the supreme court to challenge their own overlord. As the County of Flanders was formally part of the French Kingdom, the French supreme court, known as the Parliament of Paris, could hear appeals from the county. Flemish subjects could seek recourse against their prince before his feudal overlord, the French king. In doing so, the king could exploit this mechanism to assert authority over the county.[3]

The cities and the prince slowly negotiated a new judicial reality. However, this focus on the powers that be overlooks one of the key drivers of legal change: the litigants themselves, who sought resolution and utilised the options available to them.

With the establishment of the Council of Flanders in 1386 and the Great Council in the 1440s, princely courts emerged and began taking formal notice of commercial cases. However, it was not the princely courts that initiated cases (a process known as *evocatio*); rather, it was the merchants who chose to bring their cases to these courts. This choice was significant, as when merchants opted for princely courts, they effectively shifted the legal framework governing their case.

Thus, the question of whether and how merchants used princely courts in their litigation strategies is key to understanding the choices they made, why they made them, and the political climate that allowed such decisions. In this chapter, we argue that merchants were not always restricted to the legal framework of their merchant community, or even to that of the city of Bruges. It examines these preconditions, the practical considerations, and the effectiveness of navigating between available courts, commonly referred to as 'forum shopping'. The term suggests that merchants used the legal complexity of late medieval Flanders to make the system work in their favour. Or, in the words of an English merchant before the Parliament of Paris: 'to follow a case before a judge that was to his liking'.[4] However, it was not a free for all. Merchants needed a comprehensive knowledge of the legal system in Flanders (and beyond) to understand how, when and to what extent they could use these courts. I will assess this in three ways: the relationship between Bruges and the princely courts and how litigants used them, and how this impacted medieval Bruges.

NOTES

1. . . . *Imperatoriam maiestatem non solum in armis decoratam sed legibus oportet esse armatam* . . .; Probatio pennae on SAB 165, *Civiele Sententiën Kamer*, 1474–1475, fol. 54b v.
2. See on the adagium: Berkvens, 'Imperatoriam maiestatem', 1–7.
3. Hilaire, 'Recherches sur le fonds', 274.
4. AN, X^{1A}, 4807, *Parliament de Paris, Plaidoires*, fol. 135 v.

8

Princely Courts. A New Framework for Late Medieval Bruges

Legal reform through princely courts was a slow and gradual process. Various stakeholders had vested interests in maintaining the status quo, and it was rare for any court to be granted a clear jurisdiction that significantly diminished the authority of another. When this did occur, as with the establishment of the Parliament of Mechelen in 1473, it was met with a lot of resistance. The Parliament of Mechelen was abolished in 1477. For the other princely courts, the process was longer but more permanent. Jurisdiction was extended on a case-by-case basis, and it took decades before the Council of Flanders felt confident in its competence to adjudicate cases originating from the major cities of Flanders. Nevertheless, this evolution did happen. The slow, creeping expansion of the courts' authority – and the potential benefits this brought to Bruges – explains why these institutions persisted. However, in the case of merchants, the advantages to Bruges were minimal. Merchants were able to use these courts to circumvent the jurisdiction of the Bruges aldermen and, in some instances, challenge local customs of Bruges. Yet, to achieve this, they needed to be acutely aware of the broader contextual factors that made such actions possible. In this chapter, I will examine the evolution of these courts and explore how merchants leveraged them to their advantage.

THE COUNCIL OF FLANDERS

The Council of Flanders was the product of the slow evolution the comital courts had made. Before the fourteenth century, the comital council (*grafelijke raad*) was able to arbitrate in conflicts but had no influence on the legal practice of the cities. This situation, however, changed slowly in the fourteenth century. From the mid-fourteenth century, the Audiëntie was still the comital advisory board but, in addition, had its own judicial section.[1] After the peace of Tournai in 1385, Philip the Bold established the 'Camere van den Rade' which would later evolve to become the Council of Flanders.[2] It was to comprise a legal chamber and a financial chamber. The first would evolve into the Council of Flanders, the latter into the Chamber of Accounts of Lille. The Audiëntie would die a silent death in 1409 when it was decreed that the councillors of the Council of Flanders could hold sessions as the Audiëntie if they deemed this necessary.[3]

As was customary for medieval courts, the jurisdictions of princely courts were poorly described.[4] This was also the case for the Council of Flanders, in which the ordinances regulating the institution seldom detail its jurisdiction. Such a thing would be almost unfeasible because of the sheer number of cases that appeared before the court. In addition, specifying a court's jurisdiction, would stand in the way of its own expansion. Rather, it made more sense keep a vague description. However, the most interesting competence the Council of Flanders possessed was safe conduct. Every person under princely safe conduct and all the claims that could follow from this were under the jurisdiction of the Council of Flanders.[5] Whereas the previous princely rights usually would not encroach on the jurisdiction of the cities, claims concerning princely safe conduct could interfere with their policy. We have to keep in mind that safe conduct was included in almost all privileges. As 'free trade' meant that merchants would not come to harm under princely safe conduct, it is not difficult to surmise that some merchants would find their way to a princely court. These privileges gave merchants access to the courts in the domains of the prince. In the fourteenth century, these courts were the aldermen courts as representatives of the Count of Flanders. In the fifteenth century, the Council of Flanders joined the club. Merchants could bring their case to this council if they believed their right of protection had been infringed. Claims of infringements against the princely safe conduct were the first crack in the sovereignty of the Bruges aldermen court.[6]

Nevertheless, we should not see this as a purely negative development for the cities. Clashes in jurisdiction could happen, but as long as the balance of power did not shift unilaterally in favour of the prince, the cities were wary but not openly hostile to the institution. At times, they even used it to their advantage.[7] The case of German merchant Henric Hoop illustrates these benefits for Bruges. Henric Hoop would try to use Hanseatic leverage in Bruges to help him, and the aldermen of Bruges would use their leverage to activate the Council of Flanders in assisting him.

In 1422 Henric Hoop had sailed to Holland to purchase several precious cloths to sell in Sluis. However, while he was sailing to the coast of Holland, he was beset by Dutch maritime plunderers who attacked him with two ships. They stole his ship, his cloths and all the money. The plunderers nevertheless did not immediately disappear from view. Somehow, Henric Hoop discovered that they had sailed along the river Scheldt to Moerzeke. He went to the Bruges Kontor, the Bruges Kontor went to the Bruges aldermen and the latter went to the Council of Flanders to remedy the situation.[8] The problem was that the seigneurial Lord of Moerzeke, the Lord of Maldegem, adopted an ambiguous stance. Bruges demanded the extradition of these maritime plunderers, but the Lord of Maldegem refused. At the request of the Council of Flanders, the comital bailiff of Dendermonde then had to intervene. The plunderers took their bounty and took refuge in the church of Moerzeke. The bailiff could not persuade them to leave the church, but the Lord of Maldegem could.[9] The lord reluctantly helped and drove them out of the church and into his prison. Nevertheless, he still refused to deliver them or their bounty to the Four Members. The Four Members asked the Council of Flanders to to take a firmer stance.[10] The Council of Flanders believed that the plunderers and their bounty fell within the jurisdiction the court[11] and decreed entirely to the advantage of the Four Members and the Hanse. The court stated that the cloths should be returned – or at least their equivalent value – in addition to the money that was stolen. If, for some reason, this were not possible, the amount would be levied on the possessions of the Lord of Maldegem, who was already liable for the escape of two of the plunderers.[12]

The affair illustrates several points. We must remember that, before the rebellion and subsequent submission of 1436–1438, the city of Bruges was still eager to influence policy. Nevertheless, its jurisdiction was also limited. Bruges had no say in seigneurial jurisdiction, and military force would be a last resort.[13] To exert pressure on the Lord of Maldegem, they used the one institution that could discipline him. They used the Council of Flanders to extend their influence and take possession of the cloths taken through the bailiff of Dendermonde. Although one case does not necessarily prove a point, there are other instances where the aldermen of Bruges uses the Council of Flanders to their advantage. In particular, cases where they had disputes with the Liberty of Bruges or with the Chapel of Sint Donaas tended to be brought before the Council of Flanders as a type of princely arbiter who could adjudicate on a given matter.[14] Hence, instead of just ignoring the Council of Flanders as an institution, a city like Bruges used it when it was to its advantage.

The issue arose when an appeal, or a request for the reconsideration of a case, was submitted. In such instances, the Council of Flanders would review the case and deliver a judgment regarding the legal proceedings that had occurred in Bruges. This process undermined the presumed independence of the aldermen.

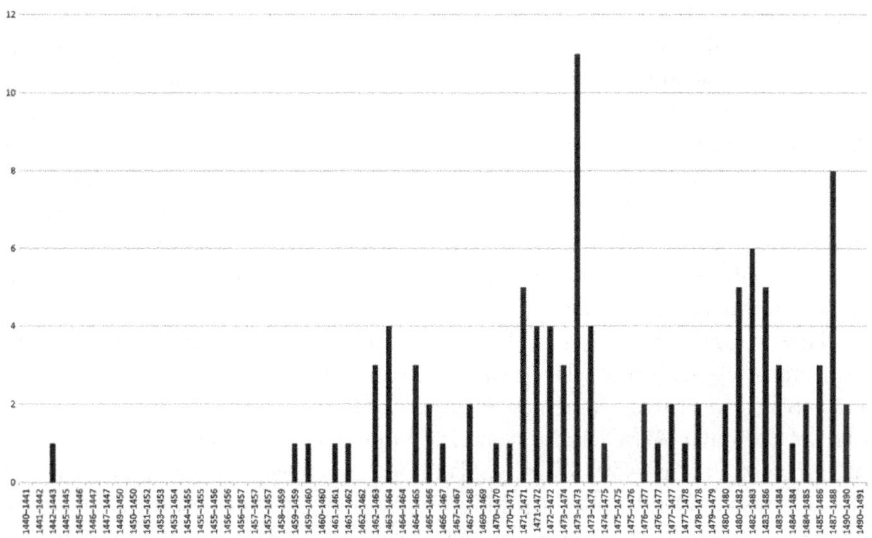

Figure 11.1 Appeals against the aldermen of Bruges

Source: RAG, Raad van Vlaanderen, Acten en sententiën, 1440–1490

We must bear in mind that an appeal was an assessment of competency and a form of control over the aldermen's legal activities. The council members did not reassess the case, but assessed whether the aldermen had delivered proper justice to the parties.[15] Instead of being a case between two parties, it was a matter between the aldermen of Bruges, the claimant and the defendant. If the aldermen of Bruges lost, they would be fined by the Council of Flanders. As Jos Monballyu has explained, the absence of the written procedure was keenly felt in this respect. If the aldermen had no written proceedings, the Council of Flanders was obliged to redo the entire procedure and could not decide *ex eisdem actis*. If this happened, parties could bring claims or evidence previously not considered.[16] As a consequence, the aldermen of Bruges could be condemned and fined 60 lib. gr. on the basis of arguments of which they were unaware.

From early on, the Four Members expressed their concerns in matters of appeals and reformations.[17] Unsurprisingly, the aldermen reacted dramatically on the first appeals that occurred. One of the first people who dared to appeal a judgment from the aldermen of Bruges before the Council of Flanders was the French merchant Jean Bridoul. In 1440, he had sold fine French wine to Florent le Blont, who operated in the name of Antonio Francesco. Although Francesco had sold the wine to the Duke of Burgundy, he never paid Jean Bridoul in the first place. When Jean Bridoul called upon Florent le Blont for the outstanding payment, the latter replied that he had already paid 2,000 pounds in Nantes. When Jean Bridoul was in Bruges, he brought his claim to the aldermen demanding payment of the full amount. Unfortunately for Jean Bridoul, the aldermen dismissed his claim due to a lack of evidence. After this, he took a bold move. He went to the Council of Flanders and asked for a '*reformacie*', or appeal, against the decision of the aldermen.[18] It was the first time merchants had actually questioned the decisions of the aldermen. Apparently, the councillors did not know what they had to do with the case and the aldermen did not even show up. The case was adjourned six times. Jean Bridoul demanded a judgment *in absentia*, but was disappointed. Most likely, he made a compromise with the aldermen of Bruges afterwards. The communal accounts mention a payment for substantive documents that were delivered to Jean Bridoul.[19] This was because Bridoul had renounced his claim before the council.[20] It is possible that the aldermen tried to make an informal deal with Bridoul to avoid a decision of the Council of Flanders. In the end, the council did not reach a final decision.[21]

However, prior to 1459, appeals of merchants against the aldermen were almost unheard of. Appeals took place before the Council of Flanders, they did just not happen against Bruges. Domenico de Rapello of Genoa appealed against the aldermen of Sluis in 1449; Dierderic van Griwe of Cologne also appealed against the aldermen of Sluis in 1450; William of Penitor from England appealed a decision of the aldermen of Dendermonde in 1450; Angelo Tani did so against the aldermen of Wervik in 1453; Abraham Sampson against Sluis in 1455; Giorgio Centurione from Genoa against the aldermen of Ostend in 1458; and Luciano Spinola from Genoa against the aldermen of Menen in 1459. Germans were present, but never in direct conflict with the aldermen of Bruges. Although it is possible that these lower aldermen benches had genuine concerns about these appeals against their authority, it is unlikely that this had greatly moved the Four Members.

The ordinance issued by Philip the Good on 15 February 1459 presents an entirely different picture of the state of appeals in Flanders. In contrast to earlier attempts at centralisation, he decreed that his princely court for the County of Flanders would only hear cases on final judgments, not on interlocutory decisions. Any rulings relating to jurisdiction or other procedural matters were no longer subject to appeal. If such an appeal was made, it could be summarily dismissed, and the vexatious appellant would be fined 60 lib. gr. In addition, the costs of an appeal were raised. Henceforth, Duke Philip decreed, litigants would have to provide a surety guaranteeing the sum for which they were condemned in the first place, and a surety to pay a possible fine in case were to be considered a vexatious appeal.[22]

Interestingly, the ordinance was requested by the cities of Flanders.[23] The Four Members lamented several existing wrongdoings. On the one hand, they claimed that the County of Flanders was endowed with rich privileges giving way to a sufficient judicial system that was perfectly capable of fulfilling its tasks. On the other, they claimed that Flanders also knew the unique situation where the land was founded on trade and commerce. The wealth of Flanders had to be preserved. However, these presumably daily appeals disrupted this beneficial equilibrium. The cities believed that if matters continued, trade would vanish from the country, and the County of Flanders would decline rapidly, impoverishing both the cities and the duke. Thus, the Four Members concluded, commercial cases should be exempt from appeals: in the preceding decade or so, appeals before the Council of Flanders were so frequent that 'it was almost impossible to reach a final decision or it was appealed'.[24] Disaster loomed on the horizon, but luckily the Duke of Burgundy was a generous ruler who immediate banned these interlocutory appeals.[25]

However, by specifying what could not be appealed, the duke also clarified what could be. Nowhere in the ordinance was it stated that foreign merchants were prohibited from appealing to the Council of Flanders. Until 1459, this had been a compromise between the city and merchants, where the city either bribed or pressured the merchant community into compliance. In the registers containing decisions from March 1459, we can see Carlo Renoncini making the first appeal against a judgment from the aldermen.[26] As the graph suggests,[27] after 1459 reformations against the aldermen of Bruges dramatically increased.[28] Although it would take some time before the aldermen were condemned in an appeal, the trend was nevertheless obvious.

Between 1459 and 1477, a trickledown effect occurred where merchants gradually found their way to the Council of Flanders. Bruges did all it could to stop this, but also accommodated itself to this new situation. Centralisation was not a linear process.[29] The councillors were not necessarily the prince's perfect representatives, but stood at an intermediate level between the cities and the prince. The councillors rarely used their right to summon cases from

Bruges to their council.[30] What did happen was that in their litigation strategies, merchants could seek a decision from the Council of Flanders and bring their case to that level. As the case was initiated, negotiations would take place on whether or not the Council of Flanders was competent to consider a case. Afterwards, it was still possible that the council members considered a case wrongly appealed. This is the relevant evolution.[31] This happened each time a case was brought before the Council of Flanders and it is apparent that the confidence of the council members grew.

The events of 1477 underline the non-linearity of this process. The death of Duke Charles the Bold gave the cities the necessary space to reclaim much of their independence. The Burgundian land complex was preserved, but the cities were now – albeit temporarily – demanding a say in government. One of those crucial moments was, of course, when the cities addressed their complaints about the previous regime and made them conditional on their acceptance of the next. The heiress, Mary of Burgundy (1477–1482), had no other choice than to comply. The Burgundian Netherlands, Flanders and several cities received privileges. These privileges insisted on the property rights of merchants, cracking down on the corruption of ducal officers and curbing centralistic tendencies.[32] It is in this light that the cities abolished the Parliament of Mechelen. Duke Charles founded the court in 1473 and apparently behaved more aggressively towards evoking cases before its court than the Council of Flanders.[33] The irony of history is that in 1477 the – by then – Three Members of Flanders favoured the survival of the Council of Flanders over the Parliament of Mechelen.[34]

The 1477 privileges stated that the Parliament transferred all pending cases to the Council of Flanders.[35] The Council of Flanders could continue, but was drastically limited. It was forbidden to take notice of cases at first instance from Flemish inhabitants. Of course, in cases of appeal, the privileges of 1477 decided that if an appeal was requested, the Council of Flanders would treat it as a case in written procedure and *ex eisdem actis bene vel male*. The 1477 privilege forbade the Council of Flanders from considering new arguments.[36] If the aldermen won the case and the Council of Flanders considered the decision to appeal vexatious, the fine remained. However, if the aldermen lost the case and the aldermen's decision was found unjust, the Council of Flanders would not demand the fine. The aldermen reasoned that since they did their best to grant good justice, they could not win or lose before the Council of Flanders. They complained that previously, if they won, they would receive no compensation but just avoid a fine. If they lost, they would pay a fine and be reprimanded.[37] Also, concerning the costs of a procedure, these should be levied on the party who won the case. Since claimants would benefit from the judgment, they should also be prepared to suffer its disadvantages.[38] In brief, the rough edges of the Council of Flanders were polished away for the different cities, while appeals turned into a more expensive and possibly more risky procedure.

Yet the cities chose to preserve the Council of Flanders. The decision to keep the council can be explained by the appearance of citizens of Bruges and even the city of Bruges before the court. Since the first half of the fifteenth century, Bruges had used the Council of Flanders as a staging ground to launch attacks against other competitors, notably the Liberty of Bruges and the Proosse of Saint-Donaas. Both had their jurisdictions within or close to Bruges while not under their authority. Obviously, most of their quarrels were fought before the Council of Flanders.[39] Furthermore, the citizens of Bruges were frequent visitors to the court. When in 1463, three citizens from Bruges Marc Despars, Nicolas Pierins, and Jan Kone were denied compensation of 12 lib. gr against Jan Salamanque from Castile before the aldermen, they tried their luck before the Council of Flanders.[40] The court accepted their case, and the citizens again tried to pressure the guarantor into paying the debt.[41] We do not know any more details, but their attempt to circumvent the aldermen of Bruges is telling.

Such cases were forbidden after 1477, but it demonstrates that even the citizens of Bruges recognised the advantages of the court. Moreover, after 1477, the Council of Flanders proved useful for Bruges. For example, Bruges did not hesitate to sue the city of Sluis when the latter threatened Bruges' interests.[42] Unfortunately for the cities, these clauses would have no lasting effect on the stream of appeals that came before the Council of Flanders. In the years immediately after 1477, Bruges received a couple of suspicious decisions from the Council of Flanders that were in the city's favour. However, quite quickly the councillors were back to their normal way of doing business. Unmistakably, by this point the Council of Flanders had become a part of the legal landscape of Flanders and the cities accepted this. Of course, this begs the question as to what the difference was with the other princely courts and why Bruges tried to avoid the influence of these institutions.

THE GREAT COUNCIL

When, in 1477, the cities chose between the Council of Flanders and the Parliament of Mechelen of the Burgundian duke, the former triumphed over the latter.

The Great Council and the Parliament of Mechelen were the results of the increasing power of the Burgundian dukes. As these dukes amassed more and more territories, their own council became more trans-regional. This was already the case by the end of the fourteenth century, but it was under Philip the Good that it became clear that regional courts like the Council of Flanders, the Council of Brabant or the Court of Holland (*Hof van Holland*), had their merits but were relics from a time when there were fewer dominions. Although we cannot convincingly attribute the foundation of a new state to the Burgundian dukes, it is clear they no longer limited themselves to a personal union between the duchies and counties.[43] The expansion of territories and the disconnection between duke and duchy resulted in a new more trans-regional elite in both jurists and advisors. It was only a logical evolution that in the 1440s – we do not know the exact date – the Great Council came into being.[44] As the Great Council was not founded by princely ordinance, but rather grew out of practice, there is no clear definition of its jurisdiction. Again, the vagueness was an asset, rather than an obstruction. The Great Council also looked after the princely prerogatives and as such became a direct competitor to the Council of Flanders. In addition to the regional courts protecting the princely prerogatives, there was now a trans-regional court doing exactly the same thing. In this section, I will question whether merchants capitalised on this complexity.

The Great Council grew out of the duke's personal council – the *Hofraad* in Dutch.[45] This council remained in existence, advised the duke and followed his movements, while the Great Council would increasingly remain stationary and had a specific legal task. Van Rompaey credits this to a transformation period of about ten years (1435–1445) in which the Great Council becomes a court in its own right, separate from the personal council.[46] For several reasons, this was a slow evolution. The establishment of a central judicial court with competence over the *pays de par-deça* (*van herwaarts over*), known as the Low Countries, would have provoked the Four Members profoundly, especially when it could hear appeals.[47] Therefore, the 1446 ordinance, when the Great Council was already functioning, was very cryptic on what it could and could not do.[48] In addition, we must understand that the creation of such a court was not part of any grand design. The Council of Flanders and the Great Council had overlapping competences, which illustrates the unplanned nature of these courts. The Burgundian duke needed a trans-regional court, but had not yet figured out how it related to the other already existing courts.

The scale of the Great Council had its advantages. This is illustrated by the actions of the Portuguese Vincente Gil, who obtained a judgment from the aldermen court of Damme. Six years before the decision, Gil had sold wine to a certain wine merchant named Jacome, but allegedly, the wine had still not been paid for. The aldermen of Damme agreed that the wine was indeed sold and therefore should be paid for. Nevertheless, Vincente Gil believed enforcement of the decision would be highly unlikely. The wine had already been resold making revindication impossible, and Jacome was nowhere to be seen. To increase his chances of indemnification, Gil went to the Great Council to make the judgment enforceable in the entire County of Flanders.[49] This way, he could proceed to seize the merchandise from the French wine merchant. The initiative Vincente Gil took is remarkable, but also closely related to the duke's own authority.[50] As Van Rompaey indicated, the activities of the Great Council were very closely intertwined with the Duke Charles the Bold, until it started to operate more as an independent court. The Parliament of Mechelen remained sedentary, but the Great Council initially followed the duke.[51]

The close link between the duke and the court was an advantage neither the Council of Flanders nor the local aldermen possessed. Therefore, these courts acted cautiously when a potential conflict arose. This is illustrated in the case of the Genoese Luigi Geno and Antoine Machet from Piedmont in 1468. Each merchant had the other imprisoned, claiming outstanding debts. Since they found themselves in the city's prison, the imprisonment was discussed by the city's aldermen. The aldermen found the imprisonment just, but Antoine Machet signalled another problem.[52] He believed that the aldermen of Bruges could not decide upon the case, because litigation before the Great Council had already been initiated.[53] Since no one could be brought to court twice in the same case, Antoine Machet believed that he should be acquitted by the aldermen.[54] The aldermen decided that the possibility of having the same case dealt with by different courts should be taken seriously, temporarily suspended their procedure, and investigated the case.[55] If the aldermen had proceeded, they risked incurring the indignation of the duke. When the aldermen found out that this had been a ruse, they proceeded under their own authority. In December 1468, they sentenced Antoine Machet for falsely imprisoning Luigi Geno.[56] Tellingly, the aldermen of Bruges were careful in their confrontations with the duke. If the aldermen believed their rights were being infringed, they did not shun confrontation. However, if the case was deemed less important, they remained more circumspect in their dealings with the Great Council.

Whereas the aldermen of Bruges were careful, the Council of Flanders harboured a different attitude. Both the Council of Flanders and the Great Council were princely courts. Appeals from these courts were nevertheless not very popular among the council members of both courts. This is one of the big mysteries of the Great Council, and further research in non-commercial cases is absolutely necessary, but all indications point towards preferring not to cross swords too frequently.[57] Because their jurisdictions overlapped, the choice was open to the litigants as to where they brought their cases. Forum shopping was something that had to be done with caution. Although possible, hopping from one court to another was frowned upon. For example, in cases of maritime plunder both courts could investigate breaches of princely safe conduct.[58] Of course, since there was a close alignment with the Burgundian duke and most cases of maritime plunder had exceptionally high stakes, parties often brought them to the Great Council.[59] But if a case was brought first to the Council of Flanders for whatever reason, it would be handled there.

For example, when Jacob Boven and six other fishermen and/or plunderers were accused of abusively taking the vessels of Breton merchants Jennet Henry and Aleyn L'Espeau, the case was brought before the Council of Flanders. The sailors nonetheless immediately appealed the case before the Great Council, while the Council of Flanders had not yet reached a decision.[60] The defendants argued that such an action seriously trespassed on the authority of the Council of Flanders.[61] The members of the Great Council agreed and fined the Flemish sailors for a vexatious appeal and remanded back to the Council of Flanders. This does not mean that they respected each other's jurisdictions, or that there was some sort of a division *ratio materiae*.[62] Rather, in the period before the Parliament of Mechelen, the Great Council and the Council of Flanders refused to cross the swords in commercial matters and thus existed side by side rather than in a hierarchical structure.[63]

The Parliament of Mechelen was another matter. The successor to the Great Council was clearly envisioned as a supreme court for the territories in the Low

Countries. We can clearly see a hierarchical structure here. It is apparent that there was a difference in attitude between the Council of Flanders and the Parliament when dealing with the aldermen of Bruges. Both would frequently accept appeals from Bruges, but whereas the Council of Flanders would seldom condemn the aldermen, the Great Council was more aggressive. In particular, the possibility of revision and evocation was loathed by the cities.[64] Revision entailed that a decision pronounced by a court could be revoked within ten years on grounds of fault in the facts (*propositie van erreur*). With it, Charles the Bold had introduced a legal figure very similar to something the French king introduced a century before. Though it was not often used by the duke, this sword of Damocles could hang over the head of a city for quite some time.[65] It is important to note that the initiative lay with the duke and not his court. Evocation, or the act of transferring a case to a higher court, could only be done with letters patent from the sovereign.[66] Admittedly, the right of evocation was used more regularly under Charles the Bold and the cities grew to dislike the Parliament.

The attitude of the Parliament of Mechelen diverged significantly from its predecessor. Take the case between the Spanish merchants Fernando de Spinosa and Alonso de Medina. They were involved in a longstanding quarrel for an unpaid debt of 238 lb. gr., which Alonso de Medina had contracted when he was younger. Nonetheless, Fernando de Spinosa demanded the repayment. In order to make the matter more pressing, he detained both the merchandise and books and letters of the firm to which Alonso de Medina belonged.[67] This was quite a drastic decision and the aldermen reacted in the most lenient way they could. On 7 September 1473, the aldermen set up a commission consisting of the aldermen Jacob Coolbrandt and Jan Van and two merchants from the Bourse.[68] This arbitration should have evaluated the case in all seriousness, taken its time, heard all the parties and inspected all relevant accounts.[69]

The intentions of the aldermen were sincere, but apparently the parties were less scrupulous. Although they both appeared before the commission, neither wanted to give in and the two aldermen saw themselves obliged to return the case to the entire college. Alonso de Medina asked for more time to make sure that his brother, who was head of the firm, could come to Bruges. He could represent him and bring the relevant accounts. In the meantime, he requested that his merchandise should not be seized. To make sure this was the case, Alonso had obtained letters from the Burgundian duke.[70]

Fernando de Spinosa, however, believed that as the merchandise was present, it was also liable for seizure. Any delay would just give Alonso the time to disappear. Furthermore, Fernando demanded a fine, as he believed that Alonso had broken off the arbitration.[71] The aldermen decided that, albeit on the condition of a surety, Alonso de Medina should be granted a delay until 5 April and the aldermen acquitted him from paying the fine for breaking the arbitration.[72] The letters from the duke nevertheless irritated the aldermen. The ducal letters granted an extension, but Alonso de Medina did not give any proof that progress had been made in bringing forward the relevant accounts. The aldermen kept postponing the case.[73] In June 1474, Alonso de Medina again asked for a delay of six months, while Fernando de Spinosa wished to proceed. The aldermen believed their good graces were being abused and decreed that Alonso de Medina should answer the claims of Fernando de Spinosa within a week, with or without these accounts.[74] Alonso appealed this decision of the aldermen before the parliament. The parliament agreed with him that the aldermen had defaulted on justice because they did not give him the chance to procure the relevant evidence.[75] Intentionally or not, Alonso de Medina had outplayed the aldermen of Bruges.

We see two different narratives. From the Bruges' proceedings, everything indicates that Alonso de Medina was *malafide* and delayed any execution of his signed obligation. From the parliament's records, we can see the aldermen of Bruges eagerly pushing for justice and denying it in the process. Of course, there are two sides to every story but we can say that the reaction of the Great Council and its interference with Bruges law was more profound than it was with the Council of Flanders. Merchants knew this, and were keenly aware that they could bypass Bruges by going directly to the duke's supreme court.

THE PARLIAMENT OF PARIS

Although the cities of Flanders had a healthy distrust of 'novelties', they certainly found the Parliament of Mechelen provocative. In particular, the right of evocation was keenly felt dearly by the cities, which raises the question of how the cities – and litigants – reacted towards the other institution employing the right of evocation.[76]

Paradoxically, the biggest ally against these princely courts was probably the Parliament of Paris. This French court had jurisdiction in Flanders, and, as Serge Dauchy has noted, in the fifteenth century the court was as much an ambiguous tool of princely power in Flanders as it was an option for the Flemish cities to countermove princely centralisation efforts.[77] By appealing judgments from the Council of Flanders and the Great Council before the Parliament, the Flemish cities tried to undermine these courts. The cities took the initiative in this respect, but the results varied. The Parliament of Paris regularly confirmed the judgments of the Council of Flanders or the Great Council, and in so doing, strengthened the position of princely courts in Flanders. Of course, the logic of the gentlemen from Paris was that the parliament was still the sovereign court over Flanders, but they also wanted these 'regional' courts to do their job and not just be bypassed.

Yet every time the Parliament of Paris did counteract the Burgundian duke, it dealt the latter's aspirations of sovereign jurisdiction a blow. In order to counteract this French influence, the Duke of Burgundy bargained with the King of France for the non-acceptance of cases from Flanders for brief periods.[78] First conceded in 1445, via a bribe of 5,000 riders, the king promised to suspend all criminal cases from the Flemish aldermen benches until 1454.[79] In 1447, all civil appeals were suspended. In 1455 a second term was initiated.[80] Although there were still some daring merchants who tried to undercut the aldermen benches of the cities, merchants rarely sought redress before the court.

Before the 1460s, two kinds of appeals from Bruges reached the Parliament of Paris: appeals made by merchants against smaller cities, and appeals by the city of Bruges made when the latter believed this to be in its own interest. In 1448, the city of Bruges did not hesitate to drag Jeanne de Bethune, Countess of Ligny, Lady of Ghistel, before the Council of Flanders and before the Parliament of Paris when this turned out unfavourable.[81] Together with the Venetian nation, the aldermen of Bruges believed the excises of Damme, a responsibility of the lord of lady of Ghistel, had surpassed the boundaries of reasonablness. When the Council of Flanders disagreed with them, they went to the Parliament of Paris. Similarly, when they believed the city of Sluis was infringing their staple privileges and the decision taken by the Duke in 1441, Sluis was summoned before the French court.[82] Again, the Parliament of Paris was mainly a court of opportunity.

Bruges used the Parliament to its advantage but when the shoe was on the other foot and when its own judgments were appealed, Bruges was not so thrilled with the French involvement.[83] In the fifteenth century, only two periods qualify where merchants could explore the full possibilities of the Parliament of Paris.[84] The first was from 1460 until 1471 and the second after 1477 until 1521.

In the first phase before 1471, we can see how the parliament was consciously used by merchants as a forum for lamenting perceived 'injustices' and in some cases, even to outrun Flemish local law. Richard Copping and Richard Heron attributed these intentions to John Valdin, John Tac and Philips Vadeban. They were all Calais staplers trading in the Low Countries, yet they had another opinion on conflict resolution. The three merchants were stopped/attacked by Richard Heron and Richard Copping on their way to Flanders. The latter seized their merchandise under the pretext of being a part of a larger debt.[85] The validity of the claim is difficult to assess, but according to the three merchants it was actually a simple robbery. Since there was a peace between England and Flanders at that moment and the Burgundian duke had given them safe conduct, they should be compensated. However, such safe conduct protected against capricious arrests and robberies, but not against distraints. Richard Heron believed that it was the latter and additionally argued that sureties had been given and a procedure was initiated before the aldermen of Bruges. Nevertheless, the three merchants believed the princely right of safe conduct was infringed and petitioned the Duke. He agreed and summoned the case before his court starting a quarrel with the aldermen of Bruges, who believed the case should be considered before their court.[86] Richard Heron tried to counteract this move and quickly appealed before the Parliament of Paris.[87]

As we can see in his arguments before the Parliament of Paris, he feared that the three merchants were trying to escape justice. Since they were merchants of the staple and because one of them was a mayor in Calais, he feared they wanted the case to proceed in Calais, under the law of the staple.[88] Richard Heron argued that they had no intention of coming to a decision.[89] It was a self-fulfilling prophecy. The other Englishmen argued before the Parliament of Paris that they were Englishmen and considered to be the traditional enemy of France. Hence, they did not owe obedience and requested that the case was considered under the law of the staple in Calais, an English enclave.[90] The Duke of Burgundy believed this was an utter affront to his jurisdiction and demanded that the Parliament of Paris remand the case.[91] Heron nevertheless maintained that the safe conduct was issued by a subject of the king (in this case the Duke of Burgundy), and should therefore be dealt by his court.[92] Without truly realising the irony of it all, Richard Heron accused the three English merchants of just choosing the judge where they wanted to litigate.[93]

After lengthy discussions, Richard Heron won his case.[94] Throughout almost the entire proceedings the quarrel was about which courts should be 'respected', which court was 'disrespected' in the procedure, and whether or not the case should even have ended up before the Parliament of Paris. At the same time as the French king once again accepted appeals from Flanders, merchants started regularly appealing the decisions from the aldermen before the Council of Flanders and the Great Council. The phenomenon of merchants appearing before the Parliament of Paris fits perfectly in the general trend of the 1460s of merchants seeking recourse at higher courts. This is confirmed by the arguments that came before the Parliament of Paris: most discussions revolved around its competence to hear cases from Flanders.[95]

This would remain so until Louis XI once again suspended appeals before the Parliament. The last suspension was a concession given by the French King Louis XI in 1468 after a short war and an even shorter 'arrest' of the king by the Burgundian duke Charles. If Louis XI were to break any of the stipulated clauses, the Parliament of Paris would have no more jurisdiction over Flanders. This clause was triggered in 1471 when King Louis declared war on Burgundy and gave Duke Charles a pretext to forbid anyone to litigate before the Parliament of Paris. Instead, litigants should direct themselves to his own Great Council and from 1473 the Parliament of Mechelen. However, this last court would not survive his creator. With the death of Charles the Bold and the abolition of the Parliament of Mechelen, the Parliament of Paris made its re-entry. First, it re-emerged informally from 1477 onwards; later on formally in 1484 when Louis re-established in the Treaty of Arras that the Parliament of Paris was a court of appeal for Flemish judgments.[96]

The Parliament of Paris is both an example of how merchants sought the best court of appeal and of how they also respected the limits of litigation. While in the 1460s merchants were questioning the decisions of the Council of Flanders and the Great Council in Paris, merchants remained silent in the 1480s and 1490s. The death of the Burgundian duke disrupted the ban on appeals between 1471–1477. Merchants and nations could once again seek recourse before the Parliament of Paris.[97]

Instead of merchants using the Parliament of Paris to their advantage, the aldermen of Bruges were the ones using the Parliament of Paris to contain the increasing influence of the Council of Flanders.[98] When Diederic Basdau and Hendrik Croesen appealed the decision made by arbiters of the Hanse, this was a sensitive case for the aldermen in the 1490s.[99] As previously explained, arbitration was a cornerstone in the conflict resolution model in late medieval Bruges. Even if appeals were becoming more frequent before the Council of Flanders, the aldermen did not condone appeals on arbitrations. According to the aldermen, arbitrations were not liable for appeal – certainly not when they were confirmed by the aldermen bench.[100] They made their stance crystal clear before the Council of Flanders, but the latter nevertheless annulled the decision of the arbiters and fined them 60 lib. parisis. For the aldermen, it was a grave intrusion on their authority, and they appealed the decision before the parliament of Paris. Curiously, when Basdau and Croesen tried to have the second appeal dismissed on the basis that it was not appealed in time, the aldermen of Bruges answered that as the Hanseatic merchants were not inhabitants of the County of Flanders, they were not bound by this rule.[101] This was a strange explanation for not respecting the proper procedure. The Parliament of Paris made a compromise between both parties. They annulled the appeal, the arbitration and all legal steps that were taken after the arbitration and sent the case back to the aldermen of the Bruges.[102] In this way, the Hanse won because it kept the dissident merchant in check, but Bruges also won because the decision of the Council of Flanders was also annulled.

The interference of the Parliament of Paris was not as straightforward as one might expect from this royal court. The court had autonomy after King Louis XI and was no longer a political instrument of the French king. The number of merchants appearing before the Parisian court was limited and thus we can never truly know the intentions of the members of parliament towards the Flemish commercial cases. It is nevertheless noteworthy that the common scheme of first appearing before the Council of Flanders and consequently appealing before the royal court had completely disappeared. Occasionally it was used by the Bruges aldermen and it still had the possibility to be used by these foreign merchants but, for some reason, they were no longer interested. An explanation can be found in the profile of these litigants.

When the appeals for Council of Flanders increased in the 1460s, the Council itself reacted quite hesitantly and did not immediately give solace to these merchants. In the 1460s, it was still quite uncommon to appeal decisions from Bruges before the Council. The possibility existed, but the actual belief as to how far this council could go was something that had to grow case by case. Therefore, the Parliament of Paris was still a viable option for merchants who understood the political relations. The French king was definitely able to accept cases before his court and although his influence on the procedure was uncertain, there was little doubt as to whether the Parliament of Paris had the confidence to 'correct' the aldermen of Bruges and even the Council of Flanders. By the 1480s and 1490s, the judicial landscape had shifted. The council members did not hesitate to correct the aldermen of Bruges and even the Great Council of Mechelen was growing in importance.[103] In 1477, the Parliament of Mechelen had been abolished, and the Great Council returned to its ambulant form. However, the court quickly re-established itself in Mechelen and regained much of its importance in the decades that followed. By the sixteenth century, the authority of the Council of Mechelen was firmly established.[104]

NOTES

1. Buntinx, *De Audiëntie van de graven van Vlaanderen,* 238–263.
2. RAG 691, *Raad van Vlaanderen, Placcaarten en ordonnantiën*; 1385 (vs); 'Instruction par les gens du conseil', 234.
3. Verfaillie, *Au coeur de la court,* 1–3.
4. Van Rhee, *Litigation and legislation,* 27; De Schepper, 'Recht en administratie', 365–367.
5. The same principle was of course in play before the Great Council; Van Answaarden, *Les Portugais devant le Conseil,* 82–83.
6. RAG 7509, *Raad van Vlaanderen, Interlocutoire Sententiën,* fol. 92 v.
7. See for political frustrations: Dumolyn, *Raad van Vlaanderen,* 39–41.
8. Also, their 1359 privileges stated that if the stolen merchandise was found in the County of Flanders, this should be restored without any form of justice; Gilliodts-Van Severen, *Inventaire des Chartes,* vol. 2, 53, art. 44.
9. As Fredirik Buylaert has mentioned, the lord of Maldegem, who depended on the Burg of Bruges, was mentioned in the convocation list for the Land van Waas and the area around Dendermonde as a certain Philippe de Maldeghem; Buylaert, *Repertorium van de Vlaamse adel,* 456; Buylaert e.a. eds., 'De adel ingelijst', edition, nr. 4; Verstraete, 'Het domein', 121–130.
10. RAG 7509, *Raad van Vlaanderen, Interlocutoire sentenciën,* 146 v.
11. The Council of Flanders combined the function of princely and feudal court: Heirbaut, *Over heren,* 192–197; Opsommer, *Omme dat leengoed,* 260.
12. The prison guardian of Dendermonde had already been imprisoned for the escape of these plunderers; RAG 7509, *Raad van Vlaanderen, Interlocutoire sentenciën,* 147 v.
13. The city of Ghent was less shy in this respect. See Boone, *Gent en de Bourgondische hertogen,* 182–183.
14. See, for example, Bruges against Sint Donaas: RAG 2359, *Raad van Vlaanderen, Acten en Sententiën,* 1441–1442, fol. 22 r., 84 r. 194 r., 321 r., Liberty, 284 v. Sluis, 431 r.–432r.
15. Ganshof, 'Etude sur le faussement de jugement', 138–140; Ganshof, 'Les transformations', 58.
16. Monballyu, 'Appelatien en Reformatien', 253–254.
17. Blockmans, *Handelingen van de Leden van Vlaanderen,* p. 413, n. 357.
18. RAG 2360, *Raad van Vlaanderen, Acten en Sententiën,* 1442–1443, fol. 117 r.; 123 v.; 131 v.; 141 v.; 166 v.; AN, X^{1A}, *Parlement de Paris, Plaidoiries,* 14799, fol. 258 v.–260 r.
19. SAB 216, *Stadsrekeningen Brugge,* 1442–1443, fol. 65 r.
20. RAG 2360, *Raad van Vlaanderen, Acten en Sententiën,* 1442–1443, 233 r.
21. It is even possible that Bruges paid for such a development. The writings cost a total of 36 Flemish pounds, making them rather expensive documents. See SAB 216, *Stadsrekeningen Brugge,* 1442–1443, fol. 65 r.
22. RAG 2377, *Raad van Vlaanderen, Acten en Sententiën,* 1458–1459, fol. 1A v.; RAG, 34280, *Raad van Vlaanderen,* fol. 16 v.–20 r.; SAB 96, *Rodenboek A,* fol. 195 r.–196 v.; Confirmed in 1515: SAB 96, *Sententiën,* fol. 116 r.–118 v.
23. SAB, *Politieke Charters,* 1082; SAB, *Rodenboek,* fol. 195 r.–196 v.
24. RAG 2377, *Raad van Vlaanderen, Acten en Sententiën,* 1458–1459, fol. 1A v.

25. In contrast, Wielant claimed that the 'reformation' was introduced '*in faveur van justicie ende van der coopmanschappe ende ooc om t'onderhouden van der rechten, previlegien ende usaigen van den Vierscharen ende Leenhoven ende ander Justitie van den Lande*'; Wielant, *Practijke civile*, 290.
26. RAG 2378, *Raad van Vlaanderen, Acten en Sententiën*, 1459–1459, fol. 109 v.
27. The graph is divided along the different registers. As some registers span multiple years, some years have multiple registers and some years have no registers at all, this division gives the fairest distribution of appeals.
28. In the redaction of the graph some choices were made. First, the registers of the Council of Flanders covered varying periods (sometimes three months, sometimes an entire year) and some registers even overlap for certain periods. In addition, they are not preserved fully. Several years are missing, while we have entire years for others. Therefore a division per year is almost impossible. We chose to group them per register and not per year because at least the reader knows how long a register is and thus how many appeals appeared. The material is too fragmentary. Furthermore, we only noted when an appeal was initiated. Some cases dragged on for years but would only inflate the graph and distort the material. Lastly, we also studied the material pre-1447 but its inclusion would make the graph unreadable.
29. Van Peteghem, *De Raad van Vlaanderen en staatsvorming*, 181–182.
30. See for example: RAG 2401, *Raad van Vlaanderen, Acten en Sententien*, 1473–1474, fol. 18 r.
31. RAG 2379, *Raad van Vlaanderen, Acten en Sententiën*, 1459–1460, fol. 306 r.; RAG 2387, *Raad van Vlaanderen, Acten en Sententiën*, 1464–1464, fol. 198 r.
32. Blockmans, 'Corruptie, patronage en makelaardij', 234.
33. SAB 96, *Zwartenboek*, fol. 12 v.–13 r., art. 26.; Although it could also happen before the Council of Flanders. For example, the case between Juan Lopez against Bruges, where Lopez obtained letters of evocation and brought the case before the Council of Flanders; RAG 2399, *Raad van Vlaanderen, Acten en Sententiën*, 1473–1474, fol. 18 r.
34. The privileges also included the destruction of the Liberty of Bruges as a Fourth Member, which was considered as too princely. The rural nobility dominated the liberty. SAB, *Politieke Charters*, 1153; SAB 96, *Zwartenboek*, fol. 40 v.–41 r.
35. SAB 96, *Zwartenboek*, fol. 14 r., art. 31.
36. SAB 96, *Zwartenboek*, fol. 13 v., art. 28.
37. SAB 96, *Zwartenboek*, fol. 13 v., art. 28.
38. SAB 96, *Zwartenboek*, fol. 13 v., art. 29.
39. See, for example, how Bruges used the Council against Bonnore Olivier. The latter was a Burgundian official and thus his behaviour was lamented before the Council of Flanders: RAG 2386, *Raad van Vlaanderen, Acten en Sententiën*, 1463–1464, fol. 56 r.; SAG 2386, *Raad van Vlaanderen, Acten en Sententiën*, 1463–1464, fol. 282 v. In the 1480s, the citizens of Bruges did the same thing to complain about their *écoutete* Pieter Lanchals.
40. RAG 2386, *Raad van Vlaanderen, Acten en Sententiën*, 1463–1464, fol. 89 v.
41. RAG 2386, *Raad van Vlaanderen, Acten en Sententiën*, 1463–1464, fol. 89 v. It was immediately appealed; RAG, 2386, *Raad van Vlaanderen, Acten en Sententiën*, 1463–1464, fol. 90 r.
42. RAG 2411, *Raad van Vlaanderen, Acten en Sententiën*, 1480–1480, 205 r. –206 r.
43. Stein, *Magnanimous dukes*, 148.

44. Although Wielant states that the Great Council was established around 1455–1456, archival research has shown that this is implausible; Wielant, 'Recueil des Antiquités', 133–134; Gaillard, 'L'origine du Grand Conseil', 267–324; Van Rompaey, *De Grote raad van de Hertogen van Bourgondië*, XI.
45. Van Rompay, 'Het ontstaan van de Grote Raad', 298; 304–305.
46. Van Rompaey, *De Grote Raad*, 22–23.
47. Gilissen, 'De grote Raad van Mechelen', 27. The Burgundian dukes were always cautious to stress the contractual relation with their subjects and not to offend them too much; Braekevelt and Dumolyn, 'Diplomatique et discours politiques', 336–337.
48. Braekevelt, 'Un prince de justice', 45–47.
49. ARA, Chartes de l'Audience 957.
50. In addition, he was a known face before the Great Council; Van Answaarden, *Les Portugais devant le Grand Conseil*, 105–109; Miranda, *Portugal and the medieval Atlantic*, 239–240.
51. Van Rompaey, *De Grote Raad*, 47–49.
52. 157, *Civiele Sententiën*, 1465–1469, fol. 170 v.
53. SAB 157, *Civiele Sententiën*, 1465–1469, fol. 170 v.
54. SAB 157, *Civiele Sententiën*, 1465–1469, fol. 170 v.
55. SAB 157, *Civiele Sententiën*, 1465–1469, fol. 171 r.
56. SAB 96, *Groenenboek ongecotteerd*, fol. 243 r.
57. In the ordonnances of 1439, 1451 and 1463, the Council of Flanders was still considered to have sovereign jurisdiction in the County of Flanders. Although this never truly manifested, it may explain why the Great Council was hesitant to reform the judgments. In the early-modern period this would be a moot point between the Council of Flanders and the Great Council of Mechelen; Monballyu, 'De Raad van Vlaanderen', 77–78, 89.
58. Wielant, 'Recueil des Antiquités', 133. See, for example, a letter from Charles the Bold in 1469 to the Council of Flanders stating the need to be firm against maritime plunderers: RAG 691, *Raad van Vlaanderen, Placcaarten en ordonnantiën*, 1469.
59. Wijffels, 'Justitia in commerciis', 32, 49–50.
60. ARA, *Fonds Grote Raad*, 796.30, fol. 62 v.
61. ARA, *Fonds Grote Raad*, 796.30, fol. 63 r.
62. See for an example regarding tolls: RAG 34288, *Collectie van de Advocaat-fiscaal J.B. Van Steenbergen*, Rekenkamer van Rijsel, Grote Raad van Mechelen en Raad van Vlaanderen: hun respectievelijke bevoegheid.
63. See on the available source material: Wijffels; 'Dutch litigation', 545; Oosterbosch, *Grote Raad*; De Smidt and Strubbe, 'Chronologische lijsten', 1–12.
64. Although we could find no commercial cases where the Great Council used this figure; Leyder, *Les archives*, 25–26. Rompaey, *Grote Raad, Ordonnance de Thionville*, 503, art. 29.
65. Miscarriage of justice was not accepted; Dauchy, *Les voie de recours*, 59–60; Wijffels en Koster, 'Les procédures en révision', 72–73.
66. Wielant, *Causes Civiles*, cap. 180; Van Rhee, *Litigation and Legislation*, 86.
67. SAB 165, *Civiele Sententiën Kamer*, 1473–1474, fol. 10 r.
68. Piero Perandrea and Nicolas de Poge.
69. SAB 165, *Civiele Sententiën Kamer*, 1473–1474, fol. 1 r.; Gilliodts-Van Severen, *Cartulaire d' ancien Estaple*, vol. 2, n. 1171.
70. SAB 165, *Civiele Sententiën Kamer*, 1473–1474, fol. 21 r.
71. SAB 165, *Civiele Sententiën*, 1473–1474, fol. 11 r.–v.

72. SAB 165, *Civiele Sententiën Kamer*, 1473–1474, fol. 11 v.
73. On 4 May another delay of a week was accorded; SAB 165, *Civiele Sententiën Kamer*, 1473–1474, fol. 19 v., 21 r., 24 v.
74. SAB 165, *Civiele Sententiën Kamer*, 1473–1474, fol. 33 v.
75. ARA, *Fonds Grote Raad*, 793.79, fol. 214 r.–215 v.
76. Although, the parliament saw itself somewhat as the guardian of the *royaute* instead of being the guardian of the *roy*; Stocker, 'Office and justice', 378; Auzary-Schmaltz and Dauchy, 'Le Parlement de Paris', 207.
77. Dauchy, 'De Vaamse appels', 279; Dauchy, 'Le parlement de Paris, juge contraignant?' 151. However Charles VII and Louis XI dared to use the parliament for political gains: Hildesheimer and Morgat-Bonnet, *Le parlement de Paris*, 241–246; UAG.HS.3795, *Extraits des Antiquits de Flandre*, fol. 71 r.–v.; RAG 3371, *Varia D.*
78. Being Bruges, Ghent, Ypres and the Liberty of Bruges.
79. SAB 96, *Groenenboek* C, fol. 220 r.–223 r.
80. Something that was of course done without *prevendicie* of his right to hear these appeals; SAB 96, *Groenenboek* C, fol. 220 v.–221 r.
81. AN, X1A, 4801, *Parlement de Paris, Plaidoiries*, fol. 221 r.; Van Caenegem, *Appels Flamands*, vol. I, 550–552.
82. See the accord: AN, X^{1C}, 172, *Parlement de Paris, Accords*, 51–54; Van Caenegem, *Appels Flamands*, vol. I, 452–455.
83. As we have seen in the case of Thomas de Marquil and Jean Bridoul. Both appealed, but were met with stiff resistance of the aldermen of Bruges.
84. Dauchy, 'Le Parlement de Paris', 372. During the English rule of Paris (1420–1436), the Parliament of Paris also functioned and accepted appeals from Flanders. However, Flemish subjects enjoyed preferential treatment, as the English king had proclaimed them to be equals to his own subjects and the parliament was partially staffed with confidants of the Burgundian duke. Therefore, the cities could probably obstruct any merchants from appealing. We could not find any examples; Allmand and Armstrong, eds. *English suits*, 6–7.
85. AN, X^{1A}, 4807, *Parlement de Paris, Plaidoires*, fol. 132 r.–132 v.
86. AN, X^{1A}, 4807, *Parlement de Paris, Plaidoires*, fol. 133 r.
87. This was a direct provocation towards the duke's authority and he had to appeal twice; Van Caenegem, *Appels Flamands*,
88. Or at least wanted to flee the aldermen of Bruges; AN, X^{1A}, 4808, *Parlement of Paris, Plaidoires*, fol. 71 r.
89. AN, X^{1A}, 4807, *Parlement de Paris, Plaidoires*, fol. 135 v.
90. AN, X^{1A}, 4808, *Parlement de Paris, Plaidoires*, fol. 13 v., 152 v.–153 r. In the early 1460s, Calais was under de facto ownership of the Count of Warwick. A possible hypothesis would be that the three English merchants were better friends of the Count of Warwick than Richard Heron. See for references to the War of Roses: AN, X^{1A}, 4807, *Parlement de Paris, Plaidoires*, fol. 133 r.; 135v–136 r.
91. AN, X^{1A}, 4807, *Parlement de Paris, Plaidoires*, fol. 133 r.
92. AN, X^{1A}, 4807, *Parlement de Paris, Plaidoires*, fol. 135 v.
93. AN, X^{1A}, *Parlement de Paris, Plaidoires*, fol. 135 v.
94. Van Caenegem, *Appels Flamands*, 421. Although he would not enjoy it for very long. In 1470, the Englishman was accused of bribery and the Great Council condemned him to eternal banishment and the confiscation of all his valuables; ARA, *Fonds Grote Raad*, 790.7, fol. 19 r.–22 r.

95. AN, X^{1A}, 4809, *Parlement de Paris, Plaidoires*, fol. 24 v., 27 v., 98 r., 102 r.–v.
96. Dauchy, *Les arrêts et jugés*, vol. III, 118–119; Dauchy, 'De Vlaamse appels', 310.
97. Influence in Flemish politics was another matter; Dauchy, *Les arrêts et jugés*, vol. III, 120.
98. A more symbolic example was the demand of the French King Charles VIII that Maximilian appeared before the parliament of Paris and answered for the 'infringements against the privileges of the Flemish cities'; SAB, *Politieke Charters*, 1233.
99. Van Caenegem listed the parties as Conrad Handeman with the *procureur-generael* of Flanders against the aldermen of Bruges and Dierderik Basdau and Hendrik Croesen, but in reality the Conrad Handeman was supported by the aldermen of Bruges, while Diederik Basdau and Hendrik Croesen were supported by the aldermen of the Hanze, of which they were also members; Van Caenegem, *Appels Flamands*, 616–617; RAG 7510, *Raad van Vlaanderen, interlocutoire sententiën*, fol. 303 r.–305 v.
100. In addition, Basdau and Croesen accused the aldermen of Bruges of poor management of their prison: RAG 7510, *Raad van Vlaanderen, Interlocutoire Sententiën*, fol. 304 r.
101. AN, X^{1A}, 8323, *Parlement de Paris, Plaidoires*, 744 v.; AN, X^{1A}, 1504, *Parlement de Paris, Conseil*, fol. 197 r.
102. Van Caenegem, *Appels Flamands*, 618.
103. De Schepper, 'De Geheime Raad', 40.
104. RAG 34280, *Raad van Vlaanderen, Collectie van de advocaat-fiscaal J.B. Van Steenberghen*, fol. 1 r.–4 r.

9

Merchants Using the Princely Courts

Knowledge is power, cash is king. Bruges and the Burgundian duke had enough resources to litigate for prolonged periods before princely and royal courts. However, this was not so straightforward for individual merchants. In our assessment of how and why foreign merchants forum shopped and how far could they use the legal complexity to their benefit, the next logical step is to determine who these merchants appearing before the courts actually were. This group of 'forum shoppers' had to overcome two main problems. To begin with, these merchants had to have the resources to keep a case pending before a court for several years and had to incur a potential liability to pay for the trial costs, while at the same time keeping their own expenses in check.[1] There can be little doubt that litigation before a princely and royal court was a protracted and expensive activity.[2] In addition, these forum shoppers needed to have the (legal) knowledge to appear before these courts. In contrast to the aldermen court, the princely courts were the playing field of jurists. Roman-Canonical law was thoroughly known in the Great Council and the Parliament of Paris used its own legal structures that were not so easily understood.[3] Did foreign merchants forum shop? I will argue that some did and others did not. There was a small group who went forum shopping and this group did their utmost to extract the maximum return from their cases. However, these forum shoppers were a small group of merchants who had the financial means and knowledge to bring their cases to the different courts of the County of Flanders in the hope of bringing them to a satisfactory conclusion. As mentioned above, they needed to know the political context, understand the workings of these courts and estimate their response towards such an appeal. The majority of merchants lacked this knowledge and could not risk the drain on their finances, making them vulnerable to these *forum shoppers*.

FORUM SHOPPERS? MERCHANTS SEIZING THE INITIATIVE

To begin with, one had to possess capital before embarking upon litigation. Princely courts, such as the Council of Flanders, demanded a provisional sum to be deposited before litigation could proceed. Parties needed to pay for procedural documents that were produced, and litigants had to be careful not to incur exorbitant expenses, fines and damages to the other party. We do not possess any accounts that indicate the costs of these proceedings, but for medieval Bruges, the city accounts were scattered with notes about Bruges incurring judicial costs.[4] These costs could range from small notations for writs or the payment of the proctors who litigated on behalf of the city, to vast sums intended for the 'advancement of cases'.[5] It would be naïve to believe that the city was the only one bribing officials. Also, for merchants, the expenses could spiral seriously out of control.

For Bruges, the case against the English Richard Moyn, Willem Moor, Willem Borgoys and Thomas Cost probably remained a painful memory. The English merchants claimed they had sold the Castilian, Barthelemy Ribe, cloths in Antwerp in 1443, but never saw any payment.[6] The Castilian merchant had a different opinion, and stated that he had already satisfied the Englishmen and would not do so again. When the English initiated their case before the aldermen of Bruges, they were left frustrated. The Bruges aldermen concluded that there was not enough evidence for a condemnation, and provided the Castilian merchant with the option to give an oath that he had paid the amount.[7]

The English merchants did not plan to leave it at that. They demanded a reprisal letter from the English king and subsequently used the same letter to leverage the Burgundian duke into reopening the case. This was a smart move from the merchants. Whereas it was unlikely that the aldermen of Bruges would have been blackmailed, the Burgundian duke had little stomach for a potential international incident. He evoked the case before the Council of Flanders. Bruges refused to appear before the Council of Flanders, but nonetheless, the council members agreed with the Englishmen that there were indeed irregularities and condemned both Barthelemy Ribe and the Bruges aldermen to pay a fine.[8] Bruges in turn, appealed the decision before the Parliament of Paris. The English argued that this was an absurdity, since the city's representatives failed to show up at the Council of Flanders in the first place. The aldermen of Bruges fought back and claimed that as the commissioners did not hear the witnesses or see the correct letters, their decision was without merit.[9] In so doing, the aldermen gave a curious twist to their nonappearance before the court. The Parliament of Paris was not won over by such tactics and after twenty years of litigation, the Parliament decided the complaint of the Englishmen was justified.[10] Bruges was ordered to pay the costs of the case, an advance payment on the sum to be claimed from Barthelemy Ribe, as well as the customary fine for a vexatious appeal.[11] The Bruges aldermen had lost in dramatic fashion and Serge Dauchy calculated the city had to pay 920 lib. 8 s. 7 d. as honoraria for the proctors and advocates, 13 lib. 3 s. for advice, 76 lib. 13 s. 4 d. as travel reimbursements, 39 lib. 3 s. for the drafting of several documents, and 9 s. 5 d. for the services of the bailiff of Amiens.[12] In addition, they had to pay a fine of 60 lib. parisis (which was 11 lib. 2 s. 9 d. gr.) and they had to pay 513 lib. 11 s. gr. in advance to the English merchants.[13] Luckily for Bruges, they could negotiate a deal with the claimants in which a percentage was paid to end the case. The aldermen rightfully feared the 'rigorous execution of the sentence', and only paid 200 lib. from the 513 lib. 11 s. gr.[14]

After all of this, they also had to intervene in the procedural costs the English had made for over 2,000 lib. gr. Bruges only paid after the heirs of the merchants threatened to drag Bruges before the Parliament of Paris once again. A compromise was found on a sum of 400 lib.[15] The case ended with a total cost of 1,969 lib. 13 s. 1 d. gr. or about 157 years' work for a master mason.[16] Bruges was a wealthy city, but we can only wonder how far merchants were willing to go. In this case, these merchants had to be careful that the expenses did not rise above the actual stakes of the case. Of course, one could claim before the court that the expenses were paid by the adversary but this could also – once again – entail years of litigation.

Unsurprisingly, some merchants arguably used these aspects of the courts in order to raise the stakes.[17]

There is little doubt that a case before a princely court was an expensive matter, not least because legal knowledge came at a price. Merchants appearing before princely courts had to rely upon proctors and advocates who charged handsome honoraria.[18] They pleaded before the Council members and made sure the correct procedural steps were taken. While advocates were schooled in law, this was not expected of the proctors who had to be familiar with the necessary procedural steps and the customary law of the County.[19] They were not part of the princely court, but were private individuals, who swore an annual oath of good conduct before the prince and offered their services to individuals.[20] Jan Dumolyn estimates that their number never exceeded a dozen at the Council of Flanders and that the cities and towns always came back to the same three or four proctors, including Jan van Overbeke, Lodewijk Hauweel and Rogier de Mol.[21] They were the key to litigating before the Council of Flanders.

Yet these proctors only facilitated access to princely courts to a limited degree. They made the procedural steps of submitting the necessary documents, but the decision to appear before a court and to keep a case was still made by the litigants themselves.[22] The choice to litigate before these courts was one made in the belief that they would bring more reward than the previous ones. Undoubtedly, there were abundant procedures where cases were dismissed on the basis of procedural faults like 'not respecting the terms' or 'disrespecting princely ordinances'. Nevertheless, from the proceedings of those who did litigate frequently, we can see how they must have had precise knowledge of the procedures and even the law that was practised.

Such differences may have motivated litigants to go forum shopping. For example, the Bruges' aldermen were allowed to make a claim against either the principal or the guarantee. The Council of Flanders' custom entailed that a creditor first had to make a claim against the principal and only when this failed, make a claim against the guarantor.[23] The presence of Roman law is an uncertainty here. Since the aldermen never registered the motivation for their decisions and almost all arguments are lost, we can never precisely know how far the average merchant knew Roman-Canonical law. This notwithstanding, there are clear indications that it was something that could be used before the aldermen as an argument.

Of course, these merchants never reached the level of those who were university-trained lawyers. However, these merchants, in particular the Italians, were inclined to use Roman law in their arguments.[24] Strubbe even believed that merchants used Roman law not only to supplement the existing law, but also to confront customary law at the high courts. As such, the presence of *ius commune* at these princely courts gave foreign (mostly southern) merchants an advantage they did not have in Bruges.[25] For Bruges, the only case where we have evidence of those arguments is the earlier discussed Pazzi-bank case from 1480. The merchants litigating the case were in no way legal scholars and the aldermen court of Bruges did not demand any knowledge of the *ius commune*. Yet the parties used whatever was at their disposal to bring their case home. On several occasions, this also included founding their arguments on excerpts from the *ius commune*. This is not to say that the aldermen of Bruges were completely convinced by them, or requested their application; Roman law just stood among the other arguments based on Flemish customary law, Florentine law, the statutes of the nation, letters from the pope, and common sense.[26]

These considerations indicate that a group of merchants combined financial capital with knowledge of how these courts reacted, interacted and sometimes even overreacted. Members of the Lomellini family are a great illustration of the specialisation of one family that would henceforward litigate persistently between the different courts of the Burgundian Netherlands. The family was already well entrenched in the Bruges market and social life from the beginning of the fifteenth century.[27] They most likely started in the alum trade; they appear frequently as insurers, and quickly had several members present in Bruges.[28] As knowledge was transferred from generation to generation, we can also presume that they were well aware of the political context of the Burgundian Low Countries.

In 1459, Paolo Spinola appealed a decision of the aldermen in favour of Carlo Lomellini. The case was dismissed and Spinola was fined the usual fine of 60 lib. par., but the Lomellini quickly had a taste for more.[29] A year later Jeronimo Lomellini would appeal a judgment of this aldermen of Bruges and Jan de Baenst.[30] The Genoese would do so with success.[31] Tommaso Lomellini lodged claims in 1461 against Jacop vander Poele before the council,[32] Jeronimo Lomellini against the aldermen of Bruges and Jacques Philips in 1461,[33] Ottobono Lomellini as representative of the Genoese nation against several members of the Spanish nation in 1472–1473, and as representative of the family against Joos van Varsenare and Anselmus Adoorne in 1473.[34] The pride of the family, at least in matters of litigation, must have been the brother of Ottobono, Lazzaro Lomellini. The latter would appeal decisions from the aldermen with such regularity that one can only assume that he was either an incredibly persistent man, or that he achieved some success in litigating before princely courts.[35] In 1474, he immediately summoned the Four Members of Flanders before the Council of Flanders after they had dared to seize his corn. Technically Lazzaro Lomellini was at fault because he had used princely letters to transfer corn from one ship to another, without intending to bring it to Flanders. This was a grave infringement against the corn staple, which entailed that all corn arriving in Flanders also had to be sold in Flanders.[36] The Four Members promptly took possession of Lazzaro's corn, and the latter subsequently brought his case before the Council. Once there, the Four Members had to soften their stance and allowed the corn to be sold this time out of Flanders, without prejudice (damage) towards their corn privileges.[37]

Most of the judgments we have from these cases are mere procedural matters that do not reveal the reason for the quarrel.[38] This is complicated by the fact that most cases did not lead to a final decision, and it is very difficult to make a formal assessment of the Lomellini before the Council of Flanders.[39] They nevertheless fit into a general scheme where mainly Italian and other merchants with poor privileges took the initiative in the post-1459 period. They were the first to actively lodge claims against the aldermen of Bruges or other princely officials. In the 1460s and 1470s the families of the Lomellini, Doria,[40] Spinola,[41] Dandulo[42] pursued the most aggressive strategies in this respect.[43] These families combined their networks and their knowledge of the Bruges system, as noted in earlier chapters, with the fixed residence and necessary capital to run to the Council of Flanders and elsewhere.[44] Some of them had already used the Council of Flanders to sue smaller cities and their consequent reappearance suggests some success.[45] As final decisions are rare, it might have been a tactic used by these families to outbid their opponents. They were the most efficient before these princely courts, having the expertise and financial capital.

Their victory was, of course, not a given and depended on the counterparty. Domenico de Rapello was a merchant who knew his way around the different courts, but would also meet his match in the form of Jan van Stillebeke.[46] De Rapello had arrested Jan van Stillebeke as a guarantor of the Catalan merchant François de Casesage in 1443. De Rappelo held him accountable for the debt and imprisoned him to press him for payment. Apparently, De Rapello had no interest in initiating a procedure before the aldermen of Bruges, since he kept it in Sluis. The Sluis aldermen nevertheless believed that the arrest was made abusively and ordered the release of Jan van Stillebeke. Domenico de Rapello felt poorly treated and appealed the decision before the Council of Flanders.[47] Before this princely court, de Rapello apparently made a convincing case. The Council members annulled the decision of the aldermen of Sluis and stipulated that the aldermen had to pay a fine. However, Jan van Stillebeke appealed the judgment of the Council of Flanders before the Parliament of Paris. But unfortunately for him, Domenico de Rapello was again able to convince the members of the parliament of his righteousness. The case was sent again to the Council of Flanders and the appellant had to pay the 60 lib. par. fine.[48] The case was sent back to the Council of Flanders, but here Domenico de Rapello would again prove to be a skilled litigator.

A bitter struggle took place between Domenico de Rapello and Jan van Stillebeke.[49] The Council of Flanders quickly decided that the aldermen of Sluis made a spurious judgment, but did not determine how much the aldermen and Jan van Stillebeke should pay to the Domenico de Rapello. Domenico demanded the additional payment of the expenditures he had made, in addition to the payment of the surety (which he valued at 300 lib par.).[50] Eventually, the Council of Flanders gave him a hundred golden riders, because Jan van Stillebeke had abused the law.[51] Yet still this was not the end of the case. After ten years of litigation, Jan van Stillebeke had found an irregularity where he claimed that Domenico de Rapello should have provided a surety after the judgment of the aldermen in Sluis, back in 1445, according to the local custom.[52] The Council of Flanders decided that they would tackle this matter by referring it to a procedure by the commissioners.[53] This is the last we hear of the case. Be that as it may, neither of the parties was ready to give in. Although the picture of Jan van Stillebeke is quite unclear, everything points towards a Domenico de Rapello who was keenly aware of the legal framework of his day and used it to maximum effect.[54] Although it took ten years to reach a conclusion (and we are not certain what that conclusion was), it was already an impressive feat to have the entire surety recognised, but still Jan van Stillebeke proved to be an equal match.

Although the Italians were the first to make regular visits to the different courts, they did not remain the only ones. Quite quickly, individual German, English, Spanish and Aragonese merchants and sailors used the Council of Flanders as an option in their litigation strategies.[55] These were also merchants without the extensive benefits the merchant communities gave them. Merchants like the previously mentioned Vincente Gil,[56] members of the Pardo family, or de Medina were found litigating before the Council of Flanders more than once.[57] German merchants could also appear, without having the help of the Kontor Secretary.[58] Obviously, the Hanse was not a monolith capable of controlling every action of its merchants. However, the fact that merchants who still defined themselves as belonging to the Hanse, appear before the Council of Flanders, shows the initiative they could possess. In the end, it was not nationality that defined whether or not merchants appeared before the council, it was initiative.

THE IMPACT OF FORUM SHOPPING

The forum shopping in which these merchants engaged, had an impact on Bruges. It should be emphasised that the majority of merchants still aimed to resolve their disputes before the aldermen, with only a few having recourse to princely courts. Be that as it may, when such cases did arise, they presented a significant challenge for the aldermen. When a case was brought at first instance before a higher court, it eroded the aldermen's authority to a certain extent. For example, in Bruges, the aldermen believed that matters concerning the merchant communities fell under their jurisdiction. However, what happened when a merchant community decided to present their case before a princely court, such as the Council of Flanders? Although the aldermen could request a *renvoi*, or request to bring the case back to the aldermen, they would only receive a favourable decision if all the other parties agreed. This process of *renvoi* could considerably prolong the case, potentially leading to greater costs for the aldermen. In addition, each time the aldermen failed to receive a *renvoi*, it set a precedent for the Council of Flanders to judge upon these cases.

Consequently, as the fifteenth century drew to a close, it became normalised that the merchant communities went to the Council of Flanders. We should not overstate the impact of this evolution. While it is true that these cases in the first instance were a blow to the control the Bruges' aldermen had over the different nations and their internal affairs, it did not severely undermine Bruges' legal authority. However, the appeals that were started were an important blow to their authority. Our focus on appeals can be explained by the impact they had on the legal system of medieval Bruges. As have seen, the number of appeals against the aldermen of Bruges rose in the 1460s. In case of an appeal, the Council of Flanders would assess whether the aldermen of Bruges had carried out their function as judges.[59] Accusations of poor justice, the resulting fines, and the potential for the aldermen to be condemned based on previously unknown arguments made appeals particularly difficult for them to accept.[60]

As far as possible, the aldermen were eager to minimise the impact of appeals.[61] In 1477, they prohibited the Council of Flanders from convicting them based on previously undisclosed evidence, but the court soon reverted to its old practices.[62] Appeals continued into the 1480s, leading the aldermen to realise that a more refined procedure, with an emphasis on written arguments, would provide them with greater protection in the event of appeals. Importantly, however, there were considerable differences between the legal frameworks of Bruges and the Council of Flanders. One striking example is arbitration, which the aldermen were keen to retain within their sphere of influence. As previously noted, arbitration procedures allowed for more time, expertise and authority, attributes often lacking in the more expedited chamber processes. Consequently, arbitration was among the most significant legal mechanisms in Bruges, constituting a core aspect of its judicial system. Arbiters were responsible for settling disputes, and the aldermen expected their decisions to be final. In theory appeals were not allowed, as – via the *compromissum* or agreement – both parties had committed to honour the arbiters' final ruling or face substantial penalties.

If the decision was appealed, it undermined the finality that arbitration was intended to have. In this way, arbitration's role as a mechanism for settling disputes shifted, becoming part of the merchants' litigation strategy. The aldermen could approach the merchants or their community and persuade them to bring the case back to Bruges. This informal approach had the advantage of having the case withdrawn from the princely court, thereby avoiding a final decision on the matter. However, this strategy relied on the goodwill of the merchants and their community and was not a viable solution given the number of appeals occurring in the 1470s and 1480s. For example, in 1448, Battista Gambaro appealed his arbitration decision to the Council of Flanders. Subsequently, the aldermen of Bruges engaged with the Florentine nation and persuaded them to convince Battista to withdraw his case from the Council of Flanders and return it to Bruges. When this endeavour faltered, the case was again presented before the Council of Flanders. The aldermen then appealed to the Great Council, which led to the French king – at Battista's behest – referring the case to the Parliament of Paris. The aldermen challenged this jurisdiction but were ultimately unsuccessful.[63]

The aldermen's court could attempt to persuade the Council of Flanders that such cases should remain within Bruges' jurisdiction. If a judgment was rendered in their favour, they could then use it as a precedent in future cases, arguing that all appeals related to arbitration should remain under their authority. In 1477, for instance, the aldermen succeeded in obtaining a ruling from the Council of Flanders affirming that arbitration was indeed a long-standing tradition (*prouven coustume*) and that cases involving arbitration should be brought before the Bruges aldermen, who alone had the authority to review them.[64] In the years after 1477, ducal power was restored and arbitrations of foreign merchants would again find their way to the Council of Flanders.[65] In the late 1480s and 1490s, appeals against arbitration were once again lodged before the Council of Flanders.

The cities could not control the court. In addition, if the court deemed a decision unjust, it could even increase it competence and render a judgment anyway.[66] This was also the case in the Council of Flanders when the Scottish nation and Jan and Pauwels van Kerckhove were in dispute in 1459. Some unspecified members of the Scottish nation were involved in an altercation with the Kerckhoves. The reason why is unclear, but the case itself quickly came before the Bruges aldermen's court. The Scottish nation decided not to wait for the aldermen's decision and organised a gathering where they went as a mob to the Kerckhoves' house and attacked and wounded them.[67] In the fight some Scottish merchants were also wounded, and the nation demanded reparations. Curiously, the Bruges aldermen did not intervene, but proposed an arbitration by the Bishop of Saint Andrews, who happened to be in the city at that time.[68] The bishop decided that Jan and Pauwel van Kerckhove were responsible for the disturbance and punished them. Without hearing their pleas, he condemned them to beg forgiveness before deputies of the aldermen of Bruges and the Scottish nation and to make a pilgrimage to Rome and Santiago de Compostela. The aldermen did not intervene in the case and the brothers went to the Council of Flanders. The Council of Flanders considered the arbitration as unjust and invalidated it.[69]

The third option involved modifying their own procedures. In the late 1460s and early 1470s, rather than referring cases to merchant arbiters, the aldermen began instructing the parties to submit to the judgment of 'men' (*mannen*).[70] These men were not further specified but the aldermen tended to remain in closer contact with them than in previous arbitrations. For example, if the parties could not come to an agreement within a certain time period the case was *de iure* referred back to the aldermen. The time schedule that these men had seems to have been shorter, although this is difficult to determine because the aldermen noted an 'appointment to men' instead of the *compromissum*. These men were not specified or named, but they had the same task as their predecessors. For example, in a case between Jan Dynant, a merchant from England, and Jan van Amsterdam, a merchant from Holland, it was specifically stated that the parties had to appoint men who were competent in bills of exchange.[71]

Furthermore, evidence presented before these men was also presented before the aldermen when the procedure failed.[72] The involvement of the aldermen remained clear. They kept track of the procedure, could intervene in the production of evidence and could bring the case back before their court when the arbiters could not agree, or when one of the parties did not abide by the *compromissum*.[73]

This evolution was perfectly illustrated when the aldermen passed it to their own clerks instead of referring a case to anonymous men.[74]

The Council of Flanders also posed a threat regarding debt imprisonment and the associated sureties. As previously noted, a key objective of debt imprisonment was to secure the debtor's release on the condition that proper legal procedures would be observed and the aldermen's judgment respected. Problems arose, however, when merchants refused to comply and instead appealed to the Council of Flanders. By doing so, they could evade the surety, disregard their promise to remain within the jurisdiction of the Bruges court, and grant the Council of Flanders influence over the management of Bruges' prison – a matter Bruges considered firmly within its own sphere of authority.

Take the case between Roderigo Catalan and a money changer, Nicholas de May. Catalan, an Aragonese merchant, owed money to de May. Catalan alleged that de May had extorted more than owed, resulting in his imprisonment and seizure of possessions. Catalan, fearing further imprisonment, relented and agreed to pay what de May demanded.[75] Subsequently, Catalan was freed on the condition that he should use this freedom to collect the money, but, once Catalan had left prison, discussion arose over the total amount he had to pay. Nicolas imprisoned Catalan again, and the latter brought his case before the aldermen. The aldermen confirmed his imprisonment, and Catalan appealed the decision before the Council of Flanders. The aldermen were confronted by the Council of Flanders, which had to decide whether these urban magistrates had acted correctly in their function as representatives of the count. Despite the aldermen's attempts to limit the scope of the case, the Council of Flanders decided to release Catalan from imprisonment.[76]

In cases involving imprisonment, the aldermen implemented regulations to enhance debt imprisonment and avoid appeals. The demand for using legal captors was already established during the whole of the fifteenth century, but would become more pronounced towards the end of the century, when the aldermen started systematically fining perpetrators.[77] The aldermen increasingly demanded that their consent should be secured before an imprisonment, and we can observe bigger fines for those who ignored this.[78] Furthermore, the aldermen's influence over the actual prison grew. In 1480, they published a new prison ordinance, and in 1481 they received a dispensation from Duchess Mary of Burgundy and Maximilian of Austria to purchase the basement of the city's prison, which they bought in 1481.[79] The charter specified that this acquisition aimed to 'improve and increase incarceration in the city of Bruges', undoubtedly contributing to limiting princely intervention.[80]

The aldermen became increasingly meticulous in the second half of the fifteenth century. The growing number of appeals before princely courts led to more comprehensive documentation. The registers for 1465–1469 and 1469–1471 contain significantly more detailed procedural records than earlier ones, and even the cases themselves suggest that the aldermen were more thoroughly engaged with the concerns of merchants than in previous years. In the event of an appeal, the aldermen were well-prepared with all the necessary documents. This shift also led to the aldermen curtailing certain 'liberties' that merchants had previously enjoyed.

However, the aldermen's response was characterised by increased involvement rather than fundamental change. In terms of procedural adjustments and the introduction of Roman law, there is little evidence to suggest any marked differences. Antwerp, by contrast, was undergoing rapid transformations and rendered legal mechanisms such as debt imprisonment obsolete.[81] Despite the new challenges posed by the Council of Flanders, the Bruges aldermen adapted without making significant alterations to their legal framework. This continuity becomes even more apparent in the 1490s, when Bruges resorted to various measures, including legal reforms, in a bid to attract merchants back.

NOTES

1. See, for example, RAG 2407, *Raad van Vlaanderen, Acten en Sententiën*, 1477–1477, fol. 82 v.
2. See on this: Dauchy, 'The cost of plaiding', 181–193; Dauchy, 'Quelques remarques', 49–55; Van Rhee, 'Snelheid', 27; Oosterbosch, 'Appelprocedure', 14–15.
3. It was forbidden to use Roman-Canonical law in Paris, though it might have been used less explicitly; Pashel, 'L'usage du droit romain', 457–477.
4. See for payments of documents: SAB 216, *Stadsrekeningen Brugge*, 1452–1453, fol. 33 v. See, for example, remuneration for proctors: SAB 216, *Stadsrekeningen Brugge*, 1444–1445, fol. 54 r., 75 v.; or fines; SAB 216, *Stadsrekeningen Brugge*, 1485–1485, fol. 160 r.
5. SAB 216, *Stadsrekeningen Brugge*, 1455–1456, fol. 55 r.; SAB 216, *Stadsrekeningen Brugge*, 1455–1456, fol. 48 v.; although such benevolent actions were not forbidden in the fifteenth century, they were frowned upon; Zemon Davis, *The gift*, 110–111.
6. AN, X^{1A}, 8304, *Parlement de Paris, Plaidoiries*, fol. 264 v.; Van Caenegem, *Appels Flamands*, 368.
7. AN, X^{1A}, 8304, *Parlement de Paris, Plaidoiries*, fol. 265 v.–266 r; Van Caengem, *Appels Flamands*, 368.
8. The English mainly claimed that Barthelmy Ribe had not properly fulfilled his guaranty and thus left them open for damages. The Council members researched this and agreed with this stance; AN, X^{1A}, 8304, *Parlement de Paris, Plaidoiries*, fol. 264 r.–265 r.; SAB, *Politieke Charters*, 1094.
9. AN, X^{1A}, 8304, *Parlement de Paris, Plaidoiries*, fol. 266 r.
10. The case dragged on for so long that several parties had inheritors taking up their claim in 1476 and 1478; SAB, *Politieke Charters*, 1140, 1162, 1163.
11. SAB, *Politieke Charters*, 1164, 1169, 1170; AN, X^{1A}, 8555, *Parlement de Paris, Amendes*, fol. 65 v.
12. It should be noted that we follow S. Dauchy in the above-mentioned calculation, but that it is very hard to estimate the true extent of the expenses. A messenger could, for example, be sent for information in several cases at the same time but the aldermen would still register this as a single expense; S. Dauchy, 'The cost of plaiding', 190; SAB 216, *Stadsrekeningen Brugge*, 1449–1450, fol. 46 r., 47 r.; SAB 216, *Stadsrekeningen Brugge*, 1463–1463, fol. 26 r.; SAB 216, *Stadsrekeningen Brugge*, 1464–1465, fol. 28 r.; SAB 216, *Stadsrekeningen Brugge*, 1464–1465, fol. 53

v.; SAB 216, *Stadsrekeningen Brugge*, 1465–1466, fol. 48 r.; SAB 216, *Stadsrekeningen Brugge*, 1465–1466, fol. 50 r.; SAB 216, *Stadsrekeningen Brugge*, 1465–1466, fol. 53 v.; SAB 216, *Stadsrekeningen Brugge*, 1466–1467, fol. 50 v.; SAB 216, *Stadsrekeningen Brugge*, 1468–1469, fol. 104 r.

13. This was due to the fact that the aldermen of Bruges had released Bartelmy Ribe about four hours after the Englishmen had imprisoned for the execution of the decision of the Council of Flanders. Of course, Bartelmy Ribe quickly disappeared afterwards; AN, X^{1A}, 8304, *Parlement de Paris, Plaidoiries*, fol. 266 r.; Van Caenegem, *Appels Flamands*, 371.
14. SAB 216, *Stadsrekeningen Brugge*, 1465–1466, fol. 48 r.
15. SAB 96, *Groenenboek C*, fol. 175 r.–176 r.; SAB, *Politieke Charters*, 1164; SAB 216, *Stadsrekeningen Brugge*, 1478–1479, fol. 165 r.; SAB 216, *Stadsrekeningen Brugge*, 1479–1480, fol. 51 r.; SAB 216, *Stadsrekeningen Brugge*, 1480–1481, fol. 46 r. and SAB 216, *Stadsrekeningen Brugge*, 1481–1482, fol. 45 v.
16. Dauchy, 'De Vlaamse appels', 114.
17. Dauchy, 'The costs of plaiding', 192.
18. In 1485, the aldermen appointed Pierre Duret as a proctor for the cases from Bruges before the parliament of Paris and agreed he would be paid annually 100 lib. gr. for his services; SAB 216, *Stadsrekeningen Brugge*, 1485–1485, fol. 163 v.
19. Dumolyn, *De Raad van Vlaanderen*, 84–85; Dumolyn, *Staatsvorming en vorstelijke ambtenaren*, 222–223; Wijffels, 'Procureurs et avocats', 170–172. See on the Advocates: Martyn, 'Les avocats', 105, 108, 113.
20. Strubbe, 'De verordening van 1483', art. 16.
21. Dumolyn, *De Raad van Vlaanderen*, 85; SAB 216, *Jaarrekeningen Brugge*, 1491–1492, fol. 206 r.
22. RAG 23703, Processen par Escript, Zeger Parmentier c. Thomas Stevinszone, 1467–1470.
23. RAG 1259, Varia 2, *Costumen en Privileges van de Raad van Vlaanderen*, 35 r.
24. Before these courts, they were represented by advocates or proctors; Wijffels, 'L'influence de la doctrine', 147–148.
25. Strubbe, 'De receptie in de Vlaamse rechtbanken', 614. As Alain Wijffels mentioned, it should not be mutually exclusive, but rather some forms of 'romanisation' of existing rules; Wijffels, *Qui Millies Allegatur*, 21; Wijffels, 'Mos italicus', 116–117.
26. Daniels, *Die Verschwörung der Pazzi*, 136–137; ASF, *Carte Strozziane*, serie II, 21b, fol. 33 v.; 34 v.–35 r.; 40 r.; 57 r.
27. Petti Balbi, 'I rapporti', 9–18. Together with the Guistiniani families they were among the earliest Italians to commission works of art from the famous painter Jan van Eyck; Müller, 'Visual culture', 310; Borchert, 'The impact', 35.
28. Heers, 'Les Génois', 34–35; Lambert, 'De Genuese aanwezigheid in Brugge', 134–135.
29. RAG 2379, *Raad van Vlaanderen, Acten en Sententiën*, 1459–1460, fol. 306 r.; 391 r.; 465 r.
30. Most likely Jan II de Baenst; Buylaert, 'Baenst, Jan II de', 41–44.
31. RAG 2382, *Raad van Vlaanderen, Acten en Sententiën*, 1461–1461, fol. 445 r., RAG 2383, *Raad van Vlaanderen, Acten en Sententiën*, 1461–1462, fol. 22 r., 85 r.; RAG 2383, *Raad van Vlaanderen, Acten en Sententiën*, 1461–1462, fol 262 v., 302 r.
32. RAG 2383, *Raad van Vlaanderen, Acten en Sententiën*, 1461–1461, fol. 199 r.
33. RAG 2383, *Raad van Vlaanderen, Acten en Sententiën*, 1461–1461, fol. 298 r.; RAG 2384, *Raad van Vlaanderen, Acten en Sententiën*, 1462–1462, fol. 74 r.

34. RAG 2398, *Raad van Vlaanderen, Acten en Sententiën*, 1472–1472, fol. 225 r.; RAG 2400, *Raad van Vlaanderen, Acten en Sententiën*, 1473–1473, fol. 1 v., 85 r., 161 v., 201 r., 293 v.
35. Against Bruges and the Company of Piero Merulo et co.: RAG 2398, *Raad van Vlaanderen, Acten en Sententiën*, 1472–1472, fol. 69 r., 100 v., 223 r.; RAG 2399, *Raad van Vlaanderen, Acten en Sententiën*, 1473–1474, fol. 119 v., RAG 2400, *Raad van Vlaanderen, Acten en Sententiën*, 1473–1473, fol. 21 v., 187 v., 219 v. Against Bruges and Loys Miron: RAG 2400, *Raad van Vlaanderen, Acten en Sententiën*, fol. 201 r., 256 r.; RAG 2402, *Raad van Vlaanderen, Acten en Sententiën*, 1474–1475, fol. 243 r. Against Bruges and Alfonso Conantin: RAG 2400, *Raad van Vlaanderen, Acten en Sententiën*, 1473–1473, fol. 262 v., 294 v. Against the water bailiff: RAG 2401, *Raad van Vlaanderen, Acten en Sententiën*, 1473–1474, fol. 122 v., 136 v., 196 v.; defence against Fernando de Salves: RAG 2403, *Raad van Vlaanderen, Acten en Sententiën*, 1475–1475, fol. 218 r.; defence against Willem Dapper: RAG 2411, *Raad van Vlaanderen, Acten en Sententiën*, 1480–1480, fol. 9 r., 37 r. See for the Lommelini outwitting the chambre des comptes by going directly to the duke: ADNB, 17712, *Lettres missives et dépêches*, Bruges.
36. Tits-Dieuaide, 'Le grain et le pain', 453–491.
37. A logical stance from the Four Members, because if they had allowed this, it would have set a dangerous precedent for other merchants who wanted to sell corn to the highest bidder destabilising the populous region of Flanders; RAG 2401, *Raad van Vlaanderen, Acten en Sententiën*, 1473–1474, fol. 70 v.
38. See, for example, a successful appeal: RAG 2400, *Raad van Vlaanderen, Acten en sententiën*, fol. 201 r. See for an example of an unsuccessful appeal, which was sent back to the aldermen of Bruges for a decision in fine: RAG 2400, *Raad van Vlaanderen, Acten en Sententiën*, 1473–1473, fol. 256 r.
39. However, some payments the city of Bruges had to make to these merchants indicate a couple of wins: SAB 216, *Stadsrekeningen Brugge*, 1512–1513, fol. 66 r.
40. RAG 2382, *Raad van Vlaanderen, Acten en Sententiën*, 1461–1461, fol. 273 r, 449 r.; RAG 2383, *Raad van Vlaanderen, Acten en Sententiën*, 1461–1462, fol. 223 r, 272 v; RAG 2385, *Raad van Vlaanderen, Acten en Sententiën*, 1462–1463, fol. 146 v., 230 v.; RAG 2386, *Raad van Vlaanderen, Acten en Sententiën*, 1463–1464, fol. 184 r., 412 r.; RAG 2387, *Raad van Vlaanderen, Acten en Sententiën*, 1464–1464, fol. 176 r.
41. RAG 2386, *Raad van Vlaanderen, Acten en Sententiën*, 1463–1464, fol. 428 v.; RAG 2391, *Raad van Vlaanderen, Acten en Sententiën*, 1467–1467, fol. 298 v.; RAG 2413, *Raad van Vlaanderen, Acten en Sententiën*, fol. 313 r., 340 v., 365 r., 384 r., 388 v., 458 v.–459 r.; RAG 2415, *Raad van Vlaanderen, Acten en Sententiën*, 1483–1484, fol. 40 r., 63 r.; RAG 2416, *Raad van Vlaanderen, Acten en Sententiën*, 1484–1484, fol. 143 r.; RAG 2417, *Raad van Vlaanderen, Acten en Sentenien*, 1484–1485, fol. 95 r.; RAG 2419, *Raad van Vlaanderen, Acten en Sententiën*, 1487–1488, fol. 130 r.–v., 130 v., 137 v., 176 r., 179 r.
42. RAG 2383, *Raad van Vlaanderen, Acten en Sententiën*, 1461–1462, fol. 265 v., 317 v., 336 v.; RAG 2384, *Raad van Vlaanderen, Acten en Sententiën*, 1462–1462, fol. 41 v., 230 v.; RAG 2385, *Raad van Vlaanderen, Acten en Sententiën*, 1462–1463, fol. 238 r.; RAG 2387, *Raad van Vlaanderen, Acten en Sententiën*, 1464–1464, Fol. 100 v., 143 r.; RAG 2389, *Raad van Vlaanderen, Acten en Sententiën*, 1465–1466, fol. 24 r.
43. Very often after the Council of Flanders had its last say over it, the case would also be pursued at the Great Council, the Parliament of Mechelen. In 1475 Lazzaro Lomellini even tried to have the same case before both the Council of Flanders and

the Parliament of Paris, prompting the defence to argue for malicious intent; RAG 2403, *Raad van Vlaanderen, Acten en Sententiën*, 1475–1475, fol. 218 r.

44. Obviously, the higher court supplemented their strategies. They still turned, when suitable, to the aldermen of Bruges, SAB 165, *Civiele Sententiën Kamer*, 1489–1490, fol. 34 v.–35 v.
45. See, for example, Luciano Spinola against the aldermen of Menen; RAG 2377, *Raad van Vlaanderen, Acten en Sententiën*, 1458–1459, fol. 367 v.–368 r.
46. Which might have been necessary. In 1435, the bailiff of Sluis accused him of collaborating with other maritime plunderers. ARA, CC, 13926, *Accounts of the bailiff of Sluis*, Florens Deschamps, 1435–1435, fol. 4 r.
47. Unfortunately, the court registers of the Council of Flanders for these years were lost, so we had to rely on the narration of the Parliament of Paris.
48. This was around 7 Flemish pounds, the yearly wage of a skilled laboured; AN, X^{1A}, 8854, *Parlement of Paris, Amendes*, fol. 26 r.
49. RAG 2365, *Raad van Vlaanderen, Acten en Sententiën*, fol. 408 r., 427 v.; RAG 2367 *Raad van Vlaanderen, Acten en Sententiën*, fol. 118 r., 145 v., 172 v., 189 v, 200 r., 271 v.–218 r.
50. RAG 2367, *Raad van Vlaanderen, Acten en Sententiën*, 1451–1452, fol. 217 v.–218 r.
51. RAG 2370, *Raad van Vlaanderen, Acten en Sententiën*, 1454–1455, fol. 429 v.
52. RAG 2373, *Raad van Vlaanderen, Acten en Sententiën*, 1456–1456, fol. 275 v.
53. RAG 2371, *Raad van Vlaanderen, Acten en Sententiën*, 1455–1455, fol. 182 v., 217 r., 234 v, 249 r., 270 r., 305 r., 374 v.; RAG 2372, *Raad van Vlaanderen, Acten en Sententiën*, 1455–1456, fol. 58 r.; 96 v.; RAG 2373, *Raad van Vlaanderen, Acten en Setentien*, 1456–1456, fol. 387 r.; RAG 2374, *Raad van Vlaanderen, Acten en Sententiën*, 1456–1457, fol. 60 r.
54. See also a case before the aldermen of Muide and, later, before the aldermen of Bruges; ARA, CC, 36576, *Accounts of the city of Mude*, fol. 10 v.; 14 r.; ARA, CC, 36577, *Accounts of the city of Mude*, fol. 12 r.; or against the lady of Vienne: RAG 2365, *Raad van Vlaanderen, Acten en Sententiën*, 1449–1450, fol. 408 r., 427 v.; RAG 2367, *Raad van Vlaanderen, Acten en Sententiën*, 1451–1452, fol. 118 r., 145 v., fol. 172 v., 189 v, 200 r., 271 v.–218 r.; RAG 2368, *Raad van Vlaanderen, Acten en Sententiën*, 1453–1453, fol. 6 r., 142 v.–143 r.; RAG 2370, *Raad van Vlaanderen, Acten en Sententiën*, 1454–1455, fol 424 r., RAG 2371, *Raad van Vlaanderen, Acten en Sententiën*, 1455–1455, fol. 182 v., 217 r., 234 v, 249 r., 270 r., 305 r., 374 v.; RAG 2372, *Raad van Vlaanderen, Acten en Sententiën*, 1455–1456, fol. 58 r., 96 v.; RAG 2373, *Raad van Vlaanderen, Acten en Sententiën*, 1456–1456, fol. 275 v., fol. 387 r.; RAG 2374, *Raad van Vlaanderen, Acten en Sententiën*, 1456–1457, fol. 60 r.
55. See, for example, the cases of Thomas Stevinsson (From Tetnay. There was also a Thomas from Boston): RAG 2391, *Raad van Vlaanderen, Acten en Sententiën*, 1467–1467, 298 v.; RAG 2392, *Raad van Vlaanderen, Acten en Sententiën*, 1467–1468, fol. 69 r.; RAG 2392, *Raad van Vlaanderen, Acten en Sententiën*, 1467–1468, fol. 101 r., 122 r., 125 r.; RAG 2395, *Raad van Vlaanderen, Acten en Sententiën*, 1470–1471, fol. 104 v., 164 r.; RAG 2396, *Raad van Vlaanderen, Acten en Sententiën*, 1471–1471, fol. 111 r.; RAG 2399, *Raad van Vlaanderen, Acten en Sententiën*, 1473–1474, fol. 106 r.; RAG 2400, *Raad van Vlaanderen, Acten en Sententiën*, 1473–1473, 79 v.
56. RAG 2409, 1478–1478, *Raad van Vlaanderen, Acten en Sententiën*, 1478–1478, fol. 59 r., 105 r.; RAG 2411, *Raad van Vlaanderen, Acten en Sententiën*, 1480–1480, fol. 71 v.

57. Even Medina vs. Pardo: RAG 2409, *Raad van Vlaanderen, Acten en Sententiën*, 1478–1478, fol. 207 r.; RAG 2410, *Raad van Vlaanderen, Acten en Sententiën*, 1478–1479, fol. 52 r. and 168 r.
58. RAG 2408, *Raad van Vlaanderen, Acten en Sententiën*, 1477–1477, fol. 134 v., 173 r.–v.
59. In late medieval Flanders, most appeals were in fact called reformations (*reformatiën*). The difference between appeals was that some procedures to be respected and the general aversion the Flemish cities had against appeals (so it had another name); Monballyu, 'Van appelatien ende reformatien', 237–276. See also RAG 146, 'Style van procederen', fol. 34 v.–48 v.
60. Monballyu, 'Van appelatien ende reformatien', 253.
61. SAB 95, *Zwartenboek*, art. 25 en art. 26, fol. 20 r.
62. Monballyu, 'Van appelatien ende reformatien', 254; SAB 96, *Groenenboek B*, fol. 117 v.–118 v.
63. See for more detail: Fieremans, '"In the hope to have judged a good sentence as merchants"', 9–17.
64. SAB 157, *Snaggaertsvonnissen*, fol. 73 r.–76 r.; RAG 2406, *Raad van Vlaanderen, Acten en sententiën*, 1476–1477, fol. 182 r. and 239 r.; RAG 2407, *Raad van Vlaanderen: Acten en sententiën*, 1477–1477, fol. 82 r.–83 v.
65. RAG 7512, *Raad van Vlaanderen, sentences interlocutoires*, fol. 66 v.; 84 r.–89 r. See, for example, RAG 2418, *Raad van Vlaanderen, Acten en Sententiën*, 1485–1486, fol. 143 v., 177 r.; RAG 2419, *Raad van Vlaanderen, Acten en Sententiën, 1487–1488*, fol. 11 v.; 130 v.; 137 v.; 179 r.; RAG 7510, *Raad van Vlaanderen: sentences interlocutoires*, fol. 303 r.–305 v.
66. S. Dauchy, 'Le recours contre les décisions arbitrales en perspective historique', *Revue de l'Arbitrage* 4 (1999), 771–773; S. Dauchy, 'Les recours contre les sentences arbitrales au Parlement de Paris (XIIIe et XIVe siècles) la doctrine et la législation à l'épreuve de la pratique judiciaire', Tijdschrift voor Rechtsgeschiedenis 67, nr. 3–4 (1999), 271.
67. RAG 2379, *Raad van Vlaanderen, Acten en Sentencien*, fol. 299A r.
68. In 1459, the Bishop of St Andrews was James Kennedy; Macdougall, 'Kennedy, James (c.1408–1465)'.
69. RAG 2379, *Raad van Vlaanderen, Acten en Sentencien*, 1459–1460, fol. 299A r. The Council of Flanders believed that it could 'reduce' all arbitrations that were excessive (*excessijf*); RAG 1259, Varia 2, *Costumen en Privileges van de Raad van Vlaanderen*, fol. 31 v.
70. Before the 1460s the procedure only occurred sporadically: see SAB 157, *Civiele Sententiën*, 1447–1453, fol. 47. V. This is not to say that the former type of arbitration disappeared. Both forms existed side by side, but ordering parties to submit to 'mannen' became very common. Unfortunately, the registers end in 1471, so it is difficult to investigate how this tendency developed. See for example SAB 157, *Civiele Sententiën*, 1469–1471, fol. 4 r.
71. SAB 157, *Civiele Sententiën*, 1469–1470, fol. 67 r.
72. SAB 157, *Civiele Sententiën*, 1469–1470, fol. 29 r.
73. See for example: SAB 157, *Civiele Sententiën*, 1465–1469, fol. 65 v. It was even possible that a case first handled before the *vierschaar* could be referred to arbitration, with the chamber keeping track of the procedure; SAB 157, *Civiele sententiën*, 1453–1461, fol. 25 r., 30 r. and 31 r.
74. SAB 157, *Civiele sententiën*, 1465–1469, fol. 208 v.; SAB 157, *Civiele sententiën*, 1469–1471, fol. 58 v.; 118 r.

75. RAG 7512, *Raad van Vlaanderen, Interlocutoire Sententiën*, 1483–1485, fol. 84 r.; SAB 165, *Civiele Sententiën, Kamer*, 1478–1479, fol. 15 r.
76. RAG 7512, *Raad van Vlaanderen, Acten en Sententiën interlocutoires*, 1483–1485, fol. 86 r.
77. The legal captor is also important in the symbolic image. He represented the higher authority (city or duke) entitled to make the arrests: Roussel, 'La légitimité', 47, 52–53.
78. SAB 157, *Civiele Sententiën*, 1469–1471, fol. 61 v.; SAB 165, *Civiele Sententien, Kamer*, 1479–1480, fol 9 v., 19 r.; the fine of a capture 'without commission' was 50 lib. gr. in 1479: SAB 216, *Stadsrekeningen Brugge*, 1479–1480, fol. 37 r.
79. The prison beneath the actual prison of the city was held by a Joos van Varsenare, the bailiff of Bruges, as a fief from the Count of Flanders. For the dispensation, see SAB, *Politieke Charters*, 1180; for the transfer, see SAB, *Politieke Charters*, 1182; SAB 216, *Stadsrekeningen Brugge*, 1480–1481, fol. 182 r.
80. SAB, *Politieke Charters*, 1180; SAB 216, *Stadsrekeningen Brugge*, 1492–1493, fol. 7 r.
81. De ruysscher, 'Why we need a history of collateral rights', 303–304. See for the role of the *cessio bonorum* in this regard: De Ruysscher, 'Reconciling old and new', 43–44.

10

The End of Bruges' Legal Dominance

By the fifteenth century, Bruges was no longer the only commercial hub in Northern Europe.[1] The commercial world had become increasingly multipolar with developing centres in London and Antwerp. While in the fourteenth century, Bruges had no competitors of equal size, by the fifteenth century, merchants were starting to get more options for lucrative trade. London was a commercial centre of great renown with a strong Hanseatic and Italian presence. For example, the Venetian fleet would always split between London and the Burgundian Netherlands. The itinerary towards the Burgundian Netherlands was usually to Sluis, but as the fifteenth century drew to a close, Venetian captains increasingly chose Antwerp.[2] The question of when and why medieval Bruges shifted from one of the most vibrant merchant places to a more modest Flemish city has intrigued scholars for many years. For some it was the downfall of a commercial star, for others it was the return to normality. After the sixteenth century, Bruges became less international.[3] There is no straightforward explanation as to how and why this happened. Three main theories dominate the literature: a structural, economic and events-based decline of Bruges. Needless to say, all scholars acknowledge these factors, but deem some more important than others.[4]

THE LOSS OF COMMERCE

Structurally, the Zwin silted and became less accessible. Larger ships had to dock in Sluis and transfer their merchandise to smaller vessels that would ship the wares to warehouses in Bruges. Such services demanded time and investment. Transaction costs would rise for merchants, making them think twice before sailing to Bruges.[5] However, the Zwin almost immediately began silting after the initial passage was made in the twelfth century. By the thirteenth century, Bruges had become inaccessible for bigger ships which had to dock at one of the outports closer to the sea.[6] The passage from Sluis to Bruges was difficult and filled with sandbanks, but the shippers organising this transport were experienced and capable of transferring the merchandise. In addition, the prices they could demand for their services were fixed. Hence, despite having a monopoly on the service, the shippers could not force merchants to pay more (despite possible inflation). When the shippers tried nonetheless, they were often dragged before the aldermen of Bruges who corrected them or proposed a compromise. In addition, Bruges spent considerable time and effort to convince merchants that their market was accessible.[7] Did the costs of sailing to Bruges outweigh the benefits? The city not only dug out large portions of the Zwin to improve accessibility, it also invested heavily to counter the silting and to promote this effort with the foreign nations.

Different trade flows were another important factor. Bruges relied heavily on the Hanseatic trade and the southern (Castilian, Portuguese and Italian) trade. The Hanse had lost much of its commercial influence by the end of the fifteenth century and was no longer the trade block it once was.[8] Although the organisation would not cease to exist and traded in the sixteenth century in Bruges and Antwerp, other commercial trade flows had become more vital. The English Merchant Adventurers and English draperies played a crucial role in this. English draperies were made from high-quality English wool and did not face the tolls Flemish weavers had to pay as they imported the wool. As such, English draperies presented an existential threat to the Flemish economy. The Flemish count banned English cloth from the county to protect its industry. The English, and more notably the Merchant Adventurers, sold their cloths a little further afield in Antwerp. In 1421, the Merchant Adventurers established their cloth staple in Antwerp. Via the Brabantine fairs, the English merchants came into contact with the South German merchants. The latter trade was gaining importance, with their supplies of silver and copper in the mid-1460s.[9] As these continental routes became increasingly important, Antwerp became more lucrative for merchants to visit. Antwerp was becoming slowly but steadily more attractive for the sale of merchandise.[10]

The economic vicissitudes are undeniable. Antwerp was growing as a market, but this had been the case since the fourteenth century.[11] During the Antwerp market, Bruges was a desolate place. However, the base of operations remained in Bruges. Bruges tried to hinder a permanent foreign presence in Antwerp.[12] In pursuit of this policy, it imposed punitive measures and sought promises from the nations that they would not trade in Antwerp, but this was like mopping up with the tap still running. Bruges realised this. By the 1480s, we can see several instances of English draperies entering Bruges, where the aldermen were pragmatic in enforcing the fines for staple infringements.[13] In addition, several historians have argued that brokers brought transaction costs down.[14] However, the rise in transaction costs can hardly be a sufficient explanation for the decline.[15]

Lastly, political events were vital. Although the downward spiral was a decades-long process, the eclipse of medieval Bruges happened at breakneck speed in the 1490s. Slow structural processes needed a final push to uproot the existing consensus.[16] For medieval Bruges, that push came in the person of Maximilian of Austria. The archduke and the Flemish cities shared an uneasy relationship built on mutual incomprehension. The Flemish cities were proud of their hard-fought model of political participation between the city and duke. Although the Burgundian dukes progressively tried to draw more power towards themselves, they always did so within a longstanding tradition of communication between count and city.[17] Maximilian of Austria was raised in an entirely different context. Filled with the ideals of ancient nobility and an unhealthy contempt for the populous, the archduke was amazed when he saw the splendour of the Burgundian Low

Countries. His amazement was short-lived and he immediately started bringing the Low Countries into the Habsburg fold. Personal power, dynastic considerations and an unhealthy thirst for money soon brought the suzerain into conflict with the cities who believed their privileges were undermined and disrespected. Unsurprisingly, the cities sidelined Maximilian in favour of his son Philip when the rightful heir, Mary of Burgundy, passed away in 1482. Philip the Fair (1482–1506) would be raised in the traditions of the Low Countries and prove himself a just ruler, but until then, Maximilian claimed the regency over the still young boy.[18] The Flemish cities and a considerable number of the nobles objected, and years of civil war would ensue.[19] In addition to war with France, Flanders would be the theatre for ongoing conflict, depopulating the county, annihilating industries and destroying maritime connections.[20] For Bruges, which unwisely captured and imprisoned Maximilian in 1488, destiny would strike when in that same year the archduke ordered merchants to take their leave from Bruges and transfer their services to Antwerp.[21] Although it needed repetition, the merchants eventually left Bruges for Antwerp.

Be that as it may, it should be noted that it was not the first time such an order was issued. In 1436–1438, during the Bruges rebellion, Duke Philip the Good had issued a similar charge. After 1438 and even in 1485, the merchants returned and continued their activities in Bruges.[22] Similarly, after the Flemish war ended in 1492 (for Bruges in 1489 but Sluis was still fighting), Maximilian ordered the nations to return to Bruges and continue their activities.[23] Although most would do so, they only stayed for a short period, after which they permanently left the city for the Brabantine market around the turn of the century. The Portuguese, for example, only returned briefly before they left again for Antwerp in 1510–1511.[24] As the Portuguese were emerging as leaders in the trade of colonial merchandise, Bruges felt their loss dearly.[25]

Being in Antwerp during the Flemish war (1488–1492), it is possible that the merchant communities had tasted a better market or commercial infrastructure. Antwerp was organised differently than Bruges. Whereas Bruges relied heavily on regulation, this was less the case in Antwerp. For example, Bruges' demand that each transaction should be made through a broker was not applied in Antwerp.[26] However, we should also note that in the sources in the 1490s, several complaints about the aldermen of Antwerp were recorded. For example, merchants believed that the tolls on merchandise were unjust in Antwerp.[27] It was not a simple story of the city being better in every facet.

THE LOSS OF A FRAMEWORK

Society nevertheless changed rapidly in the 1490s, including in legal affairs. Until now, we have excluded the 1490s from our analysis. The aldermen took measures to keep the merchants' communities within their city. In so doing, they uprooted the legal system that was in place in the previous decades. Whereas the source registers in the 1470s and 1480s still show the normal flow of commerce and the presence of merchants using the same techniques we have illustrated in this book, by the 1490s, there were not only fewer cases before the aldermen, but Bruges was also in a far worse bargaining position. In 1487, the money changer Willem Roelens defaulted on a debt and thus triggered the privileges of merchants protected against defaulting money changers. In particular the Portuguese believed Bruges had to indemnify the community. Bruges tried to make a deal with the Portuguese community, but the Portuguese held firm. Despite the fact that the Portuguese had no privileges stating this, they would only accept the same treatment as the Hanseatic and Castilian merchants. They demanded full compensation of all merchandise. Bruges, in decline, was eventually defeated and agreed to pay 233 lib. 13 s. 6 d. gr. over three years. Yet, apparently, the debt was not paid so easily, and six years after the decision, it was still outstanding. Alfonso Martin, the Portuguese king's factor in Antwerp, declared before the aldermen of Antwerp that the inhabitants of Bruges held collective responsibility for this debt. Arbitrarily, Jacob Despars and Hendrik Nieuwland saw their properties distrained and auctioned by the Portuguese, with the consent of the aldermen of Antwerp. Bruges tried its luck before the Great Council in Mechelen, but in 1493 the Council confirmed the decision of the aldermen of Antwerp.[28]

As Bruges lost all leverage over the communities, the attitude the aldermen harboured towards them changed drastically. It is illustrative to examine how Bruges behaved in these times of peril and how the city tried to lure merchants back during its demise. By the 1490s, the aldermen knew that commerce was slipping out of their hands. To slow this process, the aldermen of Bruges facilitated the merchant communities to the best of their abilities. It might be said that the city had few other options, with each nation holding a sword of Damocles over Bruges' head.[29] Bruges actively sought the location of foreign fleets and begged them to go to Bruges instead of Antwerp.[30] In November 1492, they visited the Spanish wool fleet in Middelburg to beg them to hold their staple 'according to ancient usage' (*naer de oude costume*) in Bruges.[31]

Whereas we saw that in earlier shakedowns from the communities, the city of Bruges would mostly hold firm and grant only small – mainly financial – concessions, such concessions multiplied rapidly in the 1490s. One could call this a snowball effect. In line with the previous traditions, Bruges was ready to concede to keep the Hanseatic trade within the city. However, before Bruges even realised it, the city was negotiating with several merchant nations about the 'bad policies in the city' in order to find 'a way to bring all the nations back to Bruges'.[32] However, other merchant communities were also making their return to the city conditional on similar concessions from Bruges, triggering other communities to demand similar terms.

This triggered a race to the bottom to secure the return of foreign merchants. Bruges could pay the sums to which merchants were previously condemned, the acquisition of property for merchants, or indemnifications for, let us say, maritime plunder.[33] For example, in 1498 the city of Bruges received a charter from the Duke Philip the Fair that his chancellor, the Great Council and the Council of Flanders would not allow any procedures of ships' captains, and merchants would not be subject to their courts in the first six months following their arrival for debts committed outside the Low Countries.[34]

A salient point in the evaluation of Bruges at the end of the fifteenth century is the political prowess of the city. The Flemish war had ravaged Bruges. The Counts of Flanders, both Maximilian of Austria and his son Philip the Fair, were reluctant to kill the goose that laid the golden eggs. Although they might have recognised the full potential of Antwerp, Bruges was still – in their memory – one of the wealthiest places in northern Europe.[35] Nevertheless, as we have seen, the power of the Council of Flanders and even the Great Council was firmly established by now. In consequence, the aldermen operated in a different political sphere than a couple decades earlier.[36] Although it was undeniable that nations could appeal decisions from the aldermen, there was still some resistance to these practices. For example, in arbitration cases, the aldermen of Bruges still endeavoured that arbitration would not be subjected to appeal or reformation.[37]

When Bruges realised that the prince's command to return would not bring back the foreign merchants, the city needed to petition the prince for new privileges.[38] In granting concessions, the aldermen changed their legal system.

In these privileges, we can find the classic demands such as reduced tolls and taxes, assurances that Bruges would indemnify merchants who endured damages on their way to Bruges, and assurances that weighters, shippers and hostellers would not abuse their position in relation to the merchants.[39] And we can recognise the – not so classic – legal concession from Bruges. As we have seen, the aldermen of Bruges were somewhat hesitant to alter their legal framework. Only a few nations were liable for arrest and it was far from certain that the aldermen confirmed the decisions of consuls.

The Spanish nation had an already firmly established nation. On 30 May 1493, the city of Bruges exempted Spanish merchants from paying brokers for transactions carried out without the intervention of a broker. Although implicit, the decision allowed the Spanish merchants to overlook the brokers in transactions, which was previously seen as one of the pillars of commerce in the city.[40] The Spaniards also received toll reductions or toll waivers, and, on 10 July 1493, the aldermen of Bruges promised that for each case of plunder that occurred in the Zwin due to continuing instability, they would pay 20 ducats for a pack of wool.[41] In addition, the nation demanded that the Bruges aldermen would continue to provide support if merchants proved rebellious against the nation and refused to follow the consul's orders.[42] Furthermore, Bruges had to acknowledge that the Castilian merchants were under the consul in Burgos. This was probably already an informal relationship, but now the aldermen of Bruges officially acknowledged the authority of the court in Burgos over affairs happening in Bruges.[43] Both the Catalan and the Biscayan nations demanded the acknowledgement that all the already extensive Castilian privileges should also be applicable to them.[44] The Biscayan nation were even granted a clause that all future privileges of the Castilians would also apply to them.[45] In addition, if a debt was settled or damage compensated to the Spanish nation, the Biscayans would also receive money.[46]

Furthermore, some new national houses were distributed to the Spanish and Biscayans, but the latter went even further and demanded a small quarter.[47] The aldermen of Bruges consented to a special legal area within their city for the Biscayan nation. There would be a Biscayan quarter between the Bridge of Saint John, the Bridge of de Kraan, the Saint John church and hostel Mareminne. The hostel was given to the nation, and in this specific area, nobody could be arrested for civil debt, making it a legal enclave.[48]

The Biscayans could not be apprehended for a debt or a crime if it did not happen in the county, if it was below 6 lib. gr. or if the crime was just ordinary fighting in the streets, without referring the case first to their consuls. Also, if a creditor apprehended a Biscayan, the debtor should be bailed out for an amount that would ensure the debtor would appear before the law; and no longer the amount that guaranteed the debt payment.[49] As these sureties were vital to Bruges' legal framework, these privileges endangered the existing mechanisms. The Spanish demanded that if merchants were apprehended, they could be released by sureties of their peers, who would be considered full citizen sureties and, in any case, were not obliged to stay incarcerated in an enclosed prison.[50] In affairs of debt imprisonment, the aldermen of Bruges were increasingly sidelined.

The nations demanded that their sureties were equal to sureties from citizens and thus sidelined the hostellers' function in the assurance a debt would be paid. Another essential element of the Bruges legal system was jeopardised.[51] In addition, the nations demanded that the aldermen court should even give these merchants preferential treatment.[52] The Aragonese, Biscayans and Castilians all demanded that their cases would be given priority: each Monday at noon, the aldermen would treat their problems first. In addition, the Spanish even received some exceptions on the Bruges customs. If someone refused to show up twice, either in person or through a proctor, the Spanish merchant could demand that this person should be condemned. The decision that would be made in the chamber, would have the value of the *vierschaar*.[53]

Furthermore, the staple right of Bruges was almost completely sidelined. The Biscayans received the right to enter Sluis, charge and recharge their ship without prior approval and move on from there to Holland, Brabant, Zeeland or elsewhere, without first bringing their merchandise to Bruges, with the notable exceptions of cloths and iron ore. The other way around, merchandise from outside the County of Flanders did not first have to pass through Bruges before going to their international destinations.[54] The Aragonese were also exempted from the staple right, except in regard to English cloths. They could use Sluis to load the cloths they had bought at Antwerp, but were forbidden to sell them in the County of Flanders.[55] The Spanish received *carte blanche* on shipping and movement within the County of Flanders, except for Spanish wool, iron and oil.[56]

Perhaps the best summary of their privileges was given by the Biscayans. The privileges end with perhaps the most ironic clause: if the Biscayans wanted a clause that would not damage the city badly, it would be granted by the aldermen without great difficulty.[57] Did this mean that minor damage was permissible so that commerce could prosper?

As we have indicated, privileges given to one nation incited others to demand the same treatment. Curiously, the Italian nations operated together and demanded privileges for one and all. The Florentine and Lucchese had no privileges, and the Genoese only the 1411 privilege, but they did not have any charters granting a nation or consular jurisdiction. However, in line with the Iberian privileges, the Italians demanded the freedom to visit the markets they wished and to relinquish the obligation to staple their wares in Bruges.[58] In addition, the Italians requested that all their merchants be freed from taxes on wine (we must remember that the Hanse fought for this clause for more than 150 years) and that they would receive the same privileges as the Spanish nation (so all the abovementioned privileges were also applicable to them).[59]

Furthermore, Italian sureties were made equivalent to those of citizens, and if a surety was given to appear before the law, the merchant giving the surety could not be held financially liable. The Italians demanded a distinction between influence and liability, while the aldermen formally did not allow this. By separating the cautions between appearing before the law and respecting the judgment, an essential authorisation of the aldermen disappeared. Perhaps the Italians feared that their privileges went too far and thus included the clause that the aldermen should respect all the stipulations without ever revoking them or going against them.[60] In additional privileges, the Italians included provisions that strengthened their positions as creditors (which the Italians often were). In cases of contumacy, or failure to appear before a court, protections for debtors were reduced. The first time a debtor failed to show up, the debtor's peremptory exception would be forfeited. The second time this occurred, the debtor would not be able to dismiss testimonies or witnesses. And after three failures, the case would be ready for judgment by the aldermen of Bruges who assured the execution or absolution of the debt of the Italians.[61] To make matters worse for the citizens of Bruges, if the aldermen passed their obligation and their creditor was an Italian, they would be liable for arrest 'like a foreigner' (*comme ung estrangier*).[62]

One of the recurring demands, however, was that the nations could monopolise an entire day, preferably Monday, where they would receive the full attention of the aldermen of Bruges.[63] The Italians demanded speedy procedures where, for example, most parts of the procedure would be handled informally by two aldermen until eventual judgment.[64] As we have seen, the numbers of cases and procedural acts in the chamber of Bruges were growing rapidly. In 1491 the aldermen of Bruges tried to modify their procedure 'because of the backlog in cases'. Each session would now have two weeks before it could be handled.[65] In brief, the legal system of Bruges was breaking down.

Bruges was eventually successful and received formal promises that several nations would return to the once prosperous city, though it would never be the same.[66] We should not forget that the city was partially successful in attracting these merchants back to Bruges. Herman van der Wee argued that the city of

Bruges remained the prime financial centre until at least 1515. Bart Lambert has pointed out that a respectable number of merchants were still present for most of the sixteenth century, especially the Spanish, who directed their successful merino-wool trade to Bruges.[67] In his description of the Low Countries, Guicciardini stated that Bruges was no longer comparable with Antwerp. The merchants had left, but thanks to the presence of the lucrative merino wool, the city could still amaze its visitors. For Guicciardini, Bruges still held claim to its former glory.[68]

A TALE OF JUSTICE, LITIGATION AND CHANGE

The influence of the princely courts was a new development for Bruges. At their foundation, these courts did not pose a significant threat to the city's legal supremacy, but they had the potential to do so. There was a very slow evolution in which the princely courts increasingly considered themselves competent to judge cases. The initiative for this was with the litigants, who were looking for alternatives to the aldermen of Bruges. Thus, merchants did not appear before the princely courts when it was theoretically possible to do so, but when the contextual circumstances allowed it. One of the most important factors in this was that other merchants litigated before these courts and the courts accepted their appeals as within their jurisdiction. There is, however, a difference between the Council of Flanders and the other princely courts. The Council of Flanders was more accessible. It was the local princely court for Flanders and allowed the aldermen to interact with it and get cases back. This happened from time to time. It was only gradually that the Council considered itself more and more competent in cases. The Great Council and the Parliament of Paris, however, were the courts of refuge of forum shoppers. These were merchants who pursued long and expensive disputes and were prepared to struggle to the bitter end to see a case through to a successful conclusion. Interestingly, the group of merchants who were most prominent in these disputes were also those who could not rely on strong communities to protect them. In Bruges, they represented themselves, defended themselves and, of course, took this initiative to the higher courts. In doing so, however, they increasingly undermined Bruges. The aldermen had to defend themselves before these courts in expensive litigations and slowly began to adapt in order to prevent further appeals. The departure of merchants from Bruges in the 1490s further disrupted this trend. In exchange for the return of their privileges, they requested new and enhanced rights that Bruges had refused for over a century. It remains to be researched how this played out in the sixteenth century, but the tendency is clear: there was an ideal of justice and a reality of justice.

NOTES

1. For a close description of these events, see: Maréchal, 'Le départ', 27–54. See, for example, Lucchese merchants on the Antwerp market: Lazzereschi, *Libro dellà comunita*, 133, 146, 190, 246.

2. See for the captain: *Venetian state papers*, 65, nr. 263. See, for example, the aldermen of Bruges complaining to the Venetian senate that their ships did not arrive in Sluis: ASV, *Comm.*, vol. 15, fol. 76 r. See for the city of Sluis complaining in 1461 that they had done nothing wrong against the Venetians and requesting that the galleys return: ASV, *Comm.*, vol. 15, fol. 76 v.
3. Dumolyn, 'Bruges in the sixteenth century', 448.
4. Moryson, *An itinerary*, vol. 4, 57; De Keyser, 'De visie van vreemdelingen', 284.
5. Gottschalk, 'Het verval van Brugge', 1–26.
6. Van Houtte, 'The rise and decline', 39.
7. Dumolyn et al. 'So one should see the good navigability', 6. See also the messengers to control, patrol and oversee the state of the Zwin: SAB 216, *Stadsrekeningen Brugge*, 1468–1469, fol. 54 r.; SAB 216, *Stadsrekeningen Brugge*, 1477–1478, fol. 48 v.; SAB 216, *Stadsrekeningen Brugge*, 1481–1482, fol. 44 r.; The octroys given in this respect; SAB 96, *Gedelf*, fol. 1 r.–3 r.
8. Wijffels, 'Le déclin de la Hanse', 275–289.
9. The Dukes of Burgundy's mint policies made silver overvalued and therefore very advantageous to sell in the Low Countries; Van Houtte, 'Rise and decline', 43; Shawn, 'Burgundian Habsburg mint policies', 1–16.
10. An argument made by Raymind van Uytven, although he places the eventual breakdown too early; Van Uytven, 'Stages of economic decline', 267.
11. Van Houtte, 'La genèse du grand marché international', 87–126; Van Houtte, 'Anvers aux XVe et XVIe siècles', 250–251. See, for example, the Hanseatic nation receiving a nation house in Antwerp: FA 1063, Privilegiekamer, Vreemde natiën, Duitse natie, 1305–1598, nr 4.
12. Von der Ropp, Hanserecesse II, vol. 4, 9. See also Schäfer, Hanserecesse III, vol. 2, 325–330, n. 292.
13. SAB 96, *Groenenboek B*, fol. 72 r. and 77 r.–v.
14. Gelderblom, 'The decline of fairs', 199–238. For example: the Italians were freed from the costs of brokers in 1493; SAB 96, *Groenenboek B*, fol. 176 v.
15. See also the numerous reductions on tolls Bruges granted: SAB 96, *Groenenboek B*, 225 r.–226 r.; RAG 175, *Brieven*, 31.
16. Maréchal, 'Le depart des marchands', 29.
17. Arnade, *Realms of ritual*, 4.
18. Cauchies, *Philippe le Beau*, 8–14.
19. Haemers, 'Factionalism and state power', 1015.
20. Van der Wee, *The growth of the Antwerp market*, 101–103.
21. SAB, *Spaans Consulaat*, nr. 42; Giliodts-Van Severen, *Consulat D'espagne*, 141–142.
22. SAB, *Presentwijnen*, 1485–1486, fol. 7 v.–8 r. See the confirmation of all staple merchandise from the Hanse in Bruges: SAB 96, *Groenenboek B*, fol. 61 r.–v.
23. One can even argue that Maximilian extended the staple privileges: SAB 96, *Groenenboek B*, fol. 137 r.–v.; SAB 120, *Register van de Hallegeboden van Brugge 1490–1499*, fol. 58 v.–59 v.; SAB 120, *Register van de Hallegeboden van Brugge 1490–1499*, 146 r., SAB, *Spaans Consulaat*, nr. 46. As Maximilian also did after in earlier rebellions in 1485 and 1487 and later confirmations in 1497, 1498 and 1499 would follow. SAB, *Politieke Charters*, 1220, 1225, 1285, 1273, 1277. Maréchal, 'Le départ de Bruges', 26–74.
24. Pohl, *Die Portugiesen*, 26.
25. Goris, *Etudes sur les colonies marchandes*, 38–39. See the Privileges the Portuguese received in 1511; FA, *Privileiekamer, Natie van Portugal*, II, fol. 59 v.

26. Although we should note that Bruges (unsuccessfully) tried to alter this system in 1465, the brokers dragged the city before the Great Council and saw their right of jurisdiction in each transaction confirmed; SAB 310, Charters Ambachten, *Oorkonden*, nr. 819 and 820; SAB, *Rodenboek*, fol. 228 v.–232 r.; SAB 299, *Makelaars, Cartularium* A, fol. 25 v.–29; the settlement: 27 r.–29 r.
27. Schäfer, Hanserecesse III, vol. 4, 543, 735; UAG.G.001979, Documents on the history of the Burgundian state, 178. See also the complaints of the Hanse and requests for better privileges: FA 1061, Privilegiekamer, Vreemde natiën, Duitse natie, 1469.
28. ARA, *Fonds Grote Raad*, 802.21, fol. 153 r.–165 r.
29. Illustrative in this respect are the emissaries sent to Antwerp to beg the merchants to return to Bruges and keep their residence there; SAB 216, *Stadsrekeningen Brugge*, 1492–1493, fol. 142 r.; 143 r.; 151 r.; 152 v., 156 v.; Blockmans, *Handelingen van de leden*, 618.
30. SAB 165, *Civiele Sententiën Kamer*, 1489–1490, fol. 30 r. See for similar pleas to the Spaniards: SAB, *Spaans Consulaat*, nr. 54; SAB 216, Jaarrekeningen, 1492–1493, fol. 142 v.
31. SAB 216, *Stadsrekeningen Brugge*, 1492–1493, fol. 143 r.
32. SAB 216, *Stadsrekeningen Brugge*, 1492–1493, fol. 153 v. See the 1487 privileges contributed by Maximilian of Austria; Confirmed in 1499: FA 1061, Privilegiekamer, Vreemde natiën, Duitse natie, 1315–1598, 1499.
33. See for the house they gave to the Portuguese nation: SAB 96, *Groenenboek B*, fol 149 r.–v. and 185 r.–186 v. Payments to the Spaniards, Germans and Venetians SAB 216, *Stadsrekeningen Brugge*, 1492–1493, fol. 169 r., 175 r.–v., 177 r., 180 v.; or a very handsome donation to the Count of Nassau, Guardian of Flanders, of 300 lib. 33 d. 8 d gr. to get the Zwin free of soldiers, ARA, CC, 32 547, *Accounts of the city of Bruges*, 1493–1494, fol. 165 v.; SAB 96, *Groenenboek B*, fol. 160 r.
34. SAB 120, *Register van de Hallegeboden*, 1490–1499, fol. 326 v.–327 r.
35. De Commynes, *Mémoire*, 400.
36. SAB 165, *Civiele Sententiën Kamer*, 1489–1490, fol. 38 r.–v.; SAB 96, *Groenenboek B*, fol. 211 r.–v.; SAB 165, *Civiele Sententiën Kamer, 1487–1488*, fol. 44 r. Nevertheless, Bruges still frequently demanded a renvoy. See for example: RAG 2426, *Raad van Vlaanderen, Acten en Sententiën*, 1494–1494, fol. 18 r., 105 r. 133 v., 152 v.
37. SAB 165, *Civiele Sententiën Kamer*, 1489–1490, fol. 21 r.–v.
38. SAB 96, *Groenenboek B*, fol. 105 r.–v.
39. See for example SAB, *Politieke Charters*, 1165.
40. SAB 96, *Groenenboek Ongecotteerd*, fol. 336 r. In 1465, the brokers guild even dragged Bruges before the great council because they believed their privileges (the right to act as a broker in all transactions) were infringed; Fonds van de Ambachten, *Oorkonden*, nr. 819 and 820; SAB 96, *Rodenboek*, fol. 228 v.–232 r.; Fonds van de Makelaars, *Cartularium* A, fol. 25 v.–29 r.
41. SAB 96, *Groenenboek B*, fol. 159 r. See also: SAB 96, *Groenenboek B*, fol. 149 r.–v. See also the important charter on wine and beer to get the Portuguese back: Braamcamp, *Noticias*, 160.
42. Gilliodts-Van Severen, *Consulat d'Espagne*, 174, art. 10.
43. See in this respect the comparison with the Florentine nation. The Florentine nation depended on the Mercanzia, but Bruges did not officially acknowledge such a relation; Gilliodts-Van Severen, *Consulat d'Espagne*, 181, art. 35.

44. Gilliodts-Van Severen, *Consulat d'Espagne*, 167, art. 26; Gilliodts-Van Severen, *Consulat d'Espagne*, 161, art. 47; *Groenenboek B*, fol. 174 v. See for a Biscayan merchant using these privileges in a conflict: SAB 165, *Civiele Sententiën Kamer*, 1501–1502, fol. 74 r.
45. As the other merchant communities left Bruges, the Castilian/Biscayan trade became more important: Priotti, 'Commerce et finance en Flandre', 81–82.
46. Gilliodts-Van Severen, *Consulat d'Espagne*, 161, art. 47, 48, 49; SAB 96, *Groenenboek B*, fol. 165 v.–166 r.
47. SAB 96, *Groenenboek B*, fol. 116 v.–117 r.; Gilliodts-Van Severen, *Consulat D'Espagne*, 156–157, art. 23 and 25.
48. SAB 96, *Groenenboek B*; Gilliodts-Van Severen, *Consulat D'Espagne*, pp. 156–157, art. 23, 24, 25; SAB 216, *Stadsrekeningen Brugge*, 1494–1495, fol. 37 r. SAB 96, *Groenenboek B*, fol. 163 v.–164 v.
49. SAB 96, *Groenenboek B*, 162 r.–163 r.; Gilliodts-Van Severen, *Consulat d'Espagne*, p. 152, 154–156, art. 4, 12, 20.
50. Gilliodts-Van Severen, *Consulat d'Espagne*, p. 180, art. 32.
51. In addition, the Spaniards received the right to become hostellers themselves: SAB, Fonds van de ambachten, nr. 832.
52. Gilliodts-Van Severen, *Consulat d'Espagne*, 165, art. 8.
53. Gilliodts-Van Severen, *Consulat d'Espagne*, 180, art. 31.
54. SAB 96, *Groenenboek B*, fol. 161 r.–v.; Gilliodts-Van Severen, *Consulat d'Espagne*, p. 152, art. 2 and 3.
55. Gilliodts-Van Severen, *Consulat d'Espagne*; 164–164, art. 6 and 10; SAB 96, *Groenenboek B*, fol. 172 v.–173 r.
56. Gilliodts-Van Severen, *Consulat d'Espagne*, 178–179, art. 26 and 27.
57. Gilliodts-Van Severen, *Consulat d'Espagne*, 161, art. 51; SAB 96, *Groenenboek B*, fol. 166 r.
58. SAB 96, *Groenenboek B*, fol. 177 r.–v.; SAB 96, *Groenenboek B*, fol. 176 r.
59. SAB 96, *Groenenboek B*, fol. 178 r.
60. SAB 96, *Groenenboek B*, fol. 178 r.
61. SAB 96, *Groenenboek B*, fol. 175 r.
62. SAB 96, *Groenenboek B*, fol. 175 v.; The question remains as to what extent these privileges were applicable in Antwerp. When several Italian nations left Bruges for Antwerp in 1501, they received a confirmation of the duke that their Bruges' privileges were also valid in Antwerp; FA 1075, Privilegiekamer, Vreemde natiën, Natie van Genua, 1501–1716, 1501. Further research is needed, but we could not find the same clauses applied in later times: FA 1075, Privilegiekamer, Vreemde natiën, Natie van Genua, 1501–1716; FA 1076, Privilegiekamer, Vreemde natiën, Natie van Lucca; FA 1078, Privilegiekamer, Vreemde natiën, Natie van Lombardie.
63. See for the Italians: SAB 96, *Groenenboek B*, fol. 175 v.
64. SAB 96, *Groenenboek B*, fol. 175 v.
65. SAB 120, *Register van de Hallegeboden, 1490–1499*, fol. 67 r.
66. See SAB, *Presentwijnen*, 1492–1493, 42 v–43 v. See for the Spanish nation: SAB 96, *Groenenboek B*, fol. 160 r.–v.
67. By the 1550s the Spanish requested to have a consul in Antwerp, Bruges opposed this; FA 1079, Privilegiekamer, Vreemde natiën, Spaanse, 1493–1685; Van der Wee, *The growth of the Antwerp market*, 109–112: Lambert, 'Steep fall or gradual decline?' 153–162. See also Brulez stressing the continuity in trade: Brulez, 'Antwerpen en Brugge', 22–23.
68. Guicciardini, *Descrittione*, 226–227.

11

Conclusion

Sopra tutto aministra buona giustitia

Guicciardini, Descrittione, 227.

When Ludovico Guicciardini professed these flattering words of Bruges as a city of justice, trade was already in a state of decline. By the 1560s, while still an important regional centre, the city of Bruges had lost its commercial status. The shadow cast by the Brabantine city of Antwerp over Bruges was long and lasting. The medieval centre of Bruges made way for the early-modern system of Antwerp. The latter had transitioned from customary (medieval) to Roman (modern) law. Antwerp changed its judicial framework, listened to the wishes of merchants and accepted a modern system based on legal professionals. Bruges chose a different path.

Proper justice was not taken for granted. It was something the aldermen had to aspire to, search for, and maintain for several decades, amidst changing contextual factors. Both Pero Tafur in 1439 and Lodovico Guicciardini in 1567 praised Bruges for its justice. However, 'justice' was a malleable term. While some travellers complimented Bruges on its system of justice, we can also find others lamenting its absence, especially after they lost a case. Whether Bruges was a city of justice is a question of opinions and viewpoints. However, the main debate we have touched upon was whether the aldermen of Bruges followed a logic where commercial interest prevailed, or one where equitable elements prevailed? Proponents of the *New Institutional Economics* have seen the city as one of the main actors in shaping the necessary conditions for a prosperous commercial climate. Although this was certainly a concern of the aldermen, it was not their most important preoccupation. The aldermen were both the rulers and the judges of the city. In that capacity, we see citizens receiving distinctly preferential treatment. Before the 1490s, all the benefits that merchants enjoyed were often already bestowed upon citizens. Citizens had access to both the *vierschaar* and the chamber procedure. They often used arbitration to resolve their cases. The aldermen applied the more lenient submission procedure more often on citizens than on merchants, and citizens were much better protected against imprisonment for debt. Merchants had to petition for those rights through privileges. Some received them, but most received these rights or even better only in the 1490s. It is clear that, in the first instance, the aldermen were more inclined to an urban logic where they protected their citizens than to a commercial logic.

When citizens experienced the full consequences of the pressure put on the aldermen, for example during a Hanseatic blockade or an English wool embargo, they began to listen to the concerns of these merchant communities. This had several consequences. Although some communities, such as the Hanseatic, Scottish, or Castilian, had many charters, their application remained questionable when the charters were clearly against the common good. In contrast, the stress on the aldermen and their court as the main venue for conflict resolution resulted in a more equal playing field. All merchants had access to the aldermen court. The consular courts were permitted to operate, as long as they did not interfere with the rights of the aldermen. With the exception of some rights involving maritime plunder, no procedural advantages were granted to any of the merchant communities. Even the Hanseatic merchants, who were able to seize maritime plunder without interference from the aldermen, did not receive any additional benefits. Even that last rule of the Hanseats was only occasionally observed.

However, it is important to note that 'good justice' should not be equated with 'equal justice'. The aldermen prioritised certain commercially sensitive groups. Although the aldermen were committed to justice, it became clear that merchants could manipulate the system to their advantage. This was especially true when their interests coincided with those of the city.

Understanding the mechanisms of customary law in the city of Bruges requires an appreciation of both the framework and the strategies employed within it. The aldermen had their vision of what justice was, and this was challenged by the vision of the merchants. The strategies of the merchants were somewhat determined by the privileges and communities to which they belonged. The Hanseatic merchants were heavily constrained within their Kontor, which was effective in keeping intra-Hanseatic conflicts within their sphere of influence. When dealing with conflicts with other merchants or citizens of Bruges, the Kontor Secretary could offer assistance, although this was not always guaranteed. The Scottish community provides a clear example of the difference between individual initiative and community support. The role of the Conservator of the Scottish Privileges was to provide legal assistance in Bruges and protect merchants in higher courts. However, merchants still had enough flexibility to develop their own litigation strategies and often relied on hostellers instead of the conservator. The example of the English community demonstrates that economic leverage alone was insufficient for attaining a privileged position in Bruges. The treatment of the English merchant differed from that of the Hanseatic and Scottish merchants, despite the fact that they possessed an essential commodity, English wool. This was due to their political sensitivity.

The Spanish (Castilian), Portuguese and Aragonese merchants could rely on political relations to receive new privileges in the 1420s and 1430s of the fifteenth century. The Spanish nation, on the one hand, used it to group together and use their consuls to defend Spanish merchants similarly to the Hanseatic Kontor. However, the dominance of the court of Burgos that informally governed the nation in Bruges was loathed by the Biscayans. A part of the Spanish nation broke loose and Bruges refused to give it privileges. The Portuguese, on the other hand, were not numerous enough to form a powerful group. However, the few merchants present in Bruges, were perhaps highly valued by the aldermen. The Portuguese trade was up-and-coming, with many luxuries desired by Bruges. The royal connection between trade and politics made the aldermen of Bruges cautious in their dealings with these Portuguese merchants. The Portugues community was a group that received several cases in submission. The Aragonese were too few in number to pressure Bruges, and did not control any important trade streams. These merchants had to find another way where leverage over the aldermen of Bruges was not an option.

In many ways, the litigation strategies of the Aragonese and Italian merchants seem very similar. Italian bankers were important, but lacked the collective power or political relations to push for extensive privileges. The Venetians could broker some privileges, and pushed Bruges for concessions for its fleet, but other groups had to operate in different ways. The Lucchese, Genoese and Florentines operated via non-privileged nations who worked informally and through peer control. The networks that were made in these communities also operated before the aldermen of Bruges.

It may be clear that these merchants could operate in groups and could push for a better legal statute. However, being a part of a group does not entirely determine the strategy certain merchants pursued. Personal initiative remained crucial. As we have demonstrated, the group to which merchants belonged were essential in shaping the context of the litigation strategy and Bruges' behaviour towards those merchants, yet the group was not the be all and end all. Several merchants tried to seek a resolution of their conflicts outside of the usual framework of Bruges. For example, in cases of maritime plunder, we see this happening between the Flemish cities, the usual source of conflict resolution, and the Council of Flanders. As maritime plunder infringed ducal promises, and the Council of Flanders protected these rights, merchants could turn to the latter if they wanted to avoid the aldermen of Bruges. Cases of maritime plunder were the first to turn up before the Council of Flanders. From the mid-fifteenth century, merchants found their way slowly but surely to the council of Flanders. Bruges always demanded a *renvoi*, but the princely ordinance of 1459 that came at the request of the cities proved to be crucial. After 1459, merchants regularly found their way to the Council of Flanders and appealed the decisions from the aldermen of Bruges.

For cases such as debt imprisonment and arbitration, the influence of the Council of Flanders proved to be an existential threat that undermined the existing legal framework. The Great Council and the Parliament of Mechelen were even more detrimental. The Council of Flanders rarely evoked cases before its court. The initiative was with the merchants. Bruges considered the Parliament of Mechelen as an instrument of princely centralisation that lifted cases from the communal level to the princely level. The solution came in the form of the Parliament of Paris. The aldermen of Bruges used this court when it suited them to confront the Great Council and the Council of Flanders. Certainly, after 1477, the aldermen of Bruges still used the parliament against the duke, while foreign merchants used the other alternatives such as the Council of Flanders.

The period after 1477 was one of changing jurisdiction. The aldermen of Bruges accepted the Council of Flanders in order to eradicate the Parliament of Mechelen. As such, proceedings before this court increased and became an aspect of the legal framework for Bruges. However, this resulted from flexible merchants who possessed the expertise and amassed the funds to litigate in these courts. This small group became very proficient and less dependent on Bruges for its conflict resolution.

It was also this group of smaller but important merchants that left the city in the 1490s. These merchants went where lucrative opportunities existed. Bruges stepped in and was ready to make significant concessions in these straitened times. The treasured, and much-defended legal framework was released to grant the merchants a truly privileged position. It kept the Castilians and Hanseatic merchants in the city; but it failed to keep the less nation-bound merchants. The Italian families, the Portuguese, and the independent English merchants could barely be controlled by their nations. The legal concessions did not keep them in Bruges for long. These merchants had never relied on privileges. They relied on networks, and as the networks shifted to Antwerp, so their litigation strategies shifted away from Bruges.

So, was Bruges a city of justice? It certainly aspired to be one, and to be regarded as such. The aldermen took their role as judges seriously and tried to provide as much adequate justice as possible. However, achieving this was challenging. The aldermen of Bruges had to govern one of the largest cities in the County of Flanders and manage the most diverse population of the time. Additionally, they understood that their prosperity depended on commerce, which gave merchants a certain level of influence over them.

The aldermen were constantly balancing the task of ensuring proper justice, while also keeping the merchant factions content. This was no easy feat, and it became even more challenging when several merchants took their cases to a princely court, outside the jurisdiction of the aldermen. In this way, some merchants could exert pressure on the aldermen to obtain favourable decisions. However, it is essential to distinguish between the individual litigation strategies of specific merchants and any structural advantages in litigating before the aldermen.

Between 1309, when the first far-reaching Hanseatic privileges were granted, and 1492, the end of the Flemish rebellion, the aldermen of Bruges maintained their own court as the primary institution for conflict resolution. While some privileges may have provided advantages before this court, none of them granted extensive advantages to any particular nation. Even the Hanseatic nation had to secure their advantage by appointing a Kontor Secretary specialised in litigating before the aldermen. However, when commerce declined in the 1490s, and all the merchant nations moved to Antwerp, Bruges found itself disadvantageously placed to negotiate their return. It is worth noting that it was during this low point that Bruges conceded major procedural advantages.

It can be argued that it was the merchants who pushed Bruges into a framework that corresponded less with the aldermen's notion of 'proper justice'. However, whether the merchant communities could enforce their privileges before the court, or whether the aldermen simply reverted to their own sense of justice, leaving these 1490 privileges aside, remains to be determined. Nevertheless, if we look at Gerard David's 'Judgment of Cambyses', it is evident that the aldermen did not relinquish their ambition. The painting they displayed in their court symbolised their ongoing endeavour to be considered as a city of justice.

Bibliography

UNPUBLISHED SOURCES

BELGIUM

ANTWERP

Felixarchief (FA)

Het groot certificatieboek

Privilegiekamer, Vreemde natiën

1061, Duitse natie (1469–1584)

1063, Duitse natie (1315–1598)

1070, Natie van Portugal (1411–1650)

1075, Natie van Genua (1501–1605)

1076, Natie van Lucca (1501–1605)

1078, Natie van Lombardie (1501–1700)

1079, Spaanse natie (1493–1685)

BRUGES

Stadsarchief (SAB)

Charters:

Politieke Oorkonden: 564, 663, 688, 945, 968, 1039, 1046, 1064, 1065, 1078, 1082, 1094, 1140, 1153, 1162, 1163, 1164, 1169, 1170, 1180, 1182, 1220, 1223, 1225, 1233, 1273, 1277, 1285

Spaans Consulaat: 4, 17, 20, 22, 23, 25, 42, 46, 54

Cartularia:

96/2 Rodenboek (1282–1548)

96/3 Rodenboek A (1240–1511)

96/4 Oude Wittenboek (1089–1546)

96/11 Groenenboek A (1408–1458)

96/12 Groenenboek B (1236–1593)

96/13 Groenenboek C (1281–1548)

96/14 Groenenboek Ongecotteerd. (1447–1512)

96/17 Zwartenboek (1477)

96/21 Sententien (1442–1676)

96/22 Purperenboek (14e eeuw–1540)

96/24 Gedelf 1470–1510

114, Wetsvernieuwingen

120, Register van de Hallegeboden, 1490–1499

157, Civiele Sententiën Vierschaar, 1423–1424
157, Civiele Sententiën Vierschaar, 1433–1436
157, Civiele Sententiën Vierschaar, 1447–1453
157, Civiele Sententiën Vierschaar, 1453–1461
157, Civiele Sententiën Vierschaar, 1465–1469
157, Civiele Sententiën Vierschaar, 1469–1470
164, Memoriaal van de Kamer, 1439–1441
164, Memoriaal van de Kamer, 1474–1475
165, Civiele Sententiën Kamer, 1473–1474
165, Civiele Sententiën Kamer, 1487–1488
165, Civiele Sententiën Kamer, 1489–1490
165, Civiele Sententiën Kamer, 1501–1502
166, Sentenciën Civiele
196, Donkere kamer
198, Klerken van de Vierschaar
216, Stadsrekeningen Brugge, 1350–1500
277, Presentwijnen
299, Makelaars
310, Charters ambachten
515, Oorkonden Veranneman
522, Sluis, Watervliet, Muide, Maldegem

Rijksarchief Brugge (RAB)
Zeerechten, 3568

BRUSSELS
Algemeen Rijksarchief (ARA)
Accounting chambre of Flanders (Chambre des comptes – CC) 13769
13769–13782, Accounts of the city bailiff of Bruges, 1414–1495
13926, Accounts of the bailiff of Sluis, 1421–1489
36550–36618, Accounts of the city of Mude, 1406–1488
3154, Account of Bonnore Olivier
21430–21449, Comptes des exploits des conseils de Justice, Exploits du grand conseil et du conseil privé, 1463–1494
21796–21829, Comptes des exploits des conseil de Justice, Exploits du Conseil de Flanders, 1416–1462

Fonds Grote Raad
Geëxtendeerde Sententiën
Grote Raad, 791, 1471–1472
Grote Raad, 794, 1479
Grote Raad, 795, 1479–1480
Grote Raad, 796, 1477–1480
Grote Raad, 797, 1480–1482

Grote Raad, 798, 1483–1485
Grote Raad, 799, 1490–1491
Grote Raad, 801, 1491–1492

GHENT

Rijksarchief Gent (RAG)

Raad van Vlaanderen

146, 'Style van procederen', in de Raad van Vlaanderen
691, Originele placcaarten en ordonnantiën, 1416–1475
2333–2447, Acten en Sententiën, Mei 1400–April 1510
7508, Interlocutoire Sententiën, 1412–1427
7509, Interlocutoire Sententien, 1437–1439 and 1421–1422
7510, Interlocutoire Sententien, 1434–1441 and 1494–1496
7511, Interlocutoire Sententien, 1447–1458
7512, Interlocutoire Sententien, 1483–1486
7513, Interlocutoire Sententien, 1490–1493
7514, Interlocutoire Sententien, 1496–1498
7515, Interlocutoire Sententien, 1498–1503
8495, Boeten, 1454–1455
8496, Boeten, 1468–1469
8497, Boeten, 1471–1472
8498, Boeten, 1473–1474
23703, Processen par Escript, Zeger Parmentier c. Thomas Stevinszone, 1467–1470
23705, Processen par Escript, Pietro de Nyeto vs. Alonso de Larmes, 1475–1482
23712, Processen par Escript, Robert Bailly vs. Jan de Deckere (arrestatie), 1496
23720, Processen par Escript Lijsbet Spapen, wed. van Willem de Ferrest c. Rodrigo Cathelaen, 1514–1516
27783, Processen in beroep, Lazzaro Lommelini c. Thomas Pierroot
34280, Collectie van de advocaat-fiscaal J.B. Van Steenberghen, Grote Raad van Mechelen
34288, Rekenkamer van Rijsel, Grote Raad van Mechelen en Raad van Vlaanderen, hun respectievelijke bevoegdheid, vooral inzake tollen en domeinen
34305, Raden van Vlaanderen, Artois en Luxemburg; Parlement van Dôle: instructies, inrichting en werking
34312, Ressort van de Raad van Vlaanderen – Exemptie Parlement van Parijs – Bevoegdheid van van versch. wetten in Vlaanderen – Bevoegdheid van versc. Vorstelijke ambtenaren

Varia 2

1259, Costumen en Privileges van de Raad van Vlaanderen

Varia D

2963/71, Afschrift van een handelstraktaat tussen de koning van Schotland en de hertog van Bourgondië
3117, Verschillende documenten m.b.t. Italiaanse handelaars
3371, Uitreksel uit de Recueil des antiquités met betrekking tot de rechten van de graaf van Vlaanderen tegenover de Koning van Frankrijk met betrekking op de instellingen van het graafschap Vlaanderen
3431, Politieke en commerciële betrekkingen tussen Vlaanderen en Engeland, Periode 1338–1420. Verzameling kopieën van bescheiden uit de Archives Departementales

Universiteitsarchief Gent (UAG)
Manuscripten
HS. 2570, Deeds regarding Bruges and Sluis
HS. 3795, Peace negotiations and other legal texts
HS. 3800, Denys Heyman, Juridische tractaten en teksten
G.001979, Documents on the history of the Burgundian state

FRANCE

PARIS
Archives nationales (AN)
Parliament de Paris
X^{1A}, Amendes, 1482
8854, 8855
X^{1C}, Accords
172
X^{1A}, Conseil
1482, 1483
X^{1A}, Plaidoiries
4798–4810; 4825, 4838, 4839, 8304, 8307, 8309, 8310

LILLE
Archives Départementales du Nord (ADN)
Chambre des comptes
Chartes, 306, 504, 513/8621, 513/3, 572
Registre des Chartes, 1602
Lettres missives, 17667–17672
Accounts of the water bailiff, 6084–6196

ITALY

PISA
Scuola Normale (SNSP)
Archivo Diplomatico

Libri di Commercio, 24
Libri di Commercio, 25

FIRENZE
Bibliotheca Nationale (BN)
Ginori Conti
Bernardo Cambi, 7, 1455–1460
Bernardo Cambi, 8, 1435–1457
Bernardo Cambi, 9, 1470–1490
Archivio di Stato di Firenze (ASF)
Carte Strozziane
Secondo, 21bis
Terzo, 127, 138
Quinto, 14
Mercanzia
Atti in causi civile 1482, 1486
Deliberazioni dell'Ufficinte forestiero, 259
Deliberazioni dell Uficiale e de' Sei di Mercanzia, 313 and 314
Sentenze de' Sei e dell' Ufficinte, 7235, 7238
Medici Avanti il Principato

VENICE
Archivio di Stato di Venezia (ASV)
Commemorandi
Senato
Misti Senato
Senato Mar

LUCCA
Archivio di Stato di Lucca (ASL)
Corte dei Mercanti, Cause civile
Archivio Guinigi

UNITED KINGDOM
ABERDEEN
Municipal Archives Aberdeen (CAA)
Council, Baillie and Guild court registers, 1 April 1448–18 July 1468
Council, Baillie and Guild court registers, 3 October 1468–30 December 1486

LONDON
National Archives Kew (NA)
Chancery, miscellanea
C 47/37/10–18, C 47/130/9/nr. 17

Municipal Archives London (MAL)
Common council
Journal 8 (1470–1482)
Journal 9 (1482–1492)

PUBLISHED SOURCES

Blockmans W.P. and I. Strubbe, 'Privilegie voor Vlaanderen', In *1477. Het algemene en de gewestelijke privilegien van Maria van Bourgondië voor de Nederlanden*, edited by M.-W.P. Blockmans. Kortrijk-Heule: UGA, 1985.

Blockmans, W.P. *Handelingen van de leden en van de staten van Vlaanderen. Regering van Filips de Goede (10 september 1419–15 juni 1467). Excerpten uit de rekeningen van de Vlaamse steden en kasselrijen en van de vorstelijke ambtenaren. Deel 1. Tot de onderwerping van Brugge (4 maart 1438)*. Brussels: Paleis der Academiën, 1990.

Blockmans, W.P. *Handelingen van de leden en van de staten van Vlaanderen. Regering van Filips de Goede (10 september 1419–15 juni 1467). Excerpten uit de rekeningen van de Vlaamse steden en kasselrijen en van de vorstelijke ambtenaren. Deel 2. Vanaf de onderwerping van Brugge (4 maart 1438)*. Brussels: Paleis der Academiën, 1995.

Blockmans, W.P. *Handelingen van de leden en van de staten van Vlaanderen (1467–1477). Excerpten uit de rekeningen van de Vlaamse steden en kasselrijen en van de vorstelijke ambtenaren*. Brussels: Paleis der Academiën, 1971.

Blockmans, W.P. *Handelingen van de leden en van de staten van Vlaanderen. Regeringen van Maria van Bourgondië en Filips de Schone (5 januari 1477–26 september 1506). Excerpten uit de rekeningen van de Vlaamse steden en kasselrijen en van de vorstelijke ambtenaren. Deel 1. Tot de vrede van Kadzand*. Brussels: Paleis der Academiën, 1973.

Blockmans, W.P. *Handelingen van de leden en van de staten van Vlaanderen. Regeringen van Maria van Bourgondië en Filips de Schone (5 januari 1477–26 september 1506). Excerpten uit de rekeningen van de Vlaamse steden en kasselrijen en van de vorstelijke ambtenaren. Deel 2. Na de vrede van Kadzand*. Brussels: Paleis der Academiën, 1982.

Bonenfant, P, J. Bartier, and A. Van Nieuwenhuysen, *Ordonnances de Philippe le Hardi et de Marguerite de Male du 16 octobre au 31 décembre 1393*. Brussels: SCT, 1965.

Bonenfant, P., J. Bartier and A. Van Nieuwenhuysen, *Ordonnances de Philippe le Hardi et de Marguerite de Male du 17 janvier 1394 au 25 février 1405*. Brussels: Ministrère de la justice, 1974.

Braamcamp, F. *Noticias da feitoria de Flandres precedidas dos brandões poetas de concioneiro*. Lissabon: Arquivo Historico Portugues, 1920.

Brown, R. *Caldendar of State Papers and Manuscripts relating to English affairs existing in the archives and collections of Venice, Italy and in other libraries of Nortern Italy. Volume I. 1202–1509*. London: Longman, Green, Roberts and Green, 1864.

Cauchies, J.-M. *Ordonnances de Jean sans Peur, 1405–1419*. Brussels, Ministrère de la Justice, 2001.

Dauchy, S. *Les appels flamands au Parlement de Paris: regestes des dossiers de proès reconstitués d'après les registres du Parlement et les sources conservées dans les dépôts d'archives de Balgique et du Nord de la France*. Brussels: Ministère de la justice, 1998.

De Commynes, P. *Mémoire*, edited by J. Blanchard. Genève: Dross, 2007.

De Damhoudere, J. *Van de Grootdadigheyt der breedt-vermaerde regeringhe van de stadt Brugge: met de plaets-beschrijvinge der selver stede; beneffens een loflijke uytsprake ter eere van 't grootdadig magistraet*. Amsterdam: Weduwe van Jan Jacobz. Schipper, 1684 [1555].

De La Marche, *Mémoires*, edited by H. Beaune and J.D. Arbaumont, vol. III. Paris: Librairie Renouard, 1885.

De Smet, J.J. *Corpus chronicorum Flandriae: sub aespiciis Leopoldi Primi serenissimi Belgarum regis*. Brussels: Hayez, 1865.

Desmoni, C. and L.T. Belgrano, *Documenti, ed estratti inediti o poco noti riguardanti la storia del commercio e della marina ligure*. Genua: Società Ligure di Storia Patria, 1867.

Despars, N. 'Cronijcke van den lande en graefscepe van Vlaendren gemaeckt', vol. III, edited by J. De Jonghe. Rotterdam: Den uitgever, 1840.

Dumolyn, J. 'Rebelheden ende vergaderinghen: twee Brugse documenten uit de Grote opstand van 1436–1438', *Handelingen van de Koninklijke Commissie voor Geschiedenis: Koninklijke Academie van België* (1996), 297–323.

Gilliodts-Van Severen, L. *Cartulaire de l'ancien consulat d'Espagne. Recueil de documents concernant le commerce maritime et intérieur, le droit des gens public et privé et l'histoire économique de la Flandre*. Bruges: De Plancke, 1902.

Gilliodts-Van Severen, L. *Cartulaire de l'ancien estaple de Bruges. Recueil de documents concernant le commerce intérieur et maritime, les relations internationales et l'histoire économique de cette ville*, vol. 1–2. Bruges: De Plancke, 1904.

Gilliodts-Van Severen, L. *Coutume du Franc de Bruges.*, vol. II (Brussels: Gobbaerts, 1879), 418;

Gilliodts-Van Severen, L. *Coutumes de petites villes et seigneuries enclavées, Ostende, Oudenburg, Sluis*, vol. 4. Brussels: Gobbaerts, 1892.

Gilliodts-Van Severen, L. *Coutumes des petites villes et seigneuries enclavées Ghistelles, Houcke, Lichtervelde, Maldeghem, Merckem, Middelbourg, Mude, Munikerede, Nieuvliet, Oostbourg*, vol. 3. Brussels: Fr. Gobbaerts, 1891.

Gilliodts-Van Severen, L. *Coutumes des petites villes et seigneuries enclavées. Cadsant, Caprycke, Damme, Dixmude, Eecloo*, vol. 2. Brussels: Gobbaerts, 1890.

Gilliodts-Van Severen, L. *Inventaire des archives de la ville de Bruges. Section 1: Inventaire des chartes*, vol. I–VI. Bruges: Gailliard, 1871–1885.

Grunzweig A. 'Le fonds du consulat de la mer aux archives de l'Etat à Florence', In *Bulletin de l'Institut historique belge de Rome* 10 (1930), 5–121.

Guicciardini, L. *Descrittione di tutti I Paesi Bassi, altrimenti detti Germania Inperiore con piu carte di Geographia del paese é colritratto natorale du piu terre principali.* Antwerp: Guglielmo Silvio, 1567.

H.P. Schaap, *Philips Wielant en diens corte instructie omme jonghe practisienen in civile zaken.* Haarlem: Tjeenk Willink, 1927.

Höhlbaum, K., K. Kunze and W. Stein, *Hansisches Urkundenbuch.* Halle: Verlag der Buchhandling des Waisenhauses, 1876–1916.

Innes, C. *The acts of the parliaments of Scotland*, vol. I. London: s. p., 1844.

Koppmann, K. *Hanserecesse. Die recesse und andere Akten der Hansetage, 1256–1430*, vol. 1. Leipzig: Duncker and Humblot, 1870.

Lazzereschi, E. *Libro della comunità dei mercanti lucchesi in Bruges.* Milan: Dott. Rodolfo Malfasi, 1947.

Masi, G. *Statuti delle colonie Fiorentine all'estero (secc. XV–XVI).* Milan: Dott. A. Giuffrè – Editore, 1941.

Monballyu, J. *Filips Wielant. Verzameld werk I, Corte instructie in materie criminele.* Brussels: Paleis der Academien, 1995.

Monstrelet, E. *La chronique d'Enguerran de Monstrelet, en deux livres, avec pieces justificatives 1400–1444*, vol. III. Edited by L. C. Douët-d'Arcq. Paris: Renouard, 1859.

Moryson, F. *An itinerary containing his ten yeeres travell through the twelve dominions of Germany, Bohmerland, Switzerland, Netherland, Denmarke, Poland, Italy, Turky, France, England, Scotland & Ireland.* Glasgow: J. MacLehose and sons, 1907.

Müller, J. *Docimenti sulle relazioni delle città toscane.* Florence: Coi tipi di M. Cellini e C, 1879.

Pardessus, J-M. *Collection de lois maritimes antérieures au XVIIIe siècle*, vol. 1 and 4. Paris: Imprimerie Royale, 1839.

Paz y Melia A. *Series de los mas importantes documentos del Archivo y biblioteca del Exmo. Señor Duque de Medinaceli/Elegidos por su encargo y publ. a sus expensas.* Madrid: Archivia y biblioteca de la casa de Medinaceli, 1922.

Predelli, R. *I Libri commemoriali della republica di Venezia. Regesti*, vol. I. Venice: A Spese Della Societa, 1876.

Prevenier, W. *Handelingen van de leden en van de staten van Vlaanderen (1384–1408). Excerpten uit de rekeningen der steden, kasselrijen en vorstelijke ambtenaren.* Brussels: Paleis der Academiën, 1959.

Romiti A., *Riformagioni della repubblica di Lucca (1369–1400). Volume primo (Marzo 1369–Agosto 1370 e aggiunte).* Rome: Accademia Nazionale dei Lincei, 1980.

Schouteet A., *De klerken van de vierschaar te Brugge met inventaris van hun protocollen bewaard op het Brugse stadsarchief.* Brugge: Gemeentebestuur Brugge 1973.

Scott, M.E. *Le cotton manuscrit galba.* B.I. Brussels: Hayez, 1986.

Sicking L.H.J. and C.H. van Rhee, *Filips Wielant verzameld werk II Briève instruction en causes civiles.* Brussels: Paleis der Academiën, 2009.

Simonetti G. and M. Tangheroni, *Lucca Repubblicana.* Lucca: Editalia-Edizioni d'Italia.

Spruit, J.E., R. Feenstra, K.E.M. Bongenaar, eds. *Corpus Iuris Civiles. Tekst en vertaling III. Digesta XI–XXX.* Zutphen: Walburg Pers, 1996.

Stalins, G., Jean de Bloys, B. van Zoomeren, *Tweeden druck van den eersten bouck der ordonnancien, statute, edicten ende placcaeten soo van weghen den keyserlyke ende koninghlyke maiesteyten, als huerlieder doorluchtighste voorsaeten, graven ende graefneden van Vlaendren, Nieuwelinghs vermeerdert met doorgaende marginale aenwysinghen ende volkommentafel.* Ghent: Anna vanden Steene, weduwe van Michiel du Laury, 1639.

Strubbe, E.I. *Pracktijke civile.* Amsterdam: Graphic, 1968.

Sutton A. and L. Visser-Fuchs, *The book of privileges of the Merchant Adventurers of England, 1296–1483.* New York: Oxford University Press, 2009.

Thomson T., *Acts of the Lords of Council in civil causes,* vol. 1, London: s.p., 1839.

Van Caenegem, *Les arrêts et jugés du Parlemnt de Paris sur appels flamands conservés dans les registres du Parlement,* vol. 1. 1320–1453. Brussels: 1966.

Van der Tanerijen, W. *Boec van der Loopender Pracktijken der raidtcameren van Brabant,* edited by Eg. I Strubbe. Brussels: Koninklijke Academie, 1952.

Warner, G. *The Libelle of Englyshe Polycye: a poem on the use of sea-power.* Oxford: Clarendon Press, 1926.

Zoete, A. *Handelingen van de leden en van de staten van Vlaanderen (1405–1419). Excerpten uit de rekeningen der steden, kasselrijen en vorstelijke ambtenaren. Deel 1 (24 maart–5 maart 1413).* Brussels: Paleis der Academiën, 1981.

LITERATURE

Abraham-Thisse, S. 'Les relations hispano-hanséates au Bas Moyen Age', *En la España Medieval* 14 (1991), 131–161.

Abraham-Thisse, S. 'Les relations hispano-hanséates au Bas Moyen Age', *En la España Medieval* 15 (1992), 249–295.

Acheri, M. *The Law of Late Medieval Italy (1000–1500).* Leiden: Brill, 2013.

Aerts, E. 'De Rekenkamer van Vlaanderen, (1386–1735)', In *De centrale overheidsinstellingen van de Habsburgse Nederlanden,* edited by E. Aerts et al., 608–615. Brussels: Algemeen rijksarchief, 1994.

Aerts, E. 'Italian presence in late medieval Bruges stock market', In *Le droit face à l'économie sans travail,* edited by L. Brunori, S. Dauchy, O. Descamps, X. Prévost, 169–221. Paris: Classiques Garnier, 2019.

Aerts, E. 'The absence of public exchange banks in medieval and early modern Flanders and Brabant (1400–1800), a historical anomaly to be explained', *Financial History Review* 18, nr. 1 (2011), 91–117.

Aerts, E. 'Wisselruiterij in de Lage Landen. De wisselbrief op de Brugse geldmarkt tijdens de late middeleeuwen', In *Ter Beurze. Geschiedenis van de aandelenhandel in België 1300–1900,* edited by G. De Clerq, 33–46. Antwerp: Tijd, 1993.

Aguiar Andrade, A., F. Miranda, 'Lisbon: trade, urban power and the King's visible hand', In *The Routledge Handbook of maritime trade around Europe, 1300–1600,* edited by W. Blockmans, 333–351. New York: Routledge, 2017.

Allmand, C.T. and C.A.J. Armstrong, *English suits before the Parlement of Paris, 1420–1436*. London: Royal Historical Society, 1982.

Anderson, J.L. 'Piracy and world history. An economic perspective on maritime predation', In *Bandits at sea: a pirate reader*, edited by C.R. Pennel, 82–106. New York: New York University Press, 2001.

Arbel, B. 'Venice's maritime empire in the early modern period', *A companion to Venetian history*, edited by E.R. Dursteler, 125–254. Leiden: Brill, 2013.

Arnade, P. *Realms of ritual. Burgundian ceremony and civic life in late medieval Ghent*. Ithaca and London: Cornell University Press, 1996.

Arnould, M.-A. 'Les lendemains de Nancy dans les "pays de par deça" (Janvier–Avril 1477)', In *1477. Het algemene en de gewestelijke privilegiën van Maria van Bourgondië voor de Nederlanden*, edited by W.P. Blockmans, 1–83. Kortrijk-Heule: UGA, 1985.

Ashtor, E. 'The Venetian supremacy in Levantine trade: monopoly or pre-colonialism', *Journal of European Economic History* 3, nr. 1 (1974), 5–53.

Aubert, J.J. 'Dealing with the Abyss: the nature and purpose of the Rhodian Sea-law on jettison (Le Rhodia de iactu, D. 14.2) and the making of Justinian's digest', In *Beyond dogmatics: law and society in the Roman world*, edited by J.W. Cairns and P.J. du Plessis, 157–172. Edinburgh: Edinburgh University Press, 2007.

Auzary-Schmaltz, B. and S. Dauchy, 'Le Parlement de Paris', In *Case law in the making. The techniques and methods of judicial records and law reports. Vol. 1 Essays*, edited by A. Wijffels 199–223. Berlijn: Duncker & Humblot, 1997.

Bader, K.S. 'Arbiter arbitrator seu amicabilis compositor. Zur verbreiting einer kanonistischen Formel in Gebieten nördlich der Alpen', *Zeitschrift der Savigny-Stiftung für Rechtsgeschichte. Kanonistische Abteilung* 46, nr. 1 (1960), 239–276.

Barros A. and F. Miranda, '"To make good peace or total war": Trade, piracy, and the construction of Portugal's maritime state in the later middle ages', In *Merchants, pirates and smugglers. Criminalization, economics, and the transformation of the Maritime world (1200–1600)*, edited by T. Heebøll-Holm, P. Höhn and G. Rohmann, 305–308. Frankfurt: Campus Verlag, 2018.

Bell, A.L., C. Brooks, and T.K. Moore, 'Cambium non est mutuum: exchange and interest rates in medieval Europe', *Economic History Review* 70, nr. 2 (2017), 373–396.

Berben, H. 'Une guerre économique au Moyen Age. L'embargo sur l'exportation des laines anglaises (1270–1274)', In *Etudes d'histoire dédiées à la mémoire de H. Pirenne par ses anciens élèves*, ed. by H. Van Werveke, 1–17. Brussels: Nouvelle société d'éditions, 1937.

Berkvens, L. 'Imperatoriam maiestatem non solum armis decoratam sed legibus oportet esse armatam . . . Notes on the influence of Justinian's Institutes on the codification of customary law in the Southern Netherlands', In *Viva vox iuris Romani. Essays in Honour of Johannes Emil Spruit*, edited by L. de Ligt, 1–7. Leiden: Brill, 2002.

Bervoets, L. and J. Dumolyn, 'Urban protest in thirteenth-century north-western Europe: a comparative approach', *Journal of Medieval History* 48, nr. 1 (2022), 75–102.

Beuken, J.H.A. *Hanze en Vlaanderen*. Maastricht: Van Aelst, 1950.

Biancalana, J. 'The legal framework of arbitration in fifteenth-century England', *American Journal of Legal History* 47 (2005), 347–382.

Bissaud, J. *Le créancier 'premier saisissant' dans l'ancien droit français*. Paris: Presses universitaires de France 1972.

Blockmans, W. 'Villes et monarchies: complémentarité et rivalité entre commerce et politique', *Histoire urbaine* 2 (2022), 7–30.

Blockmans, W. *De volksvertegenwoordiging in Vlaanderen in de overgang van middeleeuwen naar nieuwe tijden (1384–1506)*. Brussels: Koninklijke Academie, 1978.

Blockmans, W. M. Krom, and J. Wubs-Mrozewicz. 'Maritime trade around Europe 1300–1600. Commercial networks and urban autonomy', In *The Routledge Handbook of maritime trade around Europe 1300–1600*, edited by W. Blockmans, M. Krom and J. Wubs-Mrozewicz, 1–14. New York: Routledge, 2017.

Blockmans, W.P 'Mutaties van het politiek personeel in de steden Gent en Brugge tijdens een periode van regimewisselingen: het laatste kwart van de 15de eeuw', In *Bronnen voor de Geschiedenis van Instellingen in België*, edited by H. De Schepper, 193–201. Brussels: Algemeen Rijksarchief, 1976.

Blockmans, W.P. 'Corruptie, patronage en makelaardij en venaliteit als symptomen van een ontluikende staatsvorming in de Bourgondische-Habsburgse Nederlanden', *Tijdschrift voor Sociale Geschiedenis* 3 (1985), 231–247.

Blockmans, W.P. and W. Prevenier, *The promised lands. The Low Countries under Burgundian Rule, 1369–1530*. Philadelphia: University of Pennsylvania Press, 1999.

Boestad, T. 'Legitimizing interurban cooperation in the Middle Ages: the legal system of the Hanse', In *Research handbook on international law and cities*, edited by H.P. Aust and J.E. Nijman, 29–40. Cheltenham: Edward Elgar Publishing, 2021.

Boestad, T. *'Pour le profit du commun marchand': la genèse de la Hanse (XIIe siècle du XIVe siècle)*. Paris: Sorbonne Université, 2020.

Bolton J. and F. Guidi-Bruscoli, '"Your flexible friend": the bill of exchange in theory and practice in the fifteenth century', *Economic history review* 74, nr. 4 (2021), 873–891.

Bolton J. and F. Guidi-Bruscoli, 'When did Antwerp replace Bruges as the commercial and financial centre of North-Western Europe? The evidence of the Borromei ledger for 1438', *The Economic History Review* 61, nr. 2 (2008), 360–379.

Bonduel, E. 'Late medieval Bruges as an international market for eastern and African goods', In *Underneath the shade we lay grounded*, edited by O. Nkanga, 131–137. Veurne: Hannibal Books, 2023.

Bonner, E. 'Scotland's "Auld Alliance" with France, 1295–1560', *History* 84, nr. 273 (1999), 5–30.

Boone, M. 'Apologie d'un banquier médiéval: Tomasso Portinari et l'Etat bourguignon', *Le Moyen Age* 105 (1999), 31–54.

Boone, M. 'In defence of a medieval banker: Tommaso Portinari and the Burgundian state', In *City and state in the medieval Low Countries. Collected studies by Marc Boone*, edited by J. Braekevelt et al., 111–134. Turnout: Brepols, 2021.

Boone, M. 'Le rêve de l'État-ville. Ambitions gantoises, réalités bourguignonnes et conflits juridico-financiers (ca. 1430)', In *Le gouvernement des communautés politiques à la fin du Moyen Âge: entre puissance et négociation: villes, finances, état: actes de colloque en l'honneur d'Albert Rigaudière*, edited by C. Leveleux, A. Rousselet-Pimont, P. Bonin and F. Garnier, 375–399. Paris: Panthéon-Assas, 2010.

Boone, M. 'Les ducs Valois de Bourgogne, leur successeurs habsbourgeois et les villes: ambitions et réalités fiscales', *Société française d'histoire urbaine* 1 (2021), 95–120.

Boone, M. 'L'influence des pratiques et du savoir-faire «étatiques» dans les comptes des villes flamandes et des principautés des anciens Pays-Bas au XIV–XVe siècles', In *Classer, dire, compter. Discipline du chiffre et fabrique d'une norme comptable à la fin du Moyen âge. Colloque des 10 et 11 octobre 2012*, edited by O. Mattéoni en P. Beck, 199–215. Paris: comité pour l'histoire économique et financière de la France Ministère des Finances et des Comptes publics, ministère de l'Economie, de l'Industrie et du Numérique, 2015.

Boone, M. 'Stedelijke financiën in de laatmiddeleeuwse Zuidelijke Nederlanden', *Tijdschrift voor fiscaal recht* 102 (1991), 122–135.

Boone, M. 'Urban Space and political conflict in late medieval Flanders', *Journal of Interdisciplinary History* 32, nr. 4 (2002), 621–640.

Boone, M. *Gent en de Bourgondische hertogen ca. 1384–ca. 1453: een sociaal-politieke studie van een staatsvormingsproces*. Brussels: Koninklijke Academie voor wetenschappen, letteren en schone kunsten van België, 1990.

Borchert, T.-H. 'The impact of Jan van Eyck's lost Lomellini-Triptych and his Genoese patrons', *Colnaghi Studies* 4 (2019), 31–61.

Boumans, R. 'Wethouders en stedelijk functionarissen in de 16de, 17de en 18de eeuw', In *Flandria Nostra. Ons land en ons volk, zijn standen en beroepen door de tijden heen*, volume 5, edited by J.L. Broekx, 395–424. Antwerpen: Standaard boekhandel, 1960.

Braekevelt J. and B. Lambert, 'Bonnore Olivier, Courtier ligurien de la fiscalité bourguignonne', *Revue belge de Philologie et d'Histoire* 90, nr. 4 (2012), 1155–1191.

Braekevelt J. and J. Dumolyn, 'Diplomatique et discours politiques. Une analyse lexicographique qualitative et quantitative des ordonnances de Philippe le Bon pour la Flandre (1419–1467)', *Revue Historique* 662, nr. 2 (2012), 323–356.

Braekevelt, J. 'Entre profit et dommage: présence et privilèges de la nation Génoise à Bruges sous les ducs de Bourgogne (1384–1477)', *Publications du centre européen d'études Bourguignonnes* 49 (2009), 117–129.

Brand, H. 'Floris en Jan van Boschuijsen: Leidense edelen aan het Beierse en Bourgondische hof', *Leidschrift* 14 (2000), 64–99.

Braudel, F. *Les jeux de l'échange. Civilisation matérielle, économie et capitalisme: XVe–XVIIIe siècle*. Paris: Colin, 1979.

Breakevelt, J. 'Un prince de justice: vorstelijke wetgeving, soevereiniteit en staatsvorming in het graafschap Vlaanderen tijdens de regering van Filips de Goede (1419–1467)', PhD. Diss: Ghent University, 2013.

Brown A. and J. Dumolyn, *Medieval Bruges, c. 850–1550*. Cambridge: Cambridge University Press, 2018.

Brown, A. 'Cities, nations and divine service: identifying Spanish merchants in late medieval Bruges', *Urban History* 44, nr. 2 (2017), 166–187.

Brown, A. 'Urban jousts in the later middle ages: the white bear of Bruges', *Belgisch Tijdschrift voor Geschiedenis en Filologie* 78, nr. 2 (2000), 315–330.

Brown, A. *Civic ceremony and religion in medieval Bruges c.1300–1520*. Cambridge: Cambridge University Press, 2011.

Brulez, W. 'Bruges and Antwerp in the 15th and 16th centuries: an antithesis?' *Acta Historiae Neerlandicae. Studies on the history of Netherlands* VI (1973), 1–26.

Brulez, W. 'Brugge en Antwerpen in de 15e en 16e eeuw: een tegenstelling?' *Tijdschrift voor Geschiedenis* 83 (1970), 15–37.

Brundage, J.A. *The Medieval origins of the legal professions*. Chicago: Chicago University Press, 2008.

Bryer, R.A. 'Double-entry bookkeeping and the birth of capitalism: accounting for the commercial revolution in Medieval Northern Italy', *Critial perspectives on accounting* 4 (1993), 113–140.

Buntinx, J. 'De l'origine de l'audience du comte de Flandre', *Revue du Nord* 30, nr. 120 (1948), 210–222.

Buntinx, J. 'Wielant, Philips', *Biographie nationale*, 27 (1938), 279–298.

Buntinx, J. *De audientië van de graven van Vlaanderen: studie over het centraal grafelijk gerecht (c. 1330–c. 1409)*. Brussels: standaard Boekhandel, 1949.

Burke, P. 'Early modern Venice as a centre of information and communication', *The history and civilisation of an Italian city-state Venice reconsidered*, edited by J. Martin and D. Romano, 389–419. Baltimore: Johns Hopkins University Press, 2000.

Burkhardt, M. 'Kontors and outposts', In *A Companion tot he Hanseatic League*, edited by D. J. Harreld, 127–161. Leiden: Brill, 2015.

Burkhardt, M. 'Policy, Business, Privacy. Contacts made by the merchants of the Hanse Kontor in Bergen in the Late Middle Ages', In *Trade, Diplomacy and Cultural Exchange. Continuity and Change in the North Sea and the Baltic c. 1350–1750*, edited by H. Brand, 136–151. Hilversum: Uitgeverij Verloren, 2005.

Burkhardt, M. 'The German Hanse and Bergen. New perspectives on an old subject', *Scandinavian Economic History Review* 58, nr. 1 (2010), 60–79.

Buylaert, F. 'Baenst, Jan II de, vorstelijk ambternaar, baljuw van Brugge en het Vrije, lid van het stadsbestuur van Brugge', *Nationaal Biografisch woordenboek* 17, 41–44. Brussels: Paleis der Academiën, 2005.

Buylaert, F. 'Lordship, urbanization and social change in late medieval Flanders', *Past & Present* 227, nr. 1 (2015), 31–75.

Buylaert, F. 'The "Van Bosschuyen affair". In Leyden. Conflicts between elite networks in Late Medieval Holland', *Francia -Forschungen zur westeuropäische Geschichte* 35 (2008), 95–113.

Buylaert, F., J. De Rock and J. Dumolyn, 'La loge des bourgeois de Bruges. Les stratégies de distinction d'une élite commerçante cosmopolite', *Revue du Nord* 414, nr. 1 (2016), 37–69.

Cairns, J. 'Historical Introduction', In *A history of private law in Scotland*, vol. 1, edited by K. Reid and R. Zimmermann, 14–184. Oxford: Oxford University Press, 2000.

Camenisch, C. 'Cold, rain and famine. Three subsistence crises in the Burgundian Low Countries during the fifteenth century', In *Fifty years of medieval technology and social change*, edited by S.A. Walton, 187–197. New York: Routledge, 2019.

Cannelloni, F. 'Il commercio dell'allume di Tolfa nei Paesi Bassi borgognoni', *Archivio Storico Italiano* 175, nr. 3 (2017), 517–546.

Caravaggi, L. 'Keeping the peace in a Late-Medieval polity. Conflict and collaboration in Bologna in the Age of Dante (13th–14th centuries)', PhD. Diss. University of Oxford, 2020.

Caravaggi, L. 'Tra dialogo e conflitto. Controllare lo spazio e mantenere la pace a Bologna alla fine del Duecento', *Archivio Storico Italiano* 178, nr. 666 (2020), 677–712.

Carlier, A. 'Taaldiversiteit in de kosmopolitische stad. Taalgebruik, migratie en integratieaspecten in Brugge in de 15de eeuw', Masterthesis: UGent, 2002.

Casado Alonso, H. 'Brugge, centrum van uitwisseling met Spanje', In *Hanzekooplui en Medicibankiers. Brugge, wisselmarkt van Europese culturen*, edited by A. Vandewalle, 51–57. Oostkamp: Stichting Kunstboek, 2002.

Casado Alonso, H. 'La colonie des marchands Castillans de Bruges au milieu du XVe siècle', *Publications du Centre Européen d'Etudes Bourguignonnes* 51 (2011), 233–251.

Casado Alonso, H. 'La nation et le quartier des Castillans de Bruges (XVe et XVIe siècles)', *Handelingen van het Genootschap voor geschiedenis* 133 (1996), 61–77.

Cauchies, J.M. *Philippe le Beau. Le dernier duc de Bourgogne*. Turnhout: Brepols, 2003.

Cecchini I. and L. Pezzolo, 'Merchants and institutions in early-modern Venice', *The Journal of European Economic History* 41, nr. 2 (2012), 89–114.

Cessi, R. 'Le relazioni commerciali tra Venezia e la Fiandra nel secolo XIV', *Nuovo Archivio Veneto* XXVII (1914), 5–116.

Chavarot, M.-C. 'La pratique des lettres de marque d'après les arrêts du parlement (XIIIe–début XVe siècle)', *Bibliothèque de l'école des chartes* 149 (1991), 51–89.

Claustre, J. 'De l'obligation du corps à la prison pour dette: l'endettement privé au Châtelet de Paris au XVe siècle', In *La dette et le juge. Juridiction gracieuse et juridiction contentieuse du XIIIe au XVe siècle*, edited by J. Claustre, 121–134. Paris: Publications de la Sorbonne, 2006.

Claustre, J. 'Dette et obligation à Paris à la fin du Moyen Âge', In *Valeurs et justice. Ecarts et proximités entre société et monde judiciaire du Moyen Âge au XVIIIe siècle*, edited by B. Lemesle and M. Nassiet, 69–83. Rennes: Presses universitaires de Rennes, 2011.

Claustre, J. 'La honte de l'endetté (Paris, XVe siècle)', In *Shame between punishment and penance: the social usages of shame in the middle ages and early modern times*, edited by J. Wettlaufer, 229–246. Florence: Sismel, 2012.

Cohen, J. 'The history of imprisonment for debt and its relation to the development of discharge in bankruptcy', *The Journal of Legal History* 3, nr. 2 (1982), 153–171.

Coll Conesa, J. 'El comercio de la cerámica valenciana en Flandres y el Atlantico norte', In *A la búsqueda del Toisón de oro. La Europa de los Príncipes. La Europa de las cuidades*, edited by E. Mira and A. Delva, 316–325. Almudín: Museo de la Ciudad, 2007.

Cordes A. and P. Höhn, 'Extra-legal and legal conflict management among long-distance traders (1250–1650)', In *Oxford Handbook of European legal history*, edited by M.D. Dupper, M. Godfrey and H. Pihlajamäki, 509–527. Oxford: Oxford University Press, 2018.

Cordes, A. 'Die Regelung von Interessenkonflikten im Seerecht des späten 13. Jahrhunderts: Ein Vergleich', *Zeitschrift der Savigny-Stiftung für Rechtsgeschichte, Germanische Abteilung* 137 (2020), 52–92.

Cordes, A. 'Flandrischer Copiar Nr. 9. Juristischer Kommentar', In *Seerecht im Hanseraum des 15. Jahrhunderts: edition und kommentar zum Flandrischen Copiar Nr. 9*, edited by C. Jahnke, 119–144. Lubeck: Schmidt-Römhild, 2003.

Cordes, A. 'Litigating abroad: merchants' expectations regarding procedure before foreign courts according to the Hanseatic privileges', In *Law and disputing in the Middle Ages: proceedings of the Ninth Carlsberg Academy Conference on medieval legal history 2012*, edited by Per Andersen, 281–299. Copenhagen: JØF Pub., 2013.

Cordes, A. 'Maritime Law. Western Europe', In *Lexikon des Mittelalters* VII (1995), accessed 29.11.2022.

Cordes, A. and P. Höhn, '"Per amorem vel per iusticiam» La résolution juridique et extra-juridique des conflits en matière commerciale (1250–1650)', In *Les chimères de l'alternative? Regards croisés sur les Modes alternatifs de règlement des conflits* (Droit, Histoire, Anthropologie), edited by S. Amrani-Mekki et al., 47–58. Paris: Mare et Martin, 2018.

Craeybeckx, J. 'De wijnvaart tussen West-Frankrijk en de Nederlanden. Het ontstaan van het zeerecht van Oleron en Damme', In *Van rank tot drank*, edited by M.A. Arnould and E. Van Driessche, 140–145. Brussels: ASLK, 1990.

Crouzet-Pavan, E. 'Venice and its surroundings', *A companion to Venetian history*, edited by E.R. Dursteler, 25–46. Leiden: Brill, 2013.

Crouzet-Pavan, E. *Les villes vivantes. Italie XIIIe–XVe siècle*. Paris: Fayard, 2009.

Crouzet-Pavan, E. *Venice triumphants: the horizons of a myth*. Baltimore: Johns Hopkins University Press, 2002.

Crouzet-Pavan, E. *Venise triomphante: les horizons d'un mythe*. Paris: Albin Michel, 1999.

Crouzet-Pavan, E. *Venise: une invention de la ville (XIIIe–Xve siècle)*. Seysell: Champ Vallon, 1997.

Damaska, M. 'Rational and irrational proof revisited', *Journal of Interdisciplinary History* 4 (1974), 25–40.

Daniels, T. *De Verschwörung der Pazzi. Ein politischer Skandal und seine europäischen Resonanzen*. Stuttgart: Hiersemann, 2020.

Daru, P. *Histoire de la république de Venise*, vol. III. Paris: Firmin Didot, 1819.

Daubresse, S. 'L'obéissance du Parlement de Paris. Entre raison et nécessité', *Nouvelle revue du seizième siècle* 22, nr. 1 (2004), 89–110.

Dauchy, S. 'La non-motivation des décisions judiciaires dans l'ancien droit: principe ou usage', *Revue historique de droit français et étranger* 82, nr. 2, (2004), 171–188.

Dauchy, S. 'Le parlement de Paris, juge contraignant ou arbitre conciliant? Les conflits entre Philippe le Bon et ses bonnes villes de Flandre', *Publications du centre Européen d'Etudes Bourguignonnes* 33 (1993), 143–152.

Dauchy, S. 'Le recours contre les décisions arbitrales en perspective historique', *Revue de l'Arbitrage* 4 (1999), 763–784.

Dauchy, S. 'Les recours contre les sentences arbitrales au Parlement de Paris (XIIIe et XIVe siècles) la doctrine et la législation à l'épreuve de la pratique judiciaire', *Tijdschrift voor Rechtsgeschiedenis* 67, nr. 3–4 (1999), 255–311.

Dauchy, S. 'Parlement de Paris et les Pays-Bas Bourguignons', *Tijdschrift voor Rechtsgeschiedenis* 61, nr. 3 (1993), 367–374.

Dauchy, S. 'Quelques remarques sur les amendes prononcées par le Parlement de Paris au Moyen Age pour "fol appel» provenant de Flandre', *Tijdschrift voor Rechtsgeschiedenis* 55 (1987), 49–55.

Dauchy, S. 'The cost of plaiding in the Parlement of Paris in the fifteenth century', In *Geschichte der Zentraljustiz in Mitteleuropa. Festschrift für Bernhard Diestelkamp zum 65. Geburstag*, edited by Friedrich Battenberg and F. Ranieri, 181–193. Weimar: Böhlau, 1994.

Dauchy, S. *De Vlaamse appels bij het Parlement van Parijs. Een rechtshistoriche onderzoek naar de wording van staat en soevereiniteit in de Bourgondische – Habsburgse periode*. PhD. Diss.: Ghent University, 1990.

Dauchy, S. *Les voie de recours extraordinaires: proposition d'erreur et requête civile (de l'ordonnance de Saint Louis jusqu'à l'ordonnance de 1667)*. Paris, PUF, 1988.

Davidson, J. and A. Gray, *The Scottish staple at Veere. A study in the economic history of Scotland*. Longmans, Green and Co., 1909.

De Boodt, M. 'An instrumental take on Justitia. A dialogue of ideas in fifteenth-century Bruges', In *Normativa y autoridad en la ciudad medieval Atlántica (Y más allá)*, edited by J.A. Solórzano Telechea and J. Haemers, 139–158. Longroño: Instituto de Estudios Riojanos, 2022.

De Clercq, W., J. Braekevelt, J. Coll Conesa, H. Kaçar, J. Vicente Lerma, and J. Dumolyn, 'Aragonese tiles in a Flemish castle: a chivalric gift-exchange network in Fifteenth-century Europe', *Al Masaq: Journal of the Medieval Mediterranean* 27, nr. 2 (2015), 153–171.

De Clercq W., R. Dreesen, J. Dumolyn, W. Leloup, J. Trachet, 'Ballasting the Hanse: Baltoscandian erratic cobbles in the Later Medieval port landscape of Bruges', *European Journal of Archaeology* 20, nr. 4 (2017), 710–729.

De Clercq, W., J. Trachet, S. Delefortrie, K. Dombrecht, J. Dumolun, W. Leloup, E. Thoen, M. van Meirvenne. 'Turning back the tide: the Zwin debate in perspective. A historiographical review of the medieval port system northeast of Bruges', *Revue du Nord* 97 (2015), 305–321.

De Clercq, W., K. Dombrecht, J. Dumolyn, W. Leloup and J. Trachet. 'Monnikerede: the rise and decline of a medieval port community in the Zwin estuary', *The Medieval Low Countries. An Annual Review* 7 (2020), 97–130.

De Groote, M. 'Strandvonsten in de Bourgondische tijd. Een bijdrage tot de sociale-economische geschiedenis van de Vlaamse kust (1384–1448)', Masterthesis: UGent, 1999.

De Keyser, J. 'De visie van vreemdelingen op de verschuiving van het commerciële zwaartepunt van Brugge naar Antwerpen (14de–16de eeuw)', *Handelingen van het Genootschap voor Geschiedenis* 146, no°2 (2009), 269–307.

De Lara, Y 'The secret of Venetian success: a public-order, reputation-based institution', *European Review of Economic History* 12 (2008), 247–285.

De Larivière C.J. and B. Doumerc, 'Le rôle du patriciat dans la gestion des galères marchandes à Venise au début du seizième siècle', *Studi Veneziani* 36 (1998), 57–84.

De Larivière, C.J. 'Entre gestion privée et contrôle public: les transports maritimes à Venise à la fin du Moyen Âge', *Histoire Urbaine* 12, nr. 1 (2005), 57–68.

De Maddalena, A. 'Per la stoia delle "colonie" mercantile italiane il Libro della comunità dei mercanti lucchesi in Bruges', *Giornale degli Economisti e Annali di Economia* 7, nr. 9/10 (1948), 566–571.

De Oliveira Marques, A.H. 'Notas para a História da Feitoria Portuguesa na Flandres, no século XV', In *Ensaios de História Medieval*, edited by A.H. de Oliveira Marques, 439–476. Lisbon: Portugália Editora, 1965.

De Roover, R. 'La communauté des marchands Lucquois à Bruges de 1377 à 1404', *Handelingen van het Genootschap voor Geschiedenis te Brugge* 86 (1949), 23–89.

De Roover, R. '"Cambium ad Venetias": contribution to the history of foreign exchange', In *Business, banking and economic thought in late medieval and early modern Europe*, edited by R. de Roover, 239–259. Chicago: Chicago University Press, 1974.

De Roover, R. 'Le contrat de change depuis la fin du treizième siècle jusqu'au début du dix-septième', *Belgisch tijdschrift voor filologie en geschiedenis*, 25, nr. 1–2 (1946), 111–128.

De Roover, R. 'New interpretations of the history of banking', In *Business, banking, and economic thought in late Medieval and Early Modern Europe. Selected studies of Raymond de Roover*, edited by J. Kirshner, 200–238. Chicago and London: The University Press, 1974.

De Roover, R. 'Renseignements complémentaires sur le marché monétaire à Bruges au XIVe et au XVe siècle', *Het Genootschap voor Geschiedenis te Brugge* 109 (1972), 51–91.

De Roover, R. 'The cambium maritimum contract according to the Genoese notarial records of the twelfth and thirteenth centuries', *Explorations in economic history* 7 (1970), 15–33.

De Roover, R. 'The Scholastics, usury and foreign exchange', *The Business History Review* 41, nr. 3 (1967), 257–271.

De Roover, R. 'Tommaso Portinari', In *Nationaal Bibliografisch woordenboek*, dl. 2, 690–698. Brussels: Paleis der Academien, 1966.

De Roover, R. *Money, banking and credit in mediaeval Bruges. Italian merchant-bankers, Lombards and Money-Changers. A study in the origins of banking*. Cambridge: The Mediaeval Academy of America, 1948.

De Roover, R. *The Bruges money market around 1400*. Brussels: Paleis der Academiën, 1968.

De Roover, R. *The rise and decline of the Medici bank 1397–1494*. Cambridge: Harvard University Press, 1963.

De Ruysscher D. and J. Puttevils, 'The art of compromise. Legislative deliberation on marine insurance institutions in Antwerp (c. 1550–c. 1570)', *Low Countries Historical Review* 130, nr. 3 (2015), 25–49.

De ruysscher, D. 'Over themis en mercurius. Handelsgebruiken en-recht in Antwerpen (vijftiende-zeventiende eeuw', *Belgisch Tijdschrift voor Filologie en Geschiedenis* 88 (2010), 1105–1134.

De ruysscher, D. 'Antwerp commercial law in sixteenth century: a product of the renaissance? The legal facilitating, appropriating and improving of mercantile practices', In *Antwerp in the Renaissance*, edited by B. Blondé and J. Puttevils, 33–88. Turnhout: Brepols, 2020.

De ruysscher, D. 'Bankruptcy, insolvency and debt collection among merchants in Antwerp (c. 1490 to c. 1540)', In *The history of bankruptcy. Economic, social and cultural implications in early modern Europe*, edited by T.M. Safley, 185–199. London: Routledge, 2013.

De ruysscher, D. 'Belgium. Marine Insurance', *A comparative history of insurance law in Europe. A research agenda*, edited by Ph. Hellwege, 110–132. Berlin: Duncker & Humblot, 2018.

De ruysscher, D. 'Consulter, débattre, négocier et légiférer en matière d'assurance maritime aux niveaux central et municipal aux Pays-Bas (Anvers-Bruxelles, 1555–1571)', *C@hiers du CRHIDI* 39 (2016), 1–9.

De ruysscher, D. 'Customs and municipal law: the symbolic authority of the past (Low Countries, 16th–17th century)', *Dutch Crossing* 46, nr. 2 (2022), 95–114.

De ruysscher, D. 'From usages of merchants to default rules: practices of trade, ius commune and urban law in early modern Antwerp', *The Journal of Legal History* 33, nr. 1 (2012), 3–29.

De ruysscher, D. 'Ius commune, legal scholarship and coherence: the author's structure', *Historia et Ius* 15, nr. 1 (2019), 1–24.

De ruysscher, D. 'La lex mercatoria contextualisée: tracer son parcours intellectuel', *Revue historique de droit français et étranger* 90, nr. 4 (2012), 499–515.

De ruysscher, D. 'Normative hybridity in Antwerp marine insurance (c. 1650–c. 1700)', In *The law's many bodies, studies in legal hybrity and jurisdictional complexity c. 1600–1900*, edited by S. Donlan and D. Heirbaut, 145–168. Berlin: Duncker & Humblot, 2015.

De ruysscher, D. 'Reconciling old and new: imprisonment for debts and cession bonorum in Mechelen (c. 1500–c. 1530)', *European traditions: integration or disintegration?*, edited by J.W. Oosterhuis and E. Van Dongen, 35–48. Oisterwijk: Wolff, 2012.

De ruysscher, D. 'The struggle for voluntary bankruptcy and debt adjustment in Antwerp (c. 15200–c. 1550)', In *Between norm and practice*, edited by A. Cordes and M. Schulte Beerbühl, 77–95. Frankfurt: Peter Lang, 2016.

De ruysscher, D. 'Antwerp 1490–1590: insurance and speculation', In *Maritime insurance: origins and institutions, 1300–1850*, edited by A.B. Leonard, 79–106. London: Palgrave Macmillan, 2016.

De Schepper H. & J.M. Cauchies, 'Legal tools of the public power in the Netherlands, 1200–1600', in *Legislation and justice*, edited by A. Padoa-Schioppa, 239–246. Oxford: Clarendon Press, 1997.

De Schepper, 'Recht en administratie in de Nederlanden tijdens de zestiende eeuw', In *Recht en instellingen in de oude Nederlanden tijdens de Middeleeuwen en de Nieuwe tijd. Liber amicorum Jan Buntinx*, 369–389. Leuven: Universitaire Press, 1981.

De Schepper, H. 'De Geheime Raad als hoogste rechtscollege in de Nederlanden (1504–1580)', In *Handelingen van het tweede Hof van Holland symposium gehouden op 14 november 1997 in de Trêveszaal te Den Haag*, edited by R. Huijbrecht, 38–48. Den Haag: Algemeen Rijksarchief, 1998.

De Smet, S. 'De burgerlijke rechtspraak voor de Gentse schepenbank van de Keure. Organisatie, personeel, procedure en archief', *Handelingen der Maatschappij voor Geschiedenis en Oudheidkunde te Gent* 55 (2001), 251–295.

De Smidt J. TH. and E.I. Strubbe, 'Chronologische lijsten van de geëxedeerde sententiën', In *Miscellanea Consilii Magni. Ter gelegenheid van twintig jaar werkgroep grote raad van Mechelen*, J. Th. De Smidt, 1–12. Amsterdam: faculteit der rechtgeleerdheid, 1980.

De Win, P. 'Lalaing, Simon de, heer van Montignies-Saint-Christophe, hertogelijk raadsheer-kamerling, vliesridder', *Nationaal Biografisch Woordenboek*, XIV (1992), 389–395.

Decock, W. *Theologians and contract law: the moral transformation of the Ius Commune (ca. 1500–1650)*. Leiden/Boston: Brill, 2012.

Degryse, R. 'Brugge en de organisatie van loodswezen van het Zwin op het einde van de 15de eeuw', *Handelingen van het Genootschap voor Geschiedenis* 112 (1975), 61–130.

Degryse, R. 'Brugge en de pilotage van de Spaanse vloot in het Zwin in de XIVde eeuw, deel I', *Handelingen van het Genootschap voor Geschiedenis* 117, nr. 2 (1980), 105–178.

Del Treppo, M. *I mercanti catalani e l'espansione della corona d'Aragona nel secolo XV*. Naples, L'arte Tipografica, 1968.

Deloof, M. and J. Puttevils, 'Marketing and pricing risk in marine insurance in sixteenth-century Antwerp', *The Journal of Economic History* 77, nr. 3 (2017), 796–837.

Delumeau, J. *L 'alun de Rome, XV–XIXe siècle*. Paris: S.E.V.P.E.N, 1962.

Demets, L. 'Bruges as a multilingual contact zone: books production and multilingual literary networks in fifteenth-century Bruges', *Urban History* 51 (2024), 313–332.

Demets, L. 'De Flandria Generosa C. Een kroniek van Vlaanderen uit de Brugse Eeckhoutabdij aan het begin van de vijftiende eeuw', *Het Genootschap voor Geschiedenis te Brugge* nr. 157 (2019), 39–71.

Demets, L. 'Onvoltooid verleden. Politiek, historiografie en de handschriftelijke variatie van de Excellente Cronike van Vlaenderen (1400–1550)', PhD. Diss.: Ghent University, 2019.

Den Hollander, M. 'Comparative cultures of accountability: the Scottish exchequer and the audit chamber of Holland between 1477 and 1515', *Comparative Legal History* 6, nr. 2 (2018), 158–183.

Dendooven, H. 'De Brugse klerken in de veertiende eeuw', Master Thesis: Ghent University, 2007.

Dept, G.C. *Les influences anglaise et française dans le comté de Flandre au début du XIII siècles*. Ghent: Van Rysselberghe, 1928.

Derville, A. 'Les pots-de-vin dans le dernier tiers du XVe siècle (d'après les comptes le Lille et de Saint-Omer)', In *1477 Het algemene gewestelijke privilegiën van Maria van Bourgondie voor de Nederlanden*, edited by W.P. Blockmans and M.A. Arnould, 449–469. Kortrijk, UGA, 1985.

Derville, A. 'Pots-de-vin, cadeaux, racket, patronage: essai sur les mécanismes de décision dans l'Etat bourguignon', *Revue du Nord* 56, nr. 222 (1974), 341–364.

Desportes Bielsa, P. 'El consulado catalán de Brujas (1330–1488)', *Aragón en la Edad Media* 14–15, nr. 1 (1999), 375–399.

Devlieger, L. 'Het Oosterlingenhuis te Brugge', *Hansekaufleute in Brügge. Teil 4: Beiträge der Internationalen Tagung in Brügge April 1996*, edited by N. Jörn, W. Paravicini and H. Wernicke, 13–32. Frankfurt: Peter Lang, 2000.

Devliegher, L. 'Pero Tafur in Brugge, Sluis en Antwerpen (1438)', *Handelingen van het Genootschap voor geschiedenis* 140, nr. 3–4 (2003), 269–287.

Dierck, I. 'Hansische Älterleute und die Brügger Führungsschicht', In *Hansekaufleute in Brügge. Teil 4: Beiträge der Internationalen Tagung in Brügge April 1996*, edited by N. Jörn, W. Paravicini and H. Wernicke, 71–84. Frankfurt: Peter Lang, 2000.

Dijkman, J. *Shaping Medieval Markets. The organisation of commodity markets in Holland, c. 1200–c. 1450*. Leiden: Brill, 2011.

Dilis, E. *Les courtiers anversois sous l'ancien régime*. Antwerpen: Imprimerie J. Van Hille-De Backer, 1910.

Dillen, K. 'A paradox of maritime access. Origins and consequences of subaltern relations in a medieval portuary system in Flanders: the case of Hoeke', *The International Journal of Maritime History* 30, nr. 3 (2018), 405–421.

Dillen, K. 'Mude, de waterbajuw en het waterrecht: sleutelfactoren in de laatmiddeleeuwse Zwinhaven', *Handelingen van het Genootschap voor Geschiedenis* 159, nr. 2 (2022), 205–238.

Ditchburn, D. 'Scotland, France, and the Auld Alliance', *Medievalia et Humanistica* 41 (2015), 81–100.

Doehaerd, R. 'Les galères génoises dans la Manche et la Mer du Nord à la fin du XIIIe et au début du XIVes', *Bulletin de l'Institut historique belge de Rome*, nr. 19 (1938), 5–76.

Dollinger, P. *La Hanse: XIIe–XVIIe siècles*. Paris: Aubier, 1964.

Dollinger, P.J. A. Meijers, *De Hanze: opkomst, bloei en ondergang van een handelsverbond*. Utrecht: Het Spectrum, 1967.

Donahue Jr, C. 'Equity in the courts of merchants', *Tijdschrift voor Rechtsgeschiedenis* 72 (2004), 1–35.

Donahue, C. 'Medieval and early modern lex mercatoria: an attempt at the probation diabolica', *Chicago Journal of International Law* 5, nr. 1 (2004), 21–37.

Donlan, S. P. 'Comparative? Legal? History? Crossing boundaries', In *Comparative Legal History*, edited by O. Moréteau, A. Masferrer and K. Modéer, 78–95. Cheltenham: Elgar, 2019.

Donlan, S. P. 'To hybridity and beyond: reflections on legal and normative complexity', In *Mixed legal systems, east and west*, edited by V.V. Palmer, M.Y. Mattar and A. Koppel, 17–32. London/New York: Routledge. Taylor and Francis Group, 2015.

Doumerc, B. and D. Stöckly, 'L'évolution du capitalisme marchand à Venise: le financement des galère da mercato à la fin du XVe siècle', *Annales. Histoire, Sciences Sociales* 50, nr. 1 (1995), 33–157.

Dreijer, G. 'Identity, conflict and commercial law: legal strategies of Castilian merchants in the Low Countries (fifteenth-sixteenth century)', In *Commerce, citizenship and identity in Legal History*, edited by D. De ruysscher, A. Cordes, S. Dauchy, S. Gialdroni and H. Pihllajamäki, 118–138. Leiden: Brill, 2021.

Dreijer, G. 'Maritime averages and the complexity of risk management in sixteenth-century Antwerp', *Tijdschrift voor sociale en economische geschiedenis* 17, nr. 1 (2020), 31–54.

Dreijer, G. 'The power and pains of polysemy: general average, maritime trade and normative practice in the Southern Low Countries (fifteenth-sixteenth centuries)', PhD. Diss., University of Exeter and Vrije Universiteit Brussels, 2021.

Dumolyn J. and B. Lambert, 'Cities of commerce, cities of constraints. International trade, government institutions and the law of commerce in later medieval Bruges and the Burgundian state', *TSEG–The Low Countries Journal of Social and Economic History*, 11, nr. 4 (2014), 89–112.

Dumolyn J. and J. Haemers, 'Patterns of urban rebellion in medieval Flanders', *Journal of Medieval History* 31 (2005), 369–393.

Dumolyn J. and W. Leloup, 'The Zwin Estuary. A medieval portuary network', In *Las sociedades portugarias de la Europa Atlantica en la Edad Media*, edited by J.A. Solórzano Telechea, B. Arízaga Bolumburu, and M. Bochaca, 197–212. Longroño: Instituto de Estudios Riojanos, 2016.

Dumolyn J., W. Ryckbosh, and M. Speecke, 'Did inequality produce medieval revolt? The material position and political agency of textile workers during the Flemish Revolt of 1379–1385', *Social History* 46, nr. 4 (2021), 372–405.

Dumolyn, J. '"Our land is only founded on trade and industry": economic discourses in fifteenth-century Bruges', *Journal of Medieval History* 36, nr. 4 (2010), 374–389.

Dumolyn, J. 'Privileges and novelties: the political discourse of the Flemish cities and rural districts in their negotiations with the dukes of Burgundy', *Urban History* 35, nr. 1 (2008), 5–23.

Dumolyn, J. 'The common good. The central ideological signifier in Medieval politics', In *A cultural history of democracy in the medieval age*, edited by D. Napolitano and K.J. Pennington, 57–74. London, Bloomsbury Academic, 2021.

Dumolyn, J. *De Brugse opstand van 1436–1438*. Heule: UGA, 1997.

Dumolyn, J. *De Raad van Vlaanderen en de rekenkamer van Rijsel: gewestelijke overheidsinstellingen als instrument van centralisatie (1419–1477)*. Brussels: Algemeen Rijksarchief, 2002.

Ebert, C. 'Early modern Atlantic trade and the development of maritime insurance to 1630', *Past and Present* 213 (2011), 87–114.

Ehrenberg, R. 'Makler, hosteliers und Börse in Brügge vom 13. Bus zum 16', *Jahrhundert Zietschrift für das Gesamte Handelsrecht* 30 (1885), 403–468.

Elbl, I. 'Croscultural trade and diplomacy: Portuguese relations with West Africa, 1441–1521', *Journal of World History* 3, nr. 2 (1992), 165–204.

Elbl, I. 'Nation, bolsa and factory: three institutions of late medieval Portuguese trade with Flanders', *The International History Review* 14, nr. 1 (1992), 1–22.

Elder de Roover, F. 'A prize of war: a painting of fifteenth-century merchants', *Bulletin of the Business Historical Society*, 19, nr. 1 (1945), 3–12.

Elder De Roover, F. 'La voyage de Girolamo Strozzi de Pise à Bruges et retour à bord de la galère bourguignonne "San Giorgio"', *Handelingen van het Genootschap voor Geschiedenis* 91, nr. 3–4 (1954), 117–136.

Esch, A. 'Brügge als Umschlagplatz im Zahlungsverkehr Nordeuropas mit der römischen Kurie im 15. Jahrhundert: die vatikanischen Quellen', In *Hansekaufleute in Brügge. Teil 4: Beiträge der Internationalen Tagung in Brügge April 1996*, edited by N. Jörn, W. Paravicini, H. Wernicke, 109–137. Frankfurt: Peter Lang, 2000.

Everaert, J.G '"The Flemish Sugar Connection" Vlamingen in de Atlantische suikereconomie', *Bijdragen tot de Geschiedenis* 84, nr. 1–3 (2001), 257–264.

Fagel, R. 'Spanish merchants in the Low Countries: stabilitas loci or peregrinatio', In *International trade in the Low Countries*, edited by P. Stabel, B. Blondé and A. Greve, 87–104. Leuven: Garant, 2000.

Fagel, R. *De Hispano-Vlaamse Wereld. De contacten tussen Spanjaarden en Nederlanders 1496–1555*. Brussels: Koninklijke Bibliotheek, 1996.

Falzone, E. 'Procureurs ad litem, notaires et auditeurs jurés: autour et alentour d'une représentation en justice de l'abbaye Saint-Jean-Baptiste à Valenciennes devant l'officialité de Cambrai au XVé siècle', *Publications du Centre Européen d'Etudes Bourguignonnes* 50 (2010), 239–254.

Finlayson, W.H. 'The Scottish nation of merchants in Bruges. A contribution to the history of medieval Scottish foreign trade', PhD. Diss.: University of Glasgow, 1951.

Firnhaber-Baker, J. 'Formulating opposition to seigneural war in the Parliament of Paris', In *La Formule au Moyen Âge*, edited by E. Louviot, 209–218. Turnhout: Brepols, 2012.

Flórez, G.C. 'Vicissitudes of commercial trading: Castile and Flanders at the end of the fifteenth century (1474–1494)', *The Medieval History Journal* 6, nr. 1 (2003), 33–53.

Flume, J.W. 'Constructing the stock exchange: on the rise and fall of an iconic place of capitalism', *Rechtsgeschichte* 29 (2021), 412–430.

Fowler, L. 'Forms of arbitration', In *Proceedings of the fourth international congress of medieval canon law*, edited by S. Kuttner, 133–147. Toronto: Biblioteca Apostolica Vaticana, 1972.

Frankot, E. *'Of Laws of Ships and Shipmen' Medieval maritime law and its practice in Urban Northern Europe*. Edinburgh, Edinburgh University Press, 2012.

Frankot, E. 'De "Ordinancie van Staveren" en het Hanzeatisch zeerecht', *It Beaken* 77, nr. 1–2 (2007), 1–23.

Frankot, E. 'Der ehrbaren Hanse-Städte See-recht: diversity and unity in Hanseatic Maritime Law', In *The Hanse in Medieval and Early Modern Europe*, edited by J. Wubs-Mrozewicz and S. Jenks, 109–128. Leiden/Boston: Brill, 2013.

Frankot, E. 'Medieval maritime law from Oléron to Wisby: jurisdictions in the law of the sea', In *Communities in European history: representations, jurisdictions, conflicts*, edited by J. Pan-Montojo and F. Pedersen, 151–172. Pisa: Pisa University Press, 2007.

Friedland, K. *Die Hanse*. Stuttgart: Kohlhammer, 1991.

Fris, V. *Schets van den economischen toestand van Vlaanderen in het midden der 15de eeuw*. Gent: Siffer, 1900.

Fryde, E. 'Italian maritime trade with medieval England (c. 1270–c. 1530)', *Recueils de la société Jean Bodin* 32 (1974), 291–337.

Fusaro, M. 'Cooperating mercantile networks in the early modern Mediterranean', *The Economic Review* 65, Nr. 2 (2012), 701–718.

Fusaro, M. *Political economies of empire in the early modern Mediterranean*. Cambridge: Cambridge University Press, 2017.

Gaillard A. 'L'origine du Grand Conseil et du Conseil Privé', *Bulletin Commission royale d'Histoire* (1896), 267–324.

Galoppini, L. 'Lucchesi e uomini di comunitá a Bruges nel tardo Medioevo', In *Mercatura è arte. Uomini d'affari toscani in Europa e nel mediterranea tardomedievale*, edited by L. Tanzini and S. Tognetti, 45–79. Rome: viella 2012.

Galoppini, L. '"Nationes" toscane nelle Fiandre', In *Comunità forestiere e 'nationes' nell'Europa dei secoli XIII–XVI*, edited by G. Petti Balbi, 134–163. Napels: Liguori Editore, 2001.

Galoppini, L. 'Gli Arnolfini a Bruges nel quattrocento', In *Studi antichi e nuove recerche sulle orme di Gabriella Rossetti in occasione dei suoi settanta anni*, edited by G. Garzella and E. Salvatori, 273–291. Pisa: GISEM-ETS, 2005, 277–280.

Ganshof, F.L. *Etude sur le faussement de jugement dans le droit flamand des xiie et xiiie siècles*. Merksplas: Imprimerie administrative, 1935.

Gelderblom, O. 'The decline of fairs and merchants guilds in the Low Countries, 1250–1650', *Jaarboek voor Middeleeuwse geschiedenis* 7 (2004), 199–238.

Gelderblom, O. *Cities of commerce: the institutional foundations of international trade in the Low Countries, 1250–1650*. Princeton: Princeton University Press, 2013.

Gilissen, J. 'De grote Raad van Mechelen. Historisch Overzicht', In *Miscellanea Consilii Magni. Ter gelegenheid van twintig jaar werkgroep grote raad van Mechelen*, edited by J. Th. De Smidt, 14–43. Amsterdam: faculteit der rechtgeleerdheid, 1980.

Gilissen, J. 'L'évolution de la plévine dans le droit Flamand aux XIII et XIVe siècles', In XXXe *congres van het oudheid- en geschiedkundig verbond van België*, 171–188. Brussels: Fédération archéologique et historique de Belgique, 1935.

Gluzman, R. *Venetian shipping. From the glory to decline, 1453–1571*. Leiden: Brill, 2021.

Godding, P. 'La preuve en matière civile au XIe au XVIIIe siècle', In *Traveaux et conférences de la faculté de droit de l'université de Bruxelles*, vol. IX. Brussels: Insitut de Sociologie, 1962.

Godding, P. 'Les sûretés personnelles. Deuxième partie Moyen Age et Temps Modernes', In *Recueils de la société Jean Bodin pour l'histoire comparative des institutions XXIX*, 265–277. Brussels: Éditions de la librairie, 1971.

Godding, P. *Le droit privé dans les Pays-Bas méridionaux du 12e au 18e siècle*. Brussels: Palais des Académies, 1991.

Gonzalez Arce, J.D. 'La Universidad de mercaderes de Burgos y el consulado castellano en Brujas durante el siglo XV', *En la España Medieval* 33 (2010), 161–202.

Goris, J.A. *Etudes sur les colonies marchandes méridionales (Portugais, Espagnols, Italiens) à Anvers de 1488 à 1567. Contribution à l'histoire des débuts du capitalisme modern*. Leuven: Librairie Universitaire, 1925.

Gottschalk, M.K.E. 'Het verval van Brugge als wereldmarkt', *Tijdschrift voor Geschiedenis* 66 (1953), 1–26.

Graichen, G.R. Hammel-Kiesow, A. Hesse, *Die Deutsche Hanse: eine heimliche Supermacht*. Reinbek bei Hamburg: Rowohlt, 2017.

Greve, A. 'Brügger Hosteliers und hansische Kaufleute: Ein Netzwerk vorteilhafter Handelsbeziehungen oder programmierte Interessenskonflikte?' *Hansekaufleute in Brügge. Teil 4: Beiträge der Internationalen Tagung in Brügge April 1996*, edited by N. Jörn, W. Paravicini and H. Wernicke, 151–161. Frankfurt: Peter Lang, 2000.

Greve, A. 'Die Bedeutung der Brügger Hosteliers für hansische Kaufleute im 14. und 15. Jahrhundert', *Jaarboek voor Middeleeuwse Geschiedenis* 4 (2001), 259–296.

Greve, A. 'Hoteliers en Hanzekooplieden in Brugge in de 14de en 15de eeuw', In *Hanzekooplui en Medicibankiers. Brugge, wisselmarkt van Europese culturen*, edited by A. Vandewalle, 99–104. Oostkamp: Stichting Kunstboek, 2002.

Greve, A. *Hansen, Hosteliers und Herbergen. Studien zum Aufenthalt hansischer Kaufleute in Brügge im 14. Und 15. Jahrhundert. Teil 2. Prosopographischer Katalog Brügger Hosteliers des 14. Und 15. Jahrhunderts*. PhD. Diss.: Ghent University, 1999.

Groebner, V. 'The city guard's salute. Legal and illegal, public and private gifts in the Swiss confederation around 1500', In *Negotiating the Gift. Pre-Modern figurations of exchange*, edited by G. Algazi, V. Groebner, and B. Jussen, 247–267. Göttingen: Vandenhoeck & Ruprecht, 2003.

Groebner, V. *Liquid assets, dangerous gifts: presents and politics at the end of the Middle Ages*. Philadelphia: University of Pennsylvania press, 2002.

Guenée, B. *Tribunaux et gens de justice dans le bailliage de Senlis à la fin du Moyen Age (vers 1380–vers 1550)*. Paris: Publications de la faculté des lettres de l'Université de Strasbourg, 1963.

Gunn, S. 'State development in England and the Burgundian dominions, c. 1460–c. 1560', *Publications du centre Européen d'Etudes Bourguignonnes* 35 (1995), 133–149.

Haemers J. and B. Lambert, 'Pouvoir et argent. La fiscalité d'Etat et la consommation du crédit des ducs de Bourgogne', *Revue du Nord* 91 (2009), 35–59.

Haemers, J. 'Factionalism and state power in the Flemish revolt', *Journal of Social History* 42, nr. 4 (2009), 1009–1039.

Haemers, J. *De Gentse Opstand (1449–1453), de strijd tussen rivaliserende netwerken om het stedelijke kapitaal*. Kortrijk: UGA, 2004.

Haemers, J. *De strijd om het regentschap over Filips de Schone. Opstand facties en geweld in Brugge, Gent en Ieper (1482–1488)*. Gent: Academia Press, 2014.

Haemers, J. *For the Common Good? State power and urban revolts in the reign of Mary of Burgundy, 1477–1482*. Turnhout: Brepols, 2009.

Haggenmacher, P. 'L'ancêtre de la protection diplomatique: les représailles de l'ancien droit (xiie-xviiie siècles)', *Relations internationales* 143, nr. 3 (2010), 7–14.

Hansen, N. 'Strandrecht und Strandraub – Bemerkungen zu einem Gewohnheitsrecht an den schleswig-holsteinischen Küsten', *Kieler Blätter zur Volkskunde* 33 (2001), 51–78.

Häpke, R. *Brügges Entwicklung zum Mittelalterlichen Weltmarkt*. Berlin: Karl Curtius, 1908.

Hattenhauer, C. 'Bürgschaft', In *Handwörterbuch zur Deutschen Rechsgeschichte*, edited by A. Cordes, H. Lück, D. Werkmüller. Berlin: Erich Schmidt Verlag, 2008.

Heebøll-Holm, T., P. Höhn and G. Rohman, 'Introduction', In *Merchants, Pirates and smugglers. Criminalization, economics and the transformation of the maritime world (1200–1600)*, edited by T. Heebøll-Holm, P. Höhn, G. Rohmann, 9–32. Frankfurt/New York: Campus Verlag, 2019.

Heers, M. L. 'Les Génois et le commerce de l'alun a la fin du Moyen Âge', *Revue d'histoire économique et sociale* 32, nr. 1 (1954), 31–53.

Heirbaut, D. 'Les lois, enquêtes et jugements des pairs du castel de Lille: een unieke getuige van het Vlaamse recht rond 1300', In *De rechtspraktijk in beeld: van Justinianus tot de Duitse bezetting*, edited by B. Jacobs, 11–27. Tillburg: Tillburg University Press, 1997.

Heirbaut, D. *Over heren, vazallen en graven. Het persoonlijk leenrecht in Vlaanderen ca. 1000–1305*. Brussels: Koninlijke Academie, 1997.

Hellwege, P. 'A comparative history of insurance law in Europe', *American Journal of Legal History* 56 (2016), 66–75.

Henn V., 'Het ontstaan van de Hanze', In *Koggen, kooplieden en kantoren. De Hanze een praktisch netwerk*, edited by H. Brand and E. Knol, 10–25. Groningen: Uitgeverij Verloren, 2010.

Henn, V. 'Das Brügger Kontor', In *Die Hanse. Lebenswiklichkeit und Mythos*, edited by J. Bracker, 216–222. Lübeck: Schmidt-Römhild, 1999.

Henn, V. 'dat wie up dat gemelde kunthoer tho Brugge . . . eyn kleyn upmercken gehat und noch hebben . . .' Neue forschungen zur Geschichte des Brügger Hansekontors', *Hansische Geschichtsblätter* 132 (2014), 1–45.

Henn, V. 'Über die Anfänge des Brügger Hansekontors', *Hansische Geschichtsblätter* 107 (1989), 43–66.

Hilaire, J. 'Recherches sur le fonds du Parlement de Paris: à propos des appels Flamands au Moyen Âge', *Revue historique de droit français et étranger (1922–)* 82, nr. 2 (2004), 263–279.

Hildesheimer, F. and M. Morgat-Bonnet, *Le parlement de Paris; histoire d'un grand corps de l'état monarchique XIIIe–XVIIIe siècle*. Paris: Honoré Champion, 2018.

Hinjosa Montalvo, J. 'De Valencia a Portugal y Flandres. Relanciones durante la Baja Edad Media', *Anales de la Universidad de Alicante. Historia Medieval* 1 (1982), 149–168.

Hinjosa Montalvo, J. 'Los intercambios mercantiles entre Valencia y Brujas', In *A la búsqueda del Toisón de oro. La Europa de los Príncipes. La Europa de las cuidades*, edited by E. Mira and A. Delva, 303–314. Almudín: Museo de la Ciudad, 2007.

Höhn, P. 'Pirate places, merchant spaces? Distribution and criminalization in the Late Medieval Baltic Sea', *Merchants, pirates and smugglers Criminalization, economics and the transformation of the Maritime World (1200–1600)*, edited by T. Heebøll-Holm, P. Höhn and G. Rohmann, 127–144. Frankfurt: Campus Verlag, 2018.

Höhn, P. *Kaufleute in Konflikt. Rechtspluralismus, Kredit und Gewalt im spätmittelalterlichen Lübeck*. Frankfurt: Campus Verlag, 2021.

Hollingsworth, M. *Princes of the renaissance*. London: Head of Zeus, 2021.

Holmes, G.A. 'The Libel of English Policy', *The English Historical Review* 76, nr. 299 (1961), 193–216.

Hunt E. and J.M. Murray, *A history of business in medieval Europe 1200–1550*. Cambridge: Cambridge University Press, 1999.

Ibbetson, D.J. 'Law and custom: insurance in sixteenth-century England', *Journal of Legal History* 29 (2008), 291–307.

Jahnke, C. '"Homines Imperii" und "Osterlinge" Selbst-und Fremdbezeichnungen Hansischer Kaufleute im Ausland am Beispiel Englands, Flanderns und des Ostseeraumes im 12. Und 13. Jahrhundert', *Hansische Geschichtsblätter* 129 (2011), 1–57.

Jahnke, C. 'Lubeck and the Hansa: a queen without its body', In *The Routledge Handbook of maritime trade around Europe 1300–1600*, edited by W. Blockmans, M.M. Krom, and J. Wubs-Mrozewicz, 231–247. London: Routledge, 2017.

Jansen, H. 'Voies commerciales aux Pays-Bas à la fin du Moyen-Age: continuité et changement', *Publications du Centre Européen d'Etudes Bourguignonnes* 23 (1983), 21–26.

Janssens, A. 'Macht en onmacht van de Brugse schepenbank. In de periode 1477–1490', *Handelingen van het Genootschap voor Geschiedenis* 133, nr. 1–3 (1996), 5–45.

Jeanclos, Y. *L'arbitrage en Bourgogne et en Champagne du XIIe au XVe siecle. Etude de l'influence du droit savant, de la coutume et de la pratique*. Dijon: Centre de recherches historiques, 1977.

Jörn, N. 'Die Herausbildung der Kontorordnungen in Nowgorod, Bergen und Brügge im Vergleich – 12–17 Jahrhundert', In *Prozesse der Normbildung und Normveränderung im mittelalterlichen Europa*, edited by D. Ruhe and K.-H. Spies, 217–235. Stuttgart: Steiner Verlag, 2000.

Kadens, E. 'The myth of the customary law merchant', *Texas Law Review* 90 (2012), 1153–1206.

Kerckhoffs-De Hey, A. J.M. *De Grote Raad en zijn functionarissen 1477–1531. Biografieën van raadsheren*. Amsterdam: Franciscus de Craneveld, 1980.

Koppmann, K. *Leitfaden für die Alterleute des Deutschen Kaufmanns zu Brügge. Vefasst von einem klerk des Hansischen Kontor zu Brügge*. Hamburg: W. Mauke Söhne, 1875.

Kusman, D. 'Jean de Mirabello dit van Haelen (1280–1333). Haute finance et Lombards en Brabant dans le premier tiers du XIVe siècle', *Belgisch Tijdschrift voor Filologie en Geschiedenis* 77, nr.4 (1999), 843–931.

Labarge, M.W. 'Pero Tafur: a fifteenth century Spaniard', *Florilegium* 5, nr. 5 (1983), 237–247.

Lambert, B. '"Se fist riche par draps de soye" The intertwinement of Italian Financial interests and luxury trade at the Burgundian court (1384–1481)', In *Europe's rich fabric. The consumption, commercialisation, and production of luxury textiles in Italy, the Low Countries and neighbouring territories (Fourteenth–Sixteenth Centuries)*, edited by B. Lambert and K.A. Wilson, 91–108. Farnham/Burlington: Ashgate Publishing, 2016.

Lambert, B. 'A legal world market? The exchange of commercial law in fifteenth-century Bruges', In *Migrating words, migrating merchants, migrating law*, edited by S. Gialdroni, A. Cordes, S. Dauchy, H. Pihlajamäki and D. De ruysscher, 164–175. Leiden: Brill, 2019.

Lambert, B. 'Making size matter less: Italian firms and merchants guilds in late medieval Bruges', In *The company in law and practice: did size matter? (Middle Ages–Nineteenth century)*, edited by D. De ruysscher, A. Cordes, S. Dauchy and H. Pihlajamäki, 34–48. Brill: Leiden, 2017.

Lambert, B. 'Merchants on the margins: fifteenth-century Bruges and the informal market', *Journal of Medieval History* 42, nr. 2 (2016), 226–253.

Lambert, B. 'Offences in the outport: illicit trade in fifteenth-century Sluys and Southampton', In *Il commercio al minute: domanda e offerta tra economia formale e informale. Secc. XIII–XVIII/ Trade: supply and demand in the formal and informal economy from the 13th to the 18th centuries*, edited by G. Nigro, 167–184. Florence: Firenze University Press, 2015.

Lambert, B. 'Steep fall or gradual decline? International trade in sixteenth-century Bruges', In *Italian als Vorbild? Ökonomische und kulturelle Verflechtungen europäischer Metropolen am Voraband der 'ersten Globalisierung' (1300–1600)*, edited by J. Oberste and S. Ehrich, 153–162. Regensburg: Schnell und Steiner, 2019.

Lambert, B. 'The political side of the coin: Italians bankers and the fiscal battle between princes and cities in the late medieval Low Countries', In *Economies, public finances and the impact of institutional changes in the Low Countries and neighbouring German territories (14th–17th centuries)*, ed. R. van Schaik (Turnhout: Brepols, 2012), 103–112.

Lambert, B. *The city, the duke and their banker. The Rapondi family and the formation of the Burgundian state (1384–1430)*. Turnhout: Brepols 2006.

Lane, F.C. 'Fleets and Fairs: The Functions of the Venetian Muda', In *Scritti in onore di Armando Sapori*, edited by J. Dhondt, H. Van Werveke and F.L. Ganshof, 651–663. Milan: Ist. Ed. Cisalpino, 1957.

Lane, F.C. 'Venetian merchant galleys, 1300–1334: private and communal operation', *Speculum* 38, nr. 2 (1963), 179–205.

Lane, F.C. 'Double entry bookkeeping and resident merchants', *Journal of European Economic History* 6, nr. 1 (1977), 177–191.

Lane, F.C. 'Investment and usury in medieval Venice', *Explorations in entrepreneurial history* 2, nr. 1 (1964), 3–15.

Lecuppre-Désjardin, E. *Le royaume inachevé des ducs de Bourgogne*. Paris: Belin, 2016.

Lefebvre-Teillard, A. 'Arbiter, arbitrator seu amicabilis compositor', *Revue de l'arbitrage* 3 (2008), 369–387.

Lefebvre-Teillard, A. 'L'arbitrage en droit canonique', *Revue de l'Arbitrage*, nr. 1 (2006), 5–34.

Leigh, M. 'Quintilian on the emotions (institutio oratoria 6 preface and 1–2)', *The Journal of Roman Studies* 94 (2004), 122–140.

Leloup W. and B. Vannieuwenhuyze. 'Damme en Sluis. De oorsprong en vroege stadsontwikkeling van twee middeleeuwse Zwinstadjes', *Handelingen van het genootchap voor geschiedenis te Brugge* 150, nr. 1 (2013), 13–56.

Leloup, W. 'Een stadstichting langs het Zwin de ontstaansgeschiedenis en ontwikkeling van Sluis', *Tijdschrift voor Historische Geografie* 3, nr. 2 (2018), 104–125.

Leloux, H. 'Kirche und Caritas im Leben der Genossenschaft des Deutschen Kaufmanns zu Brügge', *Hansische geschichtsblätter* 91 (1973), 34–45.

Levy-Bruhl, H. 'Droit de naufrage', *Annales de droit commercial et industriel Français, Etranger et International* 36 (1927), 34–53.

Leyder, D. *Les archives du Grand Conseil des Pays-Bas à Mechelen (vers 1445–1797)*. Brussels: Algemeen Rijksarchief, 2010.

Liagre, L. 'Le commerce de l 'alun en Flandre au Moyen-Age', *Le Moyen Age* 49 (1955), 177–206.

Lijten, M. *Het burgerlijke proces in stad en meierij van 's Hertogenbosh (1530–1811)*. Assen/Maastricht: Van Gorcum, 1998.

Lopez, R.S. *The commercial revolution of the middle ages, 950–1350*. Cambridge: Cambridge University Press, 1976.

Lopez, R.S. 'Le marchand génois: un profil collectif', *Annales. Histoire, Sciences Sociales* 13, nr. 3 (1958), 501–515.

Lopez, R.S. 'Majorcans and Genoese on the North sea route in the thirteenth century', *Revue belge de philologie et d'histoire* 29, nr. 4 (1951), 1163–1179.

Macdougall, N., 'Kennedy, James (c. 1408–1465)', In *the Oxford Dictionary of National Biography*. Oxford: Oxford University Press, 2004.

Macquarrie, A. 'Anselm Adornes of Bruges: traveller in the East and friend of James III', *The Innes Review* 33, nr. 33 (1982), 15–22.

Mallett, M.E. 'The sea consuls of Florence in the fifteenth Century', *Papers of the British School at Rome* 27 (1959), 156–169.

Manger, C. 'Behind the scenes: urban secretaries as managers of legal and diplomatic conflicts in the Baltic region, c. 1470–1540', *Journal of Medieval History* 48, nr. 4 (2022), 571–586.

Maréchal, J. 'Het internationale karakter van de Brugsche handelsbeurs', *Bijdragen voor de Geschiedenis der Nederlanden* 1 (1946), 84–90.

Maréchal, J. 'La colonie espagnole de Bruges du XIVe au XVIe siècle', *Revue du Nord* 35, nr. 137 (1953), 5–40.

Maréchal, J. 'Le départ de Bruges des marchands étrangers (XVe et XVI siècle)', *Handelingen van het Genootschap voor Geschiedenis* 88 (1951), 26–74.

Maréchal, J. *Europese aanwezigheid te Brugge: de vreemde kolonies (XIVde–XIXde eeuw)*. Bruges: Schoonbaert, 1985.

Marinesco, C. 'Les affaires commerciales en Flandre d'Alphonse V d'Aragon, roi de Naples (1416–1458)', *Revue historique* 221, nr. 1 (1959), 33–48.

Martines, L. *April blood: Florence and the plot against the Medici*. Oxford: New York, 2003.

Martone, L. *Arbiter-Arbitrator: forme di giustizia privata nell'età del diritto comune*. Naples: Jovene, 1984.

Martyn, G. 'Cambyses aan de Vlaamse kust' *Pro memorie. Bijdrage tot de rechtsgeschiedenis der Nederlanden* 14 (2012), 126–136.

Martyn, G. 'La "purge d'héritages» dans les Pays-Bas Méridionaux: l'apport des archives du conseil privé (1577–1692)', *Tijdschrift voor rechtsgeschiedenis* 63 (1995), 273–309.

Martyn, G. 'Les avocats au Conseil de Flandre (1386–1795), à la recherche d'une déontologie', In *Les acteurs de la justice. Magistrats, ministère pulic, avocats, huissiers et greffiers (XIIe–XIXe siècle)*, edited by R. Robaye, 103–119. Namen: Presses Universitaires de Namur, 2002.

Martyn, G. 'De Portuguese natie in Antwerpen: drie eeuwen kwaliteitsbewaking van privileges en gewoonterecht', In *De achterkant van Minerva: opstellen aangeboden aan Prof. Kees Cappon ter gelegenheud van zijn afscheid van de Universiteit van Amsterdam*, edited by G.P. van Nifterik, J. de Vries and M. de Wilde, 74–87. Amsterdam: Unversity of Amsterdam, 2019.

McKelvie, G. 'The royal prisoner of Henry IV and Henry V: James I of Scotland, 1406–1424', In *Medieval hostageship, c. 700–c. 1500: hostage, captive, prisoner of war, guarantee, peacemaker*, edited by M. Bennett and K. Weikert, 158–173. New York: Routledge, 2017.

Meek, C. *Lucca. 1369–1400. Politics and Society in an Early renaissance City-State*. Oxford: Oxford University Press, 1978.

Meltzing, O. 'Tommaso Portinari und sein Konflikt met der Hanse', *Hansische Geschichttsblatter* 12 (1906), 101–123.

Mertens, J. 'De Brugse ambachtsbesturen (1363–1374), een oligarchie?' In *Recht en instellingen in de oude Nederlanden tijdens de middeleeuwen en de nieuwe tijd. Liber amicorum Jan Buntinx*, edited by G. Asaert, 185–198. Leuven: Leuven Universitaire Press, 1981.

Mertens, J. 'Twee weversopstanden te Brugge', *Handelingen van het Genootschap voor Geschiedenis* 110 (1973), 5–20.

Michienzi, I.H. 'La "nation" et les milieu d'affaires Florentins aux XIVe et XVe siècles', In *Nation et Nations au Moyen Âge, Actes du 44e congrès de la SHMESP*, edited by P. Monnet, 299–310. Paris: Publications de la Sorbonne, 2014.

Miranda, F. 'Before the empire: Portugal and the Atlantic trade in the late Middle Ages', *Journal of Medieval Iberian Studies* 5, nr. 1 (2013), 69–85.

Miranda, F. 'Commerce, conflits et justice: les marchands portugais en Flandre à la fin du Moyen Age', *Annales de Bretagne et des Pays de l'Ouest* 117, nr. 1 (2010), 1–16.

Miranda, F. 'Conflict management in western Europe: the case of the Portuguese merchants in England, Flanders and Normandy, 1250–1500', *Continuity and change* 32, nr. 1 (2017), 11–36.

Miranda, F. 'Network takers or network makers? The Portuguese traders in the Medieval West', In *Commercial networks and European cities, 1400–1800*, edited by A. Caracausi and C. Jeggle, 171–186. Oxon: Routledge, 2016.

Miranda, F. 'Portugal and the Medieval Atlantic. Commercial diplomacy, merchants and trade, 1143–1488', PhD. Diss. University of Porto, 2012.

Miranda, F. 'Portuguese traders in Atlantic Europe in the Middle Ages', *e-Journal of Portuguese History* 12, nr. 1 (2014), 120–130.

Miranda, F. 'Urban Economy in a 'kingdom without cities': population and exchange in late medieval Portugal', In *La ville médiévale en débat*, edited by A. Aguiar Andrade and A. Millán da Costa, 175–184. Lisbon: IEM – Instutio de Estudos, 2014.

Modderman, H.J.H. *De wijze van gedingvoering tegen afwezig gebleven beklaagden*. PhD. Diss.: Leiden, 1881.

Moeglin, J.M. 'A la recherche de la "paix finale". Guerre et paix dans les relations des rois de France et d'Angleterre au XIVe siècle: références normatives et pratiques politiques', In *Frieden schaffen und sich verteidigen im Spätmittelalter*, 51–82. München: Deutschen Historischen Institut Paris, 2012.

Monballyu, J. 'De gerechtelijke bevoegdheid van de Raad van Vlaanderen in vergelijking met de andere "Wetten" (1515–1621)', In *Hoven en banken in Noord en Zuid*, edited by B.C.M. Jacobs and P.L. Nève, 1–26. Assen: Van Gorcum & Comp, 1994.

Monballyu, J. 'De Raad van Vlaanderen, een soevereine justitieraad in strafzaken?' In *Handelingen van het tweede Hof van Holland Symposium gehouden op 14 november 1997 in de Trêveszaal te Den Haag*, edited by R. Huijbrecht, 77–90. Den Haag: Algemeen Rijksarchief, 1998.

Monballyu, J. 'De style ende maniere van procederen in de camere van den raede in Vlaenderen (1521) van Fransoys de Rycke (1525) ten onrechte toegeschreven aan Lambrecht van den Bryaerde, president van de Grote Raad van Mechelen', *Tijdschrift voor Rechtsgeschiedenis* 49, nr. 3 (1981), 361–387.

Monballyu, J. 'Het costumiere recht in de kasselrij Kortrijk tijdens de 15de en de 16de eeuw', In *Handelingen van de Koninklijke Geschied- en Oudheidkundige Kring van Kortrijk* 75 (1978), 135–163.

Monballyu, J. 'Het gerecht in de kasselrij Kortrijk (1515–1621)', PhD. Diss.: KULeuven, 1976.

Monballyu, J. 'Philips Wielant, Pracktijcke civile, 1508–1519', In *Pro Memorie. Juristen die schreven en bleven. Nederlandstalige rechtsgeleerde klassiekers* 21, nr. 2 (2019), 20–24.

Montemezzo, S. 'Galley routes and merchant networks between Venice and the North Sea in the Fifteenth century', In *Commercial networks and European cities, 1400–1800*, A. Caracausi and C. Jeggle, 153–170. Oxon: Routledge, 2016.

Moukarzel, P. 'The Latin traders in Egypt and Syria during the XIVth and the XVth centuries: privileged communities under a strict control', In *Mediterráneos. An interdisciplinary approach to the cultures of the Mediterranean Sea*, edited by S. Carro Martin, A. Echavarren, E. Fernández Medina, D. Riaño Rufilanchas, K. Šmid, J. Téllez Rubio, and David Torollo Sánchez, 339–354. Newcastle upon Tyne: Cambridge Scholars Publishing, 2013.

Mozejko, B. 'Maritime Danzig in the second half of the fourteenth and the fifteenth century', *New studies in medieval and renaissance Poland and Prussia. The impact of Danzig*, edited by B. Mozejko, 102–113. New York: Routledge, 2017.

Mozejko, B. *Peter von Danzig. The story of a great Caravel*. Leiden: Brill, 2019.

Mueller, R. *The Venetian money market. Banks, panics and the public debt, 1200–1500*. London and Baltimore: Johns Hopkins University Press, 1997.

Müller, R. 'Visual culture and artistic exchange', In A *Companion to medieval Genoa*, edited by C.E. Beneš, 293–319. Leiden: Brill, 2018.

Munro, J. 'The symbiosis of towns and textiles: urban institutions and the changing fortunes of cloth manufacturing in the Low Countries and England, 1270–1570', *Journal of Early Modern History* 3, nr. 1 (1999), 1–74.

Munro, J. 'Three centuries of luxury textile consumption in the Low Countries and England, 1330–1570: Trends and comparisons of real values of woollen broadcloth (Then and now)', In *The medieval broadcloth. Changing trends in fashions, manufacturing and consumption*, edited by K. Vestergard Pedersen and M.-L. Nosch, 1–73. Oxford: Oxbow Books, 2009.

Munro, J. H. 'Spanish Merino wool and the Nouvelles Draperies: an industrial transformation in the late medieval Low Countries', *The Economic History Review* 58, nr. 3 (2005), 431–484.

Munro, J. *Wool, Cloth and gold. The struggle for bullion in Anglo-Burgundian trade 1340–1478*. Toronto: University of Toronto Press, 1973.

Murray, J. 'Of nodes and networks: Bruges and the infrastructure of trade in fourteenth century Europe', In *International trade in the Low Countries*, edited by P. Stabel, B. Blondé, A. Greve, 1–14. Leuven: Garant, 2000.

Murray, J. *Bruges, Cradle of capitalism, 1280–1390*. Cambridge: Cambridge University Press, 2005.

Neto, D.M. 'As relações sociais do Prior D. Vasco de Ataíde: o priorado do Crato da Ordem do Hospital de 1453 a 1491', *Mirabilia: electronic journal of antiquity and middle ages* 24 (2017), 104–143.

Newman, L. W. 'A practical assessment of arbitral dispute resolution', In *Lex mercantoria and arbitration. A discussion of the new law merchant*, edited by T.E. Carbonneau, 1–9. Ardsely-on-Hudson: Transnational Publischers inc. 1998.

Nicholas, D. *Medieval Flanders*. Oxon: Longman Group Limited, 1992.

Niitemaa, V. *Des Strandrecht in Nordeuropa im Mittelalter*. Helsinki: Suomalaisen Kirjallisuuden Kirjapaino, 1955.

Oosterbosch, M. *Grote Raad voor de Nederlanden te Mechelen, Procesbundels beroepen uit Vlaanderen, Ordinaris Processen (Nr. 1-1000)*. Brussels: Algemeen Rijksarchief, 1998.

Oosterbosh, M. 'Appelprocedure, dossierbehandeling en registervoering bij de Grote Raad van Mechelen', In *Voortschrijdend procesrecht. Een historische verkenning*, edited by C.H. van Rhee, F. Stevens and E. Persoons, 3–25. Leuven: Universitaire pers Leuven, 2001.

Oppetit, B. *Théorie de l'arbitrage*. Paris: PUF, 1998.

Opsommer, R. *Omme dat leengoed es thoochste dinc van der weerelt: het leenrecht in Vlaanderen in de 14de en de 15de eeuw*. Brussels: Algemeen Rijksarchief, 1995.

Orella Unzué, J.L. 'Relaciones mercantiles vascas entre la edad media y el renacimiento', *Lurralde: inves. Espac.* 39 (2016), 107–198.

Ortalli, G. 'Il ruolo degli statuti tra autonomie e dipendenze: Curzola e il dominio veneziano', *Rivista storica italiana* (1986), 195–220.

Ortega Villoslada, A. 'Mallorca y el commercio atlántico siglos XIII–XIV', *Memòries de la reial acadèmia mallorquina d'estudis genealògics, heràldics i històrics* 20, 5–6 (2010), 61–80.

Paravicini, W. 'De Hanze als Europees verschijnsel', In *Hanzekooplui en Medicibankiers. Brugge, wisselmarkt van Europese culturen*, edited by A. Vandewalle, 11–24. Oostkamp: Stichting Kunstboek, 2002.

Pashel, Ph. 'L'usage du droit romain devant le Parlement médiéval (2e moitié du XIVe siècle)', In *Le Parlement en sa cour. Etudes en l'honneur du professeur Jean Hilaire*, edited by O. Descamps, F. Hildesheimer, and M. Morgat-Bonnet, 457–477. Paris: Honoré Champion éditeur, 2012.

Paviot, J. *Portugal et Bourgogne au XVe siècle (1384–1482), recueil de documents extraits des archives bourguignonnes*. Paris: Fondation Calouste Gulbenkian, 1995.

Perroy, E. 'Louis de Male et les négociations de paix franco-anglaise', In *Etudes d'histoire médiévale*, edited by E. Perroy, 305–317. Paris: Publications de la Sorbonne, 1979.

Petti Balbi, G. 'Brugge, Haven van de Italianen', In *Hanzekooplui en Medicibankiers. Brugge, wisselmarkt van Europese culturen*, edited by A. Vandewalle, 58–62. Oostkamp: Stichting Kunstboek, 2002.

Petti Balbi, G. 'I rapporti tra Genova e il mondo fiammingo', In *Primitivi: fiamminghi in Liguria*, edited by C. Cavalli Traverso, 9–18. Genova: Reti Medievali, 2009.

Petti Balbi, G. 'Le nationes italiane all'estero', In *Il Rinascimento italiano e l'Europa, vol. 4. Commercio e cultura mercantile*, edited by F. Franceschi, R.A. Goldwaite, R.C. Mueller, 397–423. Vicence: Colla Editore, 2007.

Petti Balbi, G. *Negoziati fuori patria. Marioni e genovesi in età medievale* Bologna: CLUEB, 2005.

Petti-Babli, G. 'Flottes publiques et flottes privées à Gênes au XIVe siècle', In *The sea in history. The medieval world*, edited by M. Balard, 215–224. Woodbridge: The Boydell Press, 2017.

Pezzolo, L. 'The Venetian Economy', *A companion to Venetian history*, edited by E.R. Dursteler, 255–290. Leiden: Brill, 2013.

Tits-Dieuaide, M.-J. 'Le grain et le pain dans l'administration des villes de Brabant et de Flandre au Moyen Age', In *Het openbaar initiatief van de gemeenten in België. Historische grondslagen (Acien Régime). Handelingen van het 11de internationaal colloquium. Spa 1–4 sept. 1982*, 453–491. Brussels: Gemeentekrediet, 1984.

Philips, W.D. 'Local integration and long-distance ties: the Castilian community in sixteenth century Bruges', *The Sixteenth Century Journal* 17, nr. 1 (1986), 33–49.

Phillips, W.D. 'The Spanish kingdoms and the wider world in the later Middle Ages', In *Iberia and the Mediterranean world of the Middle Ages*, edited by P. Kagay and P. Chevedden, 407–430. Leiden: Brill, 1996.

Piccinno, L. 'Genoa, 1340–1620: early development of marine insurance', In *Maritime insurance: origins and institutions*, 1300–1850, edited by A.B. Leonard, 25–46. London: Palgrave Macmillan, 2016.

Pichierri, A. *Die Hanse – Staat der Städte. Ein ökonomisches und politsches Modell der Städtevernetzung*. Opladen: Leske + Budrich, 2000.

Pifarrés Torres, D. *El Comerç internacional de Barcelona i el mar del Nord (Bruges) a finals del segle XIV*. Barcelona: Publications de l'Abadia de Montserrat, 2002.

Pirenne, H. 'Villes, marchés et marchands au Moyen Âge', *Revue Historique* 67 (1898), 59–70.

H. Pirenne, *l'Origine des constitutions urbaines au Moyen Age*. Paris: Imprimerie de F. Hayez, 1985.

Plebani, E. *I consolu del marie di Firenze nel quattrocento*. Rome: Sapienza Università Editrice, 2019.

Pohl, H. *Die Portugiesen in Antwerpen (1567–1648)*. Wiesbaden: Franz Steiner Verlag, 1977.

Prevenier, W. 'Het Brugse Vrije als vierde lid van Vlaanderen', *Handelingen van het XXIIe Vlaams Filologencongres*. Leuven: De Vlaamsche philologencongressen, 1957.

Prevenier, W. 'Quelques aspects des comptes communaux en Flandre au moyen âge', In *Handelingen van het internationaal colloquium, Blankenberge, 6–9 september 1962: Financiën en boekhouding der steden van de XIIIe tot de XVIe eeuw*, 111–151. Brussels: Gemeentekrediet België, 1964.

Prevenier, W. 'Réalité et histoire: le quatrième membre de Flandre', *Revue du Nord* 43, nr. 169 (1961), 5–14.

Prevenier, W. 'Utilitas communis in the Low Countries (thirteenth–fifteenth centuries), from social mobilisation to legitimation of power', In *De Bono Communi. The discourse and practice of the common good in the European city (13th–16th c.)*, edited by E. Lecuppre-Desjardin and A.-L. Van Bruaene, 205–216 Turnhout: Brepols, 2010.

Prevenier, W. 'Urban chanceries in the Low Countries from the twelfth to the fourteenth century', In *Stadt, Kanzlei und Kultur im Übergang zur Frühen Neuzeit*, edited by R. Suntrup and J. Veenstra, 3–15. Frankfurt: Peter Lang, 2004.

Priotti, J.P. 'Commerce et finance en Flandre au XIVe siècle. Les activités de Diego de Echavarri, consul de la nation de Biscaye', *Handelingen van het Genootschap voor Geschiedenis* 132, no°1–2 (1995), 81–95.

Puttevils, J. 'Tweaking financial instruments: bills obligatory in sixteenth-century Antwerp', *Financial History Review* 22 (2015), 337–361.

Puttevils, J. *Merchants and trading in the sixteenth century: the golden age of Antwerp*. London: Pickering and Chatto, 2016.

Puttevils, J.P. Stabel and B. Verbist. 'Een eenduidig pad van modernisering van het handelsverkeer: van het liberale Brugge naar get gereguleerde Antwerpen?' In

Overheid en economie: geschiedenissen van een spanningsveld, edited by B. Blondé, 39–54. Antwerp: University Press Antwerp, 2014.
Quertier, C. 'Les Florentins, értrangers privilégiés ou allies encombrants? Heurs et malheurs des nations Florentines (Europe, Méditerranée, XIVe–XVe siècles)', *Mélanges de l'école française de Rome* 131, nr. 2 (2019), 461–472.
Rawlinson, H. 'The Flanders galley: some notes on seaborne trade between Venice and England, 1327–1532', *Mariner's mirror* 12 (1926), 145–168.
Rediker, M. *Villains of all nations: Atlantic pirates in the golden age*. London and New York: Beacon Press, 2004.
Reid, W.S. *Skipper from Leith. The history of Robert Barton*. Philadelphia: University of Pennsylvania Press, 1962.
Rodriguez Martin, J.D. 'Moving the Judge. A legal commentary on Book VI of Quintilian's Institutio Oratoria', In *Quintilian and the law*, edited by O. Tellegen-Couperus. Leuven: Leuven University Press, 2003.
Roebuck, D. *Mediation and arbitration in the middle ages. England 1154–1558*. Oxford: Oxford University Press, 2013.
Rohmann, G. 'Jenseits von Piraterie und Kaperfahrt; Fur einem Paradigmenwechsel in der Geschichte der Gewalt im maritimen Spätmittelalter', *Historische Zeitschrift*, 304 (2017), 1–49.
Roosenboom, M. *The Scottish staple in the Netherlands: an account of the trade relations between Scotland and the Low Countries from 1292 till 1676, with a calendar of illustrative documents*. The Hague: Nijfhoff, 1910.
Rorke, M. 'English and Scottish overseas trade, 1300–1600', *The Economic Review* 59, nr. 2 (2006), 265–288.
Rorke, M. 'The Scottish herring trade, 1470–1600', *The Scottish Historical Review* 84, nr. 2 (2005), 149–165.
Rose, S. *Calais: an English town in France, 1347–1558*. Woodbridge: The Boydell Press, 2008.
Rose, S. *The wealth of England: the medieval wool trade and its political importance, 1100–1600*. Havertown: Oxbow Books, 2018.
Rossi, G. 'Civilians and insurance: approximations of reality to the law', *Tijdschrift voor rechtsgeschiedenis* 83, nr. 3–4 (2015), 323–364.
Rossi, G. 'England 1523–1601: The beginnings of marine insurance', In *Maritime insurance: origins and institutions*, 1300–1850, edited by A.B. Leonard, 131–150. London: Palgrave Macmillan, 2016.
Rossi, G. 'The abandonment to the insurers in sixteenth-century insurance practice: comparative remarks and (a few) methodological notes', In *Understanding the sources of Early modern and Modern commercial law*, edited by H. Pihlajamäki, A. Cordes, S. Dauchy and D. De ruysscher, 87–118. Leiden: Brill, 2018.
Rossi, G. 'The barratry of the shipmaster in early modern law: polysemy and mos Italicus', *Tijdschrift voor Rechtsgeschiedenis* 87, nr. 1–2 (2019), 65–85.
Rossi, G. 'The barratry of the shipmaster in early modern law: the approach of Italian and English law court', *Tijdschrift voor rechtsgeschiedenis* 87, nr. 4 (2019), 504–574.

Rossi, G. 'The liability of the shipmaster in early modern law: comparative (and practice-oriented) remarks', *Historia et Ius* 2, 12 (2017), 1–47.

Rossi, G. *Insurance in Elizabethan England: the London code*. Cambridge: Cambridge University Press, 2016.

Roussel, D. 'La légitimité de la contrainte à l'épreuve de la rue: les sergents et la prise de corps à Paris au début de l'époque moderne', In *L'arrestation. Interpellations, prises de corps et captures depuis le Moyen Âge*, edited by F. Chauvaud and P. Prétou, 45–62. Rennes: Presses Universitaires de Rennes, 2015.

Rubinstein, N. *The government of Florence under the Medici: (1434 to 1494)*. Oxford: Clarendon Press, 1998 [1966].

Ruggiero, G. 'Law and punishment in early renaissance Venice', *The Journal of Criminal Law & Criminology* 69, nr. 2 (1978), 243–256.

Russel-Wood, A.J.R. *The Portuguese Empire. A world on the move*. London: Johns Hopkins University Press, 1998.

Sabbe, J. *Vlaanderen in opstand 1323–1328: Nikolaas Zannekin, Zeger Janszone en Willem de Deken*. Bruges: Van de Wiele, 1992.

Saelens, W. 'Consignatie bij de Gentse schepenbanken tijdens het ancien régime. Een studie van het fond Vreemde Steden in het Stadsarchief Gent', *Handelingen der Maatschappij voor Geschiedenis en Oudheidkunde te Gent* 71 (2019), 123–152.

Sapori, A 'I primi viaggi di Levante e di Ponente delle galere Florentine', *Archivio Strorico Italiano* (1956), 69–91.

Schellekens, C. 'Merchants and their hometown: Florentines in Antwerp and the duchy of Florence (ca. 1500–1585)', PhD. Diss.: European University Institute, 2018.

Schnerb, B. *Jean sans peur: le prince meurtrier*. Paris: Payot, 2005.

Schubert, E. 'Novgorod, Brügge, Bergen und London: Die Kontore der Hanse', *Concilium medii aevi* 5 (2002), 1–50.

Schweitzer, J. *Schiffer und Schiffsmann in den Rôles d'Oléron und im Llibre del Consolat de Mar. Ein Vergleich zweier mitteralterlicher Seerechtsquellen*. Frankfurt am Main, Lang, 2000.

Shawn, A. 'Burgundian Habsburg mint policies and world bullion flow. A monetary interpretation of the rise and fall of Antwerp', *The Hilltop Review* 2, nr. 1 (2006), 1–16.

Sicking L. and J. De Klerk, 'The law of wreck in Flanders, Holland and Zeeland in the Late Middle Ages', In *Communities, environment and regulation in the premodern world*, edited by C. Weeda, R. Stein and L. Sicking, 201–232. Turnhout: Brepols, 2022.

Sicking, L. 'Funduq, Fondaco, Feitoria. The Portuguese contribution to the globalisation of an institution of overseas trade', In *Maritime Networks as a factor in European integration*, edited by G. Nigro, 197–207. Florence: Firenze University Press, 2019.

Sicking, L. 'God's Friend, the Whole world's enemy: reconsidering the role of piracy in the development of universal jurisdiction', *Netherlands Journal of Legal Philosophy*, 47 (2018), 176–186.

Sicking, L. 'Les marchands espagnols et Portugais aux Pays-Bas et la navigation à l'époque de Charles Quint: gestion des risques et législation', *Publications du centre européen d'études Bourguignonnes* 51 (2011), 253–274.

Sicking, L. *La naissance d'une thalassocratie. Les Pays-Bas et la mer à l'aube du siècle d'or*. Paris: Presses de l'université Paris Sorbonne, 2015.

Smail, D. 'Debt, humiliation, and stress in fourteenth-century Lucca and Marseille', *Shame between punishment and penance: the social usages of shame in the middle ages and early modern times*, edited by J. Wettlaufer, 247–262. Florence: Sismel, 2012.

Smail, D. 'Violence and predation in Late Medieval Mediterranean Europe', *Comparative Studies in Society and History* 54, nr. 1 (2012), 7–43.

Smail, D. 'Les dettes et les saissies de biens dans la région de Lucques au XIV siècle', In *La Fabrique des sociétes médievales méditerranéennes*, edited by M. Dejoux and D. Chamboduc de Saint Pulgent, 181–190. Paris: Editions de la Sorbonne, 2018.

Smail, D. *Legal plunder: households and debt collection in late medieval Europe*. Cambridge Mass.: Harvard University Press, 2016.

Sommé, M. 'Isabelle de Portugal et Bruges: des relations privilégiées', *Handelingen van het Genootschap van Brugge* 132, nr. 3 (1995), 261–280.

Sommé, M. 'Les portugais dans l'entourage de la duchesse de Bourgogne Isabelle de Portugal (1430–1471)', *Revue du Nord* 77, nr. 310 (1995), 321–343.

Sosson, J.P. *Les travaux pulics de la ville de Bruges, XIVe–Xve siècles. Les matériaux, les hommes*. Brussels: Pro Civitate, 1977.

Spindler, E. 'Between sea and city. Portable communities in late medieval London and Bruges', *London and beyond. Essays in honour of Derek Keene*, edited by M. Davies and J.A. Galloway, 181–199. London: Institute of Historical Research, 2012.

Spitzbarth, A.B. *Ambassades et ambassadeurs de Philippe le Bon, troisième duc Valois de Bourgogne (1419–1467)*. Turnhout: Bepols, 2013.

Spufford, P. 'From Genoa to London: the places of Insurance in Europe', In *Maritime insurance: origins and institutions, 1300–1850*, edited by A.B. Leonard, 271–297. London: Palgrave Macmillan, 2016.

Stabel, P. 'De gewenste vreemdeling. Italiaanse kooplieden en stedelijke maatschappij in het laat-middeleeuws Brugge', *Jaarboek voor Middeleeuwse Geschiedenis* 4 (2001), 189–221.

Stabel, P. 'Militaire organisatie, bewapening en wapenbezit in laatmiddeleeuws Brugge', *Belgisch Tijdschrift voor Filologie en Geschiedenis* 89, nr. 3–4 (2011), 1049–1073.

Stabel, P. 'Organisation corporative et production d'oeuvres d'art à Bruges à la fin du Moyen Âge et au début des temps modernes', *Le Moyen Âge* 113 (2001), 91–134.

Stabel, P. 'Schippers, wagenvoerders en kruiers: de organisatie van de stedelijke vervoersector in het laat-middeleeuws Vlaanderen', *Bijdragen tot de geschiedenis* 82 (1999), 159–185.

Stabel, P. 'Venice and the Low Countries: commercial contacts and intellectual inspirations', *Renaissance Venice and the North: Crosscurrents in the time of Bellini, Dürer and Titian*, edited by Aikema & B.L. Brown, 30–43. New York: Rizzoli, 2000.

Staelens, S. 'De schepenbank van Dendermonde onder Lodewijk van Male (1346–1384) en het huis van Bourgondië (1384–1482)', Masterthesis: Ghent university, 2005.

Stallaert, K.F. *Glossarium van verouderde rechtstermen, kunstwoorden en andere uitdrukkingen uit Vlaamsche, Brabantsche en Limburgsche oorkonden*. Leiden: Brill, 1893.

Stantchev, S. 'The medieval origins of embargo as a policy tool', *History of Political Thought* 33, nr. 3 (2012), 373–399.

Stein, R. *Magnanimous dukes and rising states: the unification of the Burgundian Netherlands, 1380–1480*. Oxford: Oxford University Press, 2017.

Stevens, F. 'The contribution of Antwerp to the development of marine insurance in the 16th century', In *Marine Insurance at the turn of the millennium*, edited by M. Huybrechts, E. Van Hooydonk and C. Dieryck, 15–20. Antwerp: Intersentia, 2000.

Stevenson, A. 'The Flemish dimension of the Auld Alliance', In *Scotland and the Low Countries, 1124–1994*, edited by G. Simpson, 28–42. East Linton: Tuckwell Press, 1996.

Stocker, C.W. 'Office and justice: Louis XI and the Parlement of Paris', *Mediaeval Studies* 37 (1975), 360–386.

Stöckly, D. *Le système de l'Incanto des galées du marché à Venise (fin XIIIe–milieu XVe siècle)*. Leiden: Brill, 1995.

Strubbe, Eg. I. 'De receptie in de Vlaamse rechtbanken van midden veertiende tot einde vijftiende eeuw', In *De Luister van ons oude recht. Verzamelde historische studies*, Eg. Strubbe, 601–615. Brussels: Elsevier – Sequoia, 1973.

Strubbe, I. 'Aantekeningen over de ivoorhandel te Brugge in de XVe eeuw', *Bijdragen voor de Geschiedenis der Nederlanden*, VII (1952–1953), 226–230.

Sutton, A. *The Mercery of London: Trade, Goods and People, 1130–1578*. New York: Routledge, 2016.

Szramkiewicz, R. and O. Descamps, *Histoire du droit des affaires*. Issy-les-Moulineaux, 2019.

Tai, E.S. 'The Legal Status of Piracy in Medieval Europe', *History Compass* 10, nr. 11 (2012), 838–851.

Teresa Ferrer, M. 'Catalan commerce in the late Middle ages', *Catalan Historical Review* 5 (2012), 29–65.

Thielemans, M.-R. *Bourgogne et Angleterre: relations politiques et économiques entre les Pays-Bas bourguignons et l'Angleterre, 1435–1467*. Brussels: Presses universitaires de Bruxelles, 1966.

Timbal, P-C. 'Les lettres de marque dans le droit de la France médiévale', *Recueil de la Société Jean Bodin*, vol. 10, 108–138, Brussels: Les éditions de la librairie encyclopédique, 1958.

Udovitch, A.L. 'At the origins of the Western commenda: Islam, Israel or Byzantium', *Speculum* 37, nr. 2 (1962), 198–207.

Unger, W.S. 'Rekening van den invoer van aluin in de Scheldedelta 1473–1475', *Economisch-Historisch jaarboek* 19 (1935), 75–88.

Van Answaarden, R. *Les Portugais devant le grand Conseil des Pays-Bas (1460–1580)*. Paris: Fondation Calouste Gulbenkian, 1991.

Van Caenegem, R.C. 'Aantekeningen bij het middeleeuwse gewoonterecht', *Tijdschrift voor Rechtsgeschiedenis* 64 (1996), 97–112.

Van Caenegem, R.C. 'La Preuve. Deuxième Partie: Moyen Age et temps modernes', *Recueils de la societe Jean Bodin pour l'histoire comparative des institutions*, 375–430. Brussels: Editions de la librairie encyclopedique, 1965.

Van Caenegem, R.C. 'Law in the medieval world', *Tijdschrift voor Rechtsgeschiedenis* 49 (1981), 15–46.

Van Caenegem, R.C. 'Notes on canon law books in medieval Belgian booklists', *Studia Gratiana*, 12 (1967), 265–292.

Van Caenegem, R.C. 'Reflexions on rational and irrational modes of proof in Medieval Europe', *Tijdschrift voor rechtsgeschiedenis* 58 (1990), 263–279.

Van den Auweele, D. 'Schepenbank en schepenen te Brugge (1127–1384). Bijdrage tot de studie van een gewone stedelijke rechts- en bestuursinstelling', PhD.Diss.: KU Leuven, 1977.

Van der Wee, H. *The growth of the Antwerp market and the European Economy. Fourteenth-Sixteenth Century*. The Hague: Springer, 1963.

Van der Velden, H. 'Cambyses for example: the origins and function of an exemplum iustitiae in Netherlandish art of the fifteenth, sixteenth and seventeenth centuries', *Simiolus Netherlands Quarterly for the History of Art* 23, nr. 1 (1995), 5–62.

Van Doosselaere, Q. *Commercial agreements and social dynamics in medieval Genoa*. Cambridge: Cambridge University Press, 2009.

Van Gassen, T. *Archiefvorming en -beheer in laatmiddeleeuws Gent. Te vindene tghuent dat men gheerne ghevonden hadde*. Ghent: Skribis, 2020.

Van Houtte J.A. et al., *De Geschiedenis van Brugge*. Tielt: Lannoo, 1982.

Van Houtte, J.A. 'Anvers aux XVe et XVIe siècles: expansion et apogée', *Annales. Histoire, Sciences Sociales* 16, nr. 2 (1961), 248–279.

Van Houtte, J.A. 'Herbergwesen und Gastlichkeit im mittelalterlichen Brügge', In *Gastfreundschaft, Taverne und Gasthaus im Mittelalter*, edited by H.C. Peyer and E. Müller-Lückner, 177–188. Vienna: R. Oldenbourg Verlag, 1983.

Van Houtte, J.A. 'La genèse du grand marché international d'Anvers à la fin du Moyen Age', *Belgisch tijdschrift voor filologie en geschiedenis* 19 (1940), 87–126.

Van Houtte, J.A. 'Makelaars en waarden te Brugge van de 13de tot de 16e eeuw', *Bijdrage voor de Geschiedenis der Nederlanden* 5 (1950), 1–30; 177–197.

Van Houtte, J.A. 'Portugal en de Brugse Handel tijdens de middeleeuwen', In *Vlaanderen en Portugal. Op de golfslag van twee culturen*, edited by J. Everaert and E. Stols, 33–52. Antwerpen: Mercatorfonds, 1991.

Van Houtte, J.A. *De opkomst van een grote middeleeuwse markt: Brugge*. Brussels: Koninklijke academie, 1985.
Van Houtte, J.A. 'Anvers aux XVe et XVIe siècles: expansion et apogée' *Annales, histoire, Sciences Sociales* 16, nr. 2 (1961), 248–278.
Van Houtte, J.A. 'Bruges et Anvers. Marches "nationaux" ou "internationaux" du XIVe au XVIe siècles', *Revue du Nord* 34 (1952), 89–108.
Van Houtte, J.A. 'Les courtiers aux Moyen Age, origine et caractéristiques d'une institution commerciale en Europe occident', *Revue historique du droit français et étranger* 4, nr. 15 (1936), 105–141.
Van Houtte, J.A. 'The rise and decline of the market of Bruges', *The Economic History Review* 19, nr. 1 (1966), 29–47.
Van Miegroet, H.J. 'Gerard David's "Justice of Cambyses": exemplum iustitiae or political allegory?' *Simiolus Netherlands Quarterly for the History of* Art 18, nr. 3 (1988), 116–133.
Van Niekerk, J.P. *The development of the principles of insurance law in the Netherlands from 1500–1800*, vol. I. Kenwyn: Juta & ca, 1998.
Van Peteghem, P. 'De verordening van 1483 voor de Raad van Vlaanderen herzien', In *Recht en instellingen in de oude Nederlanden tijdens de Middeleeuwen en de Nieuwe Tijd. Liber Amicorum Jan Buntinx*, edited by G. Asaert, 341–350. Leuven: Universitaire Press, 1981.
Van Peteghem, P. 'Raad van Vlaanderen', In *De gewestelijke en lokale overheidsinstellingen in Vlaanderen tot 1795*, edited by W. Prevenier and A. Augustyn, 44–46. Brussels: Algemeen Rijksarchief, 1997.
Van Peteghem, P.P.J.L. *De Raad van Vlaanderen en staatsvorming onder Karel V (1515–1555). Een publiekrechtelijk onderzoek naar centralisatiestreven in de XVII provinciën*. Nijmegen: Gerard Noordt Instituut, 1990.
Van Rhee, C.H. 'Snelheid en efficiency in hoger beroep. (Civiele Procedures, 16e eeuw)', In *Handelingen van het tweede Hof van Holland Symposium gehouden op 14 november 1997 in de Trêveszaal te Den Haag*, edited by R. Huijbrecht, 21–37. Den Haag: Algemeen Rijksarchief, 1998.
Van Rhee, C.H. *Litigation and legislation. Civil procedure at first instance in the great council for the Netherlands in Malines (1522–1559)*. Brussels: Algemeen Rijksarchief, 1997.
Van Rompaey, J. 'Het compositierecht in Vlaanderen van de veertiende tot de achttiende eeuw', *Tijdschrift voor Rechtsgeschiedenis*, 29 (1961), 43–79.
Van Rompaey, J. 'Het ontstaan van de Grote Raad onder Filips de Goede', *Handelingen van de Koninklijke Zuidnederlandse Maatschappij voor Taal- en Letterkunde en Geschiedenis* XXV (1971), 297–310.
Van Rompaey, J. *De Grote Raad van Boergondië en het parlement van Mechelen*. Brussels: Koninklijke Academie, 1973.
Van Rompaey, J. *Het grafelijk baljuwsambt in Vlaanderen tijdens de boergondische periode*. Brussels: Paleis der Academiën, 1967.
Van Uytven, R. 'Splendour or wealth: art and economy in the Burgundian Netherlands', *Transactions of the Cambridge bibliographical society* 10, nr. 2 (1992), 101–124.

Van Uytven, R. 'Stages of economic decline: late medieval Bruges', In *Peasants and townsmen in medieval Europe. Studia in Honorem Adriaan Verhulst*, edited by J.-M. Duvosquel and E. Thoen, 259–269. Ghent: Snoeck-Ducaju, 1995.

Van Werveke, H. *Bruges et Anvers. Huit siècles de commerce*. Brussels: Librairie encyclopédique, 1944.

Van Werveke, H. *De Gentsche stadsfinanciën in de middeleeuwen*. Brussels: Paleis van de Academiën, 1934.

Van den Aauweele, D. 'Het Brugse zeerecht, schakel in een supranationaal geheel', In *Brugge en de zee van Bryggia tot Zeebrugge*, edited by V. Vermeersch, 145–155. Antwerp: Mercatorfonds, 1982.

Vandermaesen, M. 'Curia comitis en grafelijke en hertogelijke raad', In *De gewestelijke en locale overheidsinstellingen in Vlaanderen tot 1795*, edited by W. Prevenier en A. Augustyn, 44–46. Brussels: Algemeen Rijksarchief, 1997.

Vandewalle, A. 'Brujas, centro del comercio internacional y sede de la nación Aragón-Cataluña en la baja edad media', In *A la búsqueda del Toisón de oro. La Europa de los Príncipes. La Europa de las cuidades*, edited by E. Mira and A. Delva, 291–303. Almudín: Museo de la Ciudad, 2007.

Vandewalle, A. 'Das Archiv der Hansestadt Lübeck und das Brügger Hansekontor', *Zeitschrift des Vereins für Lübeckische Geschichte und Altertumskunde* 78 (1998), 271–280.

Vandewalle, A. 'De Brugse stadsmagistraat en de deelname van de ambachten aan het bestuur, 14de.15de eeuw', In *Een privilege voor iedereen. Verzamelde studies van dr. André Vandewalle over Brugse geschiedenis, archief en heraldiek*, edited by N. Geirnaert and M. Vandebroek, 227–236. Berchem: Vlaamse vereniging voor bibliotheek-, archief- en documentatiewezen, 2008.

Vandewalle, A. 'De buerdenaars en het beheer van het Sint-Jooshuis te Brugge, 15de–16de eeuw', *Genootschap voor Geschiedenis te Brugge* 130, nr. 1–2 (1993), 145–157.

Vandewalle, A. 'Schippers, scheepsbouwers en havenarbeiders', In *Een privilege voor iedereen. Verzamelde studies van dr. André Vandewalle over Brugse geschiedenis, archief en heraldiek*, edited by N. Geirnaert and M. Vandebroek, 85–111. Berchem: Vlaamse vereniging voor bibliotheek-, archief- en documentatiewezen, 2008.

Veratelli, F. *A la mode Italienne. Commerce du luxe et diplomatie dans les Pays-Bas méridionaux, 1477–1530. Edition critique de documents de la Chambre des comptes de Lille*. Villeneuve d'Ascq: Septentrion, 2013.

Verbist, B. 'Traditie of innovatie? Wouter Ameyde, een makelaar in het laatmiddeleeuwse Brugge', PhD. Diss. University of Antwerp, 2014.

Verfaillie, J. *Au Coeur de la cour: de griffie en de griffiers van de Raad van Vlaanderen, een bijdrage tot de geschiedenis van instellingen, ambtenaren en archiefvorming tijdens het ancient regime (1386–1796)*. Brussels: Algemeen Rijksarchief, 2017.

Verhulst, A. 'Kort overzicht van de geschiedenis van de Zwinstreek in de middeleeuwen', *Handelingen van het Genootschap voor Geschiedenis te Brugge* 137 (2000), 191–198.

Verhulst, A. *The rise of cities in North-West Europe* Cambridge: Cambridge: Cambridge University Press, 1999.

Verissimo Serrão, J. 'Le Portugal et la Flandre dans le cadre de l'expansion maritime de Portugal', *Handelingen van het Genootschap voor Geschiedenis* 132, nr. 3 (1995), 231–240.

Verlinden, C. 'A propos de la politique économique des ducs de Bourgogne à l'égard de l'Espagne', *Hispania* 10 (1950), 581–715.

Verlinden, C. 'Henri le Navigateur, entrepreneur économique', *Anuario de Estudios Medievales* 17 (1987), 423–435.

Vermaseren, B. 'De Carmel van Brugge en de buitenlandse kooplieden', *Carmel* 3 (1950), 19–31.

Verstegen, R. 'The Judgment of Cambyses: a rich iconographical topic with multiple sources and a long tradition', In The art of Law, edited by S. Huygebaert, G. Martyn, V. Paumen, E. Bousmar and X. Rousseaux (Cham: Springer, 2018), 125–147.

Verstraete, D. 'Het domein van de heer van Maldegem', *Appeltjes van het Meetjesland: jaarboek van het Heemkundig Genootschap van het Meetjesland* 3 (1951), 121–130.

Von Reumont, A. 'Di alcune relazioni die Fiorentini colla città di Danzica; memoria', *Archivio storico italiano, New Series*, XIII (1861), 37–47.

Von Seggern, H. 'Fremde Kaufleute in Brügge. Zur Entstehung der Börse im 14./15. Jahrhundert', In *Mittelalterliche Kaufhäuser im europäischen Vergleich*, edited by F.J. Felten, 111–123. Stuttgart, Franz Steiner Verlag, 2015.

Walsh, R.J. *Charles the Bold and Italy. 1467–1477. Politics and personnel*. Liverpool: Liverpool University Press, 2005.

Watson, W.B. 'The structure of the Florentine galley trade with Flanders and England in the Fifteenth century', *Belgisch Tijdschrift voor Filologie en Geschiedenis* 39, nr. 4 (1961), 1073–1091.

Weber, M. *The history of commercial partnerships in the middle ages*. Oxford: Rowman & Littlefield Publishers, inc., 2003 [1889].

Weststrate, J. '"Des kopmans Hense ende vriheden", Organisatie en structuur van de Hanze, ca. 1300–ca.1450', *Leidschrift* 15, nr. 2 (2000), 21–47.

Whelan, M. '"On behalf of the city": wax and urban diplomacy in the late medieval Baltic and North Sea', *Urban History* 50, nr. 1 (2021), 1–16.

Wijffels, A. 'Dutch litigation before the Great Council of Mechlin. An additional calendar of the "Appeals from Holland"' *Tijdschrijft voor Rechtsgeschiedenis* 77 (2009), 539–550.

Wijffels, A. 'Grote Raad voor de Nederlanden te Mechelen', In *De centrale overheidsinstellingen van de Habsburgse Nederlanden (1482–1795)*, edited by E. Aerts, M. Baelde, H. Coppens, H. De Schepper, H. Soly, A.K.L. Thijs and K. Van Honacker, 448–461. Brussels: Algemeen Rijksarchief, 1994.

Wijffels, A. 'Justitia in commerciis: public governance and commercial litigation before the great Council of Mechlin in the Late Fifteenth and Early Sixteenth Century', *Understanding the sources of early modern and modern commercial law*, edited by H. Pihlajamäki, A. Cordes, S. Dauchy and D. De ruysscher, 32–54. Leiden: Brill, 2018.

Wijffels, A. 'L'histoire de la justice: les cours supérieurs dans les anciens Pays-Bas (15e–18e siècles)', *Tijdschrift voor Rechtsgeschiedenis* 61 (1993), 387–400.

Wijffels, A. 'L'influence de la doctrine sur l'argumentation judiciaire au début des temps modernes', In *Miscellanea Consilii Magni III. Essays on the history of forensic practice*, edited by A. Wijffels, 145–159. Amsterdam: Werkgroep Grote Raad van Mechelen, 1988.

Wijffels, A. 'Le déclin de la Hanse au fil des négociations avec l'Angleterre (1474–1604)', *Publications du centre Européen Bourguignonnes*, nr. 53 (2013), 275–289.

Wijffels, A. 'Mos italicus in der Anwaltspraxis des Grossen Rates zu Mecheln und des Hofes von Holland (1460–1580)', In *Höchste Gerichtsbarkeit im Spätmittelalter und der frühen Neuzeit*, edited by H. De Schepper, 105–123. Amsterdam: Universiteit van Amsterdam, 1985.

Wijffels, A. 'Procureurs et avocats au Grand Conseil de Mechelen', In *L'assistance dans la résolution des conflits, dl. 3 L'Europe médiévale et moderne, Recueils de la Société Jean Bodin pour l'histoire comparative des institutions*, 163–187. Brussels: De Boeck, 1997.

Wijffels, A. and J.M.I. Koster, 'Les procédures en révision au Grand Conseil de Mechelen, 1473–1580', *Publications du Centre Européen d'Etudes Bourguignonnes* 30 (1990), 67–97.

Wijffels, A. *Qui Millies Allegatur. Les allegations du droit savant dans les dossiers du grand conseil de Malines (causes septentrionales, ca. 1460–1580)*. Leiden: Brill, 1985.

Wood, D. *Medieval economic thought*. Cambridge: Cambridge University Press, 2012.

Wubs-Mrozewicz, J. 'De kantoren van de hanze: Bergen, Brügge, Londen en Nowgorod', In *Koggen, kooplieden en kantoren. De Hanze een praktisch netwerk*, edited by H. Brand and E. Knol, 91–108. Groningen: Uitgeverij Verloren, 2010.

Wubs-Mrozewicz, J. 'Mercantile conflict resolution and the role of the language of trust: a Danzig case in the middle of the sixteenth century', *Historical research* 88, nr. 241 (2015), 417–440.

Wubs-Mrozewicz, J. 'Mercantile conflict resolution in practice: connecting legal and diplomatic sources from Danzig c. 1460–1580', *Understanding the Sources of Early Modern and Modern Commercial Law Courts, Statutes, Contracts, and Legal Scholarship*, H. Pihlajamäki, A. Cordes, S. Dauchy and D. De ruysscher, 7–31. Leiden: Brill, 2018.

Wubs-Mrozewicz, J. 'The Hanse in medieval and early modern Europe: an introduction', In *The Hanse in Medieval and Early Modern Europe*, edited by J. Wubs-Mrozewicz and S. Jenks, 1–26. Leiden/Boston: Brill, 2013.

Wubs-Mrozewicz, J. 'The late medieval and early modern Hanse as an institution of conflict management', *Continuity and Change* 31, nr. 1 (2017), 59–84.

Wubs-Mrozewicz, J. 'The medieval Hanse: groups and networks of traders. The case of the Bergen Kontor (Norway)', In *Gentes de mar en la ciudad atlántica medieval*, edited by J.A. Solórzano Telechea, M. Bochaca, A. Aguiar Andrade, 213–233. Logroño: Instituto de Estudios Riojanos, 2012.

Wubs-Mrozewicz, J. *Traders, ties and tensions: the interactions of Lübeckers, Overijsslers and Hollanders in late medieval Bergen*. Hilversum: Uitgeverij Verloren, 2008.

Wyffels, C. 'De Vlaamse handel op Engeland voor het Engels Vlaamse konflikt van 1270–1274', *Bijdrage tot de Geschiedenis der Nederlanden* XVII (1963), 205–213.

Yante, J.-M. 'Commerce et marchands Italiens dans les Pays-Bas (XIVe–XVIe siècles)', *Publications du Centre Européen d'Etudes Bourguignonnes* 49 (2009), 87–99.

Zemon Davis, N. *The gift in sixteenth century France*. Oxford: Oxford university press, 2000.

Ziegler, K.-H 'Arbiter, arbitrator und amicabilis compositor', *Zeitschrift der Savigny Stiftung für Rechtsgeschichte: Romanistische Abteilung* 84, nr. 1 (1967), 376–381.

Zimmerman, R. *The law of obligations: Roman foundation of the civilian tradition*. Cape Town: Juta, 1990.

Index

Note on the names: In Bruges most sources are in Dutch, Latin and French. In many cases, names of Italian, Portuguese or Spanish merchants were written down in their French or Dutch forms. Famous merchants where we are certain of their original equivalent, the equivalent is given. For example, Tomase Portunare is the merchant Tommaso Portinari. For those we did not know for sure, we have given the name found in the sources.

Aardenburg, 97
account books, 130
Adornes, Anselmus, 87–8
Afrika, 101
aldermen deputation, 28–9
Algiers, 118
Aliate, Battista, 26
Alicante, 118
Allecaes, Jan, 29
Alvaro, Fernande, 104
Anguys, Stevin, 88
Aragon, 96
  nation, 106–10
  King of, 106
  merchants, 61, 75, 167, 170, 182, 189–90
arbiters, 51–3, 55, 62, 69, 105, 107, 126, 145, 155–6, 168–9
arbitration, 22–7
Archibald, Earl of Douglass, 83
Arnolfini, Michele, 55–6
audiëntie, 143
Austria, Maximilian of, 170, 178–9, 181

bailiff (*baljuw*), officer of justice, 29, 144–5
  water, 32, 101, 121–2, 125
  city, *Schout*, 40
Balbi, Jacopo, 123
Baltic, 73, 77
Bandini, Piero, 61, 123, 128–9
bankruptcy, 45, 56
Barbagialla, Niccolo, 126
Barcelona, 58, 106–7, 118
Baroncelli, Renaldo, 61
Basdau, Diederic, 155–6
Baseo, Ludovico, 123
Bastre, Loys, 52
Beneke, Paul, 73
Bentham, William, 39
Bergen-op-Zoom, 30
Bergen, 77, 80
Betrain, Franchois, 122
bills of exchange, 57–63
Biscay, 97, 100–1, 181–2, 189
Bladelin, Pieter, 44
Borgoys, Willem, 163
Boudumeris, Leonardo, 123
Bousy, Marin, 122
Boven, Jacob, 151
Brabant, 30, 119, 182
  Council of, 149
  Duke of, 124
Bridoul, Jean, 146
Brindisi, 118
brokers, 4, 26, 38, 54, 98–9, 102, 125, 178–9, 181
Brunelli, Piero, 126
Burgos, 100, 189
Burgundy
  Charles of, the Bold, 89, 141
  Duke of, 3, 53, 73, 84–6, 90, 96, 102, 106, 126, 130, 146–7, 153, 155
  John I of, the Fearless, 83, 125
  Mary of, 148, 170, 179
  Philip I of, the Bold, 86, 143
  Philip II of, the Good, 125, 83
Burk, Richard, 60

Cadiz, 118
Calais, 78
  Staple, 154–5
Cambi, Bernardo, 48, 60–1, 130
Castile, 96, 99, 116
  King, 96, 99, 101
  merchants, 51, 55–6, 60, 96–102, 109, 152, 167
  wool, 29, 180, 182
  nation, 97–101, 181–2

Catalan, Roderigo, 170, 181
Catalonia, 21, 107; *see also* Aragon
Centurione, Giorgio, 146
Ceton, Willem, 61
Champagne, 116
Cologne, 77, 80, 146
commenda, 54
compositie, 29
Conservator of the Privileges, 87–8
consul, 26, 28, 43, 99–108, 119–31, 181–3, 189
consular courts, 99–101, 104–6, 125–7, 183
Contarini, Alberto, 123
contumacia, 40
Coolbrandt, Jacob, 152
Copping, Richard, 154
Corubeas, Jehan, 56
Cost, Thomas, 163
Council of Lords, 88
Crichton, John, 38
Croesen, Hendrik, 155–6
Cups, Henric, 38

da Pasano, Giovanni di Benedicto, 128–9
da Rabata, Piero, 55–6, 130
Dalo, Christoforo, 52
Damme, 1, 31, 32, 50–1, 53, 57, 98, 103, 150, 154
Danzig, 73–4, 77
de Baenst, Jan, 44, 165
de Bardi, Bernardo, 130
de Béthune, Jeanne, 154
de Ceur, Hewin, 44
de Ceur, Pieter, 44
de Larmes, Alonso, 62–3
de Marquil, Thomas, 130
de May, Nicholas, 28, 62, 170
de Medina, Alonso, 152–3, 167
de Mol, Rogier, 164
de Nyeto, Pietro, 62–3
de Pireto, Domenico, 122
de Rapello, Domenico, 146, 166–7
de Spinosa, Fernando, 152–3
de Vega, Alvere, 56
de Viealde, Desiderius, 104
de Zaragoza, Antonio, 61
debt imprisonment, 28, 38–9, 40, 82, 119–20, 170–1, 182, 190
Despars, Jacob, 180
Despars, Marc, 149, 180
Dhont, Jan, 122
Dinis, Alvaro, 104
Dinis, Pedro, 105
Doria, Jacopo, 122
Dover, 78
Dynant, Jan, 169

Eanes, Rodrigo, 103
Edward, King of England, 79
embargo, 78–80, 91
England, 41, 60, 78–9, 82, 86, 116, 118, 127, 146, 154, 169
  cloth, 81, 178, 182
  governor of the English nation, 81–2, 90
  merchants, 39, 75, 79, 81–2, 86, 90, 142, 155, 163, 178, 189
  wool, 78, 84, 178, 188–9
Everyday, Jan, 28

factor, of the Portuguese King in Bruges, 104
Ferrier, Saldone, 21, 56, 108–10
Fiers, Johan Battista, 49
Flanders, County of, 3, 19, 30, 50, 78, 81, 84–6, 97–9, 125, 127, 141, 147, 156, 162, 182, 191
  Council of, 143–9
  Count(s) of, 3, 10, 75, 79–80, 85, 98, 108, 119, 121, 124, 126, 131, 144
Florence, 8, 75, 116–17, 124, 127–9
  merchants, 61, 73, 105, 123, 125, 127, 165, 168, 183, 190
Four Members, 6, 84–5, 87, 99, 125, 144–7, 150, 165
Francesco, Antonio, 130, 146
France, 8, 78–9, 116, 153, 179
  King, 141, 152, 155–6, 168
  merchants, 52, 146, 150
Frescobaldi, Family, 118, 137

Gambaro, Battista, 26, 168
Geno, Luigi, 150–1
Genoa, 22, 49, 54, 105, 116–17, 119, 122, 124, 146
  nation, 124–5
  merchants, 49, 52–5, 60, 104–5, 124–5, 129–30, 150
Gentile, Marco, 55
Ghent, 6, 81, 84, 97
Gil, Vincente, 150, 167
Gonçalves, Gabriel, 49
Great Council, 149–53
Guicciardini, Ludovico, 2, 184, 188
Guistiniani, Piero Battista, 49

Hamburg, 77
Hanse, 42–3, 73, 77–8, 80–1, 83, 85–9, 145, 155–6, 167, 177–8, 180, 183, 188–9
Kontor, 51, 74, 77, 87
Kontor secretary, 87–8, 131–2
merchants, 8, 43, 75, 77, 79–81, 85, 88, 96, 98–9, 101, 117, 131, 156, 189, 191
Hansetag, 77, 85, 87
Hauweel, Lodewijk, 164
Heyns, Jan, 41–2
Heyns, Vincent, 99
Holland, 182
Council of, 149
Hoochins, Henric, 62
Hoonin, Thideman, 28
hosteller, 26–9, 39, 40, 42–4, 54, 69, 78, 88, 90, 98, 100, 102, 104, 107, 109, 121, 130–1, 181–2

Isabella of Portugal, 104–6

James I, King of Scots, 83–4
Jean de Lingui, 22
Jennet, Henry, 151

Kone, Jan, 149

L'Espeau, Aleyn, 151
La Rochelle, 55–6
Larcar, Simon, 56
le Blont, Florent, 146
le Fevre, Guillaume, 122
legal framework, 2
Lem, Maarten, 105
lex mercatoria, 5
Lisbon, 103, 118
Lomellini, Carlo, 55, 165
Jeronimo, 165
Lazzaro, 52, 60, 165
Leonardo, 28
Ottobono, 165
London, 41, 60, 62, 73, 77, 80, 118, 120–1, 177
Lopez, Joao, 103
Losschaert, Jan, 122
Louppes, Jehan, 62
Loys, Fernando, 103
Lübeck, 77
Lucca, 8, 116–17, 118, 126–7
merchants, 122, 126–8, 130, 183
nation, 126–7

Machet, Antoine, 150–1
Malaga, 118
Mallorca, 106, 118
Manfredonia, 118
maritime plunder, 43, 55, 81, 83–4, 104, 120, 144, 151, 180, 189–90
Marten, Gobelinus, 87
Martines, Jehan, 51
Massado, Rui, 103
Mechelen, Grote Raad, 180
mechants, 83
Parliament, 148, 152–3, 155, 157
Medici, 59, 73–4, 118, 127–8, 130
Merchants Adventurers, 178
Metteneye, Jacob, 38
Middelburg, 121, 180
Milan, 116
Minne, Antheunis, 39
Moor, Richard, 163
Morosini, Marco, 21, 123
Morosini, Piero, 123
Moyn, Richard, 163
Moysant, Guerin, 52
Mude, 50, 125

namptissement, 57
Nantes, 146
nation, Florentine, 58, 127–31
Navarre, 96
Nieuwland, Hendrik, 180
Noel, Pierre, 55–6
Novgorod, 77, 80
Nuremberg, merchants, 61

oath, 48, 90, 100, 109, 163–4
Olivier, Bonnore, 22, 53
Oran, 118
Otranto, 118

Pagant, Claes, 38
Pardo, Alonso, 60
Paris, Parliament, 153–7
Parmentier, Zeger, 109
Penitor, William, 146
Peterszuene, Henric, 41
Philips, Jacques, 165
Pierandrea, Piero, 130
Pierins, Nicolas, 149
Pimenes, François, 109
Pinello, Sandro, 61
piracy *see* maritime plunder
Plouvier, Gérard, 56, 109

Poland, 77
Portinari, Tommaso, 32, 62, 73–5, 132
Portugal, 49, 96, 103–5, 179–80
 King, 49, 104
 merchants, 7, 29, 75, 101–6
 nation, 101–6
Priffel, Matijs, 43
proxy, 60
Pulcher, Stevin, 61

Quirino, Michele, 105

Rapondi, Dino, 126
Rau, Marian, 60
Remundo, Donato, 122
reprisal letters, also known as letters of marque, 83, 89, 98–9, 163
Ribe, Barthelmy, 163
Ribijs de Collier, Jacques, 56
Rodrigues, Gil, 104
Roetaert, Renault, 28, 62
Rôles d'Oléron, 50

safe conduct, 40, 43, 101, 121–2, 124, 144, 151, 154–5
Salamanque, Jan, 149
Salomon, Natalo, 52, 123.
Salviati, Borromei, 56
Sampson, Abraham, 146
Sandei, Francesco, 56
Sandwich, 78
Scaec, Roegier, 38
Scotland, 78–9, 84
 merchants, 38, 61, 83–6, 88–90, 117, 189
 nation, 83–4, 87–9, 169
Sevilla, 118
Sicily, 118
Sluis, 1, 29–32, 49, 83, 98, 100, 102, 106, 120–1, 123–5, 144, 146, 149, 154, 166, 177, 179, 182
sobrepotestas, 107
Sorance, Piero, 123
South German Merchants, 1, 178
Southampton, 78
Spinola, Asselin, 60
 Giorgio, 56
 Luciano, 146
staple, 29–33
Stocker, Willem, 42
Stockman, Jan, 28
Strozzi, Paolo, 105
submissie (submission), 29–33
Swin, Johannes, 87

Tac, John, 154
Tangiers, 118
Tani, Angelo, 55, 130, 146
Tripoli, 118
Tunis, 118

Utrecht, 73–4

Vaaz, Joao, 102
Vadeban, Philips, 154
Valdin, John, 154
Valencia, 106, 108
van Aertrike, Filip, 29
van Amsterdam, 169
van Attendare, Claes, 88
van Boschuysen, Jan, 89–90
van Dorle, Jacob, 42
van Griwe, Diederic, 146
van Kerckhove, Jan en Pauwels, 169
van Munten, Absalon, 100
van Overbeke, Jan, 164
van Remagen, Jan, 28
van Stillebeke, Jan, 166
van Varsenare, Joos, 44, 165
Van, Jan, 152
vande Velde, Cornille, 122
van den Berghe, Thideman, 87
Vanden Goude, Diederik, 60–1
vanden Walle, Johan, 44
vander Poele, Jacop, 165
Vas, Roys, 29
Vasques, João, 104
Venice, 116–24
 Senate, 118, 121–2
 galleys, 8, 106, 118–21, 124
 merchants, 21, 105, 117–24
 nation, 117–24, 154
von Coesveld, Goswin, 87
Vonnesse van Amsterdam, 50

written procedure, 23–4, 63, 146, 148

Ypres, 81, 97, 100

Zeeland, 182